DISCARDED

*Littleton*

*Waller*

*Tazewell*

# Littleton
# Waller
# Tazewell

*Norma Lois Peterson*

University Press of Virginia
*Charlottesville*

THE UNIVERSITY PRESS OF VIRGINIA
Copyright ©1983 by the Rector and Visitors
of the University of Virginia

*First published 1983*

*Frontispiece:* Littleton Waller Tazewell. (Virginia State Library)

Library of Congress Cataloging in Publication Data

Peterson, Norma Lois.
  Littleton Waller Tazewell.

  Bibliography: p. 299
  Includes index.
  1. Tazewell, Littleton Waller, 1774–1860. 2. Virginia
—Politics and government—1775–1865. 3. Legislators—
United States—Biography. 4. United States. Congress—
Biography. 5. Virginia—Governors—Biography. I. Title.
E340.T24P47   1983      975.5′03′0924 [B]     83-3501
ISBN 0-8139-0983-X

Printed in the United States of America

*To*
*Glennys Rugg*
*and to*
*the memory of*
*Esther H. Lyman*
*and*
*Dean Belden Lyman*

# Contents

*The world at large can never have that knowledge of him that I have; and, therefore, though I know that he looks upon mankind with an eye of benevolence, and upon his country with the spirit of a patriot; and though, in addition to this, he is certainly capable of any and every thing that demands fidelity, zeal, energy, industry the most unrelaxing, and talents the most transcendent; yet much I fear his country will never know him well enough to do him justice, or to profit herself of his powers.*

William Wirt on Tazewell
from *The Old Bachelor*

# *Preface*

In 1823 Littleton Waller Tazewell, a leading citizen of Norfolk, Virginia, began recording for the benefit of his "dear children" information concerning their lineage. For years he had collected bits and pieces of the family's past, and now, he felt, the time had arrived to organize them into a readable narrative. It was a prideful task.

"I came into life," he explained, "precisely at that period when the habits, manners, and customs of Virginia were beginning to manifest that great change, which was both the cause and effect of the political Revolution that severed this Colony from its parent Country, and gave it a name as an independent state." As a child his close associates were, for the most part, older people (his grandfather, Benjamin Waller, chief justice of the Court of Admiralty; his father, Henry Tazewell, chief justice of Virginia's General Court, justice of the Court of Appeals, and United States senator; the great teacher and jurist George Wythe; Bishop James Madison of the College of William and Mary) who related to him "by most lively description what had before occurred, some of which is even now buried in general oblivion." His own early observations and, later, his close examination of many records attested to the accuracy of those descriptions, and during his life he witnessed changes so great in some instances that posterity, he feared, scarcely would credit them. "So circumstanced, I have often been disposed to regard myself as the connecting link that was to bind the past to the future as the medium through which alone, the knowledge of what had been could be communicated to what was to be, so far at least as my own family was concerned." These words were truer and for a wider audience than even Tazewell, with his strong sense of history, realized. Beginning on the eve of the American Revolution, his life extended to the eve of the Civil War. He was an active witness to the expansion, sectional strife, and political struggles of the antebellum period and, in his own person, was a connecting link of unusual significance.

Born in Williamsburg on December 17, 1774, Tazewell spent the greater part of his adult life in Norfolk, but his reputation, especially in maritime law and statesmanship, spread far beyond the confines of the borough. A prominent intellectual of the Old South, Tazewell was a lover of books and a devotee of learning in science, history, and literature, as well as in the law. Owner of four plantations (Sandhills near Norfolk and three on Virginia's Eastern Shore: King's Creek, New Quarter, and Old Plantation) his mind-set was not solely that of an agrarian. He was an urban dweller to whom the commercial future of Norfolk was of utmost importance. He was involved in the development of banking interests, steamboat companies, and the United States Navy.

Among Tazewell's intimates were John Randolph, John Wickham, Robert B. Taylor, James Monroe, William Wirt, Stephen Decatur, Hugh Lawson White, Levi Woodbury, and Mahlon Dickerson. A confidant of John C. Calhoun, Tazewell was a vigorous opponent of nullification. He helped elect, then became disillusioned with, Andrew Jackson; Presidents John Tyler and James K. Polk sought his advice; John Quincy Adams disliked him intensely, while Henry Clay and Martin Van Buren courted his support. In appearances before the nation's highest tribunal he earned accolades that declared him more able than the illustrious Daniel Webster.

Tazewell's greatest aversion was power when used indiscriminately by an imperial president, an overly enterprising legislature, or by a popular majority. Rule by strength of numbers alone he termed "democratic despotism." This attitude was apparent as Tazewell served his state and nation in the Congress of the United States (House of Representatives, 1800–1801; Senate, 1825–32), in the Virginia General Assembly, 1804–6 and 1816–17, and as governor of Virginia, 1834–36. He never sought office. John Tyler called him the "most unambitious of men"; yet, his earnest pledge was "While I live, I will willingly render to Virginia all she may choose to require of me, to which I may be equal." He was just as loyal to the Union. However, as the country drifted, or was swept by extremists, toward disintegration, Tazewell suffered the anguish, despair, and helplessness felt by all sensitive men of balance, moderation, and integrity.

In *Cavalier and Yankee: The Old South and American National Character,* William R. Taylor portrays the southern aristocrat. In many ways Tazewell fits Taylor's description: a child of the Enlightenment, a rationalist (logical, objective, and precise) who held tenaciously to noblesse oblige, was cosmopolitan in his point of view, gave the highest priority to education, and distrusted emotion. He was uneasy about the rise of the common man with its accompanying demands for white manhood suffrage, but in no way did he consider himself antidemocratic. For him democracy meant "rule by the best," by a natural aristocracy of "talent and virtue," whose service to the country should be in the interest of the nation, not for the benefit of self.

With the advent of "King Numbers," Tazewell saw disaster for the South, a doom which he and others like him felt helpless to prevent, unless the North could be convinced of the despotic propensities inherent in unlimited majority rule. Regardless of his frustration, anger, and hurt pride, Tazewell neither joined nor encouraged the "fire-eaters" who agitated for secession, but the alienation and injured self-esteem of an entire region were reflected in his words and actions. In essence, Tazewell represents a significant aspect of southern thinking, a moderate point of view on business, slavery, and other controversial issues which, if understood and cultivated by like-minded northerners, could have gone far to ward off the tragedy of civil war.

This volume is based largely on the extensive collection of Tazewell Papers in the Virginia State Library, Richmond. Twenty-six boxes of legible letters and documents (a testimonial to Tazewell's sense of order) give at times almost a day-by-day account of the happenings in the Tazewell household as well as in the state and nation. I am deeply indebted to the excellent staff of the Virginia State Library for courteous and prompt attention to my needs.

Tazewell's most faithful correspondent was John Wickham, a Richmond attorney, who had reputedly one of the finest legal minds of his time. A microfilm copy of his papers in the University of Virginia Library was used with special permission of Wickham's descendants: Littleton Wickham, Richmond; Julia Wickham Porter, Bethesda, Maryland; Ashby Wickham, Kilmarnock, Virginia. For this study the Wickham Letters rank second in importance only to those of the Tazewell Collection. My thanks to the individuals named above and to the Manuscript Division of the University of Virginia Library for the loan of the microfilm.

Foremost among other libraries that provided indispensable services are the Library of Congress, the Maryland Historical Society, Kirn Memorial Library, Norfolk, Virginia, and the Massachusetts Historical Society.

Pertinent suggestions for improvement of this work were made by my longtime friend and mentor, Dr. Harvey L. Carter, who read the manuscript with his usual care and thoughtful consideration. My gratitude to him, as always, is immeasurable.

During difficult periods in one's life certain friends prove their mettle. In this regard I wish especially to acknowledge the assistance and support of Elizabeth Baldridge, Robin Durrance, Dr. Shirley Fredericks, and the late Esther H. Lyman. My sister Connie, whose interest in history is somewhat less than enthusiastic, but improving, provided delightful companionship during needed periods of respite from my labors. Glennys Rugg spent many hours reading and criticizing the earlier chapters. Illness prevented her from completing the task. Julie Davis-Laird willingly served as my alter ego in checking many items in the University of Virginia Library. Jean Chapman, whose devotion to the history of the Virginia Tidewater proved contagious, contributed invaluable help and encouragement in the initial stages of my research. To her I am especially indebted. My aunt, Myrtle V. Peterson, has provided a lifetime of moral support, interest, and concern. With efficiency which never ceases to amaze me, Margaret Ann Talley typed many revisions without a word of complaint. Jean Buchanan, graciously and with alacrity, typed the final changes. To these, and to numerous others, my sincere appreciation.

In his conclusion to *The Great Tom Fuller,* Professor Dean Lyman wrote: in "wisdom and humanity and mirth—he lives on." So it is with Dean and Esther, and with Glennys, to whom my work is dedicated.

N.L.P.

*Littleton*

*Waller*

*Tazewell*

## Chapter I

# "Happy the
# Parent of
# Such a Son"

Throughout his long life Littleton Waller Tazewell believed it was a stroke of good fortune to have been born in Williamsburg in 1774. The year marked the beginning of a new era, and Williamsburg, "the seat of empire" and capital of the vast lands claimed by the Old Dominion, was a focal point of upheaval. The Raleigh Tavern resounded with the voices of Patrick Henry, Edmund and Peyton Randolph, Richard Henry Lee, and others as they protested violations of their God-given natural rights. Meanwhile, Thomas Jefferson at Monticello penned his *Summary View of the Rights of British America* with its ringing declaration proclaiming the inseparability of life and liberty; "the hand of force may destroy but cannot disjoin them." In August, Virginians named delegates to the First Continental Congress, scheduled to meet in Philadelphia to discuss the grievous acts and measures perpetrated upon the colonies by His Majesty's government.

Tazewell was born on December 17 in the home of his maternal grandparents, the Benjamin Wallers, on Woodpecker Street. On both sides the family of which he now became a part was intelligent, propertied, and highly respected. The legal profession was bred in his bones. The first of his forebears to come to the Virginia colony was Nathaniel Littleton, who arrived in what is now Northampton County in the early 1630s. He was said to have been a descendant of Sir Thomas de Littleton, a judge of England's Court of Common Pleas and author of the famous *Treatise on Tenures,* so much admired by Sir Edward Coke. Nathaniel Littleton was among the first

white settlers to inhabit the region south of Old Plantation
Creek on the Eastern Shore. He presided in the county court
as one of the justices of the quorum and by mid-seventeenth
century was a member of the governor's council.[1]

Nathaniel Littleton's great-granddaughter married William
Tazewell, who made his way from England to Virginia in
1715. More Norman than Anglo-Saxon blood ran in his veins.
Also an attorney, he built an extensive practice in Northampton County. Family roots were deep in the sandy soil of the
Eastern Shore; however, Littleton Tazewell, William's son and
the grandfather of Littleton Waller Tazewell, was at the age of
seventeen placed by his father in the office of the secretary of
state in Williamsburg, an admirable preparatory school for
those who anticipated entering the legal profession. While va-
cationing during the Christmas season in Surry County, the
young man met Mary Gray. After they were married, Littleton
Tazewell in 1752 forsook the Eastern Shore and settled in
Brunswick County in southside Virginia, so that she could be
near her parents. His brother John also moved to the Tidewater, and the Tazewell name became extinct in Northampton
County. Littleton Tazewell purchased an estate on the Notto-
way River and another on the Otterdam Swamp, became clerk
of the court, and practiced law in the courts of the surrounding counties. He died at the age of thirty-three. His sole surviving child, Henry Tazewell, was placed first in the care of
relatives and later under the guidance of a stepfather, the
Reverend William Fanning. In 1770 Henry Tazewell entered
the College of William and Mary and, two years later, began
reading law in the office of his uncle John Tazewell, a reputable Williamsburg attorney.

In Williamsburg, Henry Tazewell met Dorothea Elizabeth
Waller, daughter of Benjamin Waller, whom he married in
January 1774. Scarcely twenty-one when his son was born,
Henry Tazewell already had made his mark as an attorney,
practicing in the counties of Brunswick, Southampton, Sussex,
and Surry. An active proponent of liberty and justice for the
colonists, Henry Tazewell in the summer of 1774 participated
in the Virginia convention that named representatives to the
First Continental Congress. Among Littleton Waller Taze-

well's earliest recollections were those of his father's involvement in the Revolution.

The person who had the most profound influence on the life of Littleton Waller Tazewell, however, was his maternal grandfather, Benjamin Waller, who, for a number of years, was chief justice of the Court of Admiralty. When Dorothea Waller Tazewell died in 1777, Littleton, age three, became a member of Grandfather Waller's household, while the Tazewell relatives assumed responsibility for his baby sister, Nancy. The young father, Henry Tazewell, caught up in the rush of revolutionary activities, found it impossible to establish a permanent home for his children. Fortunately, Benjamin Waller, a man of great warmth, kindness, and intelligence, was willing to devote unlimited time to a small lonely boy. "I was his companion in retirement," Tazewell remembered a half century later, "and upon me all his remaining affections were fixed. He loved me tenderly, . . . and in my little heart he held the place of the only parent it had then known."[2]

In the autumn of 1780, as British troops threatened an invasion of Williamsburg, Littleton was sent for safety to the home of Henry Tazewell's mother and stepfather, the Fannings, in Greensville County. There for the first time he met John Wickham, a nephew of the Reverend Mr. Fanning who had been driven from his home in New York by the war. Young Wickham, about seventeen, was very kind to the younger boy and for almost two years supervised his education. "He taught me first to read English better than I could do before; next, the rudiments of Latin, and lastly, to write," Tazewell recalled in 1839.[3] This was the beginning of a firm friendship of nearly sixty years' duration.

With the dangers of war past, Tazewell returned to the Waller house in Williamsburg. Grandmother Waller having died but a short time before, his grandfather devoted even more attention to Littleton's education and well-being. Although for a brief period Tazewell was sent to a private grammar school, he continued to learn much more from his grandfather, whose gentle treatment and inspired teaching brought an eager response from the shy boy.

Twice daily Benjamin Waller heard his grandson's lessons.

These finished to satisfaction, the old gentleman would relate fascinating tales, raising the boy's interest to a high pitch. At a crucial point in the story, Grandfather Waller would feign forgetfulness of some circumstance connected with the narrative and send Littleton to the study for a book to assist his memory. From the volume Littleton was expected to read aloud the entire account, which, in turn, caused his grandfather to recall other stories for the boy to pursue. Thus encouraged and stimulated, Littleton, before he reached the age of twelve, read the entire Bible, Plutarch's *Lives,* many treatises on mythology, large portions from the Greek and Roman histories, several histories of England, and many of the English poets. Grandfather Waller instilled in Tazewell a love of books and a respect for learning which were to last a lifetime.[4]

In 1784, when Walker Maury transferred his reputable grammar school from Orange County to Williamsburg, young Tazewell attended formal classes. It was here he made the acquaintance of John Randolph, an attractive, lively boy one year his senior: Together they studied Eutropius, Sallust, and Virgil, often while sitting on the base of the Botetourt statue near the Capitol.[5] The quiet, rather introspective Tazewell was amused and enthralled by the antics of young Randolph, whose intelligence, while not a match for Tazewell's, was nimble and sharp, with a strong humorous bent. Many years later, when both were in their fifties, Tazewell still listened to the speeches of John Randolph "with the relish of a schoolboy, rubbing with his hands and laughing heartily as the orator went along."[6] Tazewell was one of the few who understood Randolph, and from their correspondence there emerges a kindlier, gentler, more sensible John Randolph than usually is portrayed by historians. Tazewell remained Randolph's loyal friend until the latter's death, long after many others sought to avoid the eccentric gentleman from Roanoke plantation.

At Maury's school Tazewell met another individual who was to have an immeasurable impact on his life. It was Maury's practice to hold public examinations of his students, usually in the presence of the visitors, governors, and professors of the College of William and Mary. On one of these occasions Tazewell's class was examined by the learned classical scholar, member of the High Court of Chancery, and teacher George

Wythe, who was astonished by the ten-year-old Tazewell's knowledge of Greek history. A few months later, Wythe, while paying a visit to Benjamin Waller, again examined the boy, this time on Caesar's *Commentaries,* Roman history, and ancient geography. Tazewell answered the questions with ease, and Wythe, again amazed, turned to Grandfather Waller with an earnest request, "Mr. Waller, this is a very clever boy and when he has advanced a little further, you must let me have him." Grandfather Waller's reply was proud but wistful: "George, this boy is the sole companion and physical comfort of my old age. I feel that I cannot part with him while I live, but when I die if you will take him under your charge, I shall consider it the greatest and highest favour you can confer on each of us."[7]

Not surprisingly, Tazewell remembered precisely what he was studying at the time of his grandfather's death. His love for his grandfather and his love for books were related insepa- rably in his mind. "At this critical period of my life, just as I had begun Cicero and Virgil in the Latin, and Homer and Xenophon in the Greek," he recalled, "I sustained the heaviest misfortune I had ever felt in the loss of my much revered grandfather, who died in May 1786. . . . The shock I experi- enced in this calamity bent me to the earth, and I felt that I could never rise again. My long, intimate and endearing con- nexion with this good man, had weaned me from all other attachments, and my regard for him absorbed all my affec- tions. As he seemed to live but for me, so had I lived for him alone." Henry Tazewell returned to Williamsburg in haste to comfort his grief-stricken son, a difficult task as, having been so often absent, he was almost a stranger to the boy. Littleton had been taught to respect his parent, but not until he was almost of age did a camaraderie develop between father and son. Littleton's whole heart had been given to his grandfather, and in losing him he seemed to have lost all he valued on earth.[8]

The months of adjustment were difficult. For a while Little- ton lived in his father's home and continued to attend Walker Maury's school. After Maury became a member of the clergy, closed his school, and moved to Norfolk, Littleton idled away his time. Henry Tazewell was busy riding circuit and attending

to other duties, and even when at home he was too occupied
to pay much attention to a lad of twelve. One day, by chance,
Wythe encountered young Littleton on a Williamsburg street
and questioned him closely about his daily habits. Taking the
boy home with him, Wythe examined him on his studies. Although Littleton did not acquit himself as well as he had during the earlier examinations, Wythe seemed satisfied. Henry
Tazewell was in Richmond, but the day after his return Wythe
called on him to relate Benjamin Waller's request concerning
Littleton's education and to offer to take the boy under his
charge. Littleton continued to reside in his father's house, a
short distance from the Wythe residence, but he spent his days
and many evenings studying with the learned scholar. "I attended him every morning very early, and always found him
waiting for me in his study by sunrise," Tazewell later wrote.
At various periods during the day, whenever Wythe was free,
pupil and master turned their attention to Greek, Latin, alge-
braic equations, and mathematical problems. Mathematics
textbooks were in French in order that the student might,
while learning mathematics, perfect himself in the language.
Evenings were spent in perusing the best English authors,
either in verse or in prose, or in reading and discussing articles from the current periodicals.[9]

In 1787 Henry Tazewell purchased and took up residence at
Kingsmill, a plantation a few miles south of Williamsburg, located in a neck between Archer's Hope Creek and the James
River. Wythe, having recently lost his wife, suggested that Littleton might board in town with him. The course of study was
the same, but now Littleton was allowed free use of the large
Wythe library. In addition, letters and books arrived from
Thomas Jefferson, then American minister in Paris. Jefferson's
nephew Peter Carr also was studying with Wythe, much to the
delight of his uncle, who wrote, "I am sure you will find this to
have been one of the most fortunate events of your life, as I
have ever been sensible it was mine."[10]

Scientific experiments occupied their leisure moments, for
Wythe had acquired a very complete "electrical machine together with a fine air pump" and other "philosophical appara-
tus," including a microscope, telescope, and celestial globe.
Every person of note who passed through Williamsburg

stopped to pay his respects to George Wythe. Several other young gentlemen joined the school, and for Littleton Tazewell the experience was rich and broadening. Conversations ranged over many topics. One of the favorites was the Constitutional Convention that met in Philadelphia in the summer of 1787. Wythe was a brief participant and a strong advocate of the theory that the federal government derived its power from the states. Representative republicanism, he firmly believed, was much to be preferred over "undiluted democracy," and in 1788, representing Williamsburg in the Virginia convention, he offered the resolution to ratify the new United States Constitution. Unequivocally opposed to slavery, Wythe, by his will, freed his own slaves and supplied them with means of living until they could support themselves. Although a communicant of the Episcopal church, Wythe leaned toward deism. Quite likely the "manly and rational piety" that marked Tazewell's mature thought was an outgrowth of Wythe's influence.[11] Perhaps Tazewell was too young to profit as much from his association with this venerable gentleman as had Jefferson, who was nineteen when he began to read law under Wythe's supervision, but Tazewell learned many lessons not soon forgotten.

When Wythe found it too strenuous to have student boarders, Tazewell lived with John Wickham who, after a European tour, had returned to Virginia in 1786 to study law with Henry Tazewell and establish a practice in Williamsburg. This living arrangement continued until 1790 or 1791 when, because of the reorganization of the Virginia court system, both Wythe and Wickham moved to Richmond. After Wickham's departure, Tazewell, now a student at the College of William and Mary, resided in the home of Bishop James Madison, president of the institution. Madison, an Episcopal bishop with a touch of deism, was an ardent republican who, like Wythe, was opposed to slavery and often discussed the possibilities of emancipation. His interest in science, which ranged from mammoths and Indian mounds to meteorology and astronomy, sparked the enthusiasm of many young men of the college. Years later as Tazewell sat in the Senate of the United States, he often remembered Madison's insistence that the chief executive of the United States was only "an organ of the general will"; that it was the duty of those involved in national affairs to guard the Constitution vigilantly and insist upon its rightful application in governing the land; that checks and balances, if operating properly, should preclude the unnatural growth of power, which, in whatever guise, could destroy the "pure and sacred principles of liberty."[12]

The environment in which Tazewell lived while a young man in Williamsburg gave him ample opportunity to absorb the ideas and philosophies of some of the leading men of Virginia, men such as his grandfather, his father, Wythe, Madison, St. George Tucker (John Randolph's stepfather and a strong proponent of manumission), and many other illustrious citizens of the commonwealth. His classmates also stimulated his thinking. Among them were James Barbour of Orange County, William H. Cabell, George Keith Taylor, and Tazewell's special friend, Robert Barraud Taylor. John Randolph, too, was briefly a member of this group, until he was involved in a duel with Robert Taylor, an incident which influenced his abrupt departure from the college.[13]

For Tazewell college life was active and pleasant. On days set aside for patriotic observances the students displayed their oratorical skills, and Tazewell found that he excelled in speechmaking. His sister Nancy, fast becoming a Williamsburg belle, enjoyed being escorted to "merry balls" by her attractive brother. For the most part, however, Tazewell devoted his time to his books, acquiring a reputation as a fine and serious scholar. So well did he comport himself that in the spring of 1792 Madison, after interrogating the students in all the classes, advised Tazewell to prepare to be examined for the Bachelor of Arts degree. At first Tazewell could not believe the bishop was serious. Few dared brave the "fiery ordeal" required to obtain the coveted diploma, but encouraged by Madison, Tazewell nervously consented to make the attempt. He read constantly, scarcely allowing himself "time for necessary refreshments and repose." After a period of preparation he was subjected to several days of questioning by various professors. Having performed to their satisfaction, he was next examined on all collegiate studies by a convocation of the faculty, after which Bishop Madison directed him to prepare a thesis which he was to commit to memory, deliver as an ora-

tion, and defend before a public audience in the chapel on
August 1, the foundation day of the college. All phases of the
difficult trial were completed without complication, and Tazewell received his degree the same day before the same audience.[14]

Elated, but extremely fatigued and in ill health, he returned
to Kingsmill. Henry Tazewell, alarmed by the appearance of
his son, summoned a physician who prescribed a journey to
the northern states. Upon arrival in Philadelphia, Littleton
was exposed to smallpox and was inoculated against the disease, but in his weakened condition he reacted violently to the
inoculation and was dangerously ill for several weeks, returning to Kingsmill "more dead than alive." A regimen of "rural
sports," hunting and riding, was advised. Although Littleton
professed a definite aversion to such activities, he was forbidden to study and thus was forced to spend many hours out of
doors. In time he became a fearless horseman, performing
such feats as riding his mount to the second floor of the
Raleigh Tavern and leaping from horseback into a rapidly
moving carriage. With time to be more gregarious, Tazewell
became a popular guest at parties and balls and perhaps for
the only period of his life placed pleasure before duty. Handsome, over six feet tall, with blue eyes and auburn hair, he cut
a striking figure. Often on first meeting he gave the impression of haughtiness, but on further acquaintance his manner
relaxed to warm cordiality.[15]

A brief flurry of excitement in the fall of 1794 temporarily
interrupted this placid existence. While a student at William
and Mary, Littleton had joined the state militia. Now the militia was summoned by President Washington, at the behest of
Secretary of the Treasury Hamilton, to assist in putting down
an insurrection in Pennsylvania, commonly known as the
Whiskey Rebellion. In his youthful exuberance, Tazewell was
anxious to participate. "The novelty of this situation gave me
much pleasure," he remembered in later life, but his Antifed-
eralist father felt nothing but anxiety and uneasiness. Henry
Tazewell had gained prominence as a jurist, serving as chief
justice of Virginia's General Court and as a member of the
Court of Appeals. At this juncture, John Taylor of Caroline
resigned from the Senate of the United States, and Henry

Tazewell was being considered for the position. "His situation was such," Littleton wrote, "that he could not possibly object to my going [to Pennsylvania], and with much reluctance I was equipped for this new mode of life." But again illness struck, and Littleton, weak and too easily fatigued, was advised to return home before his company left the Williamsburg area.[16]

After his election to the Senate, Henry Tazewell persuaded his son to accompany him to Philadelphia, and late in December 1794 they traveled northward by way of Chesapeake Bay. During the hours of travel, father and son discussed the latter's future. For Littleton the future meant the law. His mind was made up, and no other career interested him, but Henry Tazewell, equally strong-willed, wanted his son to become a member of the diplomatic service. When they reached Philadelphia arrangements were made for Littleton to study with Edmund Randolph, a fellow Virginian who had succeeded Jefferson as secretary of state in Washington's cabinet. At first Littleton had the impression that he was to read law with Randolph, and when he discovered this was not the case, he became quite discontented. In another attempt to influence his son to serve in the Department of State, Henry Tazewell enlisted the aid of President Washington, who consented to interview the young man with the thought of placing him in a suitable position. Littleton was received very courteously by Washington, who questioned him about his studies and his family, particularly the Wallers with whom the president had been intimately acquainted in Williamsburg. Whether the interview was unsatisfactory or Henry Tazewell finally decided his son could not be diverted from the law, Littleton never knew. However, a few weeks later Littleton received his father's permission to return to Virginia to study law with John Wickham. Fearful that his father might have second thoughts, he left immediately, arriving in Richmond early in February 1795.[17]

The months he spent there were happy. Not since the death of his grandfather had Littleton felt so much a member of a family. Wickham had married Henry Tazewell's half-sister, Mary Fanning, who was somewhat younger than Littleton and regarded by him more as a sister than as an aunt. Littleton's paternal grandmother also lived with the Wickhams, as did his sister, Nancy. John Wickham was a concerned and careful mentor. "In looking back," Tazewell remembered, "I do not think that any period of my life ever passed so satisfactorily and profitably as that I spent in Richmond, while I was there studying the law under the direction of my good friend, Mr. Wickham."[18]

Wickham was already one of Richmond's most promising attorneys, and his associates were important, impressive, and inclined to be Federalists. Wickham leaned in that direction himself, although he never became seriously involved in politics. The Wickham home was located on Tenth Street, between Clay and Marshall, in the "Court End" of town, and was a center of social life. Not far away, on the corner of Marshall and Ninth streets, lived the John Marshalls, close friends of the Wickhams. In this setting Tazewell was exposed to points of view quite different from those espoused by his father, and he was intrigued, but not convinced, by Marshall's arguments in defense of the Jay Treaty, against which Henry Tazewell was leading the fight in the Senate. Also in the neighborhood were the residences of Alexander McRae and Benjamin Botts. A few years later, all these able men, including Littleton Tazewell, would participate, and not on the same side, in the famous treason trial of Aaron Burr. Not far from the Wickhams lived Richmond's eminent physician Dr. James McClurg, whose attractive daughter Elizabeth fast became Tazewell's "Beloved Eliza." Tazewell had lost his heart, but with his usual devotion to duty, his attention was largely on his law books. One of his few diversions was the wedding at Kingsmill of his sister Nancy and Benjamin Taliaferro.[19]

In the spring of 1796 Wickham advised Tazewell to apply for a law license. After being found "duly qualified" by three examining judges, Littleton Waller Tazewell, on May 14, 1796, was granted permission to practice as an attorney in the courts of the commonwealth of Virginia. Returning to Kingsmill, he was besieged with advice as to where he should establish a practice. His father thought he should locate in Fredericksburg, Alexandria, or Winchester; Wickham favored his returning to Richmond; and he himself was drawn to the western country, Kentucky or Tennessee. During the summer, as a trial run, he assisted one of his Waller uncles with a few cases in the Williamsburg area. Soon he was taking clients of his own and winning compliments, along with fair fees, in the hustings court in Williamsburg and in Hampton on Elizabeth City County court days. This settled the issue; he would remain in Williamsburg. A combination house and office was rented; Henry Tazewell donated his law library, a bed, chairs, and other furniture; and Littleton's career was launched. Soon his practice extended beyond Williamsburg to Yorktown, Hampton, and across the Roads to Norfolk. Glowing reports reached his father. "Your aimiable & respectable son is everyday reaping new accessions of credit & applause well merited at the different Bars," wrote Robert Greenhow. "Happy the parent of such a son."[20]

Henry Tazewell's letters from Philadelphia drew Littleton's attention increasingly to national affairs. Political parties were in the making, and Senator Tazewell was committed to the "true Republican" principles of a limited central government and of favoring France over England in the conflict then raging between those two countries. In these pre-Napoleonic days Americans who professed Republican tendencies saw in France the European fulfillment of the Declaration of Independence, or a reasonable facsimile. This attitude was not reflected in the Washington cabinet, however, where feelings ran high against France and support was strong for the Jay Treaty, designed to smooth differences between the United States and Great Britain.[21]

Among his father's friends in Philadelphia, Littleton was impressed by the senator from New York, Aaron Burr, whom the elder Tazewell favored for the vice-presidency in a possible Jefferson administration, should President Washington decline a third term. Henry Tazewell was not without influence. Although on the losing side in regard to the Jay Treaty, he was elected president pro tempore of the Senate in December 1795, a considerable compliment to one who had been a member of that body for less than a year. In Henry Tazewell's opinion, Jefferson's election was a "matter of extreme importance to republicanism and the U. States," if the ideals of individual rights and liberties, religious freedom, and limited government were to prevail.[22]

Littleton was in complete agreement, and when John

Adams's election appeared imminent, the younger Tazewell
had "alarming apprehensions" about the consequences to the
country. Adams, he was certain, would "effect a tension in the
reins of government." Perhaps, he admitted, there had been
some lack of presidential leadership during the Washington
administration, but what, he asked his father, would be the
result of a tightening of the reins by Adams. Would all the
sections of the country be forced into a pro-British stance?
Would the country witness violent struggles between conflicting interests? Could a tendency to increase the powers of the
national government result in a move to sever the Union? Was
a division of the country an absurd suggestion, or was it an
idea worthy of consideration? As the country grew and the
sections became more diverse in wealth, manners, and temper,
would it not be tempting for an oppressive central government to try to enforce conformity, through the use of a large
standing army if necessary, thus destroying the essence of republicanism? "On the other hand," he conjectured, "should a
disunion take place, we may be less wealthy, less powerful, &
therefore less feared, but we would have a better chance for a
duration of the government of freedom, & while blessed with
this, altho' at the price of a deprivation of all other blessings,
the people must continue to enjoy a greater share of comparative happiness."[23] A few days later Littleton apologized to his
father for such heretical and unorthodox opinions,[24] but many
of the questions he raised in January 1797 remained in his
mind for a lifetime. The place of the South in the Union and
the welfare of the Virginia Tidewater were ever important to
him. As he matured and became more active in political affairs, he deplored the idea of disunion and constantly sought
some other alternative as a solution for the nation's internal
difficulties. His concerns were for fair and equitable treatment
for all sections. States, he felt, must ever be on guard against
abuses of power by the federal government or by any person,
group, or branch therein.

Henry Tazewell thought his son's questions provocative but
futile, unless the querist entered politics. Voices such as his
were needed as a disastrous chain of events followed in the
wake of the ratification of the Jay Treaty. Relations between
France and the United States rapidly deteriorated, and with

the smell of war in the air state militias readied themselves. During the uneasy days of June 1797, Littleton Tazewell was appointed lieutenant of a Virginia company of light infantry, but finding this no place for an avid horseman, he requested reassignment to a cavalry troop.[25]

Within a short time, however, a more personal anxiety preoccupied young Tazewell. His father was not well. Journeys to Philadelphia were arduous, especially during the winter months, and often Henry Tazewell became ill en route with ague and fever, necessitating bleeding. Littleton was also concerned about his father's indebtedness and tried to suggest ways to liquidate at least some of the liabilities. "You will think, I fear," he apologetically explained to his father, "that I busy myself too much in your affairs, but, pardon me for so doing. It is but the effect of my solicitude to see you extricated from the seeming difficulties which at present hang over you & which appear to render you uneasy. If my anxiety offends you, I will repress it, for the first wish of my heart is to do that of which you approve."[26]

In addition to his other duties, Littleton managed his father's plantations, which included, besides Kingsmill, Capahosick on the York River. But Henry Tazewell urged his son to do more, to enter politics and join forces with the struggling Republican party. Years later when asked why he had embarked on a political career, Littleton Tazewell supposedly answered, "My father made me." Undoubtedly his father's influence was strong, but the younger Tazewell also had distinct political convictions of his own. In the spring of 1798 he was elected "by a respectable majority" to represent James City County in the Virignia House of Delegates.[27]

In retrospect, it was most fitting for Littleton Waller Tazewell to make his political debut during the debate on the Virginia Resolutions. Written to counteract national despotism, as personified in the Federalist-inspired Alien, Naturalization, and Sedition Acts, the Virginia Resolutions advocated limiting the powers of the federal government and upholding the right of states to judge the constitutionality of acts of Congress. In the United States Senate Henry Tazewell had raised his voice against Federalist usurpation: The Sedition Act, if allowed to go unchallenged, would "indulge that appetite for tyranny that alone could have occasioned the introduction of the principle." Littleton Tazewell, totally in accord with his father's views, voted with the majority in the state assembly to approve the Virginia Resolutions. During his first session in the house he also cast his ballot for the reelection of his father to the Senate of the United States.[28]

Because of ill health Henry Tazewell reluctantly postponed his departure for Philadelphia, and the short session of the Fifth Congress began without him. Remembering clearly Jefferson's impatience with "weak-kneed" Republicans who had absented themselves during the last session when crucial matters were being considered, he was troubled by the delay. As news of important business before the Senate reached him, he felt compelled to proceed to Philadelphia. Passing through Richmond, he paused briefly to exchange a few words with his son and then continued to his destination without a break. To allay Littleton's anxiety, he wrote to him immediately on arrival: "I have almost recovered [from] my fatigue, and do not lament the haste in which we travelled; indeed, I think my health has been bettered by the exercise." He had not, as yet, time to brief himself on the state of politics, but again he expressed his deep aversion for the Alien and Sedition Acts and his fears for the future of the nation. Two days later Henry Tazewell was dead of what was diagnosed as "acute bilious pleurisy." By the time Littleton received the sad news, his father had been interred in the yard of Philadelphia's Christ Church. Senators Stevens T. Mason of Virginia and John Brown of Kentucky arranged the funeral, and Littleton had some consolation in knowing that the grave site was next to that of his father's good friend James Innes, another Virginian who died far from home. James Beckley, the Virginia-born former clerk of the House of Representatives, in whose home Tazewell resided while in Philadelphia, settled the senator's affairs in the city. Along with a poignant "small bunch of keys," a message from Beckley informed Littleton that his father's clothes, trunk, and other belongings would be forwarded by ship to Norfolk, from which point Littleton could arrange to have them transported to Kingsmill.[29]

For Littleton Tazewell his father's death at the age of forty-six was a crushing blow. Only during the last five or six years had father and son developed a feeling of closeness. They were not a great deal alike. Henry Tazewell was not an abstract thinker or fond of books or study, whereas the pursuit of knowledge and the acquisition of a fine library were Littleton's chief delights; but on fundamentals there had been no disagreement. In Virginia, Henry Tazewell had fought vigorously for the abolition of primogeniture and entail and the separation of church and state. On the national scene he had not wavered from the Jeffersonian line. "In company," his son remembered, "he was generally vivacious and sprightly, but when alone with his family he was remarkable for his taciturnity, and for an apparent reserve in his manners which gave him the semblance of morose sternness." Nothing was more erroneous, however, than such an opinion, "for his temper was exceedingly mild and amiable and he was an affectionate father and kind relation."[30]

Littleton might have mentioned the financial burden bequeathed to him by his father, but he did not. In his will Henry Tazewell left to his daughter Sophia Ann ("Nancy") Taliaferro, a few slaves, a mourning ring, and two thousand pounds. Littleton inherited the remainder of the estate with the provision that he pay all his father's debts and satisfy Nancy's legacy. By the time these wishes were fulfilled, there was almost nothing left for Littleton except a strong determination to manage his own business affairs more efficiently.[31]

The winter of 1799 was grim. A week after his father's death, and very likely before the news reached him, Littleton Tazewell was saddened by the demise of Mary Wickham, John Wickham's wife and Henry Tazewell's half-sister. When she died, Littleton was in Richmond, attending to his legislative duties and residing at the Wickham home.[32] Throughout his long life he was haunted by the early deaths of his mother, father, and Mary Wickham. As a result, his own health and that of his wife and children became almost an obsession with him.

For the present Tazewell found solace in the company of Elizabeth McClurg. Whether he had spoken formally to the young lady's father is not certain, but without a doubt he assumed that he and Elizabeth would marry. Apparently the thought was mutual, for, as Tazewell expressed it, she had "deigned to approve" him. After the close of the legislative session Tazewell returned to Williamsburg and from there he wrote his "Beloved Betsy," his "Dearest Eliza," the most uninhibited and poetic letters of his lifetime. With his sister Nancy married and his father dead, Kingsmill was lonely. In a letter to Eliza, Tazewell described his return to the plantation late one evening. "The night was dark, enlightened only by the faint glimmering of a few stars, an awful stillness reigned everywhere and heightened the solemnity of the scene." As he slowly and wearily approached the house, he stopped at the gate to look about him. "At no time have I ever felt my wretchedness more keenly than then. . . . Not one there is who feel real delight in welcoming me home." Only his favorite dog was there to greet him. "You at least my little Sly-looks are pleased to see me, said I caressing the dog, & my well known voice soon drew around me a noisey pack whose deep-toned rejoicings at once awakened everyone near." This was all preliminary to telling "dear Betsy " of anticipations of far different scenes when "the dear object of my heart's best affection shall grace this habitation."[33]

Tazewell's days were busy with court sessions in Suffolk, Gloucester, and Hampton as well as in Williamsburg. His visits to Richmond were of necessity few, and by November it was obvious to him that Elizabeth's interest was waning. Communications from his friend Wickham only increased his concern. Tazewell, reading between the lines, knew something was amiss. In letters to Elizabeth he poured out his affection, hoping to dispel "the displeasure of her whom I adore," but to no avail. Elizabeth McClurg had found a new attraction. A few months later she married John Wickham.[34] The shock must have been devastating. Not only had Elizabeth rejected him, she had married his closest friend. The cordial relationship between Tazewell and Wickham cooled for a time, but as the years passed Wickham again became Tazewell's most trusted counselor. Ever after, however, Tazewell very properly and formally referred to her who had been his "heart's best affection" only as "Mrs. Wickham." Elizabeth did not completely forget the young romance. She kept a few of Tazewell's letters and a touching poem he wrote for her. These survive among the Wickham papers.

Fortunately, in the spring and summer of 1800 Tazewell was able to focus his attention on politics, a diversion needed to ease the loss of "dear Eliza." In June, John Marshall, Virginia's leading Federalist, resigned his seat in the House of Representatives to become secretary of state in the administration of John Adams. The district Marshall represented consisted of the city of Richmond and the counties of Henrico, Hanover, Charles City, James City, and New Kent. As the Federalist party was somewhat discredited by recent events, Virginia Republicans believed it possible to fill the vacancy created by Marshall's resignation with one of their own, and in casting about for a candidate, they found Tazewell's name mentioned with increasing seriousness. This was due in part to Republican devotion to the memory of Henry Tazewell, but, unquestionably, young Tazewell had acquitted himself well as a member of the Virginia General Assembly. In the courts his intellectual prowess was amazing members of the bar. His impressive appearance was an asset, as was his courteously reserved demeanor. Exposure to the Federalism of Wickham, the McClurgs, and Marshall, among others, had not lured Tazewell from the tenets of Jeffersonianism. Throughout his life Tazewell never allowed honest differences of opinion on political matters to alter a friendship. An independent spirit, he at no time considered himself a party man but consistently fostered whatever he thought was best for Virginia.[35]

When asked to stand for election to Congress, Tazewell accepted with alacrity. If elected, his term would be short. The second session of the Sixth Congress was to sit from November 17, 1800, to March 3, 1801. Tazewell, without any notion of how exciting the session would be, was anxious to prove his loyalty to the Jeffersonian cause, but the race was yet to be won and the outcome uncertain. Not quite twenty-six years old and a novice in politics, Tazewell was pitted against a seasoned and established Federalist, Colonel John Mayo. Mayo was a well-to-do planter whose estate, The Hermitage, was located about a mile from Richmond.[36]

Politically, Mayo was a determined supporter of the status quo. "With candour" he announced his unqualified advocacy of John Adams. The campaign was spirited, and Tazewell anxiously awaited the returns, which drifted in with agonizing slowness. "When the stage passed Hanover Courthouse about one o' clock yesterday," the *Virginia Argus* reported on August 1, "Mr. Tazewell had a majority of about 70 votes." In the final tally, out of 1,206 ballots cast, 778 were for the Republican candidate. "Ill news from Virginia," lamented John Marshall to Harrison Gray Otis, Massachusett's most zealous Federalist. "To succeed me has been elected by an immence majority one of the most decided democrats in the Union. . . . There is a tide in the affairs of nations, of parties, & of individuals. I feel that of real Americanism is on the ebb." Beyond the confines of Virginia other Federalists were discomfited by Tazewell's victory. Delaware's only congressman, the ultra-Federalist James A. Bayard, confided to his favorite political aspirant, Alexander Hamilton, that "Virginia is sold and past all salvation."[37]

Nationally, Republicans looked forward to the election of Jefferson as president and Aaron Burr as vice-president. The Federalists endorsed the incumbent John Adams, with Charles Cotesworth Pinckney of South Carolina as his running mate, but Jefferson's victory seemed a certainty, and with high hopes for a new era Littleton Tazewell on November 26, 1800, appeared in the House of Representatives, produced his credentials, was qualified, and took his seat.[38]

During the spring and summer of 1800, between sessions of the Sixth Congress, the federal government had moved from Philadelphia to its permanent location in the District of Columbia. President Adams arrived by coach, having been eight days en route. Most of his entourage, cabinet members, clerks, and the official records came by sloop. Tazewell, seeing the capital for the first time, found beauty in the broad sweep of the Potomac River and in the natural surroundings, but accommodations were scanty. Six or seven members of Congress, Tazewell among them, took lodgings in Georgetown. A few others located quarters near the President's House, a swampy mile and a half from the Capitol. The remainder of the lawmakers crowded into seven or eight boardinghouses on New Jersey Avenue near the north wing of the Capitol, the only completed portion. Rents were comparatively high. Albert Gallatin of Pennsylvania reported sharing a room at Conrad and McMunn's, about two hundred paces from the

Capitol, for which he paid fifteen dollars a week, "including attendance, wood, candles, and liquors." In addition to the boardinghouses, around the Capitol one could find a tailor, shoemaker, printer, washerwoman, grocery shop, stationery store, small dry-goods shop, and an oyster house.[39] Living conditions were neither pleasant nor convenient, but to one who had ridden the circuit in Tidewater Virginia for court days, the situation was bearable.

Congress convened on November 17, but members straggled in as late as January. The session was nine days old when Tazewell appeared in the small crowded room behind the Senate chamber, the temporary location of the House of Representatives. The atmosphere, the talk in the corridors, reminded Tazewell of the days he spent in Philadelphia with his father. It was good to have long conversations with John Randolph, to laugh again at his antics, to have him point out some of the major figures, Federalist and Republican, of the House and Senate. Randolph had served during the first session of the Sixth Congress and by now considered himself a veteran.[40]

Among members of the House who particularly interested Tazewell were Bayard of Delaware, the strong Hamiltonian partisan; the venerable and sometimes formidable Harrison Gray Otis, a Federalist of the staunchest variety; Edward Livingston, a wealthy New Yorker, ten years Tazewell's senior; Albert Gallatin, the Swiss-born Pennsylvanian, a friend of Jefferson's and acknowledged Republican leader of the House; and the learned and suave Thomas Pinckney of South Carolina, educated at the Middle Temple and the royal military academy at Caen. Nominally a Federalist, and a brother of Charles Cotesworth Pinckney, he nevertheless voted against the Sedition Act and was an advocate of states' rights. Randolph also introduced Tazewell to Matthew Lyon of Vermont, who had suffered prosecution under the Sedition Act, and Nathaniel Macon of North Carolina, another stalwart Republican and a future Speaker of the House. Several senators were glad to welcome the son of Henry Tazewell. John Brown of Kentucky and Stevens T. Mason of Virginia, who arranged the last rites for the elder Tazewell, and Wilson Cary Nicholas, who succeeded him in the Senate, were particularly cordial. A number of the gentlemen impressed the new congressman,

but the early business of the House did not. The almost inter-
minable discussion on a bill for erecting a mausoleum to
George Washington irritated him beyond endurance. Congress seemed only to be marking time, awaiting the outcome
of the presidential election.[41]

Throughout late October and into November the various
states, by an assortment of methods, selected members of the
electoral college. On December 3 the chosen electors, meeting
in their respective states, cast their ballots. According to the
Constitution each elector was to vote for two candidates. The
man receiving the highest number of votes would be president,
and regardless of party affiliation, the vice-presidency would
go to the runner-up. As results trickled in, the Federalist defeat
was evident, but even so, for the Republicans all was not well.
The electoral college had given an equal number of votes to
Jefferson and Burr, the two Republican candidates, thus leaving to the House of Representatives the decision as to which
should be president. A few eager Federalists, seeing an opportunity to prevent the resolution of the matter before Inauguration Day, hoped for a stopgap measure to keep their party in
power, possibly by naming John Marshall, chief justice of the
Supreme Court, temporary executive. During these anxious
weeks tempers ran high, and Tazewell was caught up in the
excitement. Rumors of secret caucuses, of Burr's maneuverings
to win the presidency, of interception of the mails by one group
or another circulated wildly. Federalists, angered by the pro-
Jeffersonian tone of the *National Intelligencer,* had the paper's
editor, Samuel Harrison Smith, ordered from the floor of the
House, where he had been permitted to sit to record debates
for the press. Three days later he was expelled from the public
gallery.[42]

The House began balloting on February 11, and by midnight the states had been polled nineteen times. At three
o'clock on the morning of February 12 Tazewell wrote to Governor James Monroe. The House, he said, had cast twenty-two
ballots with neither candidate receiving the necessary nine-
state majority. The count each time was eight states for Jefferson, six for Burr, with two state delegations divided and not
voting. To Tazewell there appeared little probability of a
change very soon. "Fatigue has worn down most of my

friends, but those who still bear up remain firm and unaltera-
ble, & the weary are now endeavoring to regain by sleep their
impaired faculties, when they will return and give us also
some relief." The eight states supporting Jefferson would remain loyal, he assured Monroe, and even though there was a
movement afoot to suspend deliberations, "We never more
adjourn but to proclaim Jefferson the President!" However,
his optimism was qualified. Should a Federalist coup d'etat
occur, Monroe must decide what course Virginia ought to
pursue. "We are prepared for every event, determined alike
neither to attempt or suffer usurpation, but should circumstances require it to throw ourselves on our state for protection, of whose support we do not permit ourselves to doubt."[43]

On Friday, February 13, after the thirtieth ballot, Tazewell
again reported to Monroe, sending the message "by a private
conveyance, apprehensive lest the mail (as heretofore) may be
interrupted."[44] A group of Federalists had tried to postpone
the next poll until March 3, the day before the inauguration,
thus almost insuring a temporary or interim arrangement.
This motion was rejected. Still, no prospect of an election
existed. Republicans and Federalists alike remained immov-
able, and on Saturday the House adjourned, out of exhaustion
and frustration, until Monday.

As the new week began, the National Intelligencer warned of
"dangers which threaten the peace of society and the existence
of the Constitution," and among members of the House the
serious implications of the situation were patently clear. Finally, the following day, February 17, on the thirty-sixth ballot, the deadlock was broken. The Federalist representatives
of Vermont and Maryland, who during previous voting had
divided their delegations and thus precluded the recording of
decisions by their states, now abstained, and Maryland and
Vermont cast ballots for Jefferson, giving him a ten-state majority. "The voice of the people has prevailed," joyfully announced the Intelligencer. Tazewell, Thomas Pinckney, and
Bayard were appointed to inform Adams and Jefferson of the
outcome.[45]

Although preoccupied with the election controversy, Congress turned its attention to two other matters of considerable
importance. The Senate, after an initial rejection, ratified the

Convention of 1800, absolving the United States from a defensive alliance with France under the terms of the Treaty of 1778 but retaining favorable commercial agreements between the two nations and, much to the credit of John Adams, returning relations with France to a normal status. While Republicans welcomed the ratification of the convention, they were dismayed by the passage of the Judiciary Act of 1801. Sponsored by the Federalists, this legislation was designed to give the defeated party significant control over the judicial branch during the next, Republican-dominated, administration. Tazewell was not present to vote against this measure.[46]

Disgusted by the machinations of some of his congressional colleagues, Tazewell, during his brief stay in Washington, acquired a distinct distaste for politics and refused to be a candidate for the Seventh Congress.[47] If a choice was possible, he preferred to emulate the life-style of Grandfather Waller rather than that of his father, and what he now desired most was a home of his own, a serene existence, a fine library, financial security, and a law practice specializing in cases of a maritime or commercial nature. For a young Virginian with such career interests, Norfolk was the ideal location. In 1801 it was the boomtown not only of Virginia but of the entire southeastern seaboard, and already Tazewell was making plans to close his Williamsburg office, sell his father's plantations, and move to the port city.

## Chapter II

# *Norfolk and*
# *a Return to*
# *Politics*

Early in 1802 Tazewell settled into his new office on Norfolk's Main Street, number 6, just a few doors from the John Nivisons, who welcomed him with generous hospitality. John Nivison, a charter member of Phi Beta Kappa and a distinguished member of the Norfolk bar, and his wife, Sarah Stratton Nivison, both had Tazewell mothers, sisters of Littleton Tazewell's grandfather. Within a very short time the unattached bachelor found himself seriously attracted to Ann, the Nivisons' charming and intelligent seventeen-year-old daughter. There were other friends and acquaintances in the vicinity: sea captains, merchants, attorneys. John Cooper, editor of the *Norfolk Public Ledger,* lived at 4 Main Street, while Robert Barraud Taylor, Tazewell's college classmate and close friend, resided at number 13.[1]

After almost total obliteration during the war years, Norfolk was experiencing a resurgence of prosperity. Renewed hostilities in Europe prevented the British navy from enforcing restrictions on trade between the United States and the British West Indies imposed after the colonies gained independence, and as a result exports, carried largely in American ships, flowed southward at an increasing rate. Commerce with the French West Indies also flourished. Opportunities for lawyers were abundant. Like any seaport, Norfolk had a fair amount of violence, and court dockets were crowded with cases involving "black eyes and cracked crowns." Disputes between masters and apprentices, landlords and tenants, or husbands and wives occupied a portion of Tazewell's time, but he was most interested in litigation concerning shipping and commerce. Wealthy Norfolk merchants who owned their own vessels were caught up in the trade revival, and as the economy expanded, maritime suits increased. Tazewell had a special hereditary affection and regard for the law of admiralty.[2]

Tazewell was a good lawyer, a "Ciceronian," according to his friends. Only lack of ambition, it was said, prevented him from becoming a prominent national figure early in his career. He was astute. There was no "broken lumber or worthless trash in his mind." In making his pleas, he drew on his vast knowledge of science, history, art, and mathematics and seemed able to grapple with the most complicated problems without difficulty. Unfortunately, at this time there were no stenographers in the inferior courts, and speeches, however eloquent or significant, were not recorded for posterity. Critics found a provoking minuteness of detail in Tazewell's arguments and a "conscious superiority" in his manner, but, reputedly, he spoke well and presented his cases with grace and efficiency.[3]

Accusations of "hauteur" stemmed in part from Tazewell's preoccupation with the "cultivation of the mind," a pursuit in which the general populace of Norfolk, including many gentlemen of the bar, did not engage. Yet, Tazewell did not lack for intellectual companionship. In addition to John Nivison there was William Pennock, shipping merchant and naval agent, who a few years earlier had given the architect Benjamin Henry Latrobe his first commission in America. The Pennock house at 16 Main Street was a joy to behold, with its grand staircase, quiet elegance, and beautiful symmetry. Moses Myers, senior partner in the firm of Myers and Pennock, was a cultured gentleman whose house, at the corner of Freemason and Catherine streets, was an oasis of charm and good taste.[4] Norfolk also had its share of literary and debating clubs. John Hamilton, the British vice-consul, hosted parties envied by larger commercial centers. A bookseller, Caleb Bonsal, established himself in Norfolk early in the 1800s, and for nearly half a century Tazewell purchased Bonsal's books to add to his ever-growing library.[5] French refugees fleeing the Santo Domingo slave revolts brought an aspect of cosmopolitanism to the borough. Often they were accompanied by their slaves, and the increasing number of Santo Domingo blacks created anxiety among the citizens of Norfolk, who feared the contagion of insurrection might spread to local Negroes. "The situation of this place," one resident informed the governor, "is such as a few hours would reduce it to ashes."[6]

Extensive foreign trade, regardless of its salutary effect on Norfolk's economy, was a mixed blessing. Always present was the danger that ships infected with smallpox and yellow fever would enter the harbor and spread sickness throughout the port. Smallpox could be contained by quarantine and inoculation, but for another century the cause and prevention of yellow fever remained a mystery. When the pestilence appeared, usually in early July, it was uncontrollable and did not abate until the first frost. Inexplicably, some years were free from the horrors of the sickness, but during fever-ridden summers those of the populace who were able to do so fled to the country, while the rest remained to die or to care for the dying. The "infection" often was confined to an area south of Main Street and west of Market Square; however, no one could be certain where death would strike, and panic was widespread.[7]

To Tazewell, attempting to outrun the disease was folly. As a child he had seen Grandfather Waller try to evade the smallpox by leaving Williamsburg whenever the British army, considered the primary carrier of the contagion, approached, only to find that "every spot to which he had fled for safety was in like manner visited, so that he had better have stayed where he was from the beginning." In this regard Tazewell was something of a fatalist, an acceptable attitude, perhaps, for a bachelor, but in the summer of 1802 his status changed. On July 15 he married Ann Stratton Nivison.[8]

Tazewell was happy. He felt as if he belonged in Norfolk and involved himself in many aspects of the town's development. He became a member of the board of trustees of the Norfolk Academy and an officer in the horse cavalry of the local militia, looking striking indeed in his scarlet and white uniform. To the elder Nivisons, he was the mainstay of the family, a devoted and dutiful son-in-law, and Ann's young brother, William, as well as her sisters, Sarah and Louisa, found him patient and understanding. Tazewell's generosity was not confined to family. When William Wirt was in need of a more lucrative practice, Tazewell, dismayed by the manner in which the brilliant young attorney was dissipating his health and reputation, offered him a partnership.[9] Tazewell was charmed by the outgoing Wirt. So lacking in effusiveness himself, Tazewell often enjoyed the antics of extroverts.

As tales of Wirt's nimble wit and pleasant personality spread throughout the borough, he did not lack for clients, but he disliked long grinding hours of preparation, preferring to spend more time in writing "causal literary pieces," such as *Letters of a British Spy* which won popular acclaim in Richmond and Norfolk in 1803. Such activity, thought Tazewell, gave Wirt a light and idle appearance, professionally detrimental. Unlike Tazewell, Wirt had no interest in the future of Norfolk, and haunted by the fear of the annually recurring yellow fever, he made plans to return to Richmond as soon as prudence would permit. He was using his experience in Norfolk, he told his wife, merely as a ladder by which they could "climb the hills of Richmond advantageously." For Tazewell, Wirt was a stimulating, entertaining, and demanding friend, forever in need of assistance in buying his winter wood, selling a servant, or preparing a case.[10] When, in 1806, Wirt forsook Norfolk for the hills of Richmond, Tazewell missed him. Although in later years they drifted apart, Wirt's brief sojourn in the Virginia seaport added zest to the intellectual life of the town, and Tazewell watched with fascination and, at times, astonishment Wirt's rapid rise to national prominence.

Other interesting and colorful people were entertained by the Tazewells. From England in November 1803 came the Anthony Merrys, accompanied by the poet Thomas Moore. Disembarking in Norfolk, the Merrys were en route to the nation's capital where Merry presented his credentials as Great Britain's envoy extraordinary and minister plenipotentiary, and where his newly acquired wife caused a minor diplomatic and social tempest.[11]

Another unusual lady entered Tazewell's life in August 1805 when the merchant ship *Planter* made its way into Hampton Roads, carrying home from England, after a prolonged absence, the eccentric Lucy Ludwell Paradise. Tazewell had never before met Mrs. Paradise; yet, it was to him she

Littleton Waller Tazewell. (*Virginia State Library*)

Ann Nivison Tazewell. (*Virginia State Library*)

directed her appeal for assistance when she decided to return permanently to her native shore. As she was entirely without funds, with "Great Debts" to pay, would Tazewell, as a "particular friend" of her dear deceased nephew, William Ludwell Lee, forward a remittance large enough to enable her to settle her accounts in London and buy passage to Virginia? "I shall bring my coach and furniture with me," she wrote, "but no servants." Tazewell did what he could, and Lucy Paradise arrived with all her worldly possessions, including her treasured black and yellow four-wheeled carriage, a pianoforte, and an assortment of household furniture. It is doubtful that Tazewell attended the Sunday morning service in Bruton Parish Church when Mrs. Paradise, nobly attired, made her grand entrance behind a turbaned black boy who held aloft a cushion on which were ensconced her prayer book and hymnal. But Tazewell may have accompanied her on one of her famous rides in the coach she brought with her from London. On such occasions Williamsburg residents worthly of an invitation from the elegant lady were conducted to the carriage house and bidden to enter the vehicle. No horses were used, and the ride was entirely indoors. Henry, the Negro servant, drew the carriage back and forth while the guests conversed on lofty subjects. From the Ludwell-Paradise house on Williamsburg's Duke of Gloucester Street, this remarkable but unfortunate lady held court until, in 1812, she was committed to the Eastern Lunatic Hospital, where she spent the last two years of her life. "When I am settled in my house in Williamsburg I hope you will honour me with you company," she had written Tazewell from London.[12] One hopes that he did.

At a reception for His Excellency Sidi Solyman Malimeli, ambassador from the Bay of Tunis (who surpassed in novelty even the colorful Mrs. Paradise), Tazewell first met the dashing Captain Stephen Decatur, fresh from his heroic feats against the Tripolitans. When Decatur was assigned to the Norfolk area as commander of a squadron of gunboats and later as head of the Gosport Navy Yard, he and Tazewell formed a close and lasting friendship, and Decatur retained Tazewell as his legal representative in the settlement of numerous prize cases.[13]

For Tazewell the early years in Norfolk were good. His expanding law practice and his excellent business sense placed him in so favorable a financial position that others often applied to him for loans. "You mentioned to me sometime past," Wilson Cary Nicholas reminded him, "that you sometimes lent money to country gentlemen. If you have any that you cannot better employ you would do me a great kindness, if you would lend me any sum from five to fifteen hundred pounds. . . . Money I shall certainly be able to repay, but I fear I shall too long remain your debtor for the good offices you have already done me."[14]

Tazewell's circle of friends grew, as did his family. In the spring of 1804 a daughter, their first child, was born to Ann and Littleton Tazewell. She was named Louisa, after Mrs. Tazewell's sister. A year later a son, Henry, followed.[15] In a few years Tazewell had established himself as a family man and as a respected member of the Norfolk bar and business community.

Then, with the approach of the 1804 presidential election, Tazewell, to his own surprise, found his political interests whetted. "For several years since we last saw each other," he reflected in a letter to John Randolph, "I have preserved this apathy as to political arrangements & have mistaken this indifference for content." But with the general rise of election-year fever, he developed symptoms of "the same sort of interest which formerly disturbed me, and am anxious, if not to mix again in the political world, to hear at least what is acting and planning there." Would Randolph please keep him informed?[16]

Several matters troubled Tazewell, matters of importance to the future of the country which could be solved only in the political arena. One was "the infernal traffic in the slave trade." While investigating charges against persons presumably engaged in the loathsome practice and examining congressional attempts to prevent the influx of foreign slaves, Tazewell was appalled to learn about "the various measures & pretexts by which it is still carried on." According to the federal Constitution, Congress could not officially ban such traffic until 1808; however, individual states could do so, and during the early years of nationhood every southern state, with Virginia taking the lead in 1778, passed laws prohibiting within its jurisdiction the ingress of foreign slaves, and in 1803

Congress, in an attempt to strengthen state laws, forbade the importation of slaves into any state where such practice was not condoned. These laws, Tazewell knew, were violated with impunity, because the penalities they prescribed were not severe enough to "prevent or sufficiently to punish this most detestable of all iniquities . . . which is still carried on to a very great extent from the New England states." The case to which Tazewell referred involved the master of a vessel which made eleven such voyages within a few years. The profit per voyage, from $9,000 to $12,000 according to Tazewell's calculations, obviously was worth the risk of apprehension. Purchased on the African coast for less than $80, a slave sold regularly in South Carolina or Georgia for $400. Tazewell urged Randolph to persuade Congress to strengthen existing laws and bring an end to the evil.[17]

But there was little Randolph could do. "The state of [South] Carolina has put it out of my power to avail myself of the information contained in your last," he replied to Tazewell's plea. "To her indelible disgrace she has legalized this abomination. All her rice, indigo, & cotton is to be converted into slaves. The labor of the miserable negro is to procure fresh companions of his wretchedness. I tremble for the dreadful retribution which this horrid thirst for African blood, which the legislators of that state are base enough to feel, and yet more base to avow, may bring upon us." The fate of the "nabobs" of Santo Domingo had not been considered with sufficient seriousness by their counterparts in South Carolina and Georgia, and, warned Randolph, "it behooves Virginia, in my opinion, to look to the consequences." If the Negroes gained possession of the lower country of those two states, Randolph believed it never could be recovered. "The climate is even worse than that of St. Domingo. What figure would an American army cut there, when the natives, who are able, fly from it every summer, against an enemy who goes naked & lives upon a handful of rice or corn & to whom the swamps are as welcome as the alligator." Despite his feeling that he could do nothing to curb the African slave trade, Randolph, constantly encouraged by Tazewell, did rail against it both before and after the congressional prohibition of 1808.[18]

Another topic troublesome to Tazewell was the caucus system of nominating candidates for president and vice-president. Late in February 1804 a caucus composed of 108 Republican members of Congress met to decide upon the party's candidates. Jefferson received unanimous viva voce support as the presidential nominee, but the choice for second place was more difficult. By a majority (67) of those present, George Clinton of New York was nominated. Aaron Burr, the incumbent, received not a single vote. Tazewell was disturbed. "Will you tell me for what it is that Burr is abandon'd?" he inquired of Randolph. "As well as I remember we both on a former occasion thought highly of this man. My opinion of him has not been alter'd by anything I have since seen, but rather strengthened by evidence which I have in my own possession." Was it not possible that many citizens still favored Burr? Did the Republican members of Congres actually know how the qualified voters of the country felt? Tazewell chided Randolph for his lack of democratic sensitivity: "How fast is this government of ours settling into aristocracy; and into aristocracy of the worst kind, the aristocracy supported by intrigue." The voting public, which supposedly possessed the power of government, had no real voice except in electing members of the lower house of Congress, after which the people were "mere tools in the hands of their Representatives, compelled to execute whatever they decide." "The manner of your late proceedings conclusively proves these positions. An unauthorized meeting, undertaken to decide that one of the old servants of the people is no longer worthy of their confidence—without specifying any charge against him, offers to the public choice a new candidate of their own [the caucus'] selection." The electorate had no option but to support this nominee. If they refused to do so, they ran the risk of splitting their vote, thus guaranteeing the election of a member of the opposition party. If an intriguing character aspired to be a presidential candidate, Tazewell pointed out, all he would have to do would be "to secure the good will of a majority of the majority of the members of Congress," and his success would be assured. Even more dangerous, he thought, was the secrecy in which the caucus was conducted. If the proceedings "were open & the sentiments of each of its members necessarily known, there would be a degree of responsibility attached to their actions. . . . Thank heaven there is yet enough of honor and virtue among you to carry you to right ends through these crooked means. But you have thrown open a door, inviting the entrance of fraud, corruption, and every other dangerous foe to Republican liberty and the time I fear is not far distant when thousands will be disposed to enter." Tazewell did not object to the results of the most recent "treasonable practice against the peoples' rights." He intended to support Jefferson "in any event with all my soul," and he believed Clinton to be a valuable and sound Republican. Nevertheless, he disliked expedient explanations. "I am not enough of a causist," he delcared, "to justify means by ends, or to extol evil when practiced for the attainment of good. Republican virtue should disdain such shifts. If liberty cannot be preserved without them, it is not worth the preservation, for too surely will this present antidote prove its bane hereafter."[19]

In reply Randolph endeavored to explain the abandonment of Burr by the Republican caucus. True, the vice-president did have a general reputation for ingenuity, eloquence, enterprise, and firmness. The éclat with which he handled the New York electorate in the election of 1800 could not be denied. It was this suavity which caused Randolph to have high esteem for Burr's political character. But a closer inspection, Randolph confided to Tazewell, "as is so often the case, diminished & finally extinguished my confidence in him. I consider him now as committed to the federal party. They will support him in N. York, except a very few who affect consistency— Hamilton for instance, who, by the way is said to have been personally wounded by B. in a manner which is not in any nature (much less his) to forgive. The MARIA is said to have been a last mistress of the V.P." Randolph savored this little piece of gossip. "The Maria" was Maria Reynolds, whose notorious affair with Hamilton some years earlier had threatened that gentleman's career.[20] If the Virginia congressmen was correct, there may have been more than political enmity between Hamilton and Burr.

Randolph found Tazewell's remarks on the caucus method of nominating candidates "forcibly striking." Yet, unless Tazewell could devise a remedy, the practice appeared to be one of "those inherent evils of our system (for what system is without them)." Surely, caucus nomination was preferable to the election of the president and vice-president by the two houses of Congress, as some advocated. "Cabal is the necessary effect of freedom," he advised his friend, and "where men are left free to act, we must calculate on their being governed by their interests & passions." Instead of reviling the system, Tazewell should enter politics and attempt to improve it.[21]

Before Tazewell received Randolph's letter, he was chosen to represent the borough of Norfolk in the next General Assembly. Randolph was pleased and had high expectations of Tazewell's political contributions. Tazewell himself was not all that confident. Although he returned to public life after vowing never again to do so, primarily for the purpose of supporting Jefferson's reelection and some of the president's programs, Tazewell's "pure Republicanism" was doubted in certain quarters. "How is it Tazewell," asked James Semple of Williamsburg, "that with some your political soundness is questioned, whilst with those who once knew you best and now know you well, you are as entirely confided in as any man in the state? Is it because you are rich, because your connections in Norfolk are not democratic, because you are silent, or why is it?" Tazewell did associate closely with Federalists as well with Republicans. His father-in-law, John Nivison, was a Federalist, as were John Wickham, Robert B. Taylor, and a number of his other lifelong friends. Also, Tazewell was an independent thinker. He believed in the future of Norfolk, and if from time to time that future could be furthered by Federalist measures, he would not hew to the "pure Republican" line. At this juncture he was a Jeffersonian liberal who realized that commercial developments were important to the economic survival of the borough. He did not consider this as heresy, and neither did Jefferson, who appealed to Tazewell to do what he could for the administration among the "mercantile men" of Norfolk. "I know of no principle in which these gentlemen differ from us," the president wrote, and he asked Tazewell to inform those engaged in trade and commerce "that we aim at preserving the public faith & paying its debts honestly, at protecting commerce & enlarging its field, at an intercourse with France & England, peaceable, friendly, and rigorously impartial."[22]

To promote the economic development of Norfolk, Tazewell during the spring and summer of 1804 worked diligently
for the establishment of a Norfolk branch of the Bank of
Virginia. Although the bank was considered "a dangerous system" by some members of the business community, others
recognized the need for financial institutions. "Our bank
shares were all taken yesterday in less than three hours," Tazewell informed St. George Tucker. "The merchants here were
very few of them indeed subscribers, but the whole stock allowed us was taken by residents of the town and neighborhood." Both Tazewell and Nivison were elected to the board
of directors of the Norfolk branch.[23]

Tazewell's interest in commerce also prompted him to seek
appointment as collector of the port of Norfolk, and he wrote
letters to John Randolph, James Madison, and Wilson Cary
Nicholas, then a United States senator, requesting their support. Not accustomed to petitioning for favors, Tazewell characteristically assured Randolph that he was not a "fawning
sycophant." "I need not say to you that in any application to
anyone on my account, you will remember me also, that I am
no begger of offices, from whom governmental subserviency
is to be expected, but a citizen, who if the Executive choose to
appoint to office, will endeavor not to disgrace either myself
or my country in the discharge of its duties." He did not
receive the appointment. Instead, it went to Nicholas, who, in
desperate need of funds, hoped to make more money as a
collector than as a senator. However, Nicholas's fear of the
yellow fever, even more intense than Wirt's, kept him from
Norfolk and his duties for several months of the year.[24] Tazewell bore no hard feelings, and when shortly after his appointment Nicholas again requested aid from Tazewell, it was given
generously. Nicholas, also a liberal Jeffersonian, wanted to
become a member of the board of directors of the Norfolk
branch of the Bank of the United States, but to be eligible he
had to be a stockholder. Would Tazewell, he asked, transfer
some shares to him, "the smallest number of shares that would
be sufficient? I will pay you immediately in money." This Tazewell did without hesitation, and Nicholas became a director.[25]

Because of Tazewell's views on banks and commerce, the
more conservative, agrarian-minded Jeffersonians considered

him a political apostate, while some Federalists disliked him because he championed Jefferson. Both sets of opponents conspired to have his election to the House of Delegates challenged in the Virginia legislature, and when he arrived in Richmond in December 1804 for the opening of the General Assembly, he found himself attacked on two counts: First, that the mayor of Norfolk had omitted to report officially the returns of the Norfolk election in which Tazewell was named to the House of Delegates; and, second, that as a notary public he was, according to the Virginia constitution, ineligible to hold legislative office. A Federalist newspaper, the *Norfolk Gazette and Publick Ledger,* came to his defense, announcing that although its political sentiments and those of Tazewell were at variance, the paper could not tolerate an injustice. Wilson Cary Nicholas was concerned that the controversy "may possibly increase your dislike of a business which I wished you to be pleased with, because I am sure you will render important service to your country if you continue in the assembly."[26]

Tazewell was not troubled. Those contesting his election, he correctly surmised, were on weak ground and would soon abandon the attack. He went about his business, serving on committees to amend the penal laws and to augment the capital stock of the Bank of Virginia. As he visited with various legislators, he discerned a favorable attitude toward the support of education. "The temper of the Legislature I find more liberal upon this head than either of us had apprehended it would have been," he delightedly informed St. George Tucker. "This I think is the auspicious moment to be seized upon for laying the corner stone of the great fabric we talked of erecting somewhere near Charlottesville. I have sounded several who have influence, & find much unanimity of sentiment upon this subject." In addition to gathering the views of key legislators, Tazewell called a caucus to discuss the financing of Jefferson's cherished dream, the University of Virginia. Long-range, solid support had to be guaranteed, he told Tucker, to protect the university against possible future "legislative caprice." "We design to obtain a donation from the state of all its interest in the Potomac, James River, & Dismal Swamp Canals, together with 1000 of its bank shares. These will be vested in Trustees for the uses we spoke of—and to this fund will be added all escheats, forfitures & other contingent interest which it is not now necessary to state."[27]

To Jefferson, Tazewell sent the same encouraging tidings, and the president's response was gratefully enthusiastic: "No one can be more rejoiced at the information that the legislature of Virginia are likely at length to institute a university on a liberal plan. Convinced that the people are the only safe depositories of their own liberty & that they are not safe unless enlightened to a certain degree, I have looked on our present state of liberty as a short-lived possession unless the mass of the people could be informed." This, he told Tazewell, would require two grades of education. First, an institution where knowledge in all its branches would be taught, "and in the highest degree to which the human mind had carried it." Such an institution would educate those to whom nature had given minds of the first order. Second, he advocated township schools whose purpose would be to give at least an introduction to learning to every member of society, enabling them "to read, to judge & vote understandingly on what is passing." Jefferson was pleased to have the Virginia legislature consider the establishment of a university, and he hoped the township schools could be "incorporated into the system at a more favorable moment." For the present, he was willing to receive with contentment what the legislature was ready to give.

In the same letter Jefferson disclosed for the first time his detailed plan for an ideal university. For countless hours during many years he had contemplated all the facets of a fine academy. Nothing escaped him, and using Tazewell as a sounding board, he made suggestions on financing, the board of visitors, the employment of a faculty. "The salaries of the first professors should be very liberal, that we might draw the first names of Europe to our institution in order to give it a celebrity in the outset, which will draw to it the youth of all the states, and make Virginia their cherished alma mater." Architect that he was, Jefferson did not neglect the buildings. An academical village, he thought, would be better than a large structure. "Large houses are always ugly, inconvenient, exposed to the accident of fire, and bad in case of infection. A plain small house for the school & lodging of each professor is best. These connected by covered ways out of which the rooms of the students should open. These may be built only as they shall be wanting. In fact a university should not be a house but a village." If a university on a worthy plan should be approved by the legislature, Jefferson promised Tazewell he would bequeath to the institution "a valuable legacy . . . to wit: my library."[28]

Unhappily, the General Assembly was not as eager to advance a program of education as Tazewell was led to believe. Upon being reelected to the 1805–6 House of Delegates, he again encouraged the establishment of a university, but the bill failed.[29] This setback did not dull Tazewell's interest, and for years, both before and after the General Assembly's favorable action in 1818, he was committed to the development of Jefferson's academical village.

The interrelated topics of slavery, emanicipation, and the free blacks were other serious considerations of the General Assembly during the 1804–5 and 1805–6 sessions.[30] Public opinion, alarmed by the abortive Gabriel insurrection of 1800, by frequent rumors of potential uprisings, and by several genuine conspiracies, placed major blame for the disturbances on the free Negroes, whose numbers were increasing at a startling rate, and on the slaves brought to Virginia by French refugees. Virginia was the only southern state that did not in some manner restrict the ingression of the Santo Domingo slaves, but there was a growing realization that the insurrectionary ideas of Toussaint L'Ouverture and his followers could be spreading through the commonwealth. As Norfolk was particularly generous to the fleeing French, greater clusters of them, accompanied by their slaves, gathered there than elsewhere in the United States, making the borough inhabitants ever more concerned about restiveness among the blacks. Always present was fear of fire, set by a disgruntled slave or hostile free Negro, and on February 22, 1804, a devastating conflagration did sweep through the town, destroying not less than 260 houses. No one was certain how the fire started, but there were those who thought they knew, and uneasiness mounted.[31]

Norfolk's commercial interests were plagued by other worries. "Large numbers of poor wretches, who were driven here from Saint Domingo by the blacks," Tazewell wrote John Randolph, "having equipped themselves in the Spanish ports of Cuba with vessels, etc., are now traversing the West Indian Seas as pirates, capturing everything they meet with. Many American vessels bound to both Jamaica & Saint Domingo have been taken, and all our trade to those quarters seems to be in instant danger." The pirates, forbidden to take their prizes into Spanish harbors, rifled the capture ships of all valuables, then either abandoned or sunk them. Losses were high. "Prompt action of the government to this occurrence is ardently desired here. Much is at stake belonging to this place, and this loss added to the dreadful devastation of the last fire here would bring us almost to ruin." Nivison reported that "cash never was so scarce" in Norfolk, and economic blight threatened. The financial and commercial problems were considered by many as warnings of the terrible consequences that would stem from racial unrest. Should disturbances escalate into rebellion, plantation owners, merchants, and shipowners would be as destitute as the refugees they recently had befriended.[32]

Petitions almost swamped the state legislature. One from Norfolk, dated December 8, 1805, deplored the tumult and alarm that was destroying the peace and quiet of the borough. Too many free Negroes roamed the streets, the signers contended, adding to the difficulty of controlling the "very formidable accession" of blacks "from the Island of Saint Domingo."[33] One partial solution posed by Alexander Smyth of Wythe County was to curb the growth of the free black population by prohibiting private manumission. Between 1782 and 1800 individual owners freed an estimated twenty thousand Virginia slaves. Usually provisions in wills specified the emancipation of one or more faithful servants, but not infrequently a master in the prime of life conferred freedom for outstanding service or extraordinary loyalty. Smyth argued against all such practices and twice introduced bills to prohibit private emancipation. These were debated bitterly. Such a law, opponents insisted, would destroy a cherished natural right, that of an individual to dispose of his own property in any way he wished, while those in favor cited "a moral maxim that no man can appropriate his property to any purpose which may

injure the interests of others. . . . Whoever emancipates a slave
may be inflicting the deadliest injury upon his neighbor. He
may be furnishing some active chieftain of a formidable
conspiracy."[34] The right to dispose of private property prevailed, and Smyth's bill lost, the first time by a vote of 77 to 70
and during the next session by a closer division, 75–73.[35]

Tazewell, with mixed feelings about the measure, did not
vote. As an attorney with unlimited respect for the common
law, he firmly believed in the right of private property, but he
also understood the anxieties of his Norfolk neighbors and
their wish to forestall insurrection. In considering another aspect of the slave question, he wholeheartedly approved a measure which made the importation of all slaves, domestic as well
as foreign, into Virginia absolutely illegal. How illogical, he
contended, for Virginians to refuse to go to the Senegal for
slaves, while willing to visit the markets of Charleston in
search of laborers, thus encouraging South Carolina's continuation of the slave traffic. This restrictive act, he hoped,
would bring a final end to the African and West Indian slave
trade. However, it took a turn which he had not anticipated.
The Senate amended the bill to include a provision which
required a slave freed by his master after May 1, 1806, to
leave the state within one year from the date of his manumission. This circumlocutory law, while protecting the individual's right to dispose of his property, obviously was designed
to discourage emancipation. The House of Delegates agreed
to the amendment, and the bill to prevent slaves being
brought into the commonwealth was accepted.[36]

Tazewell's position on slavery was not adamant. His current
primary interests were not agrarian, and his own slaveholdings consisted of a few domestic servants. In public Tazewell
appeared almost neutral toward emancipation. The threat of
insurrection, he fully realized, hung like a pall over the land,
detrimental to the economy and general welfare, but on the
question of whether the threat would be better alleviated by
freeing the slaves or by tightening their bonds, he remained
silent.

It should also be noted that in searching for solutions to
Virginia's ills Tazewell, at this stage of his life, did not hesitate
to turn to the federal government for assistance in enforcing

state laws banning the African slave trade, in suppressing pirates, and in aiding local commercial endeavors. As a young
man his states' rights views had been momentarily extreme,[37]
but these opinions seemed no longer valid, and in weighing
priorties, he was willing to risk the loss of a few state prerogatives if such sacrifices would benefit the people of the commonwealth, particularly those of the Norfolk area.

## Chapter III

# *The Trials of*
# *Burr and Barron*

In January 1807 Tazewell sent word of "serious news" to James Monroe, the American minister in London: "Our old friend Col. Burr, it is said (and appearances are much against him) is at this moment actually engaged in a treasonable project of seizing upon the city of Orleans, establishing an independent government there, and separating the western from the Eastern States. He has been arrested himself in Kentucky and indicted, but the grand jury rejected the Bill of Indictment for want of evidence. Another prosecution it is said will immediately be commenced against him. His adherents and followers have many been arrested in the state of Ohio." Tazewell doubted that Burr's activities, even if the rumors of treason were well grounded, gave cause for alarm. What he did fear was the danger of hysterical reaction to the reports. The legislature of Ohio, he informed Monroe, had passed an act suspending the habeas corpus law, thus giving the governor immense power "to repress the threatened mischief." Congress also was considering a law assigning "vast and dangerous powers" to the president and the judiciary for the same purpose. This made Tazewell uncomfortable. Even if the country actually were in danger, giving emergency dictatorial powers to executive officials created a perilous potential for future abuse, and he foresaw the possibility of governors or presidents "imagining other crises" in order "to gain more authority."[1]

A few months later Tazewell was in Richmond, summoned to serve as a member of the grand jury convened to investigate the alleged misdeeds of Aaron Burr. Tazewell held no foregone conclusions as to Burr's guilt or innocence. His prior associations with the New Yorker had been pleasant, and he had not rejoiced, as had so many, in the misfortunes that had hounded

Burr after he was dropped from the 1804 Republican ticket. Burr, demoralized by his unsuccessful bid for the governorship of New York and disgraced by the tragic duel that resulted in the death of Alexander Hamilton, had sought, by some nebulous "Grand Design," to recoup his fortune. His plans may have included the conquest of Spanish territory, the separation of the western portion of the United States from the Union, the creation of an empire with himself as chief of state, or his "expedition" may have been "simply the last resort of a forlorn and friendless man to find a new home and new friends." Whatever his scheme, which could well have been flexible enough to seek the support of several different audiences, Burr found various sources of encouragement. Anthony Merry, the British minister, was delighted with an opportunity to foster the dismemberment of the United States. General James Wilkinson, ranking officer of the United States Army and for a time governor of the Louisiana Territory, was ready for any intrigue which would lead to his own aggrandizement or line his purse. For years he secretly had been in the pay of Spain. On several occasions Burr and Wilkinson conferred. Mysterious correspondence in cipher passed between them. Burr, however, talked too freely to an inordinate number of people, and when rumors of a possible conspiracy began to circulate, Wilkinson became frightened. In a frantic effort to exonerate himself and at the same time to curry favor with the president, Wilkinson warned Jefferson of a Burr plot to dissever the country. For a long time the chief executive had believed Burr to be "a crooked gun . . . whose aim you could never be sure of," and this distrust of his former vice-president led him to place undue credence in Wilkinson's information. Perhaps too quickly, Jefferson concluded that his administration could ill afford public accusations of "supine inattention to treason stalking through the land in open day." Therefore, following a series of complicated incidents, Burr was brought to Richmond in the spring of 1807, where, after a preliminary hearing, he was ordered to appear before the grand jury of the United States Circuit Court for the District of Virginia, Chief Justice John Marshall presiding.[2] Political overtones all but obliterated the judicial aspects of the case. Between Marshall and Jefferson there was a long-held smoldering animosity, and even in Jefferson's own party there were those who delightly anticipated presidential embarrassment.

At the time of Burr's appearance before the grand jury Tazewell had not taken sides for or against the administration; however, he had written to Monroe, informing him of the "schism among our Republican friends."[3] For Tazewell the litigation held particular interest. Two of his closest friends were joined in legal battle on opposite sides of this most curious case. William Wirt was an attorney for the prosecution, while John Wickham led the counsel for the defense. Both were keen, eloquent, suave, and convincing. The United States attorney for the District of Virginia was George Hay, whom Tazewell had known for years.[4]

The grand jury session started on May 22 but proceeded at an agonizingly slow pace. Nothing really could be accomplished until the arrival of the state's star witness, General Wilkinson, supposedlly en route from Louisiana. Some were wagering, at better than even odds, that he never would appear. The jurors, to pass the time, amused themselves with dinner parties and evenings of spirited conversation. This was no ordinary group. Washington Irving saw the grand jury as "the most enlightened, perhaps, that was ever assembled in the country." Sixteen of Virginia's prominent citizens, Tazewell's friends and acquaintances of long standing, were members of the panel. John Randolph served as foreman. His request to be excused because of prepossession of evidence was denied by Marshall. Other jurors from Tazewell's circle of intimates included James Barbour of Orange County, Joseph C. Cabell of Amherst, John Mercer, Robert B. Taylor, and John Ambler, and he enjoyed their company, but long separations from his family were difficult for Tazewell, as they were always to be thoughout his life. When the grand jury adjourned for a few days, he quickly left for Norfolk to see his wife and children. Such respites were all too brief.[5]

When Wilkinson finally arrived to testify against Burr, Tazewell was prepared to dislike him. The general's precipitant extralegal actions in New Orleans several months earlier had shocked Tazewell. Wilkinson, in an effort to exculpate himself by silencing anyone who could connect him with the Burr conspiracy, arbitrarily arrested several individuals, held them

without bail, ignored the orders of the civil authorities, and
sent the prisoners out of the jurisdiction of the civil courts.
Tazewell became aware of these "enormous outrages" when
John Adair and James Alexander, both taken into custody by
Wilkinson in New Orleans, arrived under guard in Hampton
Roads, on the way to Baltimore.[6]

Shortly thereafter, while dining with friends, Tazewell voiced
his conviction that President Jefferson would never condone
Wilkinson's seizure and deportation of "respectable citizens
without any other reason or authority for so doing, than his
own suspicion & power." Such disrespect for civil law and disregard for individual rights was unpardonable. Without a doubt
Jefferson would dismiss Wilkinson from the service "for so daring an attack upon all we hold valuable." Most of Tazewell's
dinner companions concurred, but Captain John Saunders of
Fort Nelson, without any justification of Wilkinson, merely observed that he would not be dismissed, whereupon Tazewell
immediately offered to bet Saunders that Wilkinson would not
be retained. A coat made the wager, and the meeting of the
next session of Congress was the deadline fixed for the resolution of the question. Commodore Decatur, also of the party,
followed Tazewell's example, and Saunders promptly accepted
the second wager. By the time Wilkinson appeared in Richmond, however, Tazewell had cause to doubt his initial confidence in Jefferson's refusal to condone the actions of the
self-seeking general, and the president's attitude puzzled and
troubled him. Sadly he provided Saunders with a regimental
coat costing twenty-eight dollars.[7]

The grand jury interrogation of Wilkinson convinced Tazewell of the general's crass perfidiousness. Without question,
the man was a perjurer and a hypocrite. His testimony
abounded with contradictions. Moreover, Tazewell discovered
that Wilkinson had tampered with papers he had submitted to
support his testimony, "erasing, interlining," and doing whatever possible to make them less incriminating to himself. On
June 24 the grand jury reached its decision. Burr and his
alleged accomplice, Harman Blennerhassett, were indicted,
*una voce,* for treason and misdemeanor, but, moaned Randolph, "the mammoth of iniquity escaped." "Upon certain
wire-drawn distinctions" Wilkinson eluded indictment by a

vote of seven to nine, although not one member of the grand jury pretended to think him innocent.[8]

Burr was tried in Richmond on charges of treason and misdemeanor and was acquitted on both counts. The treason trial lasted from August 3 to September 1, 1807, and the misdeameanor trial from September 9 to September 15. On September 16 hearings began on Attorney Hay's motion to commit Burr for trial in another district on a new charge of treason. In the course of the latter proceedings, Tazewell and several other members of the grand jury were called as witnesses by the defense, which hoped to discredit Wilkinson's testimony. Tazewell certainly was not averse to exposing Wilkinson, but the unusual action of calling members of a grand jury as witnesses bothered him. "I wish before I am sworn in," he addressed the bench, "that the point should be determined by the court whether as a grand juror, I am bound to give evidence of what passed in the grand jury room. I do not wish that the community of the grand jury should lose any rights they may have by any acquiesence of mine, if by law a grand juryman ought not to be called upon to state what happened before the grand jury. I submit myself to the court and will act according to its judgment." Over the protest of Hay, Marshall ruled that a grand juror could be called upon to give evidence to prove the consistency or inconsistency of a witness, and Tazewell then testified concerning Wilkinson's alterations of the ciphered letters.[9]

Tazewell was not convinced that Burr's activities could be construed as treason against the United States. The grand jury's indictment on that count probably resulted from a mistaken interpretation of Marshall's definition of the term, an interpretation the chief justice clarified during the trial proper, and Tazewell was satisfied when Marshall ruled that Burr should be held for trial in Ohio on the charge of misdeameanor only. While he did not condone Burr's decision to forfeit bail and depart for Europe rather than face further litigation, Tazewell was bothered more by the government's refusal to press charges against Wilkinson or to remove him as head of the army. Adding to the annoyance was Wilkinson's violent hostility toward everyone who testified against him or hinted at the possibility of his complicity in Burr's plot. The general's threats against John Randolph, who had used several choice epithets in referring to Wilkinson, were particularly vicious, and Tazewell was relieved when Randolph refused to accept the military officer's challenge. Tazewell disapproved of dueling and viewed the thought of meeting Wilkinson on a "field of honor" as the height of absurdity. Several years later when Wilkinson attempted to goad Tazewell into a confrontation, the Virginian simply ignored him, remarking "I cannot degrade myself so far as to enter into a public vindication of myself against any insinuation which Wilkinson may choose to exhibit against me. Such an attempt I fear would give a temporary significance to him whom I consider already occupying the nadir of disgrace."[10]

Jefferson's seemingly unshakable faith in Wilkinson baffled Tazewell,[11] but he could not spend an undue amount of time pondering the problem, for on the day following the grand jury's indictment of Burr, alarming news reached Richmond from Norfolk, causing Tazewell to travel homeward as quickly as possible. On June 22, 1807, the United States frigate *Chesapeake* sailed from Hampton Roads, bound for the Mediterranean. From her masthead flew the broad forked pendant of Captain James Barron, senior officer aboard, recently appointed commodore of the Mediterranean fleet. Master Commandant Charles Gordon was the captain of the frigate. The *Chespeake* was not seaworthy, even after almost four months of repairs at the Washington Navy Yard. Between June 6 and June 21, while the ship was at anchor in Hampton Roads, a few of the deficiencies were rectified. Commodore Barron visited the vessel twice but did not assume responsibility for preparing the ship for the Atlantic crossing. This he left to her captain, Charles Gordon.[12]

When the *Chesapeake* finally glided out between the Virginia Capes on the morning of June 22, her decks still were littered with stores, cables, furniture, and other sundry items. In time of peace the practice of tidying a ship after she was underway was not unusual. The crew, as unprepared and disorganized as the ship, had been recruited with great difficulty. Rumors circulated that a few deserters from the British navy had been signed on. The British consul and British naval officers demanded the return of the absconding sailors, but no action was taken. This prompted Vice Admiral George Cranfield Berkeley, commander of the British North Atlantic Station, to direct captains under his jurisdiction, should they meet with the *Chesapeake* at sea, to hail her, show her senior officer the vice admiral's order, and search the American ship for deserters.[13]

Accordingly, off Cape Henry on the afternoon of June 22 the *Chesapeake* was hailed by H.M.S. *Leopard,* with a demand for search and seizure. Upon receiving Barron's refusal, the *Leopard* opened fire, and for ten to fifteen minutes raked the *Chesapeake* with broadsides, killing three crew members and wounding several others, including Commodore Barron. The ill-prepared *Chesapeake,* unable to retaliate, laboriously fired only one gun as Barron ordered the flag struck. She was then boarded, searched, and deprived of four seamen, accused of being deserters from the British navy. The captain of the *Leopard* declined to accept Barron's sword or take the *Chesapeake* as a prize, and the heavily damaged ship painfully made her way back to Norfolk harbor, a sanctuary from enemies on the sea but not from those who felt keenly the injury to national honor and demanded explanations.[14]

The inhabitants of Norfolk were shocked and enraged. Their initial wrath was directed against the British, and Tazewell, arriving from Richmond, was greeted with the news of a mass meeting protesting the "base and insidious murders committed by a tyrannical and arbitrary power." Local forces were mustered. The governor of Virginia was called upon to supply fifteen hundred to two thousand stands of arms. Not since Lexington and Concord had the country expressed such widespread and simultaneous anger. Newspapers in many areas called for hostilities with Great Britain. "We are," wrote William Wirt, "on tiptoe for war." On July 2 a proclamation issued by President Jefferson ordered all armed vessels of His Majesty's navy "now within the harbors or waters of the United States, immediately and without delay to depart from the same," but the British squadron at anchor in Lynnhaven Inlet remained, and its commander, John Erskine Douglas, haughtily demanded in a message to Norfolk's mayor, Richard E. Lee, that Norfolk's anti-British resolutions be rescinded and that he be allowed to communicate with the British consul.

"You must be perfectly aware," Douglas arrogantly informed Lee, "that the British flag never has, or never will be insulted with impunity. You must also be aware that it has been, and is still, in my power to obstruct the whole trade of the Chesapeake [Bay] . . . . It therefore rests with the inhabitants of Norfolk either to engage in war or remain on terms of peace."[15]

Although Tazewell was considerably younger than most of the leading citizens who spearheaded the protest movement, he quickly became spokesman for the borough, and the reply to Douglas, dated July 4, while signed by the mayor, was full of Tazewellian phrases, matching in pride and arrogance the statements in Douglas's original message. "The day on which this answer is written," began the retort to the British, "ought of itself to suffice to prove to the subjects of your sovereign that the American people are not to be intimidated by menace." They might be seduced by false sincerity or surprised and slaughtered by a supposed friend, but the hand of the British was now revealed and the people of Norfolk were prepared for the worst.[16]

Tazewell personally delivered the message to Captain Douglas aboard H.M.S. *Bellona*, now blockading Norfolk from Hampton Roads. This was the first of several visits he made during the summer of 1807 to confer with British naval officers. Consistently, his policy was to avoid a war which he believed would be devastating to the United States, weak and ill-prepared as the country was. Rushing into unnecessary hostilities while there remained a chance that matters could be resolved amicably was to Tazewell the height of unreasonableness. To his friend William H. Cabell, the governor of Virginia, Tazewell voiced a similar plea. It was, he admitted, alarming to have the state threatened by a foreign foe, but equally alarming were the imprudent acts committed by citizens in "a laudable zeal" to avenge the insult to national honor. "If such measures are not repressed, the result will be deplorable." The government could be forced into taking rash and foolish actions. Perhaps, Tazewell suggested, if the British consul in Norfolk was allowed to resume his normal functions and to communicate freely with British naval officers, hostilities might be avoided or, at least, postponed.[17]

Fortunately Jefferson was not inclined to "wield the sword of state" unless it was absolutely unavoidable, and although he was under considerable pressure to call Congress into special session, he followed Albert Gallatin's advice and procrastinated. By late July the British ships had withdrawn from Hampton Roads, thus lifting the blockade of Norfolk, and the war hysteria somewhat subsided. Throughout this tense time Tazewell maintained a polite relationship with the British naval officers, especially with Sir Thomas Hardy of H.M.S. *Triumph*, who replaced Douglas as the senior officer of the British squadron in Chesapeake Bay. As a result, Tazewell was able to arrange a mode of forwarding dispatches from the British government to its minister in the United States, and he did whatever he could to keep communication open between the British on the sea and the Americans ashore. Common sense on both sides, he hoped, would in the end prevail.[18]

As the outrage against England slightly abated, demands for internal assuagement of national honor increased throughout the land, and the navy, its pride severely damaged by what was considered to be the precipitate surrender of the *Chesapeake,* looked for someone to blame. The onus fell heavily upon Commodore James Barron, whose arrest and punishment was demanded by seven of the ship's officers. To fix the responsibility, Secretary of the Navy Robert Smith ordered an investigation of the circumstances leading to the surrender and asked Tazewell to serve as judge advocate of the court of inquiry.[19]

When Smith's request arrived, Tazewell was in Richmond testifying in the Burr trial, and he did not return to Norfolk until October 6, the day after the opening session of the court. He had no relish for the assignment. Although he was not intimate with the Barrons, he had known the prominent naval family for many years. Acting as judge advocate, Tazewell explained to Smith, "would occasion some sacrifices of my feelings as an individual." In addition, the duties would be in a measure new to him, and his own practice would have to be neglected, this being the season of the year when the courts were in session. His father-in-law had cheerfully shouldered family and business responsibilities during Tazewell's stint with the grand jury and his negotiations with the British, but in fairness to Nivison, this arrangement could not continue indefinitely. Moreover, Tazewell scarcely had seen his new son, John, born in September while he was in Richmond. Yet, if Smith believed he should act as judge advocate, Tazewell would do so as an obligation "that in common with others I owe to my country," and he promised to do his best.[20]

The court met aboard the *Chesapeake*, lying in the Elizabeth river near Craney Island. Fully realizing how high feelings were running, particularly in regard to Barron, Tazewell asked Smith if he wished to review the conduct of the court before a final determination was reached. Smith declined, stating that it had been his invariable practice not to interfere in any manner with the proceedings of courts of inquiry or courts-martial. Reputable naval officers were appointed to hear the case, and "their proceedings & their findings are left to their own sound judgment upon the laws & evidence—and it is upon their finding only that the Executive can act." Robert B. Taylor, Tazewell's close friend and fellow Norfolk attorney, represented Barron, but the commodore declined to offer a defense. Ending its session on November 4, the court unanimously directed Tazewell to transmit to the secretary of the navy charges against Commodore Barron for neglecting to prepare his ship for action, for "indecision and a disposition to negotiate, rather than a determination bravely to defend his ship," for the use of language calculated to dispirit his crew, and for prematurely striking the colors of the *Chesapeake*. However, the court exonerated him from any display of cowardice. The *Chesapeake*, the findings continued, might and ought to have been better defended than she was; yet she was not at the time of the attack prepared to make a gallant defense.[21]

On the basis of these conclusions, a court-martial was ordered for the trial of Commodore Barron, Captain Gordon, Captain John Hall of the Marine Corps, and William Hook, gunner. Again Smith requested Tazewell's services as judge advocate, and again Tazewell stated that he preferred declining the appointment. When the secretary insisted, Tazewell informed Smith that he would be available only when his private legal responsibilities permitted, such as between the middle of December and the first of March. Mindful of Taze-

well's convenience, Smith ordered the court-martial to begin
on January 4, 1808. The court appointed for the trial was an
illustrious assemblage. Presiding was the highly respected
Captain John Rodgers, renowned for his heroism in en-
counters with the Barbary pirates. Ten other officers sat with
Rodgers, including Captain William Bainbridge, Master Commandant David Porter, and Lieutenant James Lawrence, who
as captain of the ill-fated *Chesapeake* during the War of 1812
would die in the very cabin where he now heard the case
against Barron. Stephen Decatur, pleading prejudice, asked to
be disqualified from sitting on the court. "During the Court of
Enquiry," he protested to Smith, "I was present when the
evidence of the officers was given. I have since seen the opinion of the Court, which I think lenient"; furthermore, prior to
the unfortunate *Chesapeake* affair, Decatur had neither liked
nor respected Barron. But Smith refused to excuse Decatur or
others who apparently voiced much the same reasons for their
unwillingness to serve.[22]

The bill of indictment against Barron was serious. If found
guilty, he could face the death penalty. Through the captain's
cabin of the *Chesapeake* came the parade of witnesses, comprised principally of officers and men of the frigate, whose
testimony was not favorable to the commodore. Tazewell's
questions were sharp and directed at the main points of the
case. Was Barron responsible for the sorry condition of the
*Chesapeake* when she put out to sea? Did he know there were
deserters from the British navy aboard? If he was cognizant of
their presence, should he not have anticipated an attack by the
*Leopard*? In anticipation of an attack, should he not have
cleared his ship for action? Did he strike the flag with undue
haste? The deliberations went on for slightly more than a
month, with most of the time devoted to the charges against
Barron. The weather was cold and damp, and when a
nor'easter roared across the Norfolk waters the court forsook
the ice-encrusted *Chesapeake* for more comfortable quarters in
Mrs. Street's boardinghouse. Although spectators crowded
into the hearing room, whether on ship or ashore, the Norfolk
papers believed it inappropriate to comment on the course of
the trial.[23]

Barron did not testify in his own behalf, but Robert Taylor

performed brilliantly as attorney for the defense, correctly reminding those sitting in judgment that according to naval regulations it was Gordon's responsibility, as captain of the *Chesapeake,* to have his ship ready for immediate action, and it was he who should have ordered the guns exercised. In the end the court found Barron guilty of only one charge, "neglecting on the probability of an engagement to clear his ship for action," and for this negligence he was suspended from all commands for a period of five years, without pay or official emoluments of any kind.[24] The sentence was harsh, and there were those who believed the navy and the country had found a scapegoat.

As Gordon was not represented by an attorney, Tazewell and the president of the court, Captain Rodgers, instructed him of his rights and warned him against self-incrimination while giving testimony in the Barron trial. The judge advocate also read Gordon's defense statement to the court. Later these actions formed the basis for allegations that Tazewell had conspired with the court, the secretary of the navy, and others in important governmental positions to exonerate Gordon and place the entire blame on Barron. True, Gordon had friends and relatives in high places, and certainly his punishment was nothing more than a light tap on the wrist. For "negligently performing the duty assigned him," he was sentenced to be privately reprimanded by the secretary of the navy or by such persons as the secretary might appoint, but, the officers of the court added, had it been within their power they would have pardoned Gordon. Since it was not, they selected the most lenient possible punishment. The same "sentence" was meted out to Captain Hall, while Gunner Hook, found guilty of more serious negligence, was dismissed from the service.[25]

In toto, the case was a strange one. Many questions were left unanswered. Why was Gordon not reprimanded severely for the unpreparedness of his ship? Should Barron have gone down fighting against impossible odds, sacrificing scores of lives, and in all probability precipitating a war with Great Britain? Given the climate of the time, was Barron merely a victim of circumstances? Was there a predisposition to find him guilty? Were the real delinquents, as James Fenimore Cooper believed, never put on trial? Cooper, of course, was referring to President Jefferson and others responsible for the neglect and mismanagement of the naval forces of the United States.[26]

What part Tazewell played in the final decisions of the court is unknown. Did he advise the officers on the degree of punishment to be applied, or did he limit his duties to the prosecution of the accused? Observers remarked about Tazewell's insistence upon strict adherence to official procedure, and for many years the Barron court martial, in its motives and impartiality, was considered a model for others to emulate.[27] It would seem likely that Tazewell followed the instructions of the secretary of the navy in remitting to the "reputable officers" the duty of arriving at the findings of the court, based on "their own sound judgment upon the laws & evidence." Later, an unsubstantiated statement by the embittered Barron accused Tazewell of writing both Gordon's and Hall's defense,[28] but this could be attributed to the commodore's urge to strike out at anyone who contributed to his disgrace.

## Chapter IV

# "The Schism among Our Republican Friends"

Tazewell was engaged in preparations for the Barron court-martial when a disillusioned James Monroe arrived from England, disembarking at Norfolk on December 13, 1807. The commercial treaty with Great Britain, which Monroe viewed as his crowning achievement, had been rejected by Jefferson and Madison, who refused to submit the treaty to the Senate because it contained no provision for the abandonment of British impressment of American seamen. Monroe was certain the British intended to discontinue impressment, in practice if not in principle, and believed the commercial concessions included in the treaty were better than might have been expected. If they were refused, he feared it would be impossible to get so good an agreement again. "I thought I had done right in what I had done," he lamented to Tazewell, and perhaps he had. Within a few months after the treaty was declared unsatisfactory, the *Chesapeake-Leopard* clash brought Britain and the United States to the edge of war.[1]

Monroe's feeling of repudiation played into the hands of John Randolph, whose hatred of Madison bordered on the psychopathic. Early in 1806 Randolph broke with the Republicans and announced his membership in the "Quids," a third-party movement opposed to the administration. Now Randolph hoped to entice Monroe to do the same. Even before Monroe left England, letters from America, largely instigated by Randolph, warned that Jefferson and Madison were bent on diminishing Monroe's reputation and thus thwarting his chances of becoming a contender for the presidency in 1808.

Madison, everyone knew, was Jefferson's choice as his successor.[2]

While Randolph fed Monroe's resentment, Tazewell urged prudence, cautioning him to examine the motives of those who, in the name of friendship, tried to push him in one direction or another. "Distrust such efforts," he warned. "Suspect all who approach you upon this topick." Perhaps, Tazewell acknowledged, Monroe had been ill-used by Jefferson and Madison, but he entreated him to repress for a season any hurt feelings he might have and "come to us like a new man, at liberty to decide as you please, without any imputation that resentment or pique or affection have any share in forming your opinion." Diplomatically, he tried to tell Monroe how unfortunate an alliance with Randolph might be for his political future. Many Republicans, although dubious about Jefferson's administration, found Randolph's malicious tactics offensive.[3]

As early as September 1806 Tazewell had alerted Monroe to "the schism among our Republican friends throughout the continent," and by late 1807 he believed the party was shattering. On the one hand there were the "Old Republicans," as they designated themselves, strong states' rightists who held to rigid limitations on the powers of the national government and its chief executive. They were dismayed when, in their eyes, Jefferson subverted the very principles he earlier had championed. Yet, Old Republicans such as Nathaniel Macon of North Carolina and John Taylor of Virginia had no desire to associate with the eccentric and contentious John Randolph. Tazewell's own disillusionment with the Jefferson administration had grown steadily during the summer and fall of 1807, but he was not comfortable with the Old Republicans, most of whom were strictly agrarian in their outlook and could not understand the need for a strong navy, improvements of ports and harbors, or general concerns of commercial interests. These were matters of primary importance to Tazewell, and it was not surprising that his faith in Jefferson reached its nadir with the executive decision to utilize the embargo to avoid war with England and France.[4]

The Embargo Act was the United States' reaction to the *Chesapeake-Leopard* affair and other British and French violations of American rights on the high seas. Under its provisions no United States merchant vessel could depart for a foreign port, although coastwise trade was allowed. Jefferson considered trade restrictions a lesser evil than war. Within a few months, however, the eastern seaboard faced economic disaster. In Norfolk, property values declined, wharves were empty, sailors unemployed, and boardinghouses deserted. The merchants believed all these misfortunes could have been avoided had Jefferson built a first-class navy to protect commercial vessels against seizures of cargoes and impressment of seamen. The embargo, they contended, spelled the ruin of American commerce.[5]

While Randolph had no regard for the "carrying trade," denouncing it as a "fungus of war," Tazewell was certain the future of the "great agricultural nation" rested on commerce. Years later he enumerated the many disastrous results of the "short-sighted and wretched" embargo. Most harmful of all, to Norfolk and other coastal cities, was Britain's realization that its West Indian colonies were not as dependent upon trade with the United States as had been supposed, and commerce lost at this time by the American merchant fleet never was completely regained. Perhaps even more disturbing to Tazewell, the embargo forced "the premature birth" of manufacturing, which required tariff protection, thus further destroying foreign commerce and seriously injuring the agricultural interests of a large portion of "these once happy and contented states."[6]

Tazewell had mixed feelings about Great Britain. The attack on the *Chesapeake* angered him more than anything he could remember. Momentarily, the complete composure on which he prided himself gave way to angry outbursts. However, if a choice was possible, he decidedly favored an alliance with England rather than with the France of Napoleon. Of no small consequence in shaping his attitude was the matter of trade with the British West Indies, so important to Norfolk's furture prosperity. What was needed, Tazewell told Monroe, was an administration which would be "both a friend to commerce and enemy to perpetual embargoes."[7]

For more than two months after Monroe's return to the United States, Tazewell was occupied with the *Chesapeake* court-martial and had no time to dabble in political affairs.

During these weeks the proadministration Republicans hurriedly held their caucus in Washington to nominate Madison, and in Richmond two caucuses vied with one another for the spotlight by meeting on the same day. One nominated Madison, while the other named Monroe. Contrary to his private desires, Tazewell was named a Monroe elector for Norfolk, Princess Anne, and Nansemond counties and the borough of Norfolk. He was not convinced that Monroe was the right choice to oppose Madison, and Monroe's reasons for seeking the nomination concerned him. Was Monroe determined to vindicate himself, to prove to those who had rejected his latest diplomatic efforts that a sizable group of Americans had confidence in his judgment? Did he wish merely to salve his own hurt feelings? Or did he really want to be president in order to help the nation? Perhaps, Tazewell suggested, as distasteful as the idea might be, Monroe, if serious about his presidential aspirations, should court the support of the Federalists, who were enraged by the Jefferson-Madison embargo. To secure their votes Monroe need not betray his Republican principles but merely promise to repeal the hated trade restrictions.[8]

In reality, Tazewell saw little hope for the defeat of Madison. The Federalists certainly had no prospect of success. After giving consideration to nominating no one, they belatedly announced a ticket of Charles Cotesworth Pinckney and Rufus King, but enthusiasm for the candidates was less than wholehearted. If Monroe wished, for the welfare of the country, to see Madison set aside, Tazewell reasoned, he would have to make some painful concessions. A New York–Virginia alliance, including both Federalists and Republicans, offered the only possible hope. To consummate the alliance, Monroe's central committee in Richmond should instruct electors to cast their presidential ballots for George Clinton, Jefferson's vice-president, a definite contender for the top position, who had served seven terms as governor of New York and whose policies were receiving favorable attention from the Federalists. Monroe would have to be satisfied with second place, and his central committee should announce as reasons for his willingness to do so "the absolute necessity which exists of preserving the harmony among the states unimpaired, and of lessening their jealousy against Virginia, which already rages too high.

That this can be done only by selecting a president from some other state than Virginia, and thus giving to our sister states in the sacrifice of our personal wishes, and state partialities, the earnest pledge of our just appreciation of their importance."[9]

Obviously Monroe's feelings were bruised by Tazewell's suggestions. "With New York there is a good understanding," he insisted. "Clinton has said to one of my friends that if I could be elected he would decline in my favor . . . . My standing in the States Eastward of New York is said to be better than his . . . . My opinion decidedly is that he who stands the best prospect for success ought to be preferred." Monroe wanted it clearly understood that he had never broken with the Republican party, that he was running as a candidate on the regular ticket, identifying himself with neither the administration nor the Randolph dissidents.[10]

On the eve of the election the Norfolk papers portrayed Monroe as the enemy of the hated embargo. If Madison was elected, warned the *Gazette and Publick Ledger*, he would continue the measures of Jefferson, for was he not, indeed, the author of the most pernicious enactments? But Norfolk voters apparently did not attribute all their ills to Madison's policies, for the borough gave Monroe only a slight edge, while Norfolk County favored Madison. In Virginia as a whole, Madison's triumph was irrefutable. Nationally, Monroe received no electoral votes and as Tazewell predicted, the Federalists made a better showing than they had in 1804.[11]

The embargo was the root of the problem, and if the administration persisted in the trade restrictions, Tazewell saw imminent danger of civil discord, nullification, and attempts at disunion. Perhaps even more than he deplored the economic havoc, Tazewell feared the increasing necessity of arbitrary presidential powers to enforce the embargo. Merchants of Boston were on the verge of armed revolt, and from the town of Bath a ship laden with cotton had gone out in open day light, "in defiance either of the power of the government or the command of the laws." The revenue cutter that attempted to stop her was driven off by gunfire. "Bad as this news is," Tazewell sorrowfully wrote to Monroe, "still I feel consolation in understanding that *no blood* has yet been spilled." But how long would it be before the country faced anarchy or tyranny?

What then would be the fate of the rights of man? To avoid unlawful upheaval or tyrannical suppression, Tazewell asked Monroe to consider the possibility of a third party consisting of Republicans who disapproved or doubted the correctness of the present course but who could not ally themselves with Randolph. The new party members could explain "the great difference between themselves and the Federalists, and the equally great difference between their tenets and those practiced by the administration." In Congress and "here and there in the country" he saw signs of the budding of such a party.[12]

Although Jefferson still believed in the efficacy of the embargo, he was sensitive to the rising tide of opposition. It troubled him deeply, and shortly before the close of his presidency he reluctantly bowed to a partial repeal. Replacing the embargo, a Non-Intercourse Act authorized resumption of trade with all nations except England and France and provided for reopening trade with Great Britain when its government lifted the blockade of the continent or with France upon its discontinuance of the blockade of the British Isles. While these changes were debated in Congress, President-elect Madison, in his capacity as secretary of state, approached the British minister, David Erskine, suggesting an Ango-American alliance against Napoleon. Tazewell and Monroe saw this as an encouraging development. Monroe, for the sake of his political future and at the urging of Jefferson, was eager to make peace with Madison if the latter's foreign policy showed any sign of a willingness to come to terms with Great Britain, and he quickly moved to regain the confidence of Madison's Virginian supporters. Wirt was among the first to respond. Less than two months after the election he invited Monroe to dine with him, expressing the hope that the presidential contest had not "raised an insuperable barrier" between Monroe and his friends. Monroe, on his part, denied any desire to separate from those among his old friends who opposed his presidential aspirations. The "old friends," however, expected Monroe to prove his loyalty on the state level if he wished to again be a force in national politics.[13]

In 1810 the Richmond Junto, an extremely influential and socially prominent coterie of ardent Madisonians led by Wilson Cary Nicholas, William Branch Giles, Thomas Ritchie, Spencer

Roane, and William Wirt, offered Monroe a chance to return to the House of Delegates. Tazewell was suspicious of the Junto's motives. Monroe, he felt, had advanced too far in the political hierarchy to accept such a lowly position, and he wondered if "insidious political rivals" believed it safer to keep Monroe in the lower echelons of state government. He questioned how a seat in the Virginia legislature could enhance Monroe's political reputation. "There is," he told his friend, "a necessity of your advancing in order to prevent retrocession."[14] Yet, Monroe returned to the legislature and there regained the confidence of many regular Republicans.

Tazewell then thought Monroe's next logical move should be to enter the senatorial race as an opponent of the incumbent, William Branch Giles. If Monroe succeeded, he could go on "to grades of more importance."[15] Monroe, however, viewed the senatorial bid as a dangerous gamble. Giles still had too many powerful allies.[16] Instead, Monroe pursued a safer goal, the governorship of Virginia, which became available early in 1811 when John Tyler, father of the future president, accepted a federal judgeship and resigned from the executive position. The Richmond Junto was of a mood to favor Monroe, but remembering his past backsliding, the members, along with other administration Republicans, insisted upon questioning him on his party loyalty and general attitude toward Madison. Monroe agreed, but not without a twinge of conscience which prompted him to explain elaborately to Tazewell the reasons for his willingness to submit himself to the rather degrading ordeal. During the probe, he assured Tazewell, he maintained his independence and did not promise to be guided by the Junto on all matters. Neither did he completely reject or condemn the minority groups that were attacking the Madison administration with a viciousness more intense than ever directed against Jefferson. By taking a moderate stance, Monroe hoped to pull the Republican party together. At least, this was the tenor of his explanation. "I am satisfied," he told Tazewell, "that the safety of free government depends on the preservation of the Republican party, and that to make the object secure, the energies of that party ought to be united."[17]

Tazewell understood but confessed he himself would never

have consented to such an interrogation. He would have been indignant "at what I should (most improperly) have conceived as a reflection upon me. I should have instantly shrunk within my own shell, and have laconically replied 'only past conduct for more than a score of years, ought to be a sufficient pledge of my character—if you choose to confide in that pledge again, I will again (& with pleasure) receive what you desire at your hands—but if you do not, I shall give none other.' " This course of action, Tazewell admitted, would have been a mistake. Had Monroe followed it, he would have hazarded the election and exposed himself to "the imputation of much arrogance, and probably some artifice." By adopting the better plan, Monroe secured the gubernatorial position and, of more importance, placed himself in a position from which he could render great service to the country, "unclogged by the opposition of those, who in a different state of things, would have been prepared to oppose you in all things."[18]

While Madison's mode of operation frequently displeased Tazewell, he often was more upset by the actions of Randolph and his followers, and he believed that Monroe, by delicately disassociating himself from them, had "shaken off a heavy incumbrance." "For some of the members of this minority," Tazewell explained, "I feel strong personal attachments, & for their leader I entertain even a stronger sentiment than friendship." Randolph, whom he regarded almost as a brother, had high ideals, and Tazewell often sympathized with the end results that his erratic friend pursued, but not with the methods by which he tried to achieve them. Randolph's policies, even when sound, too often were presented in a manner which made moderate men cringe. The mode of warfare of the Randolph men, Tazewell sadly observed, "is so odious, their attacks so irregular, and so much the result of sudden impressions, that it requires no great foresight to perceive, that they can never produce much appeal even when successful, and that they must ultimately be vanquished by better systematized operations, more temper, and more comprehensive views." Less diplomatically, Benjamin Rush bluntly characterized Randolph as "a mischievous boy with a squirt in his hands, throwing its dirty contents into the eyes of everybody that looked at him."[19]

The Madison administration was buffeted not only by the Randolph Quids but also from within its own party by another group of vocal opponents which Nathaniel Macon dubbed the "Invisibles." Under the leadership of Senator Samuel Smith of Maryland, this rather nebulous conglomeration opposed the rechartering of the Bank of the United States (the charter of the first Bank of the United States having expired in 1811), charging it was largely under the control of England, and loudly clamored for a war with Great Britain, while the Jeffersonian-Madisonian Republicans still believed in commercial retaliation as a solution to problems of foreign policy.[20]

Tazewell, not happy with either of the two factions or with the administration adherents, believed the entire Republican cause was in jeopardy, and the cause, he told Monroe, was certainly of far greater importance than the party, the continuation of which was not indispensable to the preservation of Republican principles. Maintenance of Republican ideals, in Tazewell's mind, depended upon, first, a strict allegiance to the Constitution of the United States and, second, due attention to the interests of the nation in the implementation of the Constitution. Greater damage, he contended, was done by those who manipulated the principles of the Constitution in such a way as to oppress the people than by those who actually violated the supreme law of the land. The Embargo and Non-Intercourse Acts, while undoubtedly constitutional, had brought the country to the edge of destruction. The only solution Tazewell could suggest was the organization of an "intermediate sect," a third party which would "oppose *before the people* the disastrous course" so obstinately adhered to by the Madison administration. This should be done tactfully, with "deference and mildness," accompanied by declarations of regret at the necessity of diversity of opinion, and with the hope that causes of difference could be removed and union again restored.[21]

Monroe again rejected Tazewell's proposals. No more than two parties could function effectively in the United States, he was convinced, and he thought it far better to remain in the established structure, even as a party within the party, in the hope of fostering union and cooperation in defense of true Republican ideals. Monroe hardly could say otherwise. Before he was considered for the governorship he was asked whether, if elected, he would "carry into the Government a disposition to cooperate with the [Madison] Administration and to encourage union and harmony, for the purpose of ensuring success to their measures." Monroe replied enthusiastically in the affirmative and added with pleasure "that there is nothing of a personal nature, in the relation which subsists between the chief magistrate and myself, that can possibly impair the force of this sentiment."[22]

For the sake of his own future, if for no other reason, Monroe's stand was prudent. Less than three weeks after he voiced his opposition to Tazewell's new party proposal, Monroe discreetly was sounded out on the possibility of his joining Madison's cabinet as head of the State Department. Madison, after months of feeling undercut by the "Invisibles," finally ousted Secretary of State Robert Smith, Samuel Smith's brother and a suspected member of the malcontents.[23] Monroe immediately sought Tazewell's advice, and Tazewell lost no time in telling Monroe to indicate his interest in the position, for here was a chance to heal the breach with England, paving the way for a mutually advantageous commercial arrangement. But Tazewell counseled Monroe to declare fully and explicitly the views and principles that he would carry with him into the administration, stating "that these are the result of much reflection & experience, and therefore will not probably be changed." If Madison accepted this declaration, Monroe, as secretary of state, would be free to explore the feasibility of an Anglo-American agreement. "The recent change of ministers in England," Tazewell went on, "justifies great hope I think, that all our differences in that quarter may be readily adjusted, if a proper disposition on our part is brought into the negotiation," especially if conducted under the direction of Monroe, whose favorable attitude toward Great Britain was well known. Perhaps the United States could return to nearly the same ground it would have occupied had the Monroe-Pinkney treaty been adopted, "and our internal difficulties will soon subside of themselves." In allying with England, the United States might, of course, be brought into a collision with France, but with the support of England, this would result in "no mischievous consequences."

In presenting such terms to Madison, Tazewell was of the

opinion that Monroe could not lose. If his conditions were accepted, Monroe could lead the administration, almost be president in fact, and certainly he would be next in line to inherit the office. If his conditions were rejected, Madison's responsibility for the fate of the country would become even more burdensome, and if the nation were endangered by Madison's measures, "all the odium which attaches to them" would redound to Monroe's benefit. There was only one question troubling Tazewell. Was it possible for anyone, however skilled in diplomacy, to rescue the country from the "road to ruin" on which it had been traveling? "By accepting the proposed overture," Tazewell admitted, "some might therefore say, you are only placing yourself in a situation in which you can do no good, but are imprudently uniting yours with the destiny of those who have produced the present crisis." Regardless, if Madison acceded to Monroe's stipulations, Monroe could not decline. The country had the right to expect him to "render the most effectual aid in putting down those mad politicians, who by their past counsels have plunged the country into its present distress," thus endangering the future of free government. Madison's "native virtuous disposition" required the support of a man like Monroe. The president wanted to do right, but he was surrounded by too many designing characters. If Monroe could settle the differences between the United States and Great Britain, the nation no longer would be divided, and the great causes of Republicanism would flourish.[24]

On March 20, 1811, President Madison officially offered Monroe the State Department. Monroe replied without hesitation, but he expressed his views on foreign policy with less candor than Tazewell desired. "I was sincerely of the opinion," Monroe cautiously, almost apologetically, told the president, "that it was for the interest of our country to make an accommodation with England, the great maritime power, even on moderate terms, rather than hazard war, or any other alternative. On that opinion I acted afterwards, while I remained in office, and I own that I have since seen no cause to doubt its soundness. Circumstances have in some respects changed, but still my general views of policy are the same."[25]

Tazewell, to whom Monroe dispatched a draft of his letter

to Madison, pronounced it acceptable as an introduction, as a first step in his consideration of the president's offer, but if it was meant to be a pledge to follow wherever Madison might lead, "I cannot say that it receives my sanction." Monroe should not compromise but should state his position forcefully, leaving it up to Madison to accept or reject Monroe and Monroe's principles, but Tazewell felt he could not force Monroe to take a firm stand. If Monroe was satisfied that he could work with the president and that he was not being used merely to prop up a falling administration, then Tazewell applauded his appointment. He had hoped for a more determined stand, but given Monroe's obvious overwhelming desire to again be an important figure on the Washington scene, a bit of hedging on principles was to be anticipated. Tazewell hoped Monroe would rise to the occasion and solve the nation's problems without resorting to war with England.[26]

Not all of Tazewell's time was spent in advising prospective statesmen. In July 1808 he purchased two tracts of land in Princess Anne County, bordering Chesapeake Bay to the north and Little Creek to the west, and in 1810 he added a few more contiguous acres. This was Sandhills plantation, about twelve miles from Norfolk, where he spent many happy hours, as he said, "playing farmer." Initially the plantation was manned by an overseer and twenty-three slaves, but within a year of purchase, Tazewell, always mindful of economy, reduced the number of slaves to twelve.[27]

Although court sessions and other duties associated with his law practice often demanded prolonged absences from home, Tazewell tried never to neglect his family's welfare and happiness. Knowing from experience how much a child could suffer from parental inattention, Tazewell was determined that his own children should never feel forsaken. This led to an overprotectiveness which continued far into the adult years of the Tazewell offspring. Ann was the center of the household. Gentle, kind, and shy, she loved her home and shunned social position. In such a closely knit family, tragedy was felt with great intensity, and it struck for the first time in the summer of 1810. The children, Louisa age six, Henry five, John three, and baby Sarah not quite a year old, seemed to be flourishing when suddenly and unexpectedly Sarah died.[28]

Usually reticent about discussing personal matters of any
nature in letters, except to the closest of friends, Tazewell
twice mentioned his bereavement to Jefferson. Undoubtedly
the great man of Monticello, who knew well what pain the loss
of a child could bring, understood and sympathized with Tazewell's anguish. On July 3, 1810, two days after Sarah's death,
Tazewell informed Jefferson of "a very severe illness by which
I was long confined to my bed, from whence I only arose to
witness the unexpected death of one of my children." Again in
August he mentioned his "late domestic affliction."[29]

There were several reasons for Tazewell's correspondence
with Jefferson. For one, Tazewell represented the son and
heir of a Jefferson creditor, an English merchant, and in this
capacity he reluctantly was forced to add to Jefferson's financial woes by pressing for payment of the debt.[30] In another
role, however, he was able to help rescue the former president
from possible economic ruin, due to a situation precipitated in
the spring of 1810 when Edward Livingston brought suit
against Jefferson in the federal circuit court in Richmond.

Often referred to as the Batture controversy, the case of
*Livingston* v. *Jefferson* involved a question which arose during
Jefferson's second administration. Livingston, of the prominent New York family, after suffering extreme financial re-
verses, went to New Orleans in 1804, hoping to make a fresh
start in the new and growing region and eventually to satisfy
his creditors. His attention was drawn to the valuable river-
front area built up by silt from the Mississippi River. The land
was known as the Batture St. Marie, the alleged owner of
which, John Gravier, was under attack by the citizens of New
Orleans, who contended that the batture belonged to the
people of the community to be used as common property for
an anchorage or as a place from which they could obtain dirt
and sand. The silt land, they declared, did not belong to the
person who owned riparian property adjacent to the batture.

Livingston, on the promise of a share of the batture should
the case be successful, defended Gravier, who received a favorable judgment from the territorial court. Having now a
vested interest in this valuable real estate, Livingston set about
to improve his section of the batture, constructing a dwelling,
building a levee, and excavating a canal. The people of New

Orleans protested, riots broke out, and mobs forced canal diggers from the site. The governor of Louisiana, William Claiborne, fearing uncontrollable violence, appealed to President Jefferson for assistance in resolving the conflicting claims. Since the decision of the territorial court had no binding force on the government of the United States, Jefferson placed the matter before his cabinet. In the president's mind, land created by a river current unquestionably belonged to the United States. The cabinet agreed, and acting, in part, under the provisions of the Squatters' Act of 1807, Jefferson directed Secretary of State Madison to have Livingston and his workers removed from the land in dispute.[31]

Livingston, incensed, tenaciously held to his conviction that the president could not evict him without judicial action. The matter was unresolved when Jefferson left office. Congress refused to acknowledge Livingston's petition for relief, and Livingston, in frustration, sought satisfaction by suing Jefferson for personal liability in the Circuit Court of the United States for the District of Virginia. Jefferson, whose financial situation was, to say the least, precarious, and to whom the thought of an adverse judgment in such a case was staggering, solicited aid from the best legal minds in Virginia. He turned to the attorneys of the Burr case, George Hay, William Wirt, and John Wickham. Would they, he asked, act jointly as counsel for the defense? Hay and Wirt agreed, but Wickham declined and recommended Tazewell.[32]

Wirt was delighted to have his former partner involved. "I am very glad that you are engaged in the Batture Case," he wrote in his usual merry mood, "and still more glad to learn that we are likely to have several of the chief luminaries of the North to oppose us." Standing alone, Wirt declared, he would have "no stomach for the combat against such a phalanx," but with Tazewell at his side, these were the very adversaries he would have selected.[33]

Despite Wirt's professed eagerness to test his mettle against worthy opponents, the grueling, meticulous preparation of the case fell to Tazewell. Hay, never very energetic, was "weary of drawing pleas in this suit," and Wirt, who disliked details, was "not well enough now to undertake the task," even though he did during these weeks write the *Old Bachelor*. Initially, both Tazewell and Jefferson favored basing the defense on the merits of the case, establishing the public's right to the disputed land. This, Tazewell informed Jefferson, was "highly desirable" if it could be done "without detriment to you personally."[34] However, after considering all facets of the controversy, Tazewell concluded that it was doubtful the court would deny Livingston's claim solely on evidence or historical jurisprudence.[35] The safer way was to plead no jurisdiction, arguing an English common law precedent which held that "an action to recover damages for injuries to the land can be brought only where the land lies." Livingston supposedly did not initiate the suit in New Orleans because Jefferson was not a resident of that area and a process could not be served outside the territory. In Jefferson's mind, however, there was more than a lurking suspicion that Livingston, for obvious reasons, wanted the case heard by Jefferson's adversary John Marshall. "Nobody seems to doubt," Jefferson confided to Madison, "that he [Marshall] is prepared to decide that Livingston's right to the batture is unquestionable, and that I am bound to pay for it with my private fortune."[36]

Responsibility for the defense rested almost entirely in Tazewell's hands. When a preliminary discussion of demurrers unexpectedly was scheduled by the court, Hay begged Tazewell to drop whatever he was doing and hasten to Richmond. "I am anxious that you should be here," he entreated, "really & sincerely anxious. I am worn out—Actually broke down by a jury trial of 10 days in Powhatan & feel totally unfit for any heavy discussion. You can render us the most essential aid, and I beseech you to come."[37]

In addition to the plea of no jurisdiction, several others were presented to the court, among them an attempt to prove, on the merits of the case, the federal government's claim to the batture and, second, an endeavor to establish the immunity of a former president from prosecution for errors he may have committed, in the public interest, while in office. When the case was heard only the question of jurisdiction was argued. Interestingly, attorneys for the defense were not opposed by the "northern luminaries" whom Wirt had anticipated. Instead, John Wickham represented the plaintiff. Tazewell performed brilliantly, and in response to his argument the court unanimously chose to dismiss the case, stating "a trespass upon the land lying out of the district of Virginia is not sustainable by the Federal Court within it." "The opinion of the Chief Justice," Tazewell happily informed Jefferson, "was clear, able and most satisfactory."[38]

Jefferson was grateful. "I have learnt from all quarters," he told Tazewell, "that your argument was among the ablest ever delivered before that court." But not all comment was laudatory. Marshall's written opinion contained a severe indictment of Jefferson's good faith in utilizing a technicality to prevent the court from hearing the case. Thus the "injured party may have a clear right without a remedy" because Jefferson had resorted to the use of a "technical impediment" to escape the decision of the bench. Others agreed with Marshall, including Chancellor James Kent of New York and Joseph Story, the newly appointed associate justice of the Supreme Court of the United States.[39]

Perhaps Tazewell should have argued the point of a former president's immunity from personal liability for acts performed while in office in the line of duty. One cannot imagine the establishment of a precedent whereby a chief executive would be held responsible throughout the remainder of his life for public decisions made in good faith, but had the case gone to the Supreme Court, as Livingston, and possibly Marshall, desired, the outcome is a matter of conjecture. Tazewell, in any event, did rescue Jefferson from months of litigation, and Jefferson was "well satisfied to be relieved from it."[40]

## Chapter V

# *War and*

# *Innovation*

By the time Monroe assumed his duties as secretary of state, Anglo-American relations had worsened, and his confidence, never robust, required constant bolstering. This Tazewell tried to do, assuring him that he was the only person in the entire administration who had the slightest chance of arranging an amicable settlement with Great Britain, so imperative to the salvation of the United States. There was need for haste. Hostility toward the government resounded through every port on the eastern seaboard. "If our vessels go to any port of Europe," the *Norfolk Gazette and Publick Ledger* protested, "they are sequestered or confiscated by the orders of our friend the emperor Napoleon, and so lost to their owners. If they go to Great Britain and return back, they are seized by the laws of our own country, and thus lost to their owners .... [Caught] between the Emperor of France and Mr. Madison, our merchants, shipwrights, and all those concerned with commerce, may soon cease their avocations." And there were overt indications of anger and frustration. In April 1811 the French privateer *Revanche de Cerf* was burned in Norfolk harbor, "obviously by design." A month later the United States frigate *President* clashed with H.M.S. *Little Belt* off Cape Henry. Throughout the Virginia Tidewater there was a surge of patriotism. The *Little Belt* was forced to strike her colors. The *Chesapeake* was avenged! National rights were vindicated.[1]

Although some Americans called for increased conciliatory attempts, others were galled by what they construed as the cowardly policy of the Madison administration in the face of continued British arrogance. When the British sloop of war *Tartarus* seized two American merchant vessels in Hampton Roads and impressed three seamen, the Norfolk press was angry. To what lengths, questioned the *Herald,* should such brazen and impudent actions be allowed to continue? Should "this captain of *Hell* " be able to seize "our property at our very threshold?" Without a doubt, the time to take a stand had arrived. Monroe agreed. Writing to an English friend in the fall of 1811, he expressed dismay at the evidence of a "determined hostility in your government against this country, and a decision to push things to their worst," and he concluded that "war, dreadful as the alternative is, could not do us more injury than the present state of things. It would certainly be more honorable to the nation, and gratifying to the publick feelings."[2] Many of the newly elected members of the House of Representatives, awaiting the convening of the Twelfth Congress, were of the same opinion. The "War Hawks" swooped and soared, and the "Invisibles" became increasingly visible.

Tazewell still urged a friendly Anglo-American understanding, including a solid trade agreement. When, in early November, Congress assembled and debates on war and peace began, Tazewell was pleased with John Randolph, who challenged, hour after hour, every suggestion of an open rupture with England. But he read with alarm the remarks of Henry Clay, John C. Calhoun, Felix Grundy, and other War Hawks, who were pushing Madison toward a request for a declaration of war, and he anxiously studied Madison's annual message to the first session of the Twelfth Congress, described as voicing "the President's habitual duality of force and conciliation."[3] For Tazewell, the language of the message was entirely too strong, unless, as he told Monroe, a war with Britain already had been decided upon by the president. Even if this were true, Madison's words were dangerous, as they could "induce Great Britain to strike the first blow, which in our present situation must be terrible indeed." Tazewell pleaded with Monroe, "let us have as much and as speedy preparation for war as you please and can afford, but for God's sake not actual war, until we are prepared for it in some degree. And then no war with Great Britain, if it can be fairly and honorably avoided." Influenced no doubt by his friend Decatur and by the vulnerability of Norfolk and its merchant fleet, Tazewell believed naval preparations to be of the utmost importance.

For years he had advocated a strong navy for the precise purpose Madison voiced in a resolution to Congress, "to resume, maintain, and defend the navigation of the high seas."[4]

Perhaps impatience with what he considered to be Monroe's lack of forcefulness in withstanding the pressures of those who wanted war with Great Britain caused the thirty-eight-year-old Tazewell to lecture the secretary of state, a seasoned diplomat of fifty-two, on how an important government official in a sensitive position ought to conduct himself. As the ranking cabinet officer in a country which many believed to be on the verge of war, Tazewell scolded, it was inadvisable to tell tradesmen, no matter how casually or informally, "that if you were a merchant and had the means, you would buy up all the flour in the U.S." Such indiscreet statements, if construed as "inside information," could mean profits for a few. "I know them [the merchants] well and altho' I would trust them with my gold, nay with my life or honor, I would not confide to one of them an expression, which could be tortured even into an influence upon the course of trade." Softening his tone a bit, Tazewell reaffirmed his interest "in anything which relates to you privately or publicly . . . and shall therefore be pleased at any time to hear from you, if I can in any way be useful to you. But of public matters, altho' at the present juncture my own local situation and that of all my property fills me with much anxiety, yet I wish to gain no information, at least from you."[5]

Edwin Gray of Virginia, a former Quid and a member of the House, assured Tazewell there would be no declaration of war during the current session of Congress. Tazewell hoped Gray was right. "A war and a presidential election during that war, and farewell the liberty and constitution of this once happy land," Tazewell warned Monroe. On several occasions he expressed his concern lest a military faction attempt to unseat Madison, and he cautioned Monroe to keep a careful watch on General John Armstrong of New York, minister to France from 1804 to 1811 and son-in-law of Chancellor Robert Livingston: "Beware of Armstrong, Beware of Wilkinson, they have lately been corresponding. I know the fact, and that the latter has been inviting the former to present himself at once before the public as a candidate for the next presidency.

He assured him of the support of Giles, the Smiths, and others of the Southern people. With what authority this was done I know not, but my friend Decatur received the contents of the letter from one in New York to whom it was shown by Armstrong himself." Whenever Wilkinson's name appeared, Tazewell was certain intrigue was afoot, and in 1812 he feared a coup d'etat carried out by the Invisibles in cooperation with the military, led by Armstrong and Wilkinson. A year later, when Madison's appointment of Armstrong as secretary of war turned out to be a disaster, both the president and Monroe had reason to remember Tazewell's lack of confidence in the incompetent general.[6]

In the spring of 1812 Madison and Monroe, bowing to the intensified pressure of the War Hawks, recommended a sixty-day embargo on American shipping (increased by Congress to ninety days) preparatory to a declaration of war. Citizens of Norfolk reacted bitterly. "If [the embargo] was intended as a measure of precaution and protection," blazed the *Gazette and Publick Ledger,* "we observe that those who were intended to be benefited consider it in a very different sense, for never were such exertions made to escape an evil, as we have witnessed on this occasion . . . . Everything afloat, which could possibly get away, is gone and now going out of the road and port." The audacity of a nation "without money, without men, without a navy" declaring war on Great Britain struck John Randolph as incredible. Regardless, several supposedly intelligent members of Congress wanted to challenge France as well.[7]

Monroe now agreed with Madison that England would be satisfied with nothing short of unconditional submission to its absolute control of the seas. Therefore, there was no alternative but to fight. Monroe also realized how deeply he had disappointed Tazewell and others in failing to achieve a compromise with Great Britain. On June 18, Congress took the final fateful step of declaring war. William Wirt was exuberant. There was not a man in Richmond, he was certain, who was "not an inch taller since Congress has done its duty."[8] Tazewell was appalled. Sometime earlier John Taylor had expressed well what Tazewell feared, that "this war for honour, like that of the Greeks against Troy, may terminate in the destruction of the last experiment in . . . free government."[9]

But Tazewell was a realist, and although opposed to the war, he did not intend to hide from it. Two days after the declaration he consented to act as prize agent for Decatur and his ship, the *United States*. [10]

In Norfolk the *Herald* preached doom and foretold disaster to the city's economy as a result of the coming conflict, while the *Gazette and Publick Ledger* lamented the departure of the British consul, John Hamilton, who had filled that post for more than twenty-three years. But Norfolk, too, was forced to face the realities of the situation and turned to the enormous task of putting its defenses in order. After a flurry of activity in 1807, little had been done to prepare for an attack on the borough. Despite the initial panic, Norfolk was not in danger during the first months of the war. The coasting trade was interrupted only intermittently, and Norfolk merchants carried on business as usual, or sometimes better than usual, dispatching their vessels to Bermuda and to various British West Indies ports. When the British colonies desperately needed supplies, American commerce was welcomed, and the vessels did not return to Norfolk empty-handed. Advertisements for newly arrived English goods often were seen in the city's newspapers during the fall of 1812.[11]

Until Decatur needed his assistance in prize cases, Tazewell noticed little change in his customary routine of court sessions, legal work, and plantation business. In August 1812 another daughter was born to Littleton and Ann Tazewell. The healthy infant, called Sally by the family, was christened Sarah in memory of the child who died two years before. The presidential election of 1812 passed without any signs of the coup d'etat Tazewell feared. Although a coalition of Federalists and anti-administration Republicans sought to unseat Madison by backing DeWitt Clinton of New York, the president was narrowly reelected in the tightest race since 1800. The outcome probably indicated that a sizable number of voters believed Madison unnecessarily had led the country into war, unprepared and without sufficient cause.[12]

In February 1813, the situation in Norfolk changed rapidly when the British blockaded the entrance to Chesapeake Bay, bringing life in the borough virtually to a standstill. "Not a vessel can pass from Hampton Roads either up or down the

Bay without being intercepted, and not a vessel bound from the sea can escape capture," reported the *Virginia Argus*. Early in March there was greater cause for alarm when a force of British ships, "far exceeding the number needful for a blockade," arrived in Lynnhaven Bay. Robert B. Taylor, now a brigadier general in the Virginia militia, expected the British to swarm ashore at any moment.[13]

During this time of threatened invasion Tazewell was in New York adjudicating a $200,000 prize for Decatur and his crew, the splendid British frigate *Macedonian*, captured in December. The safety of Tazewell's wife and children thus was in the hands of John Nivison, who wrote frequently to his son-in-law informing him of the welfare of the family and of the frantic efforts being made to save the town. On March 9 rumors of the presence of a British landing force of several hundred marines and picked sailors, armed with "sabres, pistols, and tommahauks," caused panic. When the ominous alarm gun sounded, Nivison directed the removal of valuable items from the Tazewell house and attempted to salvage papers (many of which were lost in the confusion) from Tazewell's office. He then gathered the Nivison and Tazewell families for evacuation to Princess Anne County. There the refugees found that oxen, mules, horses, carts, and slaves had been impressed for use by the militia, and the security they sought was not to be found. British raiding parties, coming ashore in the vicinity of Lynnhaven Inlet to seize cattle, sheep, and various other provisions, threatened lives and dwellings. Slaves were enticed from their owners by British promises of freedom and assistance. Rumors of slave revolts, encouraged by the British, spread fear, at times verging on hysteria, throughout the Tidewater.[14]

The anticipated attack on Norfolk was delayed until June, when the city was saved at the Battle of Craney Island by the heroic stand of General Taylor and the Virginia militia, but the blockade continued, and only by laborious and persistent efforts did the Norfolk merchants carry on a limited river trade. In December 1813 Congress, in an effort to prevent the British from obtaining provisions by the capture of American merchant vessels, passed a stringent embargo which included restrictions on the movements of riverboats. The economy of

Norfolk again plummeted. The people became increasingly bitter and impoverished.[15]

Tazewell's law practice, especially in its maritime aspects, also declined, and he turned to planting peach and apple trees and buying plows. His absences from home on missions for Decatur were frequent, and he neglected many domestic responsibilities, among them the matter of Louisa's education. Nivison prescribed the usual courses of English and music until Tazewell could find time to "give more special direction." Of greater seriousness, perhaps, was Tazewell's seeming obliviousness to the needs of his older son, Henry. John was the favorite, from almost the day of his birth. Henry was slower, not as mentally alert, but he tried to please. "I am very glad to take up my pen to write to you and tell you that we are all well," the nine-year-old Henry began his first extant letter to his father. "John had got a great deal better than he was when you left him. How are you and how do you like the country that you are traveling in and about?" Regardless of Henry's touching efforts, it was John who invariably was described as "a most excellent boy."[16]

Norfolk's vulnerability to enemy attack was a constant worry, especially so in August 1814, as the British plagued the upper Chesapeake Bay area, invading and burning the nation's capital. Wirt urged Tazewell to forsake Norfolk and purchase an "inland plantation in the region of health and beyond the reach of hostile alarms," even though Jefferson was saying that "there certainly must & will be peace shortly and if he were Ambassador he would consent to peace with one article—'there shall be peace between the U.S. & his Brit. majesty.'" "Such a treaty," Wirt reflected, "might be wise as well as witty."[17]

Faced with the burning of Washington and having to take over the War Department after the Armstrong fiasco, Monroe was inundated with problems. In former times of despair he often sought Tazewell's advice and sympathy. During the war years this did not occur; Tazewell's obvious disappointment with Monroe's failure to avoid hostilities had temporarily dampened their friendship. But Tazewell's counsel was requested from another quarter. Wilson Cary Nicholas, governor-elect of Virginia, was eager for assistance: "I wish you to put upon paper in the form of a communication to the legislature everything it would be proper for me to say in the present state of our affairs, in our different relations to the U.S. government & foreign nations, & to the situation of our state as to schools & the internal improvements of the country, by roads & canals." Nicholas was worried particularly about interference of state governments in the operation of national affairs. Since 1798 he had upheld the right of an individual state to challenge actions of the federal government, but with New England, because of its opposition to the war, now threatening to destroy the Union, Nicholas questioned the current validity of his states' rights positon. "In 1798 I acted conscientiously," he explained to Tazewell. "I will do so now and will not sacrifice the interest of my country to the punctilio of consistency. If you think it will do any good to call the public attention to this subject, I will for the good of my country risque giving offence. I wish you to say what you think proper. The outrageous conduct of the N.E. states would make this a fit occasion." Nicholas wanted more than Tazewell's views. He hoped the Norfolk attorney would composed the entire message to the legislature: "If you will not laugh at me, I will request you to adapt the style of the message to what would be expected from such a clodhopper as I am, rather than from a production under your own signature."[18]

Throughout his term as governor, Nicholas solicited and seemingly tried to implement Tazewell's ideas on internal improvements and education, advocating a state-financed network of canals and roads to bind the commonwealth together economically and politically. Both Tazewell and Nicholas believed that competition among the states for federal funds would preclude cooperation in a nationally supported program of internal improvements. Nicholas's diligence in working to increase the state's Literary Fund, the source of support for education, helped move the legislature another step toward the establishment of the University of Virginia, still a concern of Tazewell's. He was pleased, too, by the governor's desire to have the naval forces of the United States strengthened; although the war came to an end in December 1814, Tazewell still felt that an adequate navy was necessary if American commerce was to command respect on the high seas.[19]

The Treaty of Ghent, which terminated hostilities, was almost as brief as Jefferson's suggested statement. The aftereffects, however, were more serious. The treaty made no provision for the abandonment of trade restrictions. The British West Indies were closed to American vessels and remained so despite a commercial agreement between the United States and Great Britain in July 1815. Norfolk shipping stagnated. As British vessels were allowed to enter American ports, Norfolk merchants could export some goods to the West Indies in British bottoms, and the merchants agreed that this, at least, was preferable to an embargo, but they longed to float their own vessels. Nivison, disturbed by the strangulation of Norfolk commerce, was filled with apprehension for the future of the borough. "Nothing new of consequence exists here," he informed his son-in-law. "We have a very dull time of it. No business, most of the ships have gone up the James River to load, others which can't get employment are going to avoid the town. Not a single arrival has taken place with dry goods at Norfolk & I believe not many above. I frequently call at your office but find nothing doing or to do."[20]

Being a man who admired precision, the lack of it in the Treaty of Ghent troubled Tazewell. Peace, under these circumstances, could be described as only the absence of war, he confided to John Randolph. Nothing had been settled, not impressment, not the matter of trade with the British West Indies. Norfolk merchants actually had lost "inestimable privileges" enjoyed "before we were placed in the experimental crucible." Nevertheless, he felt that the treaty probably saved the country from the great calamity of defeat at the hands of the British. Perhaps it was the best settlement possible, but because the war had decided nothing, he believed Monroe's chances for the presidency in 1816 were gone. Monroe "will struggle hard to obtain the office, but it will be in vain," Tazewell told Randolph. The next president would be a New Yorker, "rely on it," but whether the mantle would fall on Rufus King, DeWitt Clinton, or Governor Daniel Tompkins, "future events alone can tell."[21]

Contrary to rumors circulating in Virginia, Tazewell professed no desire to become a member of the next Congress. To Randolph he declared his unavailability: "I neither am now, nor ever have been, and (unless my opinions undergo some great change) never shall be or will be desirous, or even willing to be placed in this situation again."[22] He much preferred spending hours in his library, toiling over the task of writing a treatise, requested by Randolph, on a principle of English common law which exempted lands from being seized and sold under execution to satisfy a debt. Tazewell traced the origin of the law, then defended it eloquently as a principle "endeared to the affections of the great mass of Englishmen because it hallows the bones of their ancestors, and consecrates them from the impious violations of bailiffs or auctioneers" and "has improved the agriculture of their country and sharpened the attachment the Englishman feels to his native spot." Randolph thought the work worthy of publication, but Tazewell protested: "The matter is not fit for the publick." It would excite no interest and few would understand it. "Moreover I never did, and believe I never shall appear (even anonymously) before the public as a writer upon any subject; but when I do, I should like to exhibit myself in an attire somewhat better than the morning gown and slippers in which I am very often seen by my friends."[23]

Now that peace had come, Tazewell looked forward to more hours with his family, but this was not yet to be. There were additional hearings on prize cases, entailing long stays in New York and Philadelphia, where his yearning for domestic activities was turned toward shopping for a sideboard, chairs, and other household items. There was also the tempting offer of a position in Washington to consider, that of secretary to the newly organized Board of Navy Commissioners. An illustrious trio, Commodores John Rodgers, Isaac Hull, and David Porter, requested his services. Tazewell was pleased but declined the appointment.[24]

In May 1815 Decatur sailed out of New York harbor in command of a squadron of nine ships, bound for Algiers. His mission was to press the dey for compensation for injuries to American shipping while the United States was involved in hostilities with England and to bring an end to the practice, persisted in by Algiers, Tunis, and Tripoli, of demanding tribute from American ships. Decatur's success resulted in additional prize cases that demanded Tazewell's attention when the naval hero returned triumphantly to honors and fetes. The most splendid welcome was accorded Decatur in Norfolk where the citizens hosted a magnificent dinner. John Nivison, assisted by Tazewell and Robert Taylor, presided over the gala event and joined in the cheers for Decatur's famous toast: "Our country—in her intercourse with foreign nations may she always be in the right, and always successful, right or wrong." Tazewell, in turn, toasted Decatur with, "Our Distinguished Guest, Most admired where best known." Later in the year, as a member of the Board of Navy Commissioners, Decatur ably championed Norfolk for the designation of chief naval base in the Chesapeake. His friend Tazewell was most gratified.[25] Tazewell's support of the navy and his friendships with Decatur and other naval officers evinced love of country as well as his desire to foster the material growth of Norfolk. After the War of 1812 economic nationalism was something he could well understand, and he followed closely congressional debates on the creation of the second Bank of the United States, internal improvements, and the tariff. The transportation revolution fascinated him. On the other hand, demands of western interests for a voice in state government equal to that of the eastern sections seemed premature to him, and, along with a substantial number of his generation and class, he was skeptical about the ability of a pure democracy to sustain liberty, security, and union. Would it not be better, he wondered, to place the responsibility for the nation in the hands of a natural aristocracy, men of talent, virtue, and education, who would counteract the instability of the masses? The rise of the common man, determined to exercise his right to rule, challenged Tazewell's preconceived ideas of Jeffersonian democracy.[26]

America was changing, and all the baffling aspects associated with the transformation surfaced in the session of the Virginia General Assembly that convened in the fall of 1816. Tazewell again represented Norfolk borough in the House of Delegates. He had not been a candidate for the office and was absent from the city when, without his knowledge, he was elected. "In politics," announced the *Gazette and Publick Ledger*, "Mr. Tazewell is of the Republican party, but his talents and honorable character secured him the support of both parties."[27]

The legislative committees to which Tazewell was appointed reflected his interests. He was chairman of the Committee for Courts of Justice and served on those dealing with roads, navigation, finance, schools and colleges, and banks. Bank questions constituted the intital business of the legislature, and banking was uppermost in the minds of many of the citizens of Norfolk, as well as of primary concern to the inhabitants of the western areas of the state. Hoping to obtain a branch bank for Norfolk, Tazewell consented to be a candidate for the board of directors of the second Bank of the United States, but he was unsuccessful.[28]

In the legislature Tazewell coupled the need for banks with the development of internal improvements. During the previous session of the House of Delegates he was named to the Board of Public Works, a group of ten members including, in addition to Tazewell, Alexander Smyth of Wythe County, Charles Fenton Mercer of Loudoun, and Thomas Jefferson of Albemarle. Income from the state's shares in the Bank of Virginia and the Farmer's Bank of Virginia was to be used by the board for the development of internal improvements. Tazewell believed in this approach and did all he could to further it. Constant reminders of Norfolk's banking needs came from his father-in-law, who insisted, "The great object for Norfolk is most certainly to obtain an accession of capital in order to project a market here equal to N. York." Given the availability of adequate capital and financial services, Richmond merchants and Carolina producers would prefer transacting their business in Norfolk rather than incurring additional freight and insurance costs necessary for transporting their goods to New York. With any help at all, Nivison declared, Norfolk "will yet rise and show will."[29]

Tazewell's friends in Congress, Nathaniel Macon and John Randolph, vehemently opposed the Bank of the United States and extended their animosity to all banks. Macon thought the Bank of the United States unconstitutional, while Randolph likened a bank to a house of ill fame and expressed fear of the oppression of a monster national bank or a cluster of state banks. "However great the evil of their conduct may be," he argued on the floor of the House, "who is to bell the cat? Who is to take the bull by the horns? You might as well attack

Gibraltar with a pocket pistol as to attempt to punish them."
John Taylor of Caroline likewise considered a national bank
no better than a scheme for organized theft.[30]

Tazewell staunchly defended banks and banking. For two
decades, he announced to the House of Delegates, he had
been acquainted with the operations of banks in Norfolk and
had witnessed the blessings they had bestowed upon the populace. In the early 1800s he had seen Norfolk "rise like a phoe-
nix from its ashes, with new plumage, through the instrumen-
tality of the banks established there." While he was opposed to
wildcat banking, he recommended the immediate chartering
of additional bona fide state banks and support for the Bank
of the United States. He chided the "prophetic seers" who
forecast the death of liberty should new banks be instituted.
"Twenty-five years ago," he reminded his fellow legislators,
"the same prophecy was made by the present President of the
United States and from him down to the veriest underling
then in the opposition. How has been the fact? The bank died
a natural death. The Genius of America was the greatest
mourner. Those men who prophecied the destruction of Liberty, twenty-five years ago, have caused the resurrection of
this bank with strength superior to the other, as that of Her-
cules compared with Hylas." If Madison, Monroe, and Gallatin were wrong in fearing the ruin of republicanism by the
first Bank of the United States, small confidence could be
placed in the present dire predictions by men of lesser experience. Tazewell presented to the assembly a petition for the
establishment of another bank in Norfolk, which, he asserted,
would be beneficial in providing capital to deepen and widen
the Dismal Swamp Canal. Utilization of the canal in connection with the rivers and sounds of North Carolina would create, he argued, an entire network of transportation facilities.
Yet, if his petition for a Norfolk bank was refused, he promised he would advocate the creation of other banks, even in
the smallest hamlets of the commonwealth, and especially in
the western section of the state where many "heroic souls who
had distinguished themselves at Craney Island" were eager for
economic development.[31]

His gratitude to the citizens of the Shenandoah Valley and
the Trans-Allegheny section did not extend, however, to sup-

porting their demand for a constitutional convention. Since the turn of the century cries for political reform had been heard in Virginia. Representation in the House of Delegates based on white population and suffrage for all white male taxpayers and militia men, instead of restricting the franchise to freeholders, were the primary changes sought. After the War of 1812 democratic agitation increased, and mass meetings at Harrisonburg and Winchester resulted in the Staunton Convention of August 1816. Sixty-nine delegates representing thirty-six counties prepared a memorial to the General Assembly calling for a constitutional convention to write into law the basic concept of republicanism, that the will of the majority should prevail. "The government of the commonwealth," the Staunton gathering proclaimed, "actually is in the hands of the minority; and what is still more pernicious to the general interests, in the hands of a minority inhabiting a particular section of the state." Forty-nine eastern and southern counties adjacent to one another, including three of the boroughs situated in those counties, had a majority of the whole number of representatives in the most numerous branch of the legislature. According to the 1810 census these counties and boroughs were populated by 204,766 white inhabitants, 72,138 less than one-half the population of the state. In the upper house of the legislature the inequality was still more glaring. The area west of the Blue Ridge, constituting three-fifths of the territory of the state, with a white population of 212,036, was allocated four senators, while the Tidewater, with 162,717, had thirteen.[32]

In the General Assembly the call for a convention was championed by Alexander Smyth of Wythe County and Philip Doddridge of Brooke. By restricting suffrage to owners of the soil, Smyth charged, the Virginia constitution made a mockery of the right of representation. No longer should the people of the state be forced to live under this travesty. Rather, the legislature should call for a constitutional convention, stipulating that the delegates be elected by the free and lawful citizens of the commonwealth.[33]

Tazewell's reaction was instantaneous. For more than three hours he voiced his opposition to the demands of the western counties. The Virginia constitution gave the General Assembly no power to authorize a convention, he declared, and if the legislature acted contrary to the constitution, it acted illegally. If the existing government was abolished, whether by the legislature or the people, this would be revolution. "Revolution, Sir," Tazewell addressed the chair, "does not require bayonets and muskets, guillotines and lamp-posts. Five thousand votes will answer just as well to produce an abolition of the government; and whether it is with bloodshed or without, it is still a Revolution." The mere power of numbers should not be allowed to destroy centuries of reasonable progress. "Before you entered this hall, or nominated a doorkeeper, you went to the Council chamber, and, laying your hands upon the Holy Gospels, swore to support the Constitution of the State. That oath is registered in the chancery of Heaven." "Would to God," he shouted, "that this rage for innovation was extinguished! But the times are changed and we are changed with them. In this wild rage for innovation nothing is repected; nothing remains fixed. In this unsettled spirit, we have just sought to disturb an established system, to attack a wholesome institution, which we were told was founded on the prejudices of a thousand years. Sir, I like these prejudices. I respect the ancient institutions of my country. I, too, am ready to say with the barons of old, *Nolumus leges Anglia mutari* (We do not wish to see the laws of England changed)."

Who, he asked, were the free and lawful citizens of the commonwealth referred to by Smyth? Did they include free blacks? Women? Children? The advocates of a convention pleaded the cause of natural rights; yet, if women, blacks, and children were not listed among the free and lawful citizens, qualified to vote, the argument for natural rights was obviated from the outset. Rather than agree to the resolutions proposed by the gentleman from Wythe, Tazewell declared he would submit to a division of the state, latitudinal or longitudinal.[34]

Following Tazewell's speech, Smyth substituted "white male citizens of this Commonwealth, aged twenty-one" in lieu of "free and lawful citizens," but in no way did the revision satisfy Tazewell, who moved to postpone indefinitely the convention resolution. This caused an outcry from the western reform element. Charles Fenton Mercer of Loudoun asked, "Do we owe nothing to Revolution?" He feared, just as much as Tazewell, the tearing up by the roots the constitution of Virginia, "the venerable tree planted and nurtured by our fathers, until it had grown up to the size and strength of a majestic oak." But surely it would be permissible to prune it a little, to bring its branches into fair proportions, to dig around its roots, to enrich its soil.

Smyth was more blunt in his denunciation of Tazewell's position, reminding the gentleman from Norfolk that a convention was a mode of accomplishing a change in the form of government without the violence of insurrection. The inventors of the constitutional convention as a means of initiating change in governmental structure had conferred the greatest benefit on mankind. Without it the only remedy for governmental evils or inequality of representation would be force and effusion of blood. But occasionally even violence was necessary, and contrary to Tazewell's belief that revolutions never improved the conditions of the people, surely those of 1688 and 1776 were salutary in nature, promoting greater happiness and welfare for future generations. Smyth also challenged Tazewell's denial of the right of a legislative body to do any act tending to change the constitution, pointing to the involvement of Parliament in the Revolution of 1688 and of the legislative bodies of the various American colonies in instigating the Revolution of 1776. Interestingly, it was the Federalists from the more nationalistic western counties who championed electoral reform, including white manhood suffrage, while Tazewell and other Tidewater representatives, who fancied themselves Jeffersonians, opposed the expansion of the franchise.

Tazewell's motion to postpone indefinitely any consideration of the convention resolution lost by more than two to one; nevertheless, a convention was not called. After lengthy debate the House of Delegates agreed to a bill authorizing a popular referendum on the question of a convention which would be empowered to consider extension of the suffrage as well as equalization of representation. Although the upper house defeated the bill, everyone knew the subject was far from closed. The western Virginians would not let the matter rest.[35]

With this in mind, and smarting from the barbs aimed at
him by the reform legislators, Tazewell was determined not to
be a member of the next General Assembly, a decision deplored by many of the eastern Virginia planters. "I am really
sorry you will not be with us next winter," wrote John Wickham's son William. "You must have learnt in the last, how
much danger is to be apprehended from the unsteadiness of
the Legislature, and the very causes which would render it
unpleasant to you to be in the Legislature, make it important
that you should be there. I hope enough was done at the last
session to quiet the western counties and to prevent any mischief at the next."[36]

But other interests claimed Tazewell's attention. On his return to Norfolk he traveled aboard the steamboat *Powhatan*
and was impressed by the "handsome manner" in which the
vessel performed. Constructed in New York and tested on the
North River, the eagerly awaited steamboat had arrived in
Norfolk harbor in May 1816, "gliding up the channel in great
majesty," to provide James River transportation between Norfolk and Richmond, a boon to travelers who had been forced
to spend uncomfortable and weary hours on the stage. Tazewell, whose court and legislative duties entailed many journeys
to the capital, was delighted with the new convenience. To be
able to arrive in Richmond in twenty hours from time of departure (barring running aground, mechanical failure, lack of
wood, or a burst boiler) was phenomenal. This was an innovation which met his approval.[37]

Tazewell purchased three shares in the *Powhatan,* then
made plans to finance the first Norfolk-built steamboat. He
urged friends and relatives to invest in the project, and by
October 1817 the *Norfolk* was ready to join the *Powhatan* on
the James. William Wirt, scheduled for a court appearance in
Norfolk, was one of her first eastbound passengers. "The boat
flew at the rate of fifteen miles an hour," Wirt told his wife.
Inquiring of the captain if there were any books on board for
the use of passengers, Wirt received the answer that although
no reading material was available immediately, "Mr. Tazewell
means to have a library for *this* boat." Also for the convenience
of the patrons, Tazewell arranged to have the James River
boats connect with the Norfolk-Baltimore steamer, the elegant

*Virginia,* captained by the genial John Ferguson.[38] In April 1818 Tazewell purchased the *Powhatan* outright for thirty-five thousand dollars, selling shares to a number of stockholders and organizing the James River Steamboat Company. The *Norfolk* was transferred to North Carolina, to run between New Bern and Elizabeth City, and a new vessel, the *Richmond,* was assigned to the James River line.[39]

In the steamboat Tazewell saw the salvation of Norfolk, the return of days prior to the embargo when the harbor was so crowded with ships that "one might walk from Norfolk to Portsmouth on the decks of the vessels at anchor." For a few years, while steamboats were used only for inland navigation, Tazewell's hopes were realized. But when the coastal packets converted to steam, New York vessels were able to trade directly with Richmond and other river towns, and Norfolk's seesaw economy again languished. What the borough needed was a guarantee of foreign commerce, particularly the West Indies trade.[40] Tazewell's steamboat transactions, lasting well into the 1820s, were time-consuming and worrisome. The New Bern venture was a failure. The panic of 1819 and competition from another steamboat, the *Petersburg,* brought near financial disaster to the James River line but, due to his good business sense, Tazewell managed to extricate himself unscathed from the venture.[41]

## Chapter VI

# "In the Shade
# of My Own
# Fig Tree"

While Tazewell grappled with the "convention crisis" in the House of Delegates, Monroe, contrary to Tazewell's prophecy, succeeded Madison as chief executive. Although dubious about the advisability of elevating yet another Virginian to the presidency, Tazewell did not go so far as to echo John Adams, who petulantly remarked that no one from any other state had a chance to become president "till all Virginians shall be extinct." Tazewell was impressed, as were many others, with the potential of William H. Crawford of Georgia, but in the end he loyally supported Monroe, who won handily over Rufus King.[1]

Within a year of his election Monroe appointed William Wirt, an 1808 Madisonian, attorney general of the United States, another indication of the passing of the Quid schism in Virginia. Tazewell, who had no yearning for a governmental post, happily made arrangements for transporting the Wirt family to Washington aboard the Baltimore steamboat.[2] Had he desired a position, opportunities were available. "We expect a Judge Advocate General for the navy will be appointed," wrote Decatur, "would you take it?" "Do undertake it," Wirt urged from Washington. "The path is new here & you would tread it I am sure, with great honor to yourself & advantage to your country."[3] Tazewell declined. He cherished his privacy and resented any invasion of it. A few years earlier he undoubtedly winced as he read one of Wirt's inimitable essays, a part of a series entitled collectively *The Old Bachelor*, which described Tazewell in his early twenties when Wirt first met him. Beginning with verbose praise, Wirt depicted his friend as a "master-spirit; cool, collected, firm, vigorous, and self-balanced," standing like an eagle upon the rocks of Norway's coast, defying with equal composure the storm that raved and rent the atmosphere above and the surging elements that towered and dashed and roared below.

But there were harsh statements too, as Wirt criticized Tazewell's determination to win his court cases, no matter how; his willingness "to support error with more vivacity and appearance of enjoyment" than he did truth; his pleasure in every victory, whether the cause be right or wrong. To some, Wirt observed, Tazewell seemed cold, conveying a conscious superiority, a hauteur, a disdainful indifference toward others; however, on proper occasion, no man could be more "charitable, generous, or munificent, none more alive to the misfortunes and even solicitudes of a virtuous sufferer." The author concluded with the lament that Tazewell's country would "never know him well enough to do him justice or to profit herself of his powers."[4] To a man who avoided publicity as assiduously as did Tazewell, appearance of the essay must have been painful, but he registered no complaint.

Francis Walker Gilmer, Wirt's young protégé, also included Tazewell in a series of sketches written in 1815, describing him as he appeared at the age of forty-one. If any credence can be placed in Wirt's evaluation, Tazewell must have mellowed considerably in twenty years, for Gilmer saw him as a man of great boldness, but of no insolence or sense of superiority. Physically and mentally he had, said Gilmer, all the necessary attributes for greatness. He was tall and well proportioned, and his features were all finely developed. His eyes were large, full, and dark blue, "shaded by thick black brows a little raised, as if looking on a vast expanse of distant prospect." His comprehension was great and clear, and his perceptions "as intuitive and as strong as those of Judge Marshall." Without a doubt, Gilmer declared, Tazewell could surpass the greatest advocates of the federal bar, but he lacked ambition to aspire to fame or high office. Rather, he avoided the limelight and courted obscurity.[5]

This was true. Temperamentally Tazewell was a private person, but there were more immediate reasons for his reticence to seek public acclaim. With the birth of another son, Little-ton, in 1815, and a daughter, Ann, in 1817, his children now numbered six, and he keenly felt the responsibility for his growing family. Moreover, John Nivison was seriously ill, and accompanied by his only son, William, he futilely sought resto-ration of health in the most highly recommended watering places. During his absence he depended on Tazewell's atten-tion to Mrs. Nivison, the unmarried Nivison daughters, and his business affairs. Nivison's health did not improve, but from Saratoga and Balston Spa the gentle, humorous William wrote with levity, in an effort to dispel the family's concern. "Imagine to youself," he told his sister, "a large house with fifty or sixty people in it, who rise at five o'clock in the morn-ing to drink a nauseous salt water from a spring . . . whereof they swallow from five to eight half pint tumblers." The springs, he observed, were resorted to not only for health but also for husbands. Anxious mothers promenaded their eligible daughters up and down the piazzas, and the daughters "as they sit at the meals look wonderfully like goods at auction, or crops sent to the quickest market."[6]

The panic that struck the country in 1819 forced Tazewell to use all his ingenuity to keep the Nivison-Tazewell losses at a minimum. He spent long hours laboring over plantation and steamboat company records, bank investments, and the affairs of the law firm, trying to salvage what he could. The second Bank of the United States, which earlier initiated a liberal credit policy to appease the agricultural interests of the South and West, suddenly retracted its credit, plunging the agrarian sectors into economic chaos. "The times! The times!" one of Tazewell's debtors lamented. "No Dividends! Tobacco down to nothing. Wheat nothing. Corn nothing. We are all broke, I believe, in the country as well as in the towns. No prudence, no foresight could guard against the unexampled wickedness of those who have had the management of our money in the banks."[7]

On their journey homeward from the health spas John and William Nivison observed the effects of the economic crisis. They found Richmond gloomy, where a few months before there had been glitter, bustle, and fashion. "Almost all the high-flyers have been struck to the earth by the hardness of the times," William noted. Soon there were more personal reasons for sadness. En route from New York to Norfolk, the Nivisons stayed several days in Washington with the Decaturs in their lovely new home on President's Square. A few months later the handsome, heroic Decatur was dead, killed in a duel by Commodore Barron, who for years bitterly brooded over the court-martial of 1808 and had been further provoked by Decatur's recent opposition to the commodore's reinstatement in the naval service. In the death of Decatur, Tazewell lost a favorite friend, but several weeks later there was another, heavier, blow. The kindly John Nivison, to whom Tazewell was so devoted, died and was buried in St. Paul's churchyard beside the grave of his granddaughter Sarah Tazewell.[8]

Sweeping changes were affecting the nation, but while eastern Virginia reacted violently to the provisions of the Missouri Compromise restricting slavery in the Louisiana Territory to an area south of latitude 36°30′, Tazewell was preoccupied. Complicated legal matters regarding the Decatur estate required his attention, and the death of John Nivison left the settlement of property in land and slaves in his hands. Moreover, his court docket was filled, a consequence of his growing reputation throughout the state. "He is, without exception, the most powerful advocate I ever heard," Joseph C. Cabell told Thomas Jefferson.[9]

Certainly Tazewell was not oblivious to the hostility engendered by the Missouri Compromise. William F. Gordon, a member of the Virginia legislature, advised Senator James Barbour to oppose it, "not perhaps on account of the value of the territory or the disadvantage of the bargain so much as that it is against principle, & manifests what we consider is a spirit of injustice & want of faith in the Northern politicians, which if yielded to would lead only to farther & more daring & vital usurpations." Surely, he hoped, northern politicians would pause before they "let slip the dogs of war."[10] To Tazewell, overextension of the power of the federal government outweighed all his other concerns about the compromise. As the intensity of the turmoil increased, he sought peace and refuge on his Sandhills plantation, where, he informed John Randolph, "I look with the indifference of a mere spectator upon all the passing events both of the great and little world around me." He was forty-seven, and apprehensions of growing old now had an annoying way of surfacing. Increasingly his thoughts turned to his father, dead at forty-six, and he wondered if the time had not arrived in his own career "to retire from the fatigues and bustle of a busy life" to spend his remaining days in tranquility. In a reminiscent mood, he assured Randolph of his high regard for his friendship and vowed to "strive to keep bright the chain which for so many years has linked us together."[11] But Tazewell's "mere spectator" role was of short duration. Within a few months he was summoned to Washington to help unravel a series of complicated legal tangles.

On February 22, 1821, the Spanish government ratified the Adams-Onís Treaty, by which Secretary of State John Quincy Adams skillfully acquired Florida for the United States. Under Article XI of this treaty, the United States assumed liability for five million dollars in legitimate claims of its own citizens against the government of Spain. A three-man commission was to examine each claim and decide upon the amount to be awarded. President Monroe assigned the task to Hugh Lawson White of Tennessee, William King of Maine, and John Greene of Virginia. Greene declined the appointment, and Monroe turned to Tazewell. Tazewell was reluctant. The salary of three thousand dollars a year was several times less than his law practice alone netted him, but more disturbing was the prospect of being away from home for long intervals during the three years of the commission's incumbency. On the other hand, the cases involved maritime law, Tazewell's speciality, and Monroe, fully aware of his friend's keen sense of duty, urged him to use his talents in the service of the nation. The strategy succeeded. "If I know myself," Tazewell later remarked, "there is no situation within the power of the government to bestow which I covet or desire, nor is there one which I would not accept, if the discharges of its duties by me was deemed necessary or useful to my country. I have no ambition to gratify, although I have duties to fulfill."[12]

The assignment complicated his life. A major concern was his Norfolk law practice. No longer able to turn to John Nivison for assistance, Tazewell believed his only alternative was to "quit the bar," with the exception of a few appeals which he felt obliged to see through the proper courts.[13] Late in May 1821 he entrusted his family to his amiable brother-in-law, William Nivison, and sadly left for Washington. There the commission was assigned to the building that until recently had served as temporary quarters for Congress, while the Capitol, burned by the British during the War of 1812, was reconstructed. To facilitate their labors, the three commissioners took lodgings in the same boardinghouse. Tazewell was not fond of such close living quarters, but there were compensations. He immediately like Hugh Lawson White. The feeling was mutual, and a strong and lasting friendship was formed. White was a contemplative man, whose love and knowledge of the law equaled Tazewell's. He had been a member of the Tennessee legislature and had earned a fine reputation as presiding judge of the state's supreme court. Tazewell admired White's honesty and gentlemanly demeanor and enjoyed discussing with him their many common concerns. While he did not feel as comfortable with William King, Tazewell found him to be well informed and a good conversationalist. A half brother of the eminent Federalist Rufus King, William was at one time the foremost shipbuilder in Maine. He had been a member of the state's constitutional convention and had resigned as Maine's governor to participate in the claims commission. Although lacking in formal schooling, he was an ardent proponent of higher education and served as a trustee of both Waterville (now Colby) and Bowdoin colleges. As a prosperous merchant, King was as disturbed by the problems of the British West Indian trade as Tazewell was, and the two spent hours exchanging views on the subject. Tazewell was least impressed with Tobias Watkins, a Maryland physician, who was named secretary of the commission supposedly because of his proficiency in French and Spanish.[14]

The claims, which involved damages to maritime shipping resulting from the Spanish royalists' blockade of the South American coast, were engrossing, but Tazewell worried about his wife and children, especially when the press reported a devastating hurricane or the spread of the "malignant fever" in the Norfolk area. Fortunately, he was at home when the family received staggering news. While on a short journey to Petersburg, William Nivison, age thirty-two, died from a hemorrhage of the lungs, a victim of consumption. Tazewell, attempting to console his wife, her sisters, and his mother-in-law, had little time for grief, but the hurt was deep. The talented, promising William had been like a younger brother. Tazewell had fashioned William's education after his own, placing him under the care of Bishop James Madison at the College of William and Mary and then having him read law with John Wickham. Upon the death of John Nivison, William had given up his law practice to manage his father's estate.[15] Now the entire burden fell on Tazewell, and his first thought was to resign from the commission.

Tobias Watkins urged him to reconsider, for where could the commission find a replacement so well-versed in the theory of commercial law, one who understood mercantile usage and customs, who knew firsthand the thousand frauds that daily were exposed in the courts of maritime jurisdiction? Tazewell not only possessed these attributes to a prominent degree, Watkins insisted, but, equally important, he had the reputation for possessing them. "To you, therefore, though the youngest of the commission, the whole country looks for the equity of the decisions which are hereafter to be made by the board .... Persevere to the end; for in truth I know of no individual in the United States capable of supplying your place." Finally Tazewell agreed to return, hoping that he could locate a furnished house so Ann and the children could accompany him, but none was available. Moreover, Ann was determined not to uproot the children or leave her bereaved mother.[16]

Generally the commission was in session for a month during the summer, a month in the fall, and two months in the winter or early spring. During the last year, however, the group met continuously from November 1823 until it disbanded in June 1824. The work was arduous. Every claim was examined meticulously, some several times as new evidence was acquired. Testimony was heard, and voluminous masses of proof were scrutinized before the validity and the amount of a claim were decided.[17]

During the course of these proceedings Tazewell had his first unpleasant encounter with John Quincy Adams. Intellectually, Tazewell and the secretary of state should have had many common interests. Both were brilliant, well read, urbane, and not too far apart on some issues, but from the time of their first meeting they disliked each other intensely. Their initial disagreement was over whether or not claims of insurance companies or underwriters should be admitted for compensation under Article XI. Adams adamantly declared they should, while Tazewell and White were convinced that no insurance company should be awarded one cent. The companies had assumed the risk of insuring individual shippers. This was their business, and they had been more than compensated for their losses by their profits in large premiums. To expect the United States government to reimburse the insurance companies for the money they were forced to pay their clients was absurd. Tazewell also pointed out that the treaty provided for the claims only of American citizens and that several stockholders in the insurance companies were foreigners.

Adams pressed White and Tazewell to reconsider. Under the terms of the treaty, he asserted, the claims of the insurance companies were of primary importance. He accused Tazewell of a "direct fraud" in using the "subtle device that among fifty or a hundred owners of stock in an insurance company there might be one or two foreigners." Watkins suggested that instead of accosting White or Tazewell verbally, Adams should write out his ideas on the subject, but the secretary of state declined, saying "it might have the appearance of interfering with the proceedings of the Commissioners."[18]

Tazewell and Adams were as incompatible socially as they were professionally. On one occasion, while Tazewell and the other commissioners were dining with the secretary of state, the Virginian and his host had a difference of opinion concerning wines. According to Adams, "Mr. Tazewell asserted and perseveringly insisted that Tokay was a species of Rhenish wine." Adams contradicted him, but Tazewell persisted. In the heat of the argument Adams sharply retorted, "why, you never drank a drop of Tokay in your life." Tazewell made no reply, but looked hurt, and as soon as the company rose from the table he departed without joining the rest of the party in the drawing room. "I have no good apology to make to myself for this incivility," Adams confessed to his diary, "for that Tazewell himself is not sparing of feelings in the clash of conversation, and had been much otherwise even at this dinner, is no justification to me." As Benjamin Perley Poore, at a much later date, related the incident, Tazewell earlier that evening had provoked Adams by offensively asserting that he had "never known a Unitarian who did not believe in the sea-serpent."[19] Poore's reliability is questionable, but if Tazewell did make the statement, it was in poor taste, even if in jest, for as everyone knew, Adams's sense of the ludicrous was not well developed.

While in Washington Tazewell also turned his attention to legal matters. "Tazewell and Webster," Wirt informed Francis Gilmer, "have been reaping laurels in the Supreme Court . . . . North of the Potomac, I believe, to a man, they yield the palm to Webster; South to Tazewell. So, you see, there is a *section* in everything." The particular action to which Wirt referred was the *Santíssima Trinidad* Case, sometimes known as the Cochineal Case. Tazewell had been involved in this litigation since the spring of 1817 when the Spanish consul in Norfolk, Don Pablo Chacon, filed a libel in the District Court of Virginia against eighty-nine bales of cochineal, two bales of jalap, and one box of vanilla, originally part of the cargoes of the Spanish ships *Santíssima Trinidad* and *St. André.* Allegedly the items listed were taken unlawfully and piratically from the vessels on the high seas by crew members from the *Independencia del Sud* and the *Altravida,* under the command of James Chaytor, a native citizen of the United States who now called himself Don Diego Chaytor. Chaytor claimed he had expatriated himself upon accepting a commission from the United Provinces of Rio de La Plata (Argentina), whose 1816 declaration of independence from Spain was recognized neither by the mother country nor by the United States.[20]

Tazewell, representing Spanish interests, had argued the complicated case in the district court in Norfolk and the circuit court in Richmond. His presentations, forceful and beautifully organized, attracted considerable attention. In both courts he received the favorable ruling that the seized property must be returned to the Spanish government. When the case was appealed to the United States Supreme Court, Tazewell notified Chacon that points connected with the 1819 treaty with Spain might be raised, and, therefore, because of

his position as a commissioner under the treaty, he wished to
have associated with him another attorney who could address
himself to such issues, thus ruling out any charge of conflict of
interest. Tazewell suggested Daniel Webster.[21]

In Washington the none too spacious Supreme Court chamber was crowded. John Randolph was there, as was Attroney
General William Wirt, and Robert Taylor traveled from Norfolk to observe Tazewell's performance. Randolph was
alarmed by the obvious nervousness that Tazewell invariably
suffered when he first arose to address a court, especially in
an important case and in unfamiliar surroundings, but when
he began to speak, his uneasiness faded.[22]

His task was to counter the opposition's contention that the
courts of the United States had no jursidiction over an incident which occurred outside the country's territorial limits,
involving citizens and property of two other sovereign nations.
Carefully, step-by-step, he structured his case. The capturing
vessels, he argued, were under the command of a citizen of
the United States, prohibited by a 1795 treaty with Spain from
taking a commission to cruise against that power. The capturing vessels were owned in the United States, fitted, repaired,
equipped, and manned in Baltimore, with their force and ar-
mament augmented illegally in that same port. The sovereignty of the United Provinces of Rio de La Plata was not a
matter of discussion, nor was the place of capture. The pertinent fact was the source from which the exerted force proceeded. Consequently, a capture made on the high seas by
vessels outfitted in Baltimore and commanded by a citizen of
the United States unquestionably involved the jurisdiction of
the courts of that nation. Webster likewise argued that the
government of the United States was a party to the suit. No
pretended act of naturalization, he contended, could cover
Chaytor's crime in confederating with one of the belligerents
to violate the laws, treaties, and the most solemn obligations of
his own country.

Justice Joseph Story, who delivered the decision of the
court, agreed. Expatriation could never be asserted as a cover
for fraud, as a justification for the commission of a crime
against the country, or for a violation of its laws, when this
appeared to be the intention of the act. "Upon the whole, it is

the opinion of the court that the decree of the Circuit Court be affirmed."[23]

Tazewell and Webster were opposed by David Bayard Ogden, a distinguished New York attorney, an almost last-minute replacement for William Pinkney, whose reputation in admiralty law was unchallenged. Gentlemen of the bar eagerly had anticipated a Tazewell-Pinkney confrontation, but Pinkney died shortly before the case was heard. Randolph attributed his demise to "his hard training to meet Tazewell." The latter quickly refuted such an idea, explaining that Pinkney succumbed to an inflammatory disease, that the case was not difficult, and even if it had been, Pinkney would have had no reason for excessive concern. Randolph was not satisfied, insisting that "Tazewell is second to no man that ever breathed; but he has taken almost as much pains to hid his light under a bushel as [Pinkney] did to set his on a hill."[24]

While Tazewell belittled the complexity of the case, his ability was recognized by all who observed his performance, and he now found himself a better-known figure in Washington circles. However, he had never lacked companionship. The aged and amiable Nathaniel Macon of North Carolina was still in the Senate, John Randolph continued to hold forth in the House of Representatives, and a new senator from the recently admitted state of Missouri, Thomas Hart Benton, attracted Tazewell's favorable attention. As well as being a fascinating conversationalist, Benton was kind to Randolph, whose moods, increasingly fluctuating from exhilaration to deep melancholy, distressed those devoted to him. Tazewell often dined with the senators and congressmen who made up the "southern mess" at Dawson's Number Two, but even when surrounded by interesting and stimulating people, Tazewell suffered from acute loneliness. A gloomy day could impart its hue to his spirits, and unpleasant news from home upset him for weeks. All he desired, he confided to John Wickham, was to quit Washington forever and spend the balance of his days under the shade of his own fig tree, from which he planned seldom to emerge.[25]

The deaths of John and William Nivison had increased Tazewell's family responsibilities. When the Nivison estate was settled, Littleton and Ann Tazewell inherited Old Plantation, 735 acres of bayside property on Virginia's Eastern Shore. In 1824 Tazewell purchased the adjoining King's Creek plantation of 600 acres. Meanwhile, he managed New Quarter plantation, 772 acres, for his mother-in-law until her death, at which time the Tazewells inherited the property. Thus, by 1830, in addition to Sandhills plantation in Princess Anne County, Tazewell owned 2,107 acres in Northampton County across Chesapeake Bay from Norfolk.[26]

Oats, corn, and hogs constituted the principal products, and an ordinary man would have been hard pressed to manage the plantations even without the burden of other duties. Tazewell relied on first-class overseers whom he selected carefully, not only for their good business judgment but also for their ability to handle slaves without resorting to harsh treatment. But overseers' requests required attention, and in the midst of official duties or as he prepared to depart Norfolk for Washington, Tazewell frequently had to answer an appeal for a barrel of whiskey for harvest or "the cart wheels you will please to send as quick as you can." By careful utilization of the yields of vegetables, pork, beef, and fish, Tazewell hoped to make his plantations, as well as his household in Norfolk, nearly self-sufficient. This required hours of meticulous planning.[27]

There were other decisions to be made, such as the selection of a college for Henry and John, ages seventeen and fifteen. During a recess of the claims commission in the late summer of 1822, Tazewell and his two sons traveled northward to investigate the choices and select the most suitable institution. Ann Tazewell, impatiently awaiting news of the boys, sent a servant to the post office three or four times a day. When Harvard was chosen, Ann was disappointed. She had hoped the boys would select Yale as she had heard "that New Haven was a more retired place; of course, a better place for study, that the charges were much more reasonable, which," she told Henry and John, "would have suited your Papa best, (as he complains a good deal of the difficulty of getting money) and you would have been nearer home." When her husband assured her of Harvard's superior academic reputation, she accepted the decision and expressed her willingness to curtail expenses at home rather than have the boys' education neglected for want of funds.[28]

In her letters to her sons, Ann Tazewell was warm, humorous, and loving, including news of the family dog ("Sapho is quite well, very fat and frisky"), friends, and the younger children. Littleton, age seven, inheritor of his brothers' hand-me-downs, "cuts a dash in your green jackets and white pantaloons." The boys were eager for the latest descriptions of baby Mary, born in June 1822. From both parents came pages of advice on a variety of subjects, particularly on how to cope with the evils of a northern winter. As the climate of Cambridge made one more susceptible to ague and fever, it was imperative that flannel gowns be worn at night. A record of all expenses should be kept with habitual and systematic regularity, "not for the purpose of retrenching or limiting them in any way," Tazewell explained, "but merely to make it necessary for you to acquire the habit of keeping regular accounts." He did not wish to pry into their concerns, he assured them, and "should there be anything in your accounts that you do not feel disposed to state to me, extend the sum without saying what it is for otherwise than by some general expression such as 'sundries,' 'petty expenses,' or the like." Tazewell hoped his sons would attend the Protestant Episcopal church, but if they preferred any other for reasons not known to him, they had his permission to make their own choices. "Altho' I prefer my own to any other sect of Christians, yet I prefer your attending any place of Christian worship to your neglecting all."[29]

When Mrs. Tazewell's sister, Sally Skipwith, died suddenly, Tazewell's letter to Henry and John was filled with solicitude for his wife. "This new affliction renders it indispensibly necessary," he firmly instructed them, "that you should write immediately to your Mama, informing her of your own health, & to your grandmamma & Aunt Louisa, condoling with them in their present misfortune."[30]

Perhaps Tazewell's favorable consideration of Harvard was influenced by the presence on the faculty of George Ticknor, the brilliant professor of modern languages and literature. Tazewell had either known or known of Ticknor through John Wickham and William Wirt, for in 1815 Ticknor had visited Richmond where he was entertained by those two gentlemen and by John Marshall. Tazewell liked the New Englander immensely and was delighted when he offered to act as adviser and friend to Henry and John. "I am very grateful to Mr. Ticknor for his attention to you, and so ought you to be," Tazewell counseled his sons. "Don't intrude upon him, but omit no fair opportunity for seeing him and enjoying the benefits of his society whenever you can . . . . He is an accomplished gentleman well worthy of your imitation." "Be governed by what he suggests, precisely as you would be by myself."[31]

Aboard vessels bound from Norfolk to Boston the Tazewells sent a variety of Virginia delicacies: hams, bacon, sweet potatoes, and ground peas. Ann Tazewell, writing to inform John of the shipment of a barrel of a dozen hams, directed him to "have them all taken out and hung in the shade to dry, and send Mr. Ticknor four, in your own name; telling him that I had sent you a dozen; (and you must pick four of the largest too) for four hams all the way from Virginia, from your Papa or myself, would appear but a small present, on the contrary from you, they might be duly appreciated, as you are so fond of it yourself." Ann, always frugal, consistently warned the boys to care for the kegs and boxes in which they received their homegrown provisions. The kegs cost two and three cents each, and "maybe you may have a chance of sending them back to be refilled next year." "We are endeavoring to practice economy at home, on account of the expenses which are necessarily incurred for the repairs of the lot over the bridge, and also the expense your Papa will have to be at, on Henry's and your account."[32]

"The lot over the bridge" was the Granby Street site of a large frame house built by John Boush shortly after the Revolutionary War and purchased by Tazewell in 1821. In late 1822 the family moved from their Main Street residence of twenty years to their new home. Tazewell especially liked the extensive grounds, sloping gently to the Elizabeth River, and the unobstructed view of ships entering or leaving Norfolk harbor. For Ann there was almost unlimited space for gardens. Busily planning her greenhouse, she instructed Henry and John, "whenever you see handsome flowers, if you are acquainted with the owners, endeavor to procure some of the seeds." Tazewell was uncharacteristically enthusiastic when he described for John the spring activities in the new surroundings: "Your mother lives in her large gardens, which she is decorating with every plant & flower that is rare, and in her green house . . . . The little children sport over the lawn, and gambol unrestrained through our spacious grounds, to the very visible improvement of their health, spirits & activity. Even little Mary (our beauty) spends much of her time under the shade of our numerous trees." He was eager for John's companionship. "I have half a dozen secluded shady spots where we can sit and read and meditate together." Never had he felt more happy and contented. Henry was his only anxiety.[33]

Uninterested in books and susceptible to trouble, Henry left Harvard early in 1823. Aware of his oldest son's learning difficulties, Tazewell was unwilling to admit them and complained to Ticknor about the Harvard course of study, on which he wanted to blame Henry's failure. Ticknor was sympathetic. "I have the misfortune, as you are quite aware, to think too ill of the system furnished at our arms, as well as at the other colleges yet established in the country, to permit me to feel any degree of sensibility, whatever complaints may be made against them." Although he did not believe all of Tazewell's objections well founded, Ticknor agreed that a system which left no beneficial choice as to the studies to be pursued and which placed an entire class of seventy or eighty students in a rigid curriculum and compelled them to go on together for four years, without the possibility of individual initiative, was radically wrong. Approving of such sentiments, Tazewell tried to induce Ticknor to join the faculty of the University of Virginia, then about to open. Ticknor expressed gratitude for the thought, but declined: "Some years ago when Mr. Jefferson made me a similar proposition, which I received in Europe, I almost hesitated," but now, well-established at Harvard, with his new course of lectures on Spanish literature prospering, he believed a change would be inadvisable.[34]

The warm-hearted Ticknor was concerned about Henry and repeatedly asked Tazewell to send reports on his progress. Henry was a worry. "I do not know what to do with him," Tazewell anxiously wrote John, "he cannot read, and will not work. Heedless, thoughtless, childish still, with no vice that I know of save idleness, he seems not to think of futurity, and is quite indisposed to do anything for himself." Obviously Henry rapidly became increasingly difficult. A month later Tazewell, preparing to leave for Washington for a stay of several weeks, informed John, "I shall take Henry with me, as I dare not leave him at home during my absence." This anxiety, plus the increased burden of plantation affairs, prompted Tazewell again to consider resigning from the commission, a consideration vetoed by Wirt. "You are the master of the whole subject," the attorney general argued, "and the work is almost over. No one else could take your place without great disadvantage both to himself and the country." He reminded Tazewell of his public trust. The acceptance of an office, especially one so limited in time, implied a commitment to carry the duties to completion.[35]

In the fall of 1823 illness forced John also to withdraw from Harvard, a disappointment for both father and son, for according to Ticknor, John had promise of becoming a fine scholar. However, with John at home and improving in health, Tazewell, during the long final session of the commission, could entrust to him many plantation duties, as well as some investment and banking business. Henry too made a pathetic effort to be helpful. John impatiently wished to return to college. He would be willing to settle for William and Mary, he told his father, if the family believed the rigorous climate of Cambridge unduly dangerous, but Tazewell objected to any premature return to the sedentary regimen of a scholar. For the time being, life in the open air would be more beneficial. Besides, William and Mary was a "declining institution" about to relinquish "its flickering blaze." If John chose to enter there he should be in good health, ready to do his best, for it would be doubly disgraceful to lose his hard-won Harvard reputation at an inferior institution. Meanwhile, in answer to John's persistent requests, Tazewell prescribed a curriculum which he could pursue independently. "Give six hours during the early day to severe study," he directed. In this category he placed mathematics, experimental philosophy, metaphysics, and languages. He classified history as light reading and suggested a series of books ranging from ancient to modern times. When John wearied of these, he should take up anything well written upon any subject. Mandatory inclusions were Locke's *Essay Concerning Human Understanding* and the writings of Addison, Swift, and Johnson, "probably the most various & most excellent writers of English prose," and he was not to neglect the poets Milton, Pope, and Dryden.[36]

Depite these suggestions, Tazewell did not want John to devote his entire time to study, lest his health be further impaired. To encourage outdoor activities, Tazewell assigned numerous duties. "Tell me," he wrote, "what you know concerning the plantations, particularly as to the time when they finish planting corn, as to the number of young stock such as lambs, calves & pigs." "So soon as they have finished sowing oats at the Bay-side, let me know the quantity seeded in each of the two cuts." "If you can dispose of any of the salt fish at the plantation you had better do so. The price is $6 per barrel for spots, and $8 for trouts."[37] The sixteen-year-old boy received frequent instructions that he was to transmit to the overseers. It was important, his father enjoined, that the new overseer for Old Plantation should be there before New Year's Day, "as Floyd will then quit, & the Plantation will have nobody on it." At Sandhills, "all I want is some careful body merely to take care of things until I return." Abdall, a Negro, could be hired by the month as overseer, and for the time being Tazewell preferred him to anyone else. "I don't want the Negroes or anything else disturbed for the present. They may remain where they now are until my return, and after the holydays may be employed in such occupations as William Smith [the new overseer at Old Plantation] shall direct. In him I have full confidence and in case any unforeseen difficulty arises you will consult him and be governed by his advice, which I know will be for the best." John also was warned to be careful in buying supplies for the plantations: "I regret that you purchased any pork for the Eastern Shore, as there is more than enough at the Bayside (with the fish there) to serve that plantation, and I intend to supply the wants of one plantation with the superfluity of the other."[38]

For the sake of added efficiency Tazewell likewise planned to shift slaves from one plantation to another, as needed. "So soon as the weather is warm enough and quite settled let Kate and her children and Bob be sent over to the Eastern Shore—and whenever Jonathan Smith [the overseer at Sandhills] can spare them, your mamma can order in any of the men from the plantation to weed out her gardens." When Kate and Bob objected to leaving Sandhills, Tazewell patiently suggested that the overseer might substitute Jack, although this would mean "giving up a prime fellow for a boy and a breeding woman."[39]

Accounting for his father's various business enterprises was difficult and complicated for John. Tazewell insisted upon absolute accuracy, believing such training and experience indispensable for a young man of John's station. At times Tazewell wrote despairingly, "I begin to believe that we never shall get our statements to agree until we meet. We seem to be like two persons meeting in a narrow entry, each changes his position toward the same side at the same moment, in order to allow the other to pass, and by so doing they find themselves constantly 'vis a vis.' So it is with us." But John improved, and his father was pleased: "Our accounts correspond (within one cent) and your statements of them are perfectly clear and entirely satisfactory."[40]

Along with the multitude of detailed orders, instructions, and suggestions, Tazewell never failed to warn John against overtaxing himself. The moment assignments became either irksome or hazardous to his health, John was to refrain from attending to them. Health was an obsession with Tazewell, and although he often consulted the family physician, Dr. William Selden, Tazewell had no faith in the medical profession's too frequent resort to purgatives and bleeding. He preferred home remedies. For the prevalent malady of ague and fever, Ann prescribed a mixture of sixty grains of powdered snakeroot, forty grains of salts of wormwood, one ounce of Peruvian bark, and a pint of Madeira wine. Well-shaken, an ounce glass of the concoction was to be taken every two hours. "We have tried your mother's recipe often this last summer and always with success," Tazewell told John. "I, myself, when at your time of life, was relieved from the attack of a tedious quartan ague, which had long distressed me, by the use of Peruvian bark, covering myself in woollen clothes, next only skin from head to foot, taking a great deal of fatiguing bodily exercise, and drinking three or four glasses of rich new Madeira every day."[41] When a slave child died, Tazewell regretted "very much the death of poor little Charlie," but his compassion for the child was overshadowed by fear of contagion, and he was apprehensive for weeks "to know whether any of the other parts of the family (either black or white) are affected in the same manner." "Don't fail therefore," he instructed John, "to mention this whenever you write, and desire your mamma to do the same."[42]

From Washington, Tazewell sent guests to be entertained in his Norfolk home. Contrary to Benjamin Perley Poore's unflattering description of Tazewell as "an avowed hater of New England," the Tidewater gentleman had numerous friends in the northeastern states, many of whom, curious about the South, traveled through Virginia. The Tazewell-Ticknor friendship and correspondence continued long after John left Harvard, and many New Englanders sought out Tazewell in the nation's capital at Ticknor's behest. Among them was young Joseph Coolidge, whom Tazewell thought to be "one of the most accomplished scholars and gentlemen I have met with lately, and very well meriting indeed the high character which Mr. Ticknor gives him in his letter." Coolidge, recently returned from a four-year tour of Europe, was journeying throughout the United States. As Norfolk was included in his itinerary, Tazewell gave Coolidge a letter of introduction to John, and carefully instructed his son on how to receive the guest: "I shall give him an introduction to you and hope that you will so represent me in relation to this young stranger, as will mark our respect for Mr. Ticknor . . . . Tell your mamma that if she is well enough, and does not find it too inconvenient, I wish she would shew Mr. Coolidge some of the Norfolk belles, and not to worry him too much with inspecting her garden. As to a young gentleman at his time of life, the budding beauties of the animal will be a little more attractive than those of the vegetable kingdom."[43] While in the commonwealth Coolidge did succumb to the charms of a Virginia belle, and a year later he married Ellen Wayles Randolph, Thomas Jefferson's granddaughter.

On June 8, 1824, the claims commission adjourned sine die, after examining over eighteen hundred cases. Originally the commission was confident that the five million dollars provided by the treaty would be more than sufficient to cover the total amount of the claims. Watkins even complimented Adams for not agreeing to the larger sum demanded by the Spanish minister, Nuis de Onís. However, the prognosis proved incorrect. When all the justifiable claims finally were adjudicated, the total provable indemnification amounted to $5,454,545.13, necessitating the reduction of each award by 8.5 percent to bring the allotments within the five-million-dollar limit. The commission's task was a thankless one. No claimant was satisfied, and some engaged in bitter controversy with the United States government for years. Even so, when announcing the adjournment of the commission the *National Intelligencer* was complimentary, praising the board for its ability, assiduity, and devotion to business: "The President could not have made a more judicious choice of persons to execute the arduous and responsible trust which these gentlemen have just finished."[44]

Tazewell was glad he had completed the task. Now he longed to relax, visit with friends, and play with the children. He looked forward to walking in his Norfolk garden and sailing across the bay to inspect his Eastern Shore plantations. Upon returning home he had another public duty, but one which he anticipated with pleasure, welcoming "the Guest of the Nation," the marquis de Lafayette, to Norfolk. On a bright autumn day the borough delegation met the French general at Jamestown, and after a speech by Tazewell, the general, accompanied by Secretary of War John C. Calhoun, was conducted on board the steamboat *Petersburg* and escorted down the James River by two navy barges. For several days and nights Norfolk and Portsmouth entertained the distinguished guest in a "blaze of joy" with grand balls, receptions, and banquets.[45]

Tazewell happily anticipated spending the remainder of his days on his own turf, doing whatever he could for the benefit of Norfolk and Virginia, while savoring the good life in the midst of his adoring family. Already, though, disturbing rumors were in the air. On August 21, 1824, John Taylor of Caroline, United States senator from Virginia, died at his Hazelwood plantation. Many considered Littleton Waller Tazewell his logical successor.[46]

## Chapter VII

# *In the Senate of*
# *the United States*

Tazewell had no wish to become a member of the United States Senate. During the months he had spent in Washington serving on the commission, he had observed with repugnance the intrigues, conspiracies, rumors, alliances, and deals calculated to elect one candidate or another to the presidency in 1824. The demise of the Federalist party and the monopolitical system of the "Era of Good Feeling" spawned numerous factions. Never before were so many hopefuls eager to enter the presidential race.[1]

The Richmond Junto, which had endeavored to guide Virginia politics for almost a quarter of a century, favored Secretary of the Treasury William H. Crawford, whose home state was Georgia. Crawford also was supported by the powerful Albany Regency, represented on the national scene by Senator Martin Van Buren, whose most cherished dream was a union of the Regency and the Junto, a New York–Virginia alliance which could control the country and send him to the presidency. In the 1820s the states' rights views of the Junto were more pronounced than they had been during the Jefferson administration when it had favored the Embargo Act and the purchase of the Louisiana Territory. During the intervening years, faced with the evolving power of the national government, Virginia had become increasingly sensitive to the states' rights issue. Particularly disturbing was the ever-growing influence of the United States Supreme Court, under the guiding hand of Chief Justice John Marshall. As decision after decision struck directly at Virginia's pride in its state sovereignty, those sons of the commonwealth who considered themselves Old School Republicans rose to defend the state and the "principles of '98." They shuddered to contemplate what further ruin might be wrought to southern agrarianism if Congress continued to raise the tariff in favor of manufacturing interests.[2] In Virginia, John Marshall told Justice Story, "the tendency of things verges rapidly to the destruction of the government and the re-establishment of a league of sovereign states." Thomas Ritchie, editor of the *Richmond Enquirer* and a pervading influence in the Junto, objected strenuously to Monroe's list toward mild nationalism. The president's approval of the tariff of 1816, his willingness to accept limited federally financed internal improvements, and his sanction of the Missouri Compromise all came under fire in Ritchie's paper.[3]

Rather than entertaining any ill will toward Monroe, Tazewell found his personal regard for him returning; when a man was in trouble, it was time to remember past kindnesses. "I respect the dignity of his station," Tazewell explained. "I respect his advanced years and long service," and perhaps of even greater significance, "I value the national character as the dearest possession of my country," and national character was "in some measure involved in the character of the chief magistrate. I cannot read and hear the language in which he has been spoken of without pain."[4]

In 1824 the Junto favored the congressional caucus as a means of nominating a presidential candidate, believing Crawford would have the advantage in such a gathering, as, indeed, he did. Of the sixty-six congressmen participating in the caucus, sixty-two voted for Crawford. The action brought widespread opposition. From state legislatures, mass meetings, and local conventions came other nominations. The chief contenders, in addition to Crawford, were Andrew Jackson, now a United States senator from Tennessee, John Quincy Adams, Henry Clay, and John C. Calhoun.[5]

Tazewell found none of the candidates to his liking. To Wickham he confided his indifference to the outcome of the canvass and his disgust with the crude tactics employed in the process: "The grossest terms are freely applied to all in office or aspiring to it, and if foreign nations shall judge us by the account we give of ourselves, they cannot but consider us the legitimate issue of unworthy sires whose crimes brought them thither—Rogues all. I think it clear that let who will succeed, before he gets warm in his seat a new canvass will begin for a successor." If the election was brought to the House of Representatives, he thought either Adams or Crawford would be victorious. Tazewell's good friend Hugh Lawson White was a strong and early advocate of his fellow Tennesseean Andrew Jackson, while William Wirt thought highly of Calhoun, recommending him as "the very character to strike a Virginian: ardent, generous, high-minded, brave, with a genius full of fire, energy and light;—a devoted patriot—proud of his country, and prizing her glory above his life."[6]

The field was narrowed when Calhoun, failing to gain the backing of Pennsylvania, withdrew from the presidential race to become the favored candidate for the vice-presidency. Finally the contest was between Adams and Jackson. Crawford was ill; felled by a paralytic stroke in the fall of 1823, he suffered a relapse in the spring of 1824. As had been anticipated, the multiplicity of candidates resulted in no one contestant receiving a majority in the electoral college; therefore, it devolved on the House of Representatives, each state having one vote, to decide among the three candidates having the highest number of electoral votes: Jackson, Adams, and Crawford.[7]

In the midst of all this uncertainty, the Virginia legislature met to consider the urgent matter of electing a United States senator to replace John Taylor of Caroline. Tazewell had been beset with repeated requests to allow his name to be placed in nomination. Several members of the Richmond Junto were prepared to back him if he would assure them of his political orthodoxy. Such questioning of his beliefs and principles incensed Tazewell, and one of the Junto set, Richard E. Parker, a highly regarded judge of the General Court, hastened to inform him that no insults to his integrity were intended. "On the contrary I found with pleasure that your *general conduct,* character & opinions, were understood & fully appreciated, and that by the most respectable members of both houses the strongest solicitude was felt to engage your services in the critical posture of our public affairs." Do not, Parker implored, "deny to your 'own Virginia' the benefit of your services if she requires it. Believe me she stands in need at the present moment of the talents of all her gifted sons."[8]

Still, questions were raised. Was Tazewell a friend of states' rights? Was he opposed to the Bank of the United States? How did he stand on internal improvements and the tariff? Criticisms came from various sources, all based on Tazewell's past refusal to follow a party line or, more specifically, the line of the Richmond Junto.[9] Tazewell shrank from the invasion of his privacy. He would serve Virginia if called upon to do so, but he did not seek the office, would not solicit support, and expressly refused to give his friends permission to nominate him. Aware that the Junto favored Crawford for the presidency, he hoped to "put an effectual stopper" upon his own candidacy by announcing his "fixed and immutable" intention of backing Jackson. Crawford, he declared, "is out of the question." Even this did not thwart his supporters.[10]

Tazewell's name was placed in nomination by George Loyall of Norfolk, who spoke of Tazewell's international reputation and intellectual prowess, saying he was almost without a rival in the realm of the mind. Noting the charges made against Tazewell for not paying attention to the lines that divided the political parties, Loyall contended that public documents belied such insinuations. But accusations of political apostasy did not die. When John Tyler was named to oppose Tazewell, John Armistead of Charles City stressed Tyler's undeviating Republicanism, which, during the younger man's career, had turned neither to the left nor the right. In retort, Thomas Mann Randolph begged the legislature to remember the crisis at which the nation had arrived. Undoubtedly General Jackson would win the presidency. Of all men in the Commonwealth, who but Tazewell could withstand the acts of the military chieftain if his administration should prove to be mischievous. Abel Parker Upshur, a representative from the Eastern Shore's Northampton County, also emphasized the crisis theme: "A party is rising to the North, which will tax and grind us for the establishment of their own manufactures. Can it be doubted that the tariff will be agitated?" Tazewell would stand against the tariff, Upshur promised, and against "the grand system of internal improvements, now in embryo." To protect the destiny of Virginia and the South, "let us encourage one of the first men in the commonwealth. Of all her great men, there is not one who is so well qualified to support her interests as Littleton Waller Tazewell."[11]

Tazewell was the victor, with 139 votes to 80 for Tyler, certainly not a resounding triumph considering Tyler's comparative youth and inexperience. The *Enquirer* announced the outcome on December 9, and in an editorial in the same issue, Ritchie spelled out to Tazewell what was expected of him. To the world he must demonstrate in a strong tone the spirit of '98, so cherished by Virginians. Virginia would continue true to its principles, "and we trust Tazewell will remain true to her . . . . No man is more capable of serving her, for his talents are of the *first order*." But he feared Tazewell was too nationalistic.[12]

A cousin, Waller Taylor, United States senator from Indiana, commiserated with Tazewell: "I am well aware that you have accepted this appointment with reluctance. A man of your domestic habits, and having as much private business to attend to as you have, cannot wish to embark on the tempestuous sea of politics. You will pardon me however for being so selfish as to rejoice that your state has conferred this honour upon you." Men of Tazewell's ability were needed in the Senate, but there was no reason for him to leave home before the holidays. "It has been the practice of Congress, since I have been a member, never to enter seriously upon business before Xmas."[13] The Eighteenth Congress was three weeks into the second session when Tazewell presented his credentials and took his seat on December 29, 1824, but as Taylor had predicted, little had been accomplished.

Although Tazewell temporarily lodged elsewhere, the boardinghouse of Mrs. Ann Peyton, conveniently located at the corner of Pennsylvania Avenue and 4½ Street, was his residence during most of his eight years in the capital. Mrs. Peyton's was one of the finest of such establishments, and during Tazewell's first year, it became the headquarters of the Jackson supporters in Congress. To Tazewell's great satisfaction Hugh Lawson White, Jackson's replacement in the Senate, was among the Tennesseans lodging at Mrs. Peyton's, as was the young freshman congressman James K. Polk. Irresistibly impressed by Tazewell's urbanity and intelligence, Polk frequently sought the Virginian's advice, a practice he continued throughout his political career. Even during his presidency, no man's judgment and regard meant more to Polk than Tazewell's.[14]

Senators Levi Woodbury of New Hampshire, Mahlon Dickerson of New Jersey, and Powhatan Ellis of Mississippi contributed a variety of views to the debates of the Peyton ménage, as did Congressman Gulian Verplanck of New York and John Bell of Tennessee. But the man about whom ideas revolved at a dizzying pace was Vice-President John C. Calhoun. Subsequently dubbed "Fort Jackson," Mrs. Peyton's domicile was indeed the center of anti-Adams activity, and to the "Fort" came visitors of like mind to seek allies and plot strategy. Not infrequently were Martin Van Buren, John Randolph, and Thomas Hart Benton closeted in the Peyton front parlor, hatching schemes and airing them to the lively group held together by a hearty dislike of the policies of John Quincy Adams.[15]

Tazewell's first few weeks in Washington were relatively quiet, but the calm was short-lived. Soon he was besieged by requests of various kinds from his Virginia constituents, and in the Senate "a flood of very interesting business" pressed upon him. Of primary importance was the election of a president. The Virginia delegation in the House, while still favoring Crawford, was "a good deal divided as between Jackson and Adams," and Tazewell exerted every effort to implement his prior declaration of a "fixed and immutable" determination to elevate Jackson to the presidency. The one thing Tazewell feared was a "sudden, open, and avowed coalition of Clay and his friends with Adams."[16]

There were those who thought it strange that Tazewell would champion Jackson, a man who often acted arbitrarily and with disregard for proper legal procedures, and who as senator in 1824 voted for federally financed internal improvements and for the tariff. But Jackson had been a friend of Tazewell's father in the 1790s and had supported Monroe in 1808. He heartily dislike General James Wilkinson and during the Burr litigation had furnished information against him.[17] Still, Tazewell's choice seemed inconsistent with his political philosophy and his personal taste. Regardless of the reasoning behind his preference for Jackson, many in Washington were influenced by his opinion, for, though new to the Senate, Tazewell was not without prestige. His reputation as an attorney was acknowledged nationally. As a member of the claims commission he had clearly demonstrated his erudition and judgment, and the esteem in which he was held by eminent men of differing political persuasions added to his stature. He rapidly gained the respect of his Senate colleagues, even those who did not agree with him, by the manner in which he expressed his views on executive power and responsibility, internal improvements, and maritime and international law.

On January 21, 1825, he delivered his first major address on the Senate floor, speaking for more than two hours on a bill to suppress piracy in the West Indies. The section to which he objected authorized the president to declare a blockade against any Cuban or West Indian port allowing sanctuary to a pirate ship being pursued by an armed vessel of the United States. Remembering very well the British blockade of Chesapeake Bay, in time of peace as well as war, and the resultant anguish and suffering inflicted on the citizens of Norfolk, Tazewell strenuously objected to improper use of coercion against a friendly power. "A blockade is a war measure. If we have just cause for war, so be it, but we cannot in times of peace adopt a measure which belongs to war alone. . . . A blockade acts on the innocent." Piracy must be suppressed, but the moral force of the United States should not be sacrificed to accomplish this end. "We cannot do what public law forbids."[18]

When Senator James Lloyd of Massachusetts argued strongly that even though there were doubts about the piracy bill, it ought to be approved because it came from the executive, Tazewell was again on his feet. No measure, he countered, should ever be presented to the Senate with the inference that it must be passed because the president so desired. According to the Constitution, the Senate's duty was to act as a check on the executive. John Wickham, eargerly scanning the Richmond papers for news of Tazewell, was pleased with the tenor of his remarks and complimented the senator for "supporting the rather unpopular doctrine that other nations have rights as well as our own."[19]

Perhaps in response to the criticisms directed against him in the General Assembly preceding his election, Tazewell's sensitivity to the extension of federal power in any form was more obvious in the early months of his senatorial career than ever before. When the matter of nationally supported internal improvements again arose, he reluctantly felt it necessary to take a position detrimental to the best interests of his own borough. Because of the inability of the United States to arrive at a West Indian commercial agreement with Great Britain, trade in Norfolk continued to languish. For a time Tazewell counted on steam power to alleviate the problem, but this did not bring the anticipated salutary effect. In desperation, merchants and shippers of the borough considered again the prospect of utilizing the Dismal Swamp Canal to increase Norfolk's commercial traffic. Begun before the turn of the century, the canal was now woefully inadequate, but widened and deepened, it could give the Hampton Roads area hope for a flow of trade from North Carolina and points south.[20]

When a bill was introduced in the Senate calling for the purchase by the federal government of a significant portion of stock in the Chesapeake and Delaware Canal, the people of Norfolk saw their chance. Why not also sell Dismal Swamp Canal shares to the federal government? Prominent Norfolk citizens pleaded with Tazewell to attach a rider to the bill authorizing this. The letter writers indicated their awareness of Tazewell's objections to federal financing of internal improvements; nevertheless, they begged him, this once, to set aside his principles and support their request. George Newton, a wealthy Norfolk merchant, warned that the decision to establish a naval dock at Gosport could very well rest on the development of better transportation routes in the area that would speed shipments of masts and other needed supplies from the North Carolina forests to shipbuilding firms. It was imperative for the South to have navy yards, both at Gosport and Charleston, "for if our Northern neighbors (brethern, as the phraze is, I cannot call them) should get ahead of us, they will not permit us to overtake them, and we must be satisfied to follow at an immeasurable distance in their wake."[21]

Caught in the dilemma of wanting to see Norfolk prosper, yet unwilling to forsake his principles, Tazewell attempted to betray neither. Twice, in the Eighteenth and Nineteenth Congresses, he spoke in behalf of federal involvement in the Dismal Swamp Canal improvement project, stressing its importance to the welfare of southeastern Virginia and drawing a parallel between it and the Chesapeake and Delaware Canal request. The Dismal Swamp Canal, he reasoned, was one link in a great transportation chain which could join the eastern and southern regions of the nation. The Chesapeake and Delaware Canal could provide another link, and the Senate should give careful consideration to the merits of an inland waterway system. After speaking eloquently and at length, Tazewell was asked by a fellow senator if he would vote for the measure that he had introduced. Tazewell replied that he would not support federal subsidization of such a project. "I never did vote for a proposition of this kind," he retorted, "and, so help me God, I never will." Regardless, the bill passed the Senate, 21 to 16. Tazewell had done his duty, and the people of Norfolk were pleased.[22]

The concept of federally supported internal improvements had bothered Jeffersonian Republicans for twenty years or more. During his presidency Jefferson had unsuccessfully proposed a constitutional amendment authorizing Congress to fund general welfare projects: public education, canals, river improvements, and roads. Even without the amendment numerous precedents for federal funding were established, including the coastal survey, the Cumberland Road, lighthouse construction, and harbor improvements. Clay's "American System" of the period following the War of 1812, calling for a second Bank of the United States, a protective tariff for the benefit of American industry, and vast internal improvements, had found considerable support in the South. Speaking in favor of the proposal, Calhoun termed internal improvements mandatory to strengthening the sinews of the nation's prosperity. A great country, rapidly and fearfully growing, needed strong connecting links to bind it together; a national system of roads and canals would provide the linkage. By the 1820s, however, many old-line Republicans were increasingly skeptical about federal projects. The national government was becoming too powerful too rapidly. The panic of 1819 increased antipathy toward the Bank of the United States, and the protective tariff of 1824 was considered detrimental to the South.[23] As an astute businessman, Tazewell was farsighted enough to realize the advisability of binding the country together and promoting the economic development of the nation, but he professed a genuine attachment to the Constitution and refused to violate its sanctions by voting for the use of federal funds in a manner which he believed was unauthorized. John Taylor of Caroline had fought the same fight with similar arguments. Now Tazewell was sitting in Taylor's place in the Senate, closely watched by Thomas Ritchie and other Virginians who had considered him too nationalistic to represent them in Washington. Ritchie was determined to pounce upon any deviation from the states' rights line and publish his findings in the *Enquirer*. This did not bother Tazewell. His reputation as a man of independent judgment was well established, and independent judgment, his friend Wickham believed, was precisely what was needed "in the present state of affairs."[24] But Tazewell was not completely impervious to the temper of the times, and from the South came dire predictions of the fearful consequences of unchecked nationalism.

A year earlier, in January 1824, John Randolph had startled the House of Representatives and the nation by coolly and bluntly declaring that if Congress could appropriate money to fund a survey for a general system of roads and canals, "they may not only enact a sedition law—for that there is precedent—but they may emancipate every slave in the United States." This was not a new thought, but never before did anyone have the audacity to say it, straight out, on the floor of the House. In private Nathaniel Macon voiced the same sentiment: "if Congress can make banks, roads, and canals under the Constitution, they can free any slave in the United States."[25] If this was one of Tazewell's fears, and it may have been, he did not admit it, publicly or privately. His arguments were strictly constitutional. The specter of slavery haunted neither his speeches nor his personal correspondence. On the slavery question, he was firmly convinced, unchecked emotionalism was perhaps more dangerous than unbridled national power.

Undoubtedly, it was well that the discussion on internal improvements was set aside for the main event of the session. At noon on February 9, 1825, in the midst of a driving snowstorm, the two houses of Congress assembled to perform the perfunctory duty of opening and counting the votes of the electoral college. Tazewell served as teller for the Senate. Calhoun was pronounced vice-president-elect. This was followed by formally relegating to the House of Representatives the responsibility of deciding whether the nation's president should be Jackson, Adams, or Crawford. The senators then withdrew to allow the House to proceed with the election.[26]

The *National Intelligencer,* anticipating the casting of innumerable ballots before a president was named, promised extra issues of the paper to keep the public abreast of developments. Excitement in Washington was high, and only the dampening effect of the snowstorm, according to one citizen, prevented violence. Contrary to all expectation, Adams received a bare majority on the first ballot, thirteen states voting for Adams, seven for Jackson, and four for Crawford. The Clay-Adams alliance, fearfully anticipated by Tazewell, had been hatching for months, and Clay successfully delivered the necessary support to the Adams camp. As John Randolph observed, it was impossible for anyone else to win; "gentlemen, the cards were stacked." Inside the Virginia delegation sentiment was divided, with one vote for Adams, one for Jackson, and nineteen for Crawford.[27]

The manner in which he was elected troubled Adams, but his desire for the highest office of the land overcame the pricklings of his conscience, and the following day he turned his attention to staffing his cabinet. Obviously, most, if not all, of the decisions had been made weeks before the House vote. Calhoun's preferences were ignored; the South Carolinian was to be given no opportunity to use his position as a springboard to the presidency. The appointment of Clay to the top cabinet post, though not surprising in view of the Kentuckian's tremendous efforts in Adams's behalf, was a shock to many. In Virginia the news was received with disbelief. Adams, acting contrary to the advice of several of his close associates, provided a needed rallying cry for the anti-Adams forces and speeded the amalgamation of diverse groups hostile to the incoming president, groups more than willing to believe that Adams had traded the office of secretary of state for sufficient votes to make him chief executive. A bargain, most corrupt and unholy, had been consummated, they contended. "Mr. Clay (*like Judas of old* it is said), *sold himself and his influence* to Mr. Adams, and collected his thirty pieces of silver," was Jackson's bitter charge. "Was there ever witnessed such a bare faced corruption in any country before?"[28]

Wishing to conciliate Virginia, Adams named Senator James Barbour to head the War Department. Monroe, disturbed by the indelicacy of the Clay appointment, warned Adams that such tokens would have little influence. Virginia's support or opposition would depend on the measures pursued by the executive; "if sound they would be approved, &, if not, opposed, & for no other cause." Richard Rush, son of Dr. Benjamin Rush, was offered the Treasury Department, while three members of Monroe's cabinet, Samuel Southard, John McLean, and William Wirt, were retained as secretary of the navy, postmaster general, and attorney general. Troubled by Wirt's willingness to serve in the Adams cabinet, Tazewell believed his old friend was placing ambition ahead of principle.[29]

In his inaugural address Adams called upon the members of Congress to discard "every remnant of rancor against each other" and to embrace as "countrymen and friends," a foolish expectation in the wake of events of the previous months. A strong southern contingent, including Jackson and Tazewell, refused to approve Adams's choice of secretary of state. To the peevish president this was "the first act of the opposition from the stump which is to be carried on against the administration under the banner of General Jackson."[30] The opposition was not yet organized, but Adams, by his actions and attitudes, already had contributed vastly to the consolidation of a resistance movement. Van Buren of New York, the Richmond Junto, and other former Crawfordites, along with the Jacksonians, watched the new adminisration with skepticism, which within a matter of months solidified into a new political coalition with Jackson as the standard-bearer.

A few days before Adams's inauguration Tazewell, in a letter to John, eagerly anticipated his return to Norfolk as soon as the Senate had acted upon the president's new appointments.[31] John's education was again a matter of concern. Announcements of the opening of the University of Virginia appeared in the Washington papers in February 1825, and Tazewell at once wondered if his second son wished to enroll. Not that he would reap much benefit from the classes, still in their early stages of organization, but the climate might have a salutary effect on John's "debilitated constitution," and he undoubtedly would find good books, stimulating conversation, and examples of the necessity of correct manners and proper subordination. "Of many of these advantages you, I am happy to know, stand in no need," he explained, "but I think your health will be much improved, as well as your taste and that your pride will probably be gratified by spending some time at Charlottesville. Do as you please however." Shortly after Tazewell's return home, John did matriculate, under the guidance of Francis Gilmer whom Jefferson earlier had sent abroad to recruit faculty members for the university. John was in Charlottesville less than a day before he made his way up the winding mountain road to Monticello to pay his respects to Jefferson and confer with him on a course of study.[32]

Jefferson had recently requested the senator's aid in a matter considered by the former president, now rector of the university, to be of utmost importance to his model institution in the foothills of the Blue Ridge Mountains. The Carrara marble bases and capitals ordered from Italy to grace the columns of the Rotunda's portico were being held in Boston awaiting payment of a duty too large for the university's pocketbook. According to an 1816 statute, Jefferson explained to Tazewell, all specimens of sculpture or of modeling imported for the use of any seminary of learning or for the encouragement of the fine arts were expressly exempted from an import tax. Although the 1824 act imposed a duty on such items, the Carrara marble for the university had been ordered before he enactment of the new tariff. Jefferson's desire to impart to the students an appreciation for "chaste models of the orders of architecture, taken from the finest remains of antiquity," found a sympathetic audience in Tazewell, who willingly interceded to speed the art objects to their destination. When Jefferson for the last time stood on the Lawn, he watched as the Carrara marble capitals were hoisted into place above the columns.[33]

Tazewell was happy to be home in April when the Virginia Tidewater was aglow with dogwood, yellow jasmine, redbud, and azaleas. Pottering among the flowers and shrubs and playing with the children, he found relaxation and contentment. "Papa has made gardening so complete a hobby," Ann delightedly told John, "that I believe at present it engrosses most of his thoughts." Of course, routine plantation business needed attention, especially now that John was away. In addition, the purchase of King's Creek had to be finalized, but the usual trips across the bay often were made more pleasant by the company of Louisa, now a young lady of twenty-one busily learning the duties of plantation mistress, including the wearisome task of cutting garments for the slaves from yards of oznaburg.[34]

The tranquillity was broken only by the receipt of an occasional letter voicing fears of further demands by western counties for a state constitutional convention. Benjamin Watkins Leigh, the brilliant conservative Richmond attorney, patently was distressed as he reported to Tazewell actions taken by the "Jacobins" at the most recent meeting of the westerners: "I do hold it all important to disappoint that Staunton Convention—totally. If it shall succeed to ever so small an extend, we shall have Staunton Conventions so long as there are discontents and malcontents to engender them." Leigh chose to see in the movement only a love of novelty, a passion for notoriety, and the "vanity of constitution making and mending." By proposing to equalize the representation, by demanding apportionment on the basis of free white population, the westerners, he was certain, planned to exclude slaveholders from the government, while burdening eastern counties with the expense of the state. The planting counties could survive only by opposing a constitutional convention "with all their might."[35]

Tazewell, not as excitable as Leigh, was no less anxious about the future. Western Virginians favored internal improvements and other aspects of federal support deemed necessary for the development and defense of their section. Yearly they were becoming increasingly impatient with the Richmond government as it thwarted their aspirations. Leigh, Tazewell, Wickham, and other like-minded Virginians feared that the stampede toward "democracy" in the western counties would contribute to excessive nationalism in Washington, which, if controlled by the North, would destroy the South. The Missouri Compromise had given clear warning of that possibility, and protective instinct turned many Jeffersonians, Tazewell included, from moderate nationalism to a more parochial states' rights philosophy. The survival of a united nation, they believed, rested on curbing the twin evils of despotic centralization of government and the tyranny of the majority.[36]

More immediate and practical matters diverted Tazewell's attention during the summer of 1825. In June a violent, destructive hurricane left his cherished gardens and grounds in shambles. Trees were uprooted or split to pieces, outbuildings were blown away, immense logs, planks and other debris washed ashore, bridges collapsed, and vessels were driven aground. Ann vividly described the catastrophe in a letter to John: "We sat at the front windows witnessing the destruction all the time it was going on. Our front lot here was two thirds cover'd by the tide." As the house rocked she thought of her flowers but could not "expose anyone" to look after flowers, cows, or anything else. The rain fell in torrents, and the "wind came in flaws, which made it like thunder." During the storm Tazewell was in Richmond, confined at the Wickhams' by a serious illness. Sensitive about imposing on their hospitality and concerned about Ann's anxiety should she learn of his indisposition, Tazewell insisted upon returning to Norfolk before he was strong enough to travel. For the remainder of the summer and well into the winter, his activities were inhibited by recurrences of his malady, which Wickham attributed to visits made to the Eastern Shore during the sickly time. "Next season you ought to be more careful," he scolded.[37]

## Chapter VIII

# J. Q. Adams

# and the

# "Factious Opposition"

Because of the state of his health, Tazewell was not present for the opening of the first session of the Nineteenth Congress, but he was informed of pertinent happenings, particularly the states' rights advocates' angry reaction to Adams's first annual message to Congress. Never, they charged, had there ever been a more exaggerated assumption of the authority of the national government. Even members of Adams's cabinet had cautioned him against his "excessively bold" recommendations, all designed, as the president said, to move with "the spirit of improvement abroad in the land": the establishment of a national university and an astronomical observatory (a "lighthouse of the sky"), laws to promote agriculture, commerce, manufactures, the cultivation and encouragement of the mechanic and elegant arts, the advancement of literature, and the progress of the sciences.[1]

As he studied the message, Tazewell undoubtedly had grave forebodings. Bureaucratic paternalism, however benevolent, increased the danger of despotic governmental power. And for what purpose was this "Grand Magnificent Government" being devised? Was the president merely bidding for the support of the masses? Never before had Adams evinced any particular sympathy for the plight of the "common man." Was his goal the elimination of sectional differences? If so, what was the future of the South?[2]

Arriving in Washington shortly after the holidays, Tazewell found his situation somewhat altered. He was now the senior senator from Virginia, for James Barbour had resigned to enter the cabinet. To replace Barbour, the Virginia legislature elected John Randolph, who was determined to be the sharpest thorn in the presidential flesh. Wickham was certain Tazewell would enjoy having Randolph as an associate, but privately Tazewell had reservations.[3] Although throughout his entire career he never publicly criticized his longtime friend, Tazewell could not help being concerned about Randolph's erratic temperament.

Problems of another sort were not long in surfacing. Tazewell, as a member of the powerful Foreign Relations Committee, soon was in direct conflict with the president over a statement in the annual message that at the invitation of Colombia, Mexico, and the Central American republics, he had appointed delegates to a congress to convene in Panama. Uncertain about the purpose of the Panama meeting, Adams suggested that it presented an opportunity for the United States to promote religious liberty in the Latin American nations, "which are even yet so far under the domination of prejudice that they have incorporated with their political constitutions an exclusive church, without toleration of any other dominant sect." He also wished to promote commercial relations with neighbors to the south. Adams made no mention of Senate confirmation of the delegates. Responding to senatorial indignation, the president claimed his procedure to be "within the constitutional competency of the Executive"; however, under pressure he belatedly and condescendingly asked the Senate to approve the appointees and requested the House and Senate to sanction necessary appropriations.[4]

The president's high-handedness was precisely the catalyst needed to coalesce the anti-Adams factions. Immediately his adversaries swung into action. Van Buren sought out Calhoun (never a particular favorite of the New Yorker's) who assured him Adams's treatment of Congress would rally Jacksonian states' righters in a drive to curb presidential power. Crawford, in Georgia, sent angry remarks about Adams's behavior. To further arouse the ire of southerners, Van Buren quickly warned of the probability of discussions on the African slave trade at the Panama meeting and of pressure for the opening of diplomatic relations between the United States and the black republics of the Caribbean.[5]

When the nominations of delegates were referred to the Foreign Relations Committee for consideration and recommendation to the Senate, the constitutional implications of Adams's tactics were debated at length. With Tazewell leading the discussion, the committee emphatically concluded that it was the Senate's prerogative not merely to act on the approval or disapproval of delegates but also to decide upon the expedience of the mission itself. Macon was chairman of the committee, but because of his infirmities he turned over many of the responsibilities to Tazewell, including writing the majority report that advised against entangling connections with or internal interferences in the affairs of other nations. The most caustic criticism was directed against Adams's statement regarding the possibility of advancing religious freedom in other countries. "If there be any subject more sacred and delicate than another, as to which the United States ought never to intermeddle, even by obtrusive advice, it is that which concerns religious liberty." The committee advocated retention of the "present unconnected and friendly position towards the whole of the new republics," commercial treaties arranged on an individual basis, and no involvement in the Panama meeting. Macon presented the report to the Senate, but when complimented on it, he invariably replied, "Yes, it is a good report. Tazewell wrote it." This made Tazewell the focal point of the first open confrontation between the Adams and anti-Adams forces on the floor of the Senate. The division was close. Approximately sixteen senators unreservedly were hostile to the president, while another eight or ten heartily disliked him but were instructed by their state legislatures or advised by constituents not to oppose him. Adams and Clay counted on the votes of at least three or four of the latter, thus giving the administration the necessary two-thirds majority to approve the nominees and their participation in the congress.[6]

The persuasive powers of Tazewell, as chief spokesman for the Foreign Relations Committee, were essential to victory over the Adams-Clay forces. Tazewell had the arguments at his fingertips, he was a master debater, and his influence over hesitant members was impressive. Fate, however, intervened. Five days before the president's nominees were to be considered in executive session, Tazewell received chilling news from home.

Ann was at the point of death. Frantic inquiries revealed that no steamboat was scheduled to depart for Norfolk for several days. Tazewell could not bear to wait, and he made arrangements to board the first stage going south, even though it would reach Norfolk about the same time as the steamboat. "I must leave you," he scribbled a hurried note to Randolph, "most probably never more to return here again. . . . My future course must depend on events of which I cannot judge at present." Before the note reached him, Randolph, while riding horseback near the Georgetown bridge, met James Hamilton, Jr., of South Carolina, who informed him of Tazewell's disturbing news. At once Randolph rushed off to Mrs. Peyton's, only to find Tazewell already gone. On the way to the boarding-house Randolph met Van Buren, and the two senators agreed to try to delay a vote on the Panama matter in the hope of Tazewell's early return.[7]

While detained in Alexandria awaiting the midnight departure of the stage, Tazewell wrote a long letter to Randolph, enclosing papers relating to the Panama debate. Apologizing for the distraught tone of his earlier note, he begged Randolph to write to him frequently, with news of occurrences in the Senate. "If upon reaching home I shall find my wife still living, I will return so soon as I think her out of danger, provided in the Senate my presence is in any way necessary or useful," he promised. "But should a reverse state of things exist, I shall never return to Washington again." During a brief stop between stages in Richmond, Tazewell hoped to ascertain if members of the legislature believed, as he himself did, that Virginia ought not to be minus one senator at such a crucial time. If they concurred, he would resign immediately.[8]

As Tazewell made his agonizingly slow journey overland to Norfolk, Randolph sent letter after letter in the same direction. For Tazewell not to return to the Senate would be tragic for Virginia and the nation, Randolph pleaded. Perhaps Mrs. Tazewell's condition was not so serious as was feared, but even if the worst happened, Tazewell must not forsake his post. "Since the death of Gen'l Washington Virginia will not have sustained such a blow as your resignation at this time will be. . . . If you go, I go too, but that is a small matter. Let them [the Virginia legislators] send two others of congenial feelings.

There are some of them I could not act with to any beneficial purpose." Two days later he wrote, "I can't bear the thought of your resignation. It will leave me in a hopeless & forlorn state of political widowhood." The following day he continued to implore, "Do not resign. You can do Virginia more good in Norfolk than anybody else can do here. Besides, you can be here at succeeding sessions, if not before the close of this."[9]

Arriving in Norfolk shortly before midnight on February 16, Tazewell found Ann still alive but so weak he feared she would not last the night. Seventy-two ounces of blood had been drawn during the last few days. "You may therefore form some idea of the state of debility to which a delicate female must be reduced by this process alone, if there was no other cause of exhaustion," Tazewell unburdened himself to Randolph. Ann Tazewell was in the eighth month of pregnancy when struck with what was diagnosed as a severe pleurisy. Although physicians assured Tazewell that the crisis had passed, her condition was critical. The bleeding had weakened her to such a degree that should the birth be premature, she could not live.[10]

There was yet another cause for grief, and while sitting exhausted by his wife's bedside, Tazewell, in a letter to Randolph, wrote a moving tribute to a slave: "My faithful friend and servant John departed this life a few hours before I reached home. For seventy years had he filled his place in society with a fidelity which nothing could corrupt, and with an affection for his master which knew no bounds. I have never seen a better man, and never can I have a truer friend. He died suddenly and without pain. His last words were 'Doctor keep me alive if you can until I can see master, & then I am willing to die.' Poor fellow, his wish could not be gratified here, but we shall meet again hereafter, if I shall live like him, blameless, steady and true to my trusts."[11]

While Mrs. Tazewell slowly improved, strain and fatigue took their toll of her husband's health. Chilled on the journey from Washington, he succumbed to a severe cold which led to serious complications. An infection settled in one eye, and for a time he feared for his sight. "The distension of the eyeball is so great, that I suppose it will burst, & I shall lose the eye itself. . . . I begin to think I am sinking pretty fast." "Broken down in health and spirits," Tazewell tried to bolster family morale, badly damaged when Ann, on the point of recovery, suffered a relapse after the birth of a daughter, Ella. For a time her legs were paralyzed, and she developed an ugly cough. Tazewell believed she had contracted pulmonary consumption, a disease which had taken the lives of her father, brother, and sister. "The ordinations of the most high are dark and mysterious," he wearily philosophized to Randolph. "It belongs not to ignorant and imperfect man to develop their causes, or to murmur at their effects. Reason and Religion combine to teach him to submit with fortitude to dispensations he cannot avert."[12]

Almost daily letters from Randolph and White brought temporary relief from the unbearable emotional strain. Tazewell was eager to know the fate of the Panama mission, an impersonal matter which could be faced with greater equanimity than the suffering or loss of a loved one. He had not favored the tactic of delaying consideration of the question, believing this would only give the administration an opportunity to use patronage to influence votes. Also, the longer the postponement, the more vicious tempers could become, and topics better ignored would be introduced. The fundamental truths on which the great fabric of society rested should not be examined too frequently, he cautioned Randolph, lest they, like quack medicine, be applied to the cure of all diseases. "The measure in question is doubtless an important one, but not so important as the dignity of the body to which we belong, or its proper relations to the other departments of the government." Balance and separation of powers must be maintained. Too powerful a Senate was just as undesirable as an excessively dominant executive. But Tazewell's warnings were not heeded, and during his absence the Senate heard a series of speeches aimed at delaying the vote, defeating the mission, and embarrassing Adams and Clay. Van Buren orchestrated the operation. Randolph, when it was his turn to speak, again brought up the incendiary and uncomfortable slavery question. The topic could not be ignored, he insisted. The problem should not be hidden. "It is not a dry rot that you can cover with your carpet." The operation of natural economic development would in time bring about the emancipation of

American slaves, but Latin American influence could precipitate slave insurrection in the South, with consequences too horrible to mention. Robert Y. Hayne of South Carolina was even more adamant.[13]

By early March, Tazewell was sleeping without the aid of laudanum, his swollen eye had returned to normal, and Ann was recovering. Spring came early to the Tidewater, and Tazewell was able to walk in the garden a little and "to enjoy the fragrance of every tree and shrub now in full bloom." Convinced that Ann was out of danger, he returned to Washington, arriving in time to hear Randolph deliver a diatribe against Adams and Clay on March 30. The nominations had been approved on March 14, late enough to prevent the delegates from reaching Panama before the congress adjourned. Nevertheless, Randolph refused to drop the matter. Insinuating that the invitation to the Panama meeting was manufactured in the State Department ("a Kentucky cuckoo's egg, laid in a Spanish American nest"), Randolph accused Clay of destroying the Constitution. Becoming increasingly frenzied, he hurled again the charge of "corrupt bargain," this time with an added allusion to "the coalition of Blifil and Black George . . . of the Puritan with the black-leg." The prolonged debate, as Tazewell predicted, had heated tempers to the point of explosion. Clay demanded vindication on the field of honor. Tazewell, who disapproved of dueling, did not witness the confrontation, which fortunately resulted only in a hole in Randolph's coat.[14]

Tazewell felt compelled to return the Senate's attention to the issue of presidential power, which, after all, was the heart of the matter. His speech was long and involved. Later he apologized for the inclusion of sarcasms "utter'd in the heat of debate." "My regret at having used them," he admitted to Wickham, "springs not from any belief that they were unmerited, but from the whispering of my own vanity, that it did not become me to employ such a weapon, in such a place." In his speech Tazewell took Adams to task for his contention that the appointment of envoys without the advice and consent of the Senate was within the president's "constitutional competency." If this assertion were true, and Adams had consulted the Senate only as a matter of expediency, then the Senate acted on the gracious good will of the president alone, and not on rights and responsibilities accorded to that body by the Constitution. The privileges of the Senate and the rights of sovereign states had to be defended against such flagrant and unqualified assertions of presidential power, acknowledged even by the president's advocates never to have been made before, and "against the use of which this people ought to revolt." Not once did Tazewell invoke the institution of slavery to excite his audience, for, as he remarked to Wickham, he did not always choose to steer his course by Randolph's compass.[15]

The first session of the Nineteenth Congress was scheduled to end on May 22, a date which Tazewell contemplated with considerable relief. His continued resistance to the administration and his disagreements with the majority in the Senate made his situation unpleasant. He was disturbed, too, by acceleration of the movement toward Van Buren's desired New York–Virginia coalition. The "rash obstinacy" of Adams led more pragmatic Virginians to view the president as a "dangerous man, whom we must get rid of as soon as possible." If this could be accomplished by allying with Van Buren, so be it. But Tazewell did not trust the little New Yorker.[16]

Also realizing the benefits of cooperation, the followers of Calhoun and Jackson together underwrote a newspaper, the *United States Telegraph*, edited by Duff Green, an experienced journalist closely associated with both the vice-president and the Tennessee general. Calhoun's knowledge of men and politics intrigued Tazewell, who considered the South Carolinian "gifted almost abundantly by nature, with the quickest perception and with a faculty of condensation which few possess." But Tazewell's heart did "not cling" to Calhoun. What the brilliant vice-president said sounded right. However, Tazewell wondered about his sincerity. "Ambition is his ruling passion," Tazewell told Randolph, "and, if I mistake him not, he will never be scrupulous as to the means of gratifying it." As he departed Washington in the spring of 1826, Tazewell was not committed to any political combination, but of one thing he was certain: Jackson was the only man who could drive John Quincy Adams from the White House.

Reunited with his family, Tazewell rejoiced in Ann's improved health. She gained strength daily, and baby Ella, fat and well, was the delight of her older brothers and sisters. The weary senator, not fully recovered from his own illness, again sought solace among his plants and trees, often dispatching rare specimens to favorite friends. "The arrow roots you sent me have thus far succeeded beyond my expectations," Wickham graciously informed Tazewell. "A dozen of them having vegetated. . . . I suppose they must be taken up before the winter sets in." Unlike President Adams, who stoically walked briskly around Capitol Square each morning, Tazewell did not maintain a regimen of exercise, preferring instead a rather sedentary existence. As a result, and despite his abstemious eating habits, his bulk increased. Ann encouraged gardening as beneficial to his well-being.[17]

Tazewell found many reasons for contentment in the summer of 1826, but life was not altogether idyllic. Henry continued troublesome. Sent by his father to the Eastern Shore to assist on the plantations there, his demands and erratic behavior upset the overseer. Sometimes he disappeared for days, causing the family untold worry. On the agricultural scene the oats market was extremely dull, and late in the summer a number of slaves became ill with ague and fever, but otherwise the plantations flourished. In late September yellow fever again struck Norfolk, impelling many of the inhabitants to leave for the country, but as the malady seemed to affect only a narrow district of the borough, Tazewell doggedly refused to flee. The proximity of the Tazewell household to "the seat of so dreadful a disorder" was cause for anxiety among the Wickhams, who pleaded with their friend to use every discretion to avoid contact with the disease. "The old maxim with regard to infected places I think a very good one: Go soon enough, go far enough, stay long enough," was William Wickham's sage advice.[18]

While the yellow fever was confined to Norfolk and surrounding coastal areas, another infectious disorder, this one of a political nature, spread throughout the state. Jefferson's death on July 4 elicited innumerable eulogies and political orations, many of which recalled not the "Spirit of '76" but the "Spirit of '98." The ills of the administration of John Adams were remembered and compared with similar actions of the second Adams presidency. The Richmond Junto, badly embarrassed by the election of 1824, looked ahead to recouping its losses in 1828. Next to Crawford, John Quincy Adams had been the 1824 preference of the Junto, the Virginia Assembly, and even of Jefferson, but once he was in office, Adams's ideas, attitudes, and actions, especially the "corrupt bargain," undermined this support. "Virginia is changing fast," one traveler to Virginia informed Jackson. "The western part of the state was always disposed to support you, and in the Eastern section of the state a change is gradually taking place. . . . Virginia may be calculated upon as being friendly to your election." Polk, traveling from Tennessee to Washington, learned that certain leading Virginia citizens were interested in Jackson's opinions on federally supported internal improvements as well as on other sensitive constitutional issues. Whether they were searching for reasons to support or to criticize the general, Polk was not sure, and he warned Jackson to answer all inquiries with guarded caution.[19]

Several of Tazewell's close friends were less than enthusiastic about the military man from Tennessee. Benjamin Watkins Leigh voiced an "insuperable dislike" of Jackson, declaring "I mean to hold myself at perfect liberty to oppose Adams so long as he is in, and Jackson whenever he shall be put in, with all my might." John Wickham believed aversion to Jackson was "very general in the country east of the Blue Ridge at least, but the dislike of the administration and its measures is so much stronger that unless some great change takes place I have hardly a doubt but the vote of Virginia will be given however reluctantly to Jackson." Adams, he thought, had more friends west of the Blue Ridge and in the Potomac area where the "mania" for internal improvements was strong, "but the western part of the state will I think settle down in favor of Jackson, the people of that part of the country not having that habitual respect for the law that prevails here will feel less repugnance to Jackson."[20]

This last statement troubled Tazewell, whose reverence for the law was the primary motivating force of his life. Several dilemmas resulted from his desire to use Jackson to defeat Adams, and this was one of them. He was well aware of Jackson's proclivity to ignore the law and to act arbitrarily on the slightest provocation. Also, some Jacksonians, endeavoring to build mass support for their candidate, encouraged the "common man" to demand from the state governments a greater share in political matters. In Virginia this played into the hands of those who favored calling a constitutional convention, a movement which Tazewell vigorously resisted. On the other hand, many Jacksonians reaffirmed the principle of states' rights as a basic concept of political philosophy. Tazewell saw this as a useful antidote to Adams's insistence on increasing the power of the federal government and, more particularly, the power of the president.[21]

In a somewhat defensive letter to Wickham, Tazewell tried to justify his stand for Jackson. Perhaps he was trying to convince himself. Adams had to be removed, he told Wickham, and Jackson was the man who could accomplish the task. How could Virginians who abhorred the present administration doubt this? There was no place in the contest for neutrals, for Hamlets who would rather bear the ills they had than fly to others that they knew not of. None but a schoolboy could expect to find perfection or see his "beau ideal" realized. "Such a monster as a perfect statesman never did and never can exist," and while Jackson was not the best imaginable candidate, he was the only one capable of defeating Adams.[22]

This was a persuasive selling point, one that was catching on in the area east of the Blue Ridge, and in December, Tazewell returned to Washington in excellent spirits. Adams, understandably, was glum. "The days of trial are coming again," he lamented as the second session of the Nineteenth Congress was about to convene. The gavel that called Congress to order on December 4, 1826, also signaled the commencement of open hostilities. In the Senate forty-two members were present, and of these a coalition of twenty-three was poised, ready to vote administration supporters into control of all committees. No longer was it the vice-president's prerogative to name committee members; during the last session Adams's supporters, recognizing the danger of such power in the hands of Calhoun, amended the rules. Standing committees were now to be chosen by majority vote. Thus, with twenty-three out of forty-two votes determining the outcome in every case, the opposition was overwhelmed. Tazewell, not surprisingly, found himself on the "proscribed list" of those the administra-

tion most wanted to eclipse. In the same category were Van
Buren, Woodbury of New Hampshire, Dickerson of New
Jersey, Macon of North Carolina, Hayne of South Carolina,
White of Tennessee, and John Berrien of Georgia. Instead of
the usual two committee assignments, each of these senators
was given only one, and Randolph, most despised of all, was
ignored entirely. The Adams faction controlled all standing
committees. Macon no longer chaired the Foreign Relations
Committee, and although he and Tazewell remained members, their influence was curbed considerably. "In that branch
of Congress where it [the administration] was the weakest, it is
now entirely safe," was Clay's delighted conclusion.[23]

The opposition immediately arranged a political meeting for
the Christmas holiday. From a fellow Virginian, William Fitzhugh of Ravensworth, Tazewell received a friendly note, dated
December 18: "Mr. Calhoun, and with him, we hope some
others of your friends, will do us the favor to ride over on
Sunday afternoon next, and spend the following day (Christmas) with us." At Ravensworth on Christmas Day 1826 the
Democratic party might be said to have been, if not born, at
least conceived, for it was here that Van Buren and Calhoun
agreed to form an alliance in behalf of Andrew Jackson.[24]
Neither Calhoun nor Van Buren was close to Tazewell's heart;
nevertheless, he realized how important their combined effort
would be in electing Jackson and writing finis to the hated
Adams administration. For this reason he was willing to play a
major role in arranging the alliance, even though he understood the ambitious natures of both the New Yorker and the
South Carolinian, each caring not at all about the success of
Jackson per se but instead preening himself for the presidency
in 1832, and each on guard against the other.

For the present, however, Tazewell had more immediate
worries. Randolph, who had finished out the Senate terms of
James Barbour, now faced reelection. As early as December
1826 Tazewell began hearing rumors of opposition to Randolph, and setting aside his earlier reservations about Randolph's membership in the Senate, he at once took steps to aid
his friend. Randolph must be retained, he insisted. Congress,
the nation, and certainly the administration knew him to be a
sworn enemy of the president. Unless Virginia meant to an-

nounce to the country that the state supported Adams and no longer approved of Randolph's policies, it was bound to sustain him. "It is vain to say that she may send some other representative of these opinions. This may be understood at home, but it will not be seen so abroad."[25]

Until the eve of the election the *Richmond Enquirer* confidently believed Randolph would be unopposed, despite the flurry of activity on the part of his adversaries, who approached Philip P. Barbour, John Floyd, and John Tyler with offers of support. Barbour and Floyd categorically refused to enter the race. Tyler, now governor of Virginia, did not specifically agree to accept the nomination, but neither did he absolutely reject the idea. On January 13, 1827, the names of both Randolph and Tyler were submitted to the legislature, and during the ensuing debate attacks on Randolph's reputation were devastating. Every rumor and piece of gossip about Randolph's behavior were aired. The Senate of the United States, one Adams backer charged, had been the most august and dignified body in the world until Randolph became a member and "cut the capers of a Merry Andrew" on the Senate floor. The vote was close: Tyler, 115; Randolph, 110; scattering, 2; blank, 1.[26] Tazewell regarded Randolph's defeat as a triumph for Adams. Randolph felt disgraced, and Leigh attributed the outcome, at least in part, to resentment of Randolph's brilliance: "Folly, stupidity, ineptness, pass without blame, but genius excites envy always, and its errors or extravagancies never are pardoned." Furthermore, Leigh warned Tazewell, the administration "would be very glad to see you substituted by any piece of mediocrity that could be picked up."[27]

Though slow to surface, certain Jacksonian benefits did result from the Virginia senatorial election. The low tactics used by those responsible for Randolph's downfall angered Ritchie and made him more receptive to Van Buren's effort to bring Virginia into the Jacksonian fold. On the day of Randolph's defeat Van Buren wrote to Ritchie, professing a serious commitment to a "substantial reorganization" and rejuvenation of the old Republican party, with emphasis on states' rights, low tariffs, and a New York–Virginia alliance. Would not Ritchie and the Richmond Junto pledge themselves anew to a union of the planters of the South and plain Republicans of the North? Once more, as in the days of Jefferson, they could be joined in the cause of liberty. Such a coalition, he hinted, could prevent the polarization of sectional interests, ward off hostilities between free and slave states, and curb any danger of northern interference with the institution of slavery. Here too was a chance to abandon the caucus and turn to the convention as a method of nominating the next presidential candidate. Van Buren portrayed the Adams faction as the old Federalist party resurrected, while he likened a North-South alliance to the Jeffersonian Republican organization of yesteryear.[28]

Prompted by Van Buren, Tazewell appealed to Ritchie to board the Jackson bandwagon by coming to Washington and establishing a newspaper that would be "a suitable organ of the views and opinions of the opposition in Congress." The great principles of the old Republican party "as they were manifested and expressed prior to 1801" must be kept alive by frequent repetition and argument. Would not Ritchie assume this responsibility in the nation's capital? Tazewell was dubious about the steadfastness of Van Buren's devotion to the South. What promises, he wondered, would the ambitious New Yorker make in order to capture the presidency for himself? Would the Jacksonians be in danger of dividing? Tazewell thought so, and in his usual careful, farsighted manner, he prepared to meet this contingency. "I feel solicitous," he confided to Ritchie, "that a Southern editor should have acquired and established the reputation of the proposed journal before that day arrives. What may be Mr. Van Buren's views upon this point of the subject I know not, nor does he know mine. In your reply, therefore, to this letter (which I shall be compelled to show him) you will not of course notice this." As Tazewell realized, Van Buren was searching for an editor willing to compete with Duff Green of the *Telegraph,* whose efforts were directed to furthering the political career of Calhoun. The southern element most opposed to Calhoun was the pro-Crawford faction; therefore, Ritchie, a strong proponent of Crawford in 1824, was a likely choice. Although Tazewell was anxious to have Ritchie establish a newspaper in Washington, he wanted the paper to act as a voice of the South, not of any one candidate or political organization.[29]

In replying to Tazewell, Ritchie acknowledged the advisability of setting up "an independent paper at the seat of the government." Should Jackson win the presidency in 1828, Ritchie shrewdly observed, his administration "will be the most important era our country has witnessed. It will be the crisis of our Constitution. Principles will then be fixed, which will cast their shadows or their lights for years to come." An independent press could "arrest the march of bad principles, or assist the establishment of good ones"; it could "recommend a good administration to the support of the people, or expose a bad one to the censure of public opinion." Ritchie, pleading a large family and approaching old age, was reluctant to take the risk, but he did come out in favor of the general for president.[30]

Important matters before the Senate turned Tazewell's attention to less purely partisan considerations. Calhoun, late in December 1826, had predicted that "the great topic of the session will be the W. India Trade, which I fear we have permanently lost by the neglect of the administration, and their opposition to its adjustment at the last session." Tazewell feared so too. For many years he followed with apprehension all aspects of the trade controversy, and in his opinion Adams, both as secretary of state and as president, had bungled the entire West Indies trade matter by trying to force undue concessions from the British with the threat of retaliatory measures. Restoration of reasonably regulated commerce, Tazewell firmly believed, could best be attained by accepting the limited trade allowed by Parliament as a first step toward a more mutually satisfactory agreement. Norfolk merchants, anxious to maintain some contact with this lucrative market, acceded to stipulations that required merchandise bound for the British West Indies to be carried in British ships. Even though this meant idle ships, unemployed seamen, and the decline of shipyards, it was preferable to no trade at all. Retaliation, such as closing American ports to British vessels, Tazewell argued, was not the answer.[31]

While Tazewell spoke for reconciliation, Adams called for reprisals. To Adams, bowing to British trade regulations would be a disgrace to American nationalism. Even when he gained a few concessions, he was not satisfied. Unable to resist one more twist of the lion's tail, he demanded that American goods and vessels be allowed to enter British colonial ports on the same footing as Canadian, Irish, or English goods and vessels. Great Britain considered this demand excessive (as did Tazewell), and to relieve the economic distress of the West Indian planters, His Majesty's government concluded commercial agreements with Prussia, Denmark, Sweden, and the new Latin American nations. "In the years after 1822" America did, indeed, as Bradford Perkins has observed, "throw away positive advantages in a chimerical search for total victory."[32]

Attempting to salvage some commerce for the United States, Tazewell, during the first session of the Nineteenth Congress, called for congressional repeal of all discriminatory duties on British imports and moved to refer the matter to the Senate Finance Committee, chaired by Samuel Smith of Baltimore, whose solicitude for the welfare of his merchant and shipping constituents was as great as Tazewell's. Deferring to the president's wishes, however, Congress adjourned without taking action. During the summer of 1826 Britain closed the West Indies to all United States commerce and declared the matter no longer open to discussion. What many considered to be the clumsy handling of the trade problem was laid at Adams's door, and faultfinding was rampant.[33]

In Norfolk there was strong opposition to further retaliatory measures, and the *Richmond Enquirer,* calling for reconciliation, declared Tazewell correct in insisting "that Britain had made a fair overture to us and that it was in our interest to meet it by a corresponding law." But Adams still considered reconciliation inappropriate. He recommended that Congress pass an act "totally interdicting trade with all the British colonies, both in the West Indies and in North America," and reopening trade upon terms of reciprocity "whenever the British government shall be disposed to assent to them." The opposition countered with a bill, written by Samuel Smith and strongly backed by Tazewell, proposing only a reciprocal agreement. After December 31, 1827, no other or higher duties would be levied by the United States on British ships and goods from British colonial ports than were levied on American vessels and goods arriving in West Indian ports. In the Senate the opposition bill was adopted by a majority of 32 to 10, but a House amendment was not acceptable to the Senate. A conference failed to break the impasse, and the second session of the Nineteenth Congress adjourned without relieving the plight of merchant and commercial interests. The opposition blamed presidential interference for preventing favorable action, not merely on this bill but throughout the entire ten years of negotiation conducted under Adams's "special superintendence." According to the strongly pro-Adams *Norfolk Herald*, Tazewell poured out "his accustomed bitterness upon the administration." Indeed, the *Herald* complained, Tazewell "seems to have borrowed Randolph's gall, to add to the large share of which he can boast himself."[34]

After Congress adjourned, Adams, using authority granted him by an act of 1823, issued a proclamation closing all American ports to British vessels arriving from any of Great Britain's colonies in the Western Hemisphere. Dated March 17, 1827, the proclamation became effective immediately, but for several months enforcement was negligible. "The President's Proclamation is at length issued. The direct trade to the British colonies is lopt off," was the angry comment of the *Richmond Enquirer*. The paper accused Adams of "wretchedly sporting with the whole question of American commercial interests." Norfolk was rendered a "pensive and desponding city." Even the *Norfolk Herald* was disturbed, but true to its pro-Adams leanings, it placed the blame on Congress rather than on the president.[35]

Under the name "Senex," Tazewell defended Congress in a series of twenty articles which the *Herald* agreed to print. Beginning in the March 28, 1827, issue, articles appeared periodically through May 30, giving a meticulously written account of commercial negotiations between Britain and the United States since the American Revolution. Dispassionate and factual in his approach, Tazewell detailed the president's lack of skill in the conduct of commercial diplomacy. He denounced the recent presidential proclamation, a "measure so important in itself and so ruinously injurious to a large portion of the population of the United States that it cannot fail to be a matter of much examination and discussion among them." True, the president legally could use his discretionary power to interdict trade. This was granted to him in the 1823 legislation. But he was under no mandatory obligation to exercise the right, and both houses of Congress had asked that he take no action before December 31, 1827, hoping in the meantime to resolve the deadlock. The president's issuance of the proclamation contrary to the clear and decisive wishes of the House and Senate was to Tazewell a most wanton and indiscreet exercise of presidential power. That "two nations in profound peace" should have been induced, "without one single known point of disagreement between them," to interdict a mutually beneficial commercial relationship was beyond comprehension. Unless immediate steps were taken to rectify the situation, the West Indies trade would be lost forever. There were those who welcomed the trade problem as almost a God-sent issue, a political stick with which to beat the president, but Tazewell, who certainly felt no sympathy for Adams, was genuinely disturbed. Like the Embargo Act of 1807, the interdict, he believed, could inflict a deadly blow to the nation's shipping industry and to the economy of Norfolk and other port cities.[36]

On the subject of the West Indies trade the anti-Adams coalition managed to maintain an almost united front, thus avoiding any serious schisms, but this was not true in regard to the tariff. In mid-February a bill increasing the protective duty on wool and woolen goods was introduced in the Senate, having won approval by the House, "after a protracted and desperate struggle." Textile manufacturers and wool growers strongly favored the measure. The southern states, aside from a few sheep-raising areas, resolutely opposed it, and Tazewell at once moved to table the bill. Bitter Senate debate on the tariff, he feared, would endanger the fragile North-South alliance, so recently and delicately arranged, but his motion was defeated, 28 to 17, with Van Buren and Benton siding with the majority. Invectives for and against tariffs and the American System in general flew back and forth across the chamber. Van Buren, the "little magician," summoned all his wizardry to avoid being squeezed between opposing pressures, on the one side from New York, which insisted on his firm support of the bill, and on the other from the South, which expected him to hew to the old Republican line, to which he professed great loyalty and devotion. Van Buren was in an unhappy position, and when, on February 28, Hayne of South Carolina again moved to table, the New Yorker, deciding the best solution was to absent himself before the vote was taken, found it urgently necessary to accompany a friend on a tour of the Congressional Cemetery. This time the result was a 20-to-20 tie, with Vice-President Calhoun casting his deciding vote against protection.[37]

During the closing days of the Nineteenth Congress, Tazewell was optimistic about the possibility of unseating Adams, but there was cause for sadness, too. John Randolph became increasingly morose as he faced the termination of his senatorial career, and during a brief executive session of the Senate, just before adjournment on March 3, 1827, he made his dramatic exit. As Van Buren later described the incident, Randolph, in the midst of a violent argument over a minor rule change, deliberately walked from his place, "passed in front of the Chair to the door, exclaiming as he walked along, 'I will have no more of this! I am off for England! Good bye, Tazewell! Good bye, Van Buren! They are all against me! They are all against me, Tazewell, in Virginia too!'—and still uttering these words the doors of the Senate closed behind him."[38]

After his departure from Washington, Randolph stopped briefly in Richmond, and Wickham, aware of Tazewell's concern, at once sent word that Randolph's "spirits were lower than I have almost ever seen them, but he seemed very glad to meet his friends and was kind and cordial in his deportment. To me he appeared in full possession of all his faculties and in better health than I have seen him for some time before, but strongly impressed with the notion that both his mind and body are declining."[39] Although Randolph's congressional district immediately elected him to the House of Representatives, the Senate defeat had been a painful blow to his pride.

Adams, too, was nursing political wounds. The "factious opposition" in the Nineteenth Congress had all but destroyed the president's program of "liberty through power," of a national government resplendent in increased strength and services. The Richmond Junto, at least a goodly portion of its membership, decided without enthusiasm to support Jackson. Ritchie's "conversion" was influential in this development. Now the

Jacksonians had the blessings of perhaps the strongest newspaper in the South, and Van Buren counted on the beneficence of the *Enquirer* to assist him in his struggle with Calhoun for control of the party.[40] The North-South alliance, held together by the coalition of the Richmond Junto and the Albany Regency and manipulated by Van Buren, if successful in making the Nashville connection and elevating Jackson to the presidency, could also, Van Buren hoped, work the same magic for him. But the brilliant Calhoun had other plans, and Tazewell trusted neither. Moreover, he wondered where Tyler would stand when the time came for a showdown.

## Chapter IX

# *The Tariff,*

# *Nullification, and*

# *Colonization*

In the months following adjournment of the Nineteenth Congress Tazewell was courted by followers of both Calhoun and Van Buren. Often the letters began with an appeal to Tazewell's horticultural interests. "I send you three plants of the sweet flowering current," Mahlon Dickerson wrote, "which were bro't by Lewis and Clark from the Rocky Mountains—they are very hardy." Jackson's prospects, he thought, were better in New Jersey "than I supposed when I left Washington." Calhoun's first letter ostensibly was to remind Tazewell "of the cantalope seed which you promised me before we left Washington. It is fruit of which I am very fond. What soil do you prefer, and what is your mode of treatment?" He then turned to a discussion of politics and the nature of government. "Any revolution in favor of liberty in our system," any struggle against a too-powerful national government or a president who usurped the rights of Congress or the people or who abused his power, must "be effected by the South, and I may add, the South headed by Virginia. There is something in her character well-calculated to give an impulse to such a struggle, and I trust she will be found in her true position in the pending one, in all the majesty of her power."[1]

Finding comfort in "unburthening" his mind in an exchange of ideas with Tazewell, Calhoun repeated the same message all summer long: Political reforms must come from the South, but without the leadership of Virginia the South was impotent. Reflecting with despair and anxiety on the state of the government, Calhoun considered the current presidential contest "but an incident which at best affords the *means* of reform, which must take place, or we are ruined." The administration forces, he was certain, had given up hope of separating Virginia from Jackson, and as a result, they now were scheming to detach Pennsylvania by bidding for the protectionist interests of that state. Calhoun was positive of Pennsylvania's loyalty to Jackson, just as he was sure the South would be "cordially united" in overthrowing the "wicked conspiracy which brought Mr. Adams and Mr. Clay into power." However, a larger problem occupied his thoughts. Was there any way, he wondered, to guarantee permanency to the southern way of life, to the great agricultural interests of the South?[2]

On this score there was increasing cause for alarm. During the summer of 1827 one hundred delegates from thirteen northern and western states gathered in Harrisburg, Pennsylvania, and drew up a memorial to Congress recommending an increase in duties on woolens, both raw wool and woolen textiles, on iron, flax, hemp, and distilled spirits. The convention frightened, angered, and frustrated southerners. Van Buren, who promised an alliance between planters and plain Republicans of the North, seemingly had betrayed them by declaring he would sponsor any tariff which was "temperate and wise and therefore salutary," one which would promote "every branch of domestic production and industry."[3] If this was what Van Buren meant by a "substantial reorganization of the old Republican Party," the South wanted none of it.

Tazewell and Calhoun regarded the Harrisburg Convention as a "portentious sign of the times." How, in an extensive country with diverse and opposing interests, could one portion of the people be protected against the other, Calhoun asked. All the time-honored remedies—freedom of debate, freedom of the press, division of the power of government into three branches—failed to prevent the formation of combinations that fostered what Calhoun feared most, the tyranny of the majority. Tyrannical majority rule, the South Carolinian told Tazewell, was precisely the object of the Harrisburg meeting. "It is the selected instrument to combine with greater facility the great geographic northern manufacturing in order to enforce more effectually the system of monopoly and extortion against the consuming states." Tazewell agreed, but he found Calhoun's "one effective remedy" against despotism equally frightening. What Calhoun suggested to Tazewell was the negation of an act of Congress by an individual state.[4]

Tazewell had nothing but distaste for the nullification idea. If the desired end result was southern security within the Union, Calhoun's way was not the proper course to take. Nullification was unworkable and unconstitutional. Unless the laws of the land were so structured as to command respect and obedience, the nation would cease to exist. Tazewell, too, feared the growing tyranny of a northern majority, with its latent ability to devastate the southern economy, but only by standing firmly together and refusing to go along with the machinations of northern politicians who sought to dominate the North-South alliance could the slaveholding states hope to protect their interests. The permanency of the Union "in its present form," as well as the survival of the southern states, depended on how the South reacted to the tariff issue. For now, at least, Tazewell preferred a more moderate recourse than Calhoun's, one less fraught with danger to the Union. What he hoped for was a president willing to protect southern interests; a man, whether from North or South, who respected regional differences and the doctrine of states' rights. But was Jackson the right man? Wickham was dubious. Many respectable people who disapproved of the Adams administration also were skeptical about Jackson, he cautioned, and "have such strong apprehensions of misrule under Jackson, should he be elected president, that they prefer that of Mr. Adams as the lesser evil." Perhaps there was a good chance Jackson would do nothing to harm the slaveholding states. "Still, he will have a nice game to play." In Tazewell's opinion too many people already were playing games. Even though he realized how Van Buren was caught between North and South in the tariff dilemma, he was upset by the New Yorker's propensity for manipulation and intrigue, and he wondered how far Jackson would allow himself to be influenced by the clever little magician.[5]

As the 1828 campaign gathered momentum, Tazewell became increasingly uncomfortable. The devices used by Jacksonian demagogues, the propaganda, coarse jokes, the crude methods of creating mass enthusiasm, the impossible promises made to attract votes, repelled him, and he felt alienated from the movement he had worked so hard to set in motion. Perhaps Jackson was the "People's Candidate," but was this crass appeal to egalitarianism necessary? Wickham warned repeatedly that a president elevated by the masses would have no choice but to conform to the will of the masses, the tyranny of the masses. This Tazewell understood. As an old-line Jeffersonian he maintained a firm belief in the aristocracy of virtue and talent, in the need for an educated leadership chosen by an educated electorate. Yet, he had been among the earliest backers of Jackson, who now was touted as a "natural man" as opposed to the "effete intellectual," John Quincy Adams. Tazewell's standard of values was in direct contrast to the anti-intellectualism propounded by the Jacksonian political hacks striving to snare the votes of the so-called "common man." Hugh Blair Grigsby, a budding young Norfolk author, called Tazewell "a monarch in the empire of the mind," a man with "no arrogant supremacy in his manner . . . no insulting superiority in his triumphs. He is mild and persuasive."[6] Undoubtedly he was too mild for a smear campaign which "splattered more filth in more different directions and upon more innocent people than any other in American history." He felt trapped and frustrated by a cause which he could not wholeheartedly endorse. The tactics of the Jackson political managers appalled him. Yet, with the South facing seemingly insurmountable difficulties should Adams again be the victor, where could one turn for succor? Calhoun's solution was not plausible. Tazewell wondered if he himself was an anachronism, out of step with his times. A trip up the Hudson River with John failed to bring any political peace of mind, and Tazewell returned to Washington in December hoping only that the session would be brief enough to avoid a renewal of the tariff controversy and a more severe North-South split.[7]

The first session of the Twentieth Congress, Tazewell soon learned, was destined not to be short. Hordes of interested people, many of whom had attended the Harrisburg Convention, were in Washington to persuade, cajole, influence, or demand protection of one sort or another. Andrew Stevenson, a Virginia Jacksonian and a member of the Richmond Junto, was elected Speaker of the House, an action which pleased

Tazewell not only because of the prestige that thereby accrued to Virginia and the southern Jacksonians, but also because it caused the president so much distress."This settles the complexion of the House," Adams bitterly commented. "There is a decided majority of both Houses of Congress in opposition to the Administration—a state of things which has never before occurred under the Government of the United States." With Vice-President Calhoun presiding in the Senate and the House under the leadership of Stevenson, Adams had reason to feel depressed. Perhaps, above all, he dreaded Randolph's return to Washington. The president could not mention the Virginian without referring to his "besotted violence," "corrosive rancor of heart," and "rabid foam."[8]

While the House of Representatives labored over a tariff bill, the Senate marked time, and in mid-January, Tazewell returned to Norfolk for a few weeks. The weather was unusually mild, hyacinths were in bloom, and trees and shrubs in bud. The oldest inhabitants of the borough had never known so warm a season. But the delightful temperatures also caused problems. Pork from the numerous hogs butchered on his Eastern Shore plantations was in danger of spoiling, and Tazewell needed to confer with his overseers about preventive measures. John, now returned from the University of Virginia and studying law in Norfolk, attempted to look after Sandhills, and Henry was on the Eastern Shore, but neither had the experience to cope with emergencies. Tazewell was glad for an excuse to quit Washington for a while. However, all was not peaceful in Norfolk, for the populace was arguing over the tariff proposals emanating from the House committee rooms, and the *Herald* was blaming him for a variety of wrongs, among them putting down domestic manufactures and preventing the march of improvement in an effort to return the United States to a condition of colonial dependence on England.[9]

Back in Washington, Tazewell complained of dullness, unusual anxiety, and lethargy. He wished a thousand times a day that he were at home.[10] The stress and strain of current controversies drained him of all energy, and tariff measures emerging from the House committee did nothing to ease his anxieties or lift his spirits. Thinking the South secure for Jackson, Representative Silas Wright, Van Buren's henchman, and other northern and western Jacksonians were determined to curry favor with the doubtful states. As a result, the South and New England (considered as safe for Adams as the South was for Jackson) became helpless pawns in the tariff struggle.

Even though the proposed increased duties presaged serious economic complications for Virginia, already experiencing widespread depression attributed to the Tariff of 1824, more than the surface issues of protection worried Tazewell.[11] In his thoughts was Wickham's oft-repeated warning: "If the time should ever arrive when the fanatical desire of the North to emancipate the southern slave will become general or those who labor among them shall obtain complete ascendency over those who would hold property—either of these occurrences perhaps singly and most probably united, will lead to the most injurious, perhaps fatal, consequences to this part of the Union."[12] Still, Tazewell refused to consider slavery a proper topic of discussion. Someday, he knew, the problem would have to be faced, something would have to be done, but when and what? He pondered the problem and said nothing. He had no suggestions, no solutions. Nevertheless, during this session of Congress he was forced to examine one aspect of this most vexing and perplexing subject.

For Tazewell this uncomfortable situation developed when several petitions from the American Colonization Society were referred to the Senate Committee on Foreign Relations. The petitions requested the United States government to set aside from the annual revenue a suitable fund for the purpose of assisting humane individuals willing to liberate and colonize their slaves and for aiding free blacks who desired to emigrate to a colony on the west coast of Africa. This measure would commit the United States to the acquisition of territory outside the continental limits, for Monrovia, purchased by the Colonization Society in 1821 and later known as Liberia, was considered too small to accommodate a large influx of blacks from the United States. Therefore, the Foreign Relations Committee had the responsibility of investigating the feasibility of the requests and making a report to the Senate. After several weeks of deliberation, Tazewell wrote and read to the Senate a lengthy report expressing the views and recommendations of the members.

The United States government, Tazewell told the senators, had every right to acquire new territory, either by discovery, conquest, or negotiation. The precedent was established by the procurement of Louisiana and Florida. Acquisition of territory on the west coast of Africa, however, was a different matter. This was distant land, not contiguous to the United States, and quite unlikely to be admitted into the Union as an equal member of the confederation. Nor could the senators find among the constitutionally enumerated powers of Congress any authority to possess additional domain to provide for the common defense or to promote the general welfare.

Other observations, while outside the realm of responsibilities relegated to the committee, were of particular concern to Tazewell and Nathaniel Macon, and they took this opportunity to air their views. Tazewell posed a primary question: If it were possible for the United States to possess land on the coast of Africa, did the federal government have the right to transport thither, at public expense, any part of the nation's population? He answered with a resounding no, terming the very thought a prologue for dangerous consequences. Although the Colonization Society's proposition currently applied only to a portion of the black population, and partially upon a quasi-voluntary basis, could not this precedent be used at some future time to force emigration of both blacks and whites, urging them by use of bounties and rewards to leave the country? Or could not residents of the United States be encouraged by oppression to accept financial aid to "fly from the land of their birth"? Then Tazewell raised the most sensitive issue of all: Could the federal government rightfully intrude within the confines of a state for the purpose of uprooting a portion of its inhabitants and locating them permanently elsewhere? Most emphatically not. The Constitution of the United States expressly denied to the national government the power to impair the political strength of any state by reducing its population. Moreover, the framers of that document wisely abstained from bestowing upon the government they created any power whatever over the black population of the country, whether this population was bond or free. "Any attempt to endow the federal government with such a power," Tazewell reminded the Senate, "we know as an historical fact, would have frustrated all the labours and defeated the great objects of the patriot statesmen assembled for the purpose of framing this plan of government." The proposal made by the American Colonization Society, therefore, constituted a contradiction of the very foundation of the nation's governmental principles, namely, that each state should have the exclusive right to decide not only who were black, but also who were free persons. Any attempt by Congress to assume such authority would be a direct violation of the Constitution and productive of consequences terrible beyond imagination.

From constitutional arguments Tazewell turned to the prohibitive costs of the colonization proposal. A modest estimate, he believed, would be $100 for each person, and the sum needed to transport merely the free Negroes would exceed $28 million. Using the same formula, the initial expense of colonizing the slave population would be at minimum $190 million. This figure did not include the compensation that the government would have to offer slaveowners to induce them to release their property. The amount involved in accomplishing this, Tazewell declared, would baffle all calculations.

While praising the generous feelings and philanthropic purposes of the Colonization Society, the report concluded with a stern warning against the establishment of a powerful, self-created organization which, although numbering in its ranks many distinguished government officials, could pose a dangerous threat to the future of the nation. Should there be any collusion between the society and the government to restrain or prevent the exercise of constitutional powers or prerogatives, such an organization, despite "the purity and intelligence of its members, must be looked at with suspicion and distrust." On this note Tazewell ended the report.[13]

The Foreign Relations Committee did not deal with the pros and cons of slavery as such, nor did Tazewell, even in letters to his closest friends, speculate on the future of the southern labor system. He was an indulgent master who directed his overseers to treat slaves well, and his reputation for kindness was so widespread among the Negroes, said his daughter Ann, that frequently in probate cases, when slaves had to be sold to effect a division of property, they would beg Tazewell to purchase them. Whenever possible he did so.[14] While obviously a man of humanitarian instincts, Tazewell also was engaged in agriculture for profit, and slaves were part of the system. Undoubtedly, he had conflicting emotions, as did numerous plantation owners, about the continuation of human bondage, but agitating the matter without offering concrete and realistic solutions seemed to him illogical and dangerous. Furthermore, he considered the tariff question to be of more immediate peril to the nation's future.

In stronger terms than he had ever used before, Tazewell declared his disgust with the craftiness and deception of active political life. In manipulations of the tariff he felt he was seeing men and things as they actually were, and his observations severely depressed him. If the fate of the country rested in the hands of such men, what possibly could be the outcome? Wickham tried to be more cheerful, but even he confessed to feeling a good deal of anxiety over the tariff: "The hard times we experience in this part of the country (and they have never been harder in a period of peace) are owing in great degree to the enormous taxes we pay on imports & the proportionate bounties the northern manufacturers draw from us. If the plan succeeds and is carried into full operation, I should apprehend the most disastrous consequences to the Union, unless some *countervailing force* should operate to destroy its effects."[15]

When an East-West coalition guided the tariff bill to victory, the South felt isolated, helpless, and angry. Suggestions of boycotts of northern manufactured goods or excise taxes on northern products brought "within the limits of the plundered states" reached Tazewell's desk. "Never before were any people subjected to such plunder and degradation with such ample means on their hands of doing themselves justice," was the cry of Governor William B. Giles of Virginia. Calhoun spoke of the tariff as "one of the great instruments of our impoverishment." "It is always dangerous," he wrote to Monroe, "to see the country divided, as it is, by sections," especially when the measures which divided the nation originated "in the spirit of gain on one side, at the expense of the other." Throughout the South calls for protest meetings were heard, but fear of hazarding Jackson's election prevented overt outbursts of violence.[16]

Attempting to appease southerners and calm their outrage, Van Buren spoke soothing words, promising all wrongs would be righted as soon as Jackson took the oath of office. For Tazewell, Van Buren's assurances did not ring true. Too clearly he remembered the New Yorker's pledges of loyalty to old Republicanism, to a North-South alliance with Virginia and New York in the vanguard. Tazewell, from the first, had been suspicious of Van Buren, but the double-dealing had been more flagrant than he expected. Now he was furious and bitter. Confronting the New Yorker one day shortly after the Senate vote on the tariff, Tazewell addressed him curtly. "Sir, you have deceived me once; that was your fault; but if you deceive me again the fault will be mine." For the South, the Tariff Act of 1828 was truly abominable, resulting in more serious southern alienation than had the Missouri Compromise eight years earlier. Reactions were varied, but the most consequential came from the pen of Calhoun. During the summer of 1828 he wrote his *South Carolina Exposition and Protest,* advocating in strongest terms the doctrine of nullification that Tazewell regarded with so much distaste.[17]

In Tazewell's candid opinion, the entire first session of the Twentieth Congress was a failure, perhaps even a tragedy, and as adjournment approached Tazewell's depression increased. The tariff matter, so disastrously resolved; the colonization petitions, frightening in their possible consequences; the gnawing apprehension of Jackson's malleability in the hands of his northern supporters, all these worries Tazewell took with him to Norfolk. There he found life better. The family was well, John was reading law, the crops were good. Even Henry was accepting a fair share of the responsibilities of managing the Eastern Shore plantations. For a time he had plagued the overseer with unreasonable demands, but Henry's entire outlook seemed improved. During July the weather was moderate, and the dread yellow fever had not yet appeared.[18] As usual Tazewell was busy; still, there was time to relax, to play with children, to visit friends. Then, on August 2 everything changed. On that day Henry took his own life.

Details of the incident are not clear. The Tazewells, preferring to bear their pain in stoic silence, never publicly mentioned the tragedy or Henry ever again. The Norfolk newspapers made no note of Henry's demise. However, according to a story told on the Eastern Shore, Henry had proposed marriage to Arintha Parker, "a much sought-after young lady" from a neighboring plantation, who rejected him. As Miss Parker watched, Henry mounted his horse, drew a pistol, and shot himself. He was interred in the burial ground at the King's Creek plantation, and for weeks the family was in seclusion.[19] Ann Tazewell became frighteningly despondent. Tazewell was overcome with sorrow.

Even the presidential election, which extended from September into November, failed to rouse his interest. Jackson's victory over Adams was a stunning 56 percent of the popular vote, larger than any other presidential majority in the nineteenth century. The margin in the electoral college was even greater, 178 votes for Jackson, 83 for Adams. Virginians voted well over two-to-one in favor of Jackson, 26,752 to 12,101, and although Norfolk County preferred Adams, the borough gave a narrow majority to Jackson. Calhoun's overwhelming reelection to the vice-presidency provided a ray of hope for those southerners concerned about possible northern domination of the Jackson administration. As Tazewell's friend Congressman John Floyd remarked, the president-elect had one foot in the grave, thus giving the South Carolinian a better than even chance of becoming president.[20] For Tazewell this was not a completely comforting expectation.

In fact, the entire political scene was unsettling. If, as the Albany Regency insisted, the aristocracy and the democracy of the country were arrayed against each other in the election of 1828, Tazewell belonged in neither camp. While not above some restrained mudslinging, he could not condone the "new breed of politicians," the "Hurra Boys" with their vulgar stories of sexual promiscuities, their demagogic appeals to the common man, their raucous songs, banners, and noisy demonstrations, all of which he found almost as distasteful as their pragmatism. Both parties, Jacksonian Democrats and National Republicans (as they now were designated), saw the outcome of the election as a bona fide revolution, the triumphant victory of "raving Democracy."[21] To Tazewell, the unrestricted power of the people was as dangerous as complete rule in the hands of one man or an oligarchy.

With a heavy heart he returned to Washington. His only desire was to resign from the Senate and return to his grieving wife, but as in the past, Wickham urged him to stay on: "If you should resign your seat in the Senate before the end of your term which is now so near at hand, the event would be an unexpected one by the public in Virginia and in the present state of public affairs would be generally censured by them." Resigning now would be viewed as an unkind and ungrateful rebuff of the confidence placed in Tazewell by the state legislature, as would a refusal to stand for reelection. Tazewell had to consider his duty to the state as well as his own self-respect, and in Wickham's opinion, Virginia had need of Tazewell now as never before, especially since in Washington "new combinations must be forming and new divisions taking place as personal or local interests may direct." Members of the Virginia House of Delegates echoed Wickham's sentiments. "I sympathize with you in your domestic affliction," wrote Theodore Miller of Powhatan, but he hoped that Tazewell's "private feelings & known love of retirement" would "yield to a sense of public duty & the call of your country."[22]

Reluctantly acquiescing, Tazewell stayed on at Mrs. Peyton's, living in the midst of the Tennessee delegation, sitting at table with General and Mrs. Robert Desha, Hugh Lawson White, and Mr. and Mrs. James K. Polk, listening to their plans for the reception of General and Mrs. Jackson upon their arrival in the capital.[23] When news reached them of the death of Mrs. Jackson, Tazewell, too, was saddened, and he understood the deep-seated resentment of the Tennesseeans toward the Adams faction, whose slanderous assaults may have precipitated Mrs. Jackson's fatal attack.

During these weeks, Tazewell was pathetically grateful for White's companionship. The Tennessee senator knew sorrow well, and when Tazewell and White saw each other for the first time after Henry's death, both stood silent, with tears running down their cheeks, for White recently also had lost a grown son. From his friend, Tazewell did not have to conceal his anguish and concern for his wife's state of mind, and he needed to confide in someone, for Ann was inconsolable. On Christmas Day, Tazewell spent hours writing to her, trying in some way to give hope and comfort. He was tempted to journey to Norfolk for the holiday, but because of the precariousness of the weather and the brief time he could have stayed at home, he remained in Washington. In addition, he noted, "my absence from here at this moment, would certainly have given rise to many conjectures and speculations [about his probable resignation]. These would be given to the public thro' the newspapers, in many distorted shapes, and I should be made of much more notoriety than I wish to be." She must, he told her, struggle against the influence of morbid considerations. If she persisted in indulging in such thoughts, they would become habitual, and "then their effects are truly pernicious to body and soul both." Tazewell, usually extremely reserved in referring to his religious tenets, on his occasion assured his wife that "the God whom we adore" expected from his servants constant effort in this life. "He chasteneth whom he loveth," Tazewell reminded his wife, "and the consciousness of this truth, should nerve us to endure all his dispensations, with the pious confidence, that altho' his ways are dark and mysterious to our eyes, yet they are ordained for our good." He implored Ann to begin occupying herself with exercise and other diversions. By pursuing such a course she would improve her health and her spirits. "You will become more contented, and I more happy because you are so."[24]

Tazewell had abundant time to worry about Ann, for in the capital everything was in a "dead calm," awaiting the change of administrations. Speculation about membership of the new cabinet was prevalent, and Tazewell's name figured prominently in the theorizing. While Calhoun eagerly importuned Jackson to name the Virginian secretary of state, newspapers printed rumors of Tazewell's imminent appointment, not only to the top post, but also as head of the treasury, the navy, or the Department of Justice. Early in January 1829 rumors rapidly increased when the Virginia legislature reelected him to the Senate,[25] a decision which Tazewell graciously accepted, even though his letters were filled with expressions of homesickness and longing to retire from politics.

He had not sought reelection, but neither had he instructed his supporters to withdraw his name. As usual he was torn between domestic responsibilities and public duty. If only Ann and the younger childfen would accompany him to Washington he could serve both loyalties, but this Ann adamantly refused to do, and he hated the long separations. His own preference was to decline another term, but had he done so he was certain that five or six other persons would have announced themselves as candidates, possibly causing schisms in the Jackson party in the Assembly, resulting in the election of an anti-Jackson man, and leaving the new chief executive with a weakened majority in the Senate. Having contributed so much to the elevation of the Jackson administration, he felt he ought not "to suffer it to be put in hazard at the moment of its birth." However, he pointedly assured son John, such sentiments were not to be construed as a desire on his part to become a member of the cabinet. Quite the contrary, a second term in the Senate would give him a substantial excuse for refusing an invitation, should one be proffered. The General Assembly wanted him to represent the commonwealth in the Senate of the United States. This was a high honor, one which he would not exchange for any other, and would be his justification for shunning an administrative appointment. "No man will have the right to censure me for not abandoning a post to which I have been so assigned; and Virginia will esteem me more for the sacrifice I shall make on her account." For, he observed in Periclean fashion, "in a government like this, he who declines an elevated station without a good reason, not only suffers in his reputation, but reduces himself to perfect insignificance."[26]

Contrary to his rationalization, reelection only gave added credence to stories of appointment to an important position. In Richmond there was talk of his succeeding Jackson as president, and in Williamsburg many of Tazewell's friends spoke with certainty of his plan to resign from the Senate on March 3, at which time he would be named secretary of state. His place in the Senate, they said, would be filled by John Randolph. The publicity increased Tazewell's already heavy correspondence. "It is now near 1 o'clock in the morning," he wearily wrote John. "This makes the fourteenth letter I have written since dinner, and there are at least as many more before me to be answer'd. This is but a very small part of my labor indeed; and I have no assistance in getting through it."[27]

At least he could rely upon John, now a full-fledged attorney, to attend to business matters in Norfolk.

The tempo of Washington quickened when, on February 11, Jackson unobtrusively entered the capital. Tazewell, describing the event for Wickham, said the arrival was typical of an old soldier, who "surprised all those who were watching for his approach; and was comfortably seated at the breakfast table before any of them even suspected he was on his way to the city." That afternoon Tazewell called on the president-elect to deliver officially the final tabulation of the vote of the electoral college, and very soon thereafter Ann Tazewell knew the worst, that her husband had been offered a diplomatic post, minister to Great Britain.[28]

Jackson's mention of a London assignment was unexpected, and apparently came as a consequence of Tazewell's Senate report on the West Indies trade. Tazewell was interested, but he had promised Ann he would resist all such temptations, in whatever form they might be presented, and she was not in the least reticent in opposing a foreign assignment as well as a cabinet post. "I feel no kind of ambition or desire to cross the Atlantick in any situation whatever," she declared. "On the contrary it would cause me a great deal of unhappiness to leave my aged Mother (whom I could never calculate on seeing again) without a friend or protector. Oh it would make me so truly miserable, that I think you would probably be compelled to seek a grave for me among strangers." As for being the wife of a cabinet member, she was, she protested, "of too domestic a disposition ever to wish to live in Washington, and entirely too plain both in mind and manners, either to suit, or to be pleased with the society I might meet with there." Although they were now in "easy circumstances" financially, she reminded her husband that "if Mr. Jefferson and Mr. Monroe have both been ruined by filling public situations, altho' blended with enormous salaries, how can any one expect to avoid the same fate, who occupies a station which is attended perhaps by almost as much expense, without one half the money (they were allowed) to support the same. It would reduce us to a Lottery or Beggary."[29]

For a time the wagers of knowledgeable Washingtonians were almost evenly divided on whether Tazewell or Van

Buren would be the next secretary of state, but Jackson believed the post too often had been filled by a Virginian (certainly Van Buren's exact sentiments), and the New Yorker gratefully accepted the appointment. Thomas Ritchie and other Virginians thought Tazewell should have had first place in the cabinet. Without a doubt his qualifications were better than Van Buren's. He had served on the Foreign Relations Committee for many years, his understanding of maritime law was second to none, and his service on the claims commission had given him valuable experience. Perhaps Tazewell wanted the position, but he never expressed this wish, even to his closest friends or members of his family. Jackson did consider the possibility of Tazewell's heading the War Department, replacing another Virginian, James Barbour, but if a concrete offer was made, Tazewell obviously was not interested. The diplomatic assignment in England, however, was a different matter, and he postponed his decision until after Jackson's inauguration.[30]

The second session of the Twentieth Congress adjourned on March 3. The following day was Jackson's, and the weather cooperated beautifully. From winter, the city suddenly burst into spring, and the streets were crowded with "a great concourse of strangers." Louisa and Sally had wanted to be in Washington for the event, and Tazewell willingly consented, with a warning that the crowd probably would be immense and they would be put to many inconveniences. The pleasure they would derive from their visit, he was certain, would not compensate them for the many "disagreeables" to which they would have to submit, but he remarked to Ann, "the scene is a novelty and not often presented in this country, and until they know by experience how idle and empty a pageant it is, they will certainly magnify its pleasures & overlook all its inconveniences." The Wickhams also planned to be on hand "to see the show."[31]

Perhaps they were all in the Senate gallery at eleven o'clock in the morning when the oath of office was administered to Vice-President Calhoun by Senator Samuel Smith, president pro tempore. Calhoun, in turn, swore in the new and re-elected senators. Among them were Tazewell, White, Hayne of South Carolina, and John Bell of Tennessee, and several

others. At eleven-thirty Jackson, tall and impressive, entered
the Senate chamber, followed by foreign dignitaries resplendent in their colorful costumes and members of the Supreme
Court in their somber black. At high noon the entire company
adjourned to the eastern portico of the Capitol where, facing
an immense crowd, Jackson delivered his inaugural address,
much of which pleased Tazewell. In administering the laws of
Congress, Jackson promised to keep steadily in view the limitations as well as the extent of executive power. Jackson also
acknowledged the rights of the states, promising a proper respect for those sovereign members of the Union, saying he
would take care not to confound the powers they had reserved
to themselves with those they had granted to the national government. In regard to the tariff, he called for a spirit of
equity, caution, and compromise. The great interests of agriculture, commerce, and manufacturing, he believed, should
receive equal favor, the only exception being the encouragement of any products essential to national independence. Internal improvements and the diffusion of knowledge he considered important, but only if promoted by constitutional acts
of the federal government. He declared his firm belief in liberty of conscience and of the press and pledged his administration to a just and liberal policy toward Indian tribes, with
humane and considerate attention to their rights and wants,
"consistent with the habits of our Government and the feelings of our people." To implement the program outlined,
Jackson promised to select men of diligence and talent.[32]

The inauguration was followed by a special session of Congress to confirm Jackson's cabinet appointments. This was
concluded promptly and without opposition. Van Buren officially became secretary of state; Samuel D. Ingham of Pennsylvania, secretary of the treasury; John Eaton of Tennessee,
secretary of war; John P. Branch of North Carolina, secretary
of the navy; John M. Berrien of Georgia, attorney general; W.
T. Berry of Kentucky, postmaster general. Although for the
first time since the nation's beginning Virginia was ignored,
the South was well represented. Only Ingham, however, was
considered a "Calhoun man." In the struggle between Van
Buren and the vice-president as to which would guide the
Jackson administration and eventually succeed the old gen-

eral, Van Buren already had a distinct advantage. The composition of the cabinet indicated that the wily New Yorker had been busy. Nevertheless, there were many who agreed with Webster that the majority of the appointments were incredible. Wirt announced the arrival of "the millennium of minnows," as he happily fled from the contention and confusion to a law practice in Baltimore. Margaret Bayard Smith, whose usually agile political mind failed to comprehend the Van Buren cabinet coup, reported that the New Yorker surely would not consent to head the mediocre (or worse) cabinet, but, she concluded, "if he declines it will be difficult to find another equal to the place, for Tazewell of Virginia is to go to England."[33]

But Tazewell was not to go to England. Ann's determined opposition caused him to send Jackson a letter of refusal. Family responsibilities, he said, precluded his accepting a foreign assignment anywhere. This, Tazewell thought, would end the matter. Instead, an immediate reply from the chief executive summoned him to the President's House for a conference the same morning. During the meeting Jackson used all his persuasive powers to influence Tazewell to accept the post in England. "The application," Tazewell told Wickham, "was made with so much warmth of kind feelings towards me personally, and accompanied with such liberal offers as to powers, instructions, and accommodations of every other kind, that I could not find it in my heart to repeat a blunt refusal at once." As the special session of the Senate was about to close, Tazewell asked for time to give the proposal mature consideration upon his return to Norfolk.[34]

Discussions between Ann and her husband undoubtedly were long and painful, and in the end Tazewell felt he must repeat his refusal. The state of his private affairs, he informed Jackson, was such that he could not accept the position offered. He had given serious thought to how he might have functioned, however, had he been able to accept. Tactfully, he reminded Jackson that the statesmen of Great Britain did not view his accession to the presidency with very kind feelings. "If they do not seek to embarrass you, they will at least treat with much indifference, any overtures made by the U.S. to re-open the negotiations with them." An advisable approach,

Tazewell thought, would be to initiate discussions with France with the purpose of concluding a liberal Franco-American commercial treaty. Meanwhile, the American minister in England, fully informed of all developments, should be directed to hint at the proposed treaty "upon some fit occasion, in the presence of the British Minister, and my life upon it, the tone and temper of the British cabinet towards us will be at once changed." British statesmen often were cautious, cold, and reserved by nature, almost encrusted with ice, Tazewell observed, and the American minister to the Court of Saint James's should be a man of intelligence, amiable manners, and quick and sure observation; a person who would not be offensive, but one who could hold his ground. Tazewell highly recommended for Jackson's consideration John Berrien, the new attorney general. "His present situation marks him to the world as one high in your confidence; and the appointment of one of your cabinet will be the best pledge you can offer to Great Britain of the zeal and sincerity of your wishes towards her."[35]

Upon receiving Tazewell's final refusal, Jackson expressed keen regret. "The settlement of our differences and the formation of a commercial treaty with Great Britain on the broad principles of justice and reciprocity, are objects which I have much at heart, and I know of no one so well qualified in every respect to effect them as yourself." He thanked Tazewell for his views, which he termed sound, and reserved the right to seek his advice on future Anglo-American diplomatic affairs. Jackson also immediately wrote to the attorney general, asking if he would be willing to change positions. Berrien declined, and the appointment went to another Van Buren satellite, Louis McLane of Delaware. This greatly upset Calhoun, who was deeply disappointed by Tazewell's rejection of the key diplomatic post, which, he believed, would have given the Virginian an opportunity to deal a death blow to the high tariff policy of the United States. Now, a political appointee would fill this highly sensitive position, when qualifications alone, without regard to political outlook, should have been the determining factor.[36]

Like Calhoun, Wickham thought it not improbable that Tazewell in England might have regained the ground "lost by the blundering (to say no worse) of the last administration," but understanding Tazewell's devotion to his family and his state, Wickham did not urge him to cross the Atlantic for a prolonged stay. Tazewell did not close the door completely on the possibility of participating for a limited time in the formulation of an Anglo-American commercial agreement, especially one involving the West Indies trade. Perhaps later, when the necessary groundwork was accomplished, he would be willing to do this, but he could not leave his wife and children "merely to witness an empty pageant" or for any reasons other than the attainment of some consequential object for his country.[37] Actually, a multitude of personal, domestic, political, and moral considerations induced him to refuse Jackson's current offer. In all honesty, he confessed to Wickham, he really never hesitated for a single moment but appeared to temporize only to avoid the charge of precipitate obstinacy and to escape from the too ardent solicitations of some of those who held high place in his esteem. Even so, when he announced his decision, many of his political and some of his personal friends severely censured him, but he still believed he had taken the correct action. In his own mind he was not sure of Jackson or Jackson's followers, and he wanted time to watch and weigh the actions of the new regime. His own future course would be governed by the developments of the next few months, the characters of the men, and their handling of events. For the present he wanted to stand apart, avoiding entanglements with government officials who, at first glance, seemed not entirely trustworthy. He needed time to cultivate his garden and think his own thoughts, to plant seeds in the ground and watch them grow.[38]

## Chapter X

# *The Virginia*
# *Constitutional Convention*

In Norfolk, April was cold and threatening, and spring came late to the Virginia Tidewater. "A few apricot trees blooming very slowly and reluctantly, with not a leaf to accompany the blossoms, is the only sign of Spring my garden exhibits," Tazewell commented sadly to Wickham, "unless a small mess of asparagus shoots, which we cut yesterday for the first time, may also be considered an indication of its approach." Having received a tiny parcel of casaba melon seeds from a naval officer recently returned from Smyrna, he was anxious to have Wickham plant some in the Richmond soil to see if they would grow better there than in Norfolk.[1]

A late frost on the Eastern Shore was hard on his crops, some of which were experimental. From products designed entirely for the home market, Tazewell this year, on the advice of his overseer, varied his husbandry and planted for the New York market 70,000 hills of sweet potatoes and five acres of Irish potatoes. Later he hoped to add green peas and melons. "In short," he explained to Wickham, "I shall become a horticulturist upon a large scale instead of an agriculturist." However, he did not intend to abandon his corn and oats crops altogether, at least until he was certain the change would be profitable. There were other modifications. In June the Tazewells presented John, now twenty-two, with the five-hundred-acre Sandhills plantation near Norfolk, and relieved of the responsibility of one plantation, Tazewell could devote more of his limited time to his Eastern Shore horticulture.[2] But the summer of 1829 brought many distractions.

These were restless times in Virginia. Western demands for constitutional revision reached crisis proportions in the 1827–28 legislative session, forcing the General Assembly to pass an act referring to the freeholders the question of whether or not a convention should be called. The result was an affirmative vote of 21,896 to 16,637, with Norfolk casting its lot with the majority.[3] Thomas Ritchie, who earlier had reluctantly joined the Jacksonian movement, was one of the most vocal advocates of the peoples' rights, the triumph of democratic principles. "Whatever some birds of evil omen may utter," he declared in the *Richmond Enquirer,* "we consider a convention as certain, and not accompanied by any extraordinary difficulty. The people will it, and their wills must be obliged." Philip Doddridge of Brooke County, Tazewell's adversary of the 1817 convention controversy, had lost none of his ardor, and it was he who called for an extralegal convention, without legislative interposition or aid, if the General Assembly failed to approve the measure. "He has become a finished demagogue," Theodore Miller told Tazewell. "I fear that this firebrand will produce no little evil."[4]

Unable to ignore the referendum or to stem the reformers' peremptory insistence to be heard, enough conservatives preferred to acquiesce rather than be faced with a rebellion against constituted authority. Consequently, after a quarter-century of debate and deliberate delay, the state Senate passed a convention bill, 17 to 7, followed by a house vote of 114 to 93, specifying the election of four delegates from each of the state's twenty-four senatorial districts. Among the major demands of the reformers were the abolition of property qualifications for voting, universal white manhood suffrage, representation based on white population, direct election of the governor, abolition of the Council of State, and elimination of the county courts or their extensive patronage. In short, the ingrained Virginia aristocracy was to be asked, or forced, to recognize the rise of the common man and the right of the majority to rule.[5]

Tazewell in 1829 was no more in favor of a convention than he had been in 1817, but the intervening twelve years had made him more philosophical. Wickham, on the other hand, was upset and apprehensive. After dining with John Marshall and other eastern leaders, he reported to Tazewell that "many members most opposed to a convention and friends to freehold suffrage and the protection of slave property, are of the

opinion that when the constitution is formed it must on immutable principles be submitted not to the freeholders only,
but to the people at large." This frightened Wickham. Would
this not portend the destruction of eastern interests, the
plundering of their property by raising their taxes and eman-
cipating their slaves? In reply, Tazewell told Wickham not to
despair, for the whole convention could well bog down in a
debate over abstractions. If the delegates chose to investigate
the principle of society, to discuss the question whether the
right of property was natural, social, or civil, he felt there was
no reason why either he or Wickham should be disturbed. All
speculative notions of that ilk could be regarded as harmless.
As to Wickham's fear that property, especially slave property,
would be obliterated, "is this seriously to be apprehended in
such a country as Virginia now is?" Of the state's 105 counties,
there was not one without slaves; in forty-three counties the
slave population was greater than the white; and a fair majority of the members of the General Assembly represented large
slaveholding districts. Even if representation in the legislature
was based on the white population, the relative strength of the
area east of the Blue Ridge would remain the same; and if the
slaveholding parts of the state acted together, they would have
the ability to do as they pleased. Although opposed to the
convention idea from the beginning, Tazewell did not believe
that a change in the basis for representation or in suffrage
qualifications would mean a threat to slave property. Tazewell's optimism surprised Wickham, who was positive that in
no distant day the western people would become the masters
of Virginians residing east of the Blue Ridge, an object "they
certainly have in view."[6]

John Tazewell's friend Hugh Blair Grigsby agreed with
Wickham. If western reformers succeeded in kicking up a
fuss, easterners should exclaim with one voice, "Depart from
me." If the right of suffrage was extended to the propertyless,
as even some people of the east advocated, the west, within a
few years, would have unlimited command over all the resources of the state. Then, "would that slaves were the only
article on which their heavy taxation would fall." The very day
the freeholders of Virginia agreed to call a convention, the
east was doomed. "The new constitution, be it good or bad,

our say so will have no weight." The only safeguard against oppression was to divide the commonwealth along the line of the Blue Ridge Mountains.[7]

Tazewell's philosophical composure was somewhat shaken when he found he was to be a delegate from the district that included the counties of Princess Anne, Norfolk, and Nansemond, and Norfolk borough. The call for the convention set aside the residency requirement for the delegates, and Tazewell was approached by several other districts, including Greensville, Williamsburg, and Richmond, but he had declined to stand for any of them. In his own district he was not consulted and thus was given no opportunity to refuse. He was mortified and astonished to find himself elected, he told Wickham, but being elected, he supposed he was compelled to serve; however, he anticipated no pleasure from such service. "I am too old now to be amused with building myself or admiring the structure by others of castles in the air, *or lighthouses in the skies.*" Perhaps, he conjectured, passion for notoriety and rage for innovation were inevitable in a republic, but he was weary of observing such antics and cynical about the motives of those demanding a convention. He was sure there would be as many new constitutions prepared as there were districts in the state, some to suit the market, others to perpetuate the names of their authors, and as the state could use but one of "these patent inventions" at a time, he presumed there would have to be an annual convention in order to give each of them a fair experiment. Apparently Tazewell had little understanding of the political aspirations of the people at large. To him the demands of the west were those of ambitious self-seeking individuals with no concern for the political, social, or economic stability of the commonwealth. Wickham found some solace in the fact that his friend would be at the convention. "I do not expect that you can stop the wheels of revolution but you may perhaps aid essentially in regulating their movement and checking their velocity."[8]

Tazewell hoped to spend a few days in Richmond in July or August discussing convention strategy with Wickham, but a visit to Norfolk by President Jackson interfered with his plans. Following that event, Louisa's ill health and Sally's persistent cough caused Tazewell to take his two older daughters on a "northwardly excursion" to New York and Saratoga Springs, with the possibility of going on to Niagara and Quebec. To avoid the worst of the sickly season they did not return to Norfolk until October 1, only four days before Tazewell was due in Richmond for the opening of the convention. He planned to arrive several days late, but Benjamin Watkins Leigh, a major opponent of western demands, objected: "*We shall want every member at his post from the word go. The body will no doubt be organized the first day. If Mr. Madison shall decline to serve as President (as there is the strongest reason to believe he will) Mr. Monroe will probably decline the office too, and I know the Chief Justice will*—so, we shall have to choose out of the younger men. . . . The committees will be named on the 3rd day at farthest; and I want to have *you* in full view of the chair when they are named.*"[9] Tazewell complied, and on Sunday, October 4, he boarded the steamboat for Richmond along with two other delegates from the Norfolk area, Robert B. Taylor and George Loyall. Also in the party was young Hugh Grigsby, eager to observe the workings of the constitution-makers. In Richmond, Tazewell and Grigsby found lodgings at the Eagle, while Taylor and Loyall "pushed off to Richardson's."[10]

The following day the convention assembled in the legislative hall of the Capitol, the same room where years earlier Tazewell sat as a member of the grand jury to hear the government's evidence for the indictment of Aaron Burr. Again, as in 1807, there was talent in abundance. Among the personages who, due either to past or present prestige, dominated the convention were James Madison, James Monroe, John Marshall, John Tyler, Tazewell, John Randolph, Philip P. Barbour, and William B. Giles. Robert B. Taylor was an important, although short-term, factor in the proceedings. From the Eastern Shore, Abel Parker Upshur bolstered the conservative forces, while the champion of the west, Philip Doddridge, brilliantly defended the reformers' cause. John R. Cooke of Frederick, Chapman Johnson of Augusta, Charles F. Mercer of Loudoun, William Fitzhugh of Fairfax, and James Pleasants of Goochland ably participated in this last major debate of the waning Jeffersonian era on the nature of government and the spirit of the law. Contrary to Leigh's prophecy, Monroe, upon

Madison's refusal to accept the nomination, was unanimously elected president, and he did not decline. Grigsby thought him unfit to preside, but he struggled on until ill health forced him to relinquish the gavel to Philip P. Barbour.[11]

On opening day and throughout the weeks that followed, crowds hoping to see some of the important participants blocked the paths leading to the Capitol, filled the galleries, and occupied vacant seats on the convention floor. For John Tazewell's amusement, Grigsby described the scene as one member of the throng assumed the responsibility of pointing out the "lions" as they arrived for the first session. " 'Don't you see,' says he, 'that *there* little man with his head foundered? Well, that's Madison. But look yonder,' says the same Mr. Index, 'don't you see that *there* man by the stove?' The fellow for whose benefit these questions were being propounded, after gazing as if he were really looking at a *sure enough* lion, answered in the affirmative; 'Well then,' says the fellow, 'that's Tazewell.' "[12]

From the onset of the convention Tazewell actively was involved. As a member of the committee of twenty-four (one from each senatorial district) appointed to "enquire into the best mode of proceeding," he steadfastly recommended amending the old constitution rather than discarding it completely in favor of a new one. Although his plan was rejected by the committee, he brought his motion to the convention as a whole and spoke at length in support of it. A number of voters, he declared, wanted a thoroughgoing revision of the constitution, while others, a rather large minority, believed it "better to bear the ills we have, than to fly to others that we know not of." Tazewell suggested a compromise. He also objected to the plan adopted by the committee of twenty-four of appointing several separate committees to consider specific aspects of a new constitution, such as a committee on the bill of rights, one on each of the three branches of the government, and another to devise a new constitution based on resolutions adopted by the convention. Having the work done by select committees would leave the majority of the members of the convention with nothing to do while they awaited committee reports. Also, he believed the committees could not work isolated from one another. Although the executive, legislative, and judicial branches of any government had to maintain a separation and balance of powers, "like the colors of the rainbow, they run into each other, and man has not yet found that government in which these separate branches are not in some measure connected." Despite his pleas to the convention, the organizational recommendation of the committee of twenty-four was adopted, and Tazewell was appointed to the committee on the legislature.[13]

After only two weeks Tazewell was "heartily sick" of everything. The convention, he told John, "drags on very heavily. Nothing is yet done, or likely to be done speedily, but all signs of the times indicate a most determined purpose to upturn everything from the very foundation, and a sufficient force perfectly organized for the completion of such a purpose." Initially he thought the convention would be in session for, at best, a few weeks, but now he knew otherwise. The limited amount of clothing he had brought with him was becoming quite shabby. Would John please send him the coats and trousers he ordered while in New York as soon as they arrived in Norfolk? Tazewell complained of his accommodations and of the company with whom he was forced to associate. "If you were here I could get on better, I believe, but there is nothing to attract you to this place at present, nor will there be until next week, I think, when if you wish to see what is going on you had better come up."[14]

Repeatedly Tazewell opposed the west's determination to base representation in the state legislature on white population only. If some large counties were underrepresented and smaller ones overrepresented, he suggested consolidating the smaller counties until the very least assumed a proper size or dividing the larger counties, wherever necessary. Regardless of the method, care should be taken to avoid the creation of a too large and unwieldy legislative body, and representation should not "be based on numbers of any sort *exclusively*, or taxation on property of any sort *exclusively*, or anything else *exclusively*." "Gentlemen assert that according to an eternal rule of right, the majority must govern, and then instantly exclude from the enumeration, all except *white* persons; so making the eternal rules of justice and reason, to depend not upon the condition of the population as bond or free, but

upon the accidental circumstance of the colour of their skins."
He could not comprehend the force of the argument that
disregarded all other than the free white population in establishing the basis of representation. Women, minors, aliens,
and many others who were not to be admitted to suffrage
were to be counted provided they be white, but no others,
although they be free, virtuous, intelligent, and as rich as any
white man in the whole state. He understood why slaves might
be excluded from the enumeration, as they could be considered property rather than persons, but free Negroes, in his
estimation, should be counted. In taking this stand Tazewell
was not championing the rights of the free blacks but was
attempting to point out what he considered to be the absurdi-
ties of basing representation on white population exclusively.[15]

From the Norfolk area Robert B. Taylor alone backed the
proposal for extending the right of franchise to more than the
freeholders. He had come to the convention with an open
mind, but upon examining the issues and listening to the arguments, he realized that the westerners truly had justifica-
tions for their grievances. When, early in the course of the
convention, the bill of rights was under discussion, Taylor
introduced resolutions calling for representation based on
white population and for white manhood suffrage. These
were matters of right, he contended, but the convention did
not agree, and his resolutions were tabled. Many of his Norfolk constituents, unhappy with his stand, instructed him to
modify his views; instead, Taylor resigned, explaining to the
convention: "Believing (as I conscientiously do) that the measure I am instructed to support is hostile to free institutions;
destructive to equality of right among our citizens; and intro-
ductive of a principle that a minority on account of superior
wealth, shall rule the majority of the qualified voters of the
State, I should be guilty of moral treason against the liberty of
my native land, if I allowed myself to be the instrument by
which this mischief is effected." As he was on the spot and
highly available, Hugh Grigsby was chosen to replace Taylor.[16]

In several of Tazewell's discourses he challenged those who
championed white manhood suffrage and at the same time
professed to believe in the natural right of a majority to govern. The two, Tazewell pointed out, were not one and the

same; they were not even compatible. Furthermore, the "liberalism" currently espoused by those who demanded "majority rule" was not the liberalism to which Tazewell had been devoted since early manhood. He was skeptical of the masses and saw in the growing strength of the propertyless and the uneducated a threat to cherished freedoms and minority rights. An erosion of toleration, he felt, was in the making, and undoubtedly he would have agreed with Lord Acton's observation that an intolerant majority possessed the latent power to destroy any minority which dared oppose it. "From the absolute will of the entire people," Acton warned, "there is no appeal, no redemption, no refuge, but tyranny." Tazewell feared democratic despotism as much as he feared the destructive potential of any other power monopoly. Instead, Tazewell thought the proper government a blend of various forces in a society, a reconciler of opposing elements that needed to be restrained, checked, or balanced. Capital and labor were the great components of the prosperity of every state. Each was necessary to the existence of the other, but from the beginning there had been a struggle between the two. Neither could be given undue influence in government; however, a government which respected the rights of both capital and labor would receive the support of both. Balance, order, and reason were to Tazewell the rudiments of good government.[17]

One December day, with Calhoun in attendance, Tazewell offered to the convention cogent reasons for rejecting the demand for direct election of the governor. The people, he conceded, were, of course, the sole legitimate source of power, but under consideration was the mode by which that power should be exercised. Tazewell disapproved of calling on the people to elect officials except in cases where they could do so understandingly, as in the choice of local representatives and members of the state legislature or the House of Representatives. If the populace were to choose all state officials, either numerous elections would be necessary, and the people would react negatively to being summoned frequently to the polls, or the voters would be compelled to elect all officers, state and national, at the same time. In the latter case, Tazewell warned, "the choice of the most important will invariably control all the others; the smaller offices will be lost sight of and swallowed up in the importance of the great one." Consequently, he advised continuation of the practice of having the legislature elect the governor, but with the mandatory provision that each legislator record his vote, thereby giving his constituents the opportunity to hold him accountable for his action.[18]

Along with other conservatives Tazewell argued in favor of retaining intact the county courts, those powerful entities composed of the justices of the peace in each county who sat together to hear significant cases. The courts were self-perpetuating and, as a general rule, were responsible for selecting legislative candidates and advising the governor on county appointments and the General Assembly on the selection of United States senators. They also set rates for local tax assessments. Able and interested men sat on the courts, and the system worked well, but efficiency, the reformers charged, did not compensate for its undemocratic aspects. The county courts, Tazewell agreed, did control considerable patronage; however, it was far better to have such influence widely distributed among the various counties than to have it concentrated in Richmond. For fifty-four years, he maintained, the governor had had little patronage to dispense, and the effects had been most happy. Virginia had not been plagued with excessive logrolling, conspiracies, or excitement in selecting an executive, but if county courts were obliterated and patronage was placed in the hands of the governor, the office would become so desirable that a gubernatorial election would produce "cabals and commotion throughout the community."[19]

In debates on the inviolability of judicial tenure Tazewell clashed head-on with Chief Justice Marshall. The controversy arose when Marshall objected to a suggested constitutional provision giving the legislature the right to abolish certain state courts and thereby terminate the judgeships involved. To this Marshall voiced decided opposition. He still smarted over the action of an 1802 Jeffersonian Congress which repealed the Judiciary Act of 1801, resulting in the removal of several Federalist judges. For over a quarter of a century this had infuriated him, and he had no wish to encourage the legislature of his state to take similar action. The congressional repeal, Tazewell argued, had been right and proper and completely within the province of the legislative branch, for as the United States Constitution clearly stated, "the judicial power of the United States shall be vested in one Supreme Court, and in such inferior courts as the Congress may from time to time ordain and establish." If Congress could establish inferior courts, Congress could disestablish them. Likewise, the constitution of the commonwealth of Virginia should recognize two categories of courts. A Supreme Court of Appeals and the county courts should be designated as constitutional courts, whose existence could not be terminated by the state legislature, just as Congress could not, without a constitutional amendment, abolish the Supreme Court of the United States. All other Virginia courts should be designated inferior courts, to be created or abolished by the legislature whenever the judicial system was in need of reform.[20]

Marshall countered by insisting that all judges should retain their offices, even if the courts over which they presided were abolished. This was absolutely necessary for the protection of an independent judiciary, and he charged Tazewell with suggesting that the whole criminal jurisdiction of the state be entrusted to judges removable from office at the pleasure of the legislature. "What would then be the condition of the court," demanded the chief justice, "should the legislature prosecute a man with an earnest wish to convict him?" Then addressing himself directly at Tazewell, "Will the gentleman recollect that in order to secure the administration of justice, judges of capacity, and of legal knowledge are indispensable? And how is he to get them? How are such men to be drawn off from a lucrative practice? Will any gentleman of the profession whose practice will secure him a comfortable independence, leave that practice, and come to take an office which may be taken from him the next day? You may invite them, but they will not come." Marshall, at his oratorical best, made his final appeal: "I have always thought, from my earliest youth till now, that the greatest scourge an angry Heaven ever inflicted upon an ungrateful and sinning people, was an ignorant, corrupt, or a dependent judiciary. Will you draw down this curse upon Virginia?"[21]

Not intimidated by the formidable Marshall, Tazewell persistenly pursued the subject. No one, he said, was more at-

tached to an independent judiciary than he, and he firmly
upheld the inviolability of constitutional courts; however, as a
practical matter, the legislature must have the authority to
reorganize the inferior court system as conditions and needs
dictated. Years later Grigsby recalled that "Tazewell fairly
'sunk the boat' under the Chief Justice."[22] In reality, the provision accepted by the convention was a compromise. According
to the new constitution, judicial power was to be vested in a
Supreme Court of Appeals, in such superior courts as the
legislature might establish, in the county courts and the justices of the peace, and in corporation courts and magistrates
belonging to the corporate body. The judges of the Supreme
Court of Appeals and of the superior courts were to hold their
offices during good behavior. The jurisdiction of the corporation courts was to be regulated by law, but no law abolishing
any court could be construed as depriving a judge of his office
unless two-thirds of the members present in each house concurred. The General Assembly was to have the authority to
assign other judicial duties to judges of courts abolished by
less than a two-thirds vote of the members present.[23]

A select committee of seven, including Madison, Benjamin
Watkins Leigh, Marshall, Tazewell, Doddridge, John R. Cooke,
and Chapman Johnson, drafted the proposed constitution,
which on January 14, 1830, was adopted by the convention, 55
to 40. Shortly before the meeting adjourned sine die, Tazewell
supported John Randolph's resolution to present the new constitution for ratification only to those qualified to vote under
the old document, the freeholders. The resolution failed by a
sizable majority, and those qualified to vote under the new
provisions were to be allowed to express their approval or disapproval. The following day the convention proceedings
ended.[24] The 1830 constitution took a few faltering steps in the
direction of reform, but the west was severely disappointed.
Representation based on white population was rejected. Instead, the General Assembly was to be comprised of a fixed
number of members: 134 for the House of Delegates and 32
for the Senate, to be divided among the various sections of the
state.[25] The right of franchise was moderately broadened.
Whereas the old constitution extended suffrage only to freeholders (white male citizens over the age of twenty-one who

owned twenty-five acres of settled land, fifty acres of unsettled land, or a one quarter-acre lot in town), the new constitution, in addition, included white adult males who owned land worth twenty-five dollars, leased land at an annual rate of twenty dollars for five years, or were renters who for one year paid taxes in the district where they resided. "A middle-class democracy" supposedly was the end result of the convention's proposal, a "noble advance," and certainly the improvement was substantial. Yet, under the new constitution, an estimated one-third of the white adult male citizens of the commonwealth were ineligible to vote.[26] In addition, the governor was still to be elected by the General Assembly, but triennially rather than annually; the governor's council, although reduced in size, was retained in an advisory capacity; and the county court system not only survived but was strengthened.[27]

In the referendum the new constitution was accepted by a vote of 26,055 to 15,563. The Trans-Allegheny region overwhelmingly rejected it; in Doddridge's Brooke County not one vote was cast in its favor, and only a very few affirmative votes came from Cabell, Giles, Grayson, Greenbrier, Harrison, Randolph, Tazewell, and Tyler counties of the west. Norfolk County, as was anticipated, approved the constitution by a large majority, 230 to 23, and Norfolk borough by a vote of 198 to 38. Temporarily, at least, dismemberment of the state was averted, but before many months had passed a protest meeting was held in Wheeling to discuss the possibility of annexing northwestern Virginia to Maryland. Several western newspapers carried articles and editorials recommending the formation of a new state.[28]

For more than fourteen years, as he observed the growing momentum of the west's insistence on change, Tazewell had dreaded the modifications this would bring to the entire structure of Virginia. He believed that the maintenance of good government and civilized society depended on the talent, virtue, and education of responsible citizens. These attributes, along with a deep and abiding loyalty to community and state, an interest and concern for the area in which one lived, a stake in society, created and perpetuated an enlightened body politic. Unlike many Old Republicans, Tazewell did not equate excellence in government or society solely with an agrarian economy,[29] but he was convinced that the rise of the masses threatened minority interests, that for the good of society people of talent and virtue had to be protected lest they be overwhelmed by the irresponsible majority. Similarly, if states' rights were not respected and maintained, the South would be crushed by a northern majority. The masses would seize control, and a great leveling process would ensue. Knowledge, virtue, investments, and contributions to state and nation would be thrust aside by king numbers, and an overall deterioration of the country would follow. Another worry was the West's preference for a strong national government which could provide that section with necessary internal improvements. A preponderant central government, controlled by an unchecked numerical majority, could destroy the South with high tariffs and other devices of economic exploitation. Although Tazewell was not contemptuous of the reformers, as was Randolph of Roanoke, he was equally as determined to prevent the "Jacobins" from inflicting "a deeper wound on Republican Government than it ever experienced before."[30] Power, from whatever source, had to be kept within bounds.

## Chapter XI

# *Rift in the*

# *Jacksonian Ranks*

Detained in Richmond by the Virginia convention, Tazewell did not arrive in Washington until the first week in February 1830. There he found the Senate occupied in listening to anti-climactic comments on the Foote Resolution, the spark that in January touched off the Webster-Hayne debate on the pros and cons of nullification. Webster, dramatically calling upon patriots to stand fast against the "treachery" of the nullifiers, intimated that the South sought to destroy the American dream, leaving only the "broken and dishonored fragments of a once glorious Union," the land rent with civil feuds and drenched in fraternal blood. "Liberty and Union, now and forever, one and inseparable," was his stinging challenge to the South.[1]

In his depiction of the scene, artist George P. A. Healy placed Tazewell in the foreground, intently listening to Webster's historic utterance. The Virginia senator, of course, was not present,[2] but his reaction was as explosive as if he had heard the words firsthand. Webster's charges, he told John, were unfounded and unfair. Furthermore, even if they were true, New England had no cause to assume a "holier than thou" attitude. Tazewell remembered all too clearly Massachusetts's secession tendencies during the War of 1812. Had Webster so soon forgotten the Hartford Convention? Too upset to comment on the specifics of the debate, Tazewell said he had to wait until "it shall become purified of the filth with which it is at present defiled."[3]

Tazewell was not in a happy frame of mind. He had been "summoned almost peremptorily to Washington" to lend support to the Senate's approval of several of Jackson's recess appointments, many of which were obviously party payoffs.

With the Senate almost evenly divided for and against the names submitted, the Jacksonians needed every possible vote. Tazewell came, but with a determination to resist the pressure of the Jackson machine. Both he and John Tyler were disgusted by the president's (or Van Buren's) inexorable resolve to reward or purchase the support of the nation's press by appointing newspaper editors to lucrative governmental positions. The use of the press for political purposes was by no means a unique practice, but the Jacksonians' creation of a "vast nation-wide newspaper system" to insure the election of their candidate went beyond anything previously attempted. During the months between his inauguration and the convening of the Twenty-first Congress, Jackson named a number of vigorous and friendly newsmen to well-paying offices: Amos Kendall, Isaac Hill, Henry Lee, Mordecai Manuel Noah, and others. The Virginia senators opposed them all, acting "upon the principle that the press, the great instrument of enlightenment to the people, should not be subjected, through its conductors, to rewards or punishments; and that the Sedition law was not more obnoxious than a system of rewards to be doled out from the public treasury by means of public office." Even Thomas Ritchie, now well on the way to becoming a devoted follower of Martin Van Buren, was alarmed by the blatant attempt to bring journalists under the control of the executive. "It is with great reluctance I speak upon this point," he told Van Buren, but too many such appointments had been made. "Is it not time to stop?"[4]

As the Senate day after day sat in secret executive session to consider the nominees, Tazewell became increasingly disenchanted with the Jacksonians, and to Wickham he wrote of his gloomy forebodings for the fate of the nation. Again Wickham urged patience. Governments are like individuals, he told his friend, and "though subject to disorders that to all appearances must prove fatal, sometimes survive them and often preserve a sickly existence in spite of them, long after the time which according to all calculations they should cease to exist." Of course, much depended on Jackson's real attitude toward the tariff and internal improvements, and, Wickham admitted, this was impossible to predict. However, he reminded Tazewell, "we cannot forget that the southern states are his most steady supporters." Certainly Jackson's general course of action could not be as destructive to the South as was that of Adams.[5]

But Tazewell saw no abatement of what he considered to be injurious actions, and by spring he was "utterly and painfully disgusted" with the political trickery in Washington. The Jefferson Birthday dinner of April 13, 1830, was to him simply another indication of the fanaticism abroad in the land, and he was inclined to wish a plague on Jackson, Van Buren, and Calhoun alike. The dinner, Tazewell reported to Wickham, was purely political, "given to subserve a party purpose," and he refused to attend. Precisely what the "party purpose" was he did not say, but undoubtedly those in attendance had varying and sometimes conflicting objectives in mind. There were some who wished to hasten a South-West alliance, and what could be more apropos than to use a dinner in honor of Jefferson as a springboard for launching a program of tariff reduction, cheap lands, and states' rights. Jackson was led to believe that several southerners intended to convert the occasion into a celebration of nullification. Primed to expect disunion sentiments, the president distinctly heard them in Hayne's reply to a toast, as well as in milder expressions by others from the South. Some say Jackson scribbled his reply on the back of the printed toast list. When the last of the twenty-four prearranged salutes had been made, he rose, lifted his glass, and looked angrily at Calhoun, the instigator (as Van Buren had convinced the president) of nullification, discord, and disunion. Jackson's statement was brief but forceful: "Our *Federal Union—It must be preserved.*" Again, as in Webster's reply to Hayne a few months earlier, the entire South, by implication, was made to appear unpatriotic, unanimous in its support for nullification, a nurturer of disunionism. Only this time the man who drew the inference was not an ultranational northerner but a fellow southerner in whom his compatriots had placed their hopes for understanding and fairer treatment. Calhoun's loud and clear response was almost a reflex action: "The Union—next to our liberty most dear. May we always remember that it can only be preserved by distributing equally the benefits and burthens of the Union."[6]

Jackson's willingness to follow Van Buren's lead seemed to Tazewell an act of betrayal, an indication of bad faith on the president's part. "My hopes which were not very extravagant, I think, are all blighted," he confided to Wickham. "I feel that I am much better fitted for my own fireside than anywhere else." He had resisted the cajolery of the Jackson party organization and now expected to be either vilified, traduced, and abused or subjected to bribes. In the Senate, "I hold the balance in my hand; and if I had a personal wish to gratify, it need but be expressed to be satisfied. But I have none." Faced with a multiplicity of problems, he wished to be steady and meant to be just, but he doubted his own discretion. In endorsing Jackson he had made a serious mistake. Now he had to try to stand his ground and do all which he thought a Virginia senator ought to do, "though it be to beard a lion in his lair," but he wished Wickham or some other close friend were near to give him advice, for, he sadly admitted, "my objects you will all approve, my resolution none of you need doubt, but my judgment you have all much cause to distrust." Yet he promised to stay on in Washington. "Believe, however, the watch upon the deck in such weather is not pleasant to a contented old man, whose only ungratified wish is to spend the few glasses he has to run, in great tranquillity and calm repose."[7]

As Democrats rushed to join either the Van Buren or the Calhoun clique, polarization became acute, and it was difficult to maintain a middle position. This made Tazewell's situation exceedingly uncomfortable, for he was determined to join forces with neither group. "As to the succession to the Presidency," John Quincy Adams observed, Tazewell "is for Calhoun in preference to Van Buren." Ritchie also saw him as a strong advocate of the South Carolinian, but in reality he was as disheartened by the vice-president's dangerous nullification ideas as by Van Buren's disposition to use anyone, violate any principle, betray any trust in order to achieve his own goals.[8]

In the midst of the busy session news arrived of the serious illness of Sarah Nivison. Tazewell was devoted to his mother-in-law, and he knew Ann, not recovered from her despondency, would need him during this worrisome period, but he was reluctant to leave the capital. Several items important to the welfare of the South were pending, and the Senate vote, he feared, would again be closely divided. John was to keep him informed of Mrs. Nivison's condition, sending a letter by every boat, "since I have made up my mind to come down the first moment I can learn that I ought to do so." Meanwhile, he used his time well, supporting Benton's bill to graduate the price of public lands (which passed the Senate, 24 to 22, but was killed in the House) and voting in favor of a resolution calling upon the president to communicate to the Senate the number, names, and offices of the people removed by him since the last session of the Senate, along with the reasons for each removal. Jackson's authority was being challenged. Federal sponsorship of internal improvements continued to be a vigorous item, favored by a majority of both houses, including most of the westerners. Tazewell voted against federal subscription to stock in the Fredericksburg Turnpike Road Company, but he was not present to cast his ballot against the Maysville Road bill. Mrs. Nivision died early in May, and shortly thereafter Tazewell obtained a leave of absence for the remainder of the session.[9]

The Maysville bill, providing $150,000 in federal aid to construct a road from Louisville to Maysville, Kentucky, was approved by the Senate, 24 to 18. Tazewell's presence would not have influenced the outcome of the measure, which also had substantial backing in the House. States' rights advocates waited anxiously for Jackson's decision whether or not to sign the bill. "Much of the future prosperity of the Union depends on what he may now do," a worried Hugh Lawson White informed Tazewell. White, who desperately wanted to be loyal to his fellow Tennessean, was bothered by Tazewell's disaffection. When Jackson's veto message was received in the Senate, White was elated. "Should it be the will of Providence," he immediately wrote Tazewell, "that we are again to meet in Washington, and take part in politics, I think you will find in the message of yesterday, almost a guaranty that we would wind up, as we began, side by side, contending zealously, [along] with the President, for the true political faith, as it is laid down in the Constitution." White considered the veto full compensation for all his toil and privations and vowed he would be forever proud to have "contributed something in bringing into office a President who dares to advance such opinions."[10]

Tazewell was less enthusiastic. In his shrewd mind the veto was more the work of Van Buren than of Jackson, another of the New Yorker's tricks to place Calhoun in an uncomfortable position while at the same time mollifying states' righters alienated by Jackson's Jefferson Birthday utterance. The analysis was correct. Van Buren and Jackson had discussed the advisability of making such a move. "It was understood between us," Van Buren admitted in his *Autobiography*, "that I should keep an eye upon the movements of Congress and bring to his notice the first Bill upon which I might think his interference would be preferable." By "preferable interference" Van Buren meant a veto which would not anger too many people. For the purposes of the president and the secretary of state, the Maysville bill was perfect. Although its backers looked upon the Maysville Road as part of the Cumberland national turnpike system, the highway lay entirely within the state of Kentucky, and rejection of the bill was based on the fact that the road was an intrastate rather than an interstate project, ineligible for federal funding. This reasoning made westerners, usually ardent backers of internal improvements, less upset by the quashing of the "Kentucky project" than they would have if the road had been a bona fide national undertaking.[11]

Van Buren, continuing to make a fetish of his "old Republican" principles, affirmed his sincere disapproval of federally funded internal improvements. Tazewell, remembering the New Yorker's similar denunciation of tariff measures, had no confidence in the genuineness of the declaration. Nor was he inclined to accept the veto of the Maysville bill as a guarantee of the president's future policy. But Van Buren played his cards well, and many Democrats were impressed by Jackson's stalwart defense of the Constitution in the Marysville case.[12] The "soothing & exhilarating effect throughout the South," which Van Buren anticipated the veto would produce, seemingly was accomplished, but Tazewell was not won over. Although the veto was in line with his principles, he distrusted the motives behind it and had a gnawing, intuitive feeling that the Jackson–Van Buren cabal intended to exude an aura of

Jeffersonianism while increasing the power of the national government, and especially that of the executive branch.

Basking in southern reaction to the first year of Jackson's reign, Van Buren glowed with pleasure. "The South looks better than it has done for years," he confidently reported to the president. Even Tazewell's closest friends were impressed. For John Randolph the Maysville veto fell "upon the ear like the music of other days." Wickham, too, was encouraged by the president's action, as well as by the reduction of duties on salt and a few other minor items. "Though as yet no direct approaches are made toward the outworks of the tariff system" he told Tazewell, the diminution of the duties on salt "is I hope a prelude to a regular and successful attack on it." And should Jackson recover the colonial trade, "he will come off with éclat."[13]

Calhoun was downcast. Try as he would, he could not mend his relationship with Jackson, even though it was he who saved the confirmations of both Amos Kendall and Mordecai Noah. In each case, when the Senate vote was tied, Calhoun cast his deciding vote in favor of the nominees, but for this he received no gratitude. Instead, he was being purged from the Jacksonian ranks, a victim of highly skilled intrigue. The coup de grace came on May 12 when Jackson was presented with "proof" of Calhoun's duplicity. A letter from William Crawford of Georgia (Van Buren's friend and Calhoun's bitter enemy) confirmed an earlier statement from Senator John Forsyth, also of Georgia, that in 1818, while secretary of war, Calhoun had condemned Jackson's invasion of Florida and had tried to persuade Monroe's cabinet to punish the general for disobeying orders. This revelation could not have surprised the president; he had seen Forsyth's letter the previous November. Nevertheless, his anger now rekindled, he demanded an explanation from Calhoun. For years, Jackson ranted, Calhoun had posed as his champion when the pursuit of the Seminole Indians into Florida was challenged by other members of the Monroe adminstration. "I had a right to believe that you were my sincere friend, and until now, never expected to have occasion to say to you, in the language of Caesar, *Et tu Brute*."[14] Undoubtedly Jackson's indignation was feigned. As early as December 1829 he had decided upon Van Buren as his successor, and the present controversy provided a convenient excuse to break completely with the vice-president, to whom he attributed "most of the troubles, vexations and difficulties I have encountered since my arrival in this City." Tazewell's 1827 prediction to Ritchie, of a possible separation in the Jackson ranks after the election of the general, had come true.[15]

A pleasant diversion during the summer was John Randolph's arrival in Norfolk on his way to the Russian court. Jackson, whose liking for the controversial Virginian dated back to the days of the Jefferson administration, had appointed him minister plenipotentiary to Russia. Although Tazewell realized the unsuitableness of the appointment, both for Randolph and for the United States, he voiced no objection: "Should you pass through Norfolk," he told his friend, "I shall expect to see you at my house, where we can converse on many subjects." Very likely, one of the subjects of conversation was the Jackson administration's attempt to reopen the West Indies trade. While Norfolk was optimistic over prospects of economic improvement, Tazewell was skeptical and repeated to Wickham the warning he had sounded in 1826: "The current of trade once diverted from its accustomed channel, can rarely be made to resume its former course," at least never to the same extent and advantage as before.[16] High tariffs had encouraged production of sugar and molasses in Louisiana, thus eliminating a major portion of exchange with the West Indies. Moreover, prolonged interdiction of trade forced the islands to develop considerable economic independence. No longer did they seek provisions, lumber, and naval stores in American ports. During the years of Anglo-American economic hostility many Norfolk shipowners were ruined. Those still operating in 1830 found small consolation in the resumption of commerce, for under the provisions of the "Reciprocity of 1830," as the settlement was called, restrictions were numerous and shippers realized few advantages from the negotiations. "Poor Norfolk! How thou are fallen; how different from the early days," mourned the *Herald*. "Then all was bustle, activity and life. . . . Now all appears still—still as the grave." Tazewell placed the blame on the tariffs enacted under the auspices of Martin Van Buren.[17]

Returning to Washington, Tazewell realized that the schism between the president and vice-president had passed the point of resolution, particularly in light of Jackson's accusations of Calhoun's duplicity concerning the Seminole episode. The airing of the twelve-year-old "purely personal" matter disgusted Tazewell. "The different versions which I have heard of this affair," he told John, "are so directly variant, that I know not where the truth is. It seems however to involve several other persons besides those I have named [Jackson and Calhoun], and may very possibly become one of the many pivots upon which most important public events may turn." Long before Tazewell made his observation, events already had begun to turn. In mid-November Henry Clay, contemplating (not unhappily) the rupture in the executive branch, asked, "What will—what can the Vice-President do? . . . It appears to me that Van Buren has completely outmaneuvered him."[18]

In his second annual message to Congress, Jackson pointedly referred to the unquestionable constitutionality of the tariff laws, the right of Congress to protect American industry, and the right of the majority to rule. "Every state can not expect to shape the measures of the General Government to suit its own particular interests," he warned. "Acquiescence in the constitutionally expressed will of the majority, and the exercise of that will in a spirit of moderation, justice, and brotherly kindness, will constitute a cement which should forever preserve our Union."[19] With this Tazewell could agree. However, he failed to find moderation, justice, or brotherly love toward the South in the tariff measures enacted by Congress since 1824. The message was, on the whole, conciliatory, but Tazewell awaited Jackson's actions, and while he did not consider himself one of Calhoun's partisan supporters, the Virginia senator held no brief for the Van Buren–Jackson strategy of eliminating the South Carolinian from political competition. Moreover, he wondered whether Calhoun was not at least partially blind to the slyness of Van Buren's mode of operation.

Hoping to clarify his position in the Seminole affair, Calhoun early in February 1831 decided to publish a pamphlet containing a portion of the correspondence relative to the incident. Tazewell, hearing of Calhoun's "curious pamphlet," tried to persuade him not to publish it, but on February 17 Duff Green's press completed the printing, and before the day's end the pages had "produced much excitement" in the corridors of the Capitol. Calhoun had thought the pamphlet would "direct the publick indignation against the contriver of this profligate intrigue [Martin Van Buren]," and men with such diverse outlooks as Henry Clay and Benjamin Watkins Leigh continued to insist the exposure would work to Calhoun's eventual advantage, but Tazewell disagreed. The winner, he was certain, was again the Little Magician. By early March, Calhoun was a man without a party.[20]

Meanwhile, Tazewell was having his own clash with the man in the White House. On the day following publication of Calhoun's pamphlet, Tazewell caustically criticized Jackson from the floor of the Senate. Because of the almost simultaneous occurrence of the two incidents, there were those who believed them to be parts of a concerted vice-presidential conspiracy against Jackson, but the timing was merely coincidental.[21]

Abuse of presidential power was again under Tazewell's scrutiny, and the circumstances were similar to those which precipitated his censure of President Adams's handling of the Panama mission. This time the geographic location shifted to Turkey. In September 1829, while Congress was not in session, the president had appointed three commissioners to negotiate a treaty with the Sublime Porte of the Ottoman Empire opening the Black Sea to ships of the United States, a worthy goal which in itself would not have received significant opposition from the legislative branch. However, when Congress convened in December 1829, the names of the commissioners were not submitted to the Senate for approval, and the mission was not mentioned to the Foreign Relations Committee of either house. Not until his annual message a year later, December 1830, did Jackson refer to the incident, announcing that the treaty had been agreed upon and would "be forthwith laid before the Senate" for ratification. Tazewell, as chairman of the Foreign Relations Committee, communicated to the secretary of state his disapproval of the manner in which the commissioners were appointed. His objections were ignored, and only when the appropriations bill came before the Senate did he have an opportunity to take direct action, moving to strike from the bill all remuneration for the diplomatic representatives to the Ottoman Empire. A few days later, in support of his motion, he spoke at length on the subject of executive usurpation and the abuse of power.[22]

His purpose was not, he insisted, to deny to the commissioners one single cent for services they supposedly rendered. In fact, he doubted that Congress had the moral right to refuse such compensation. On the other hand, he had a moral responsibility to object to any sanction of what he believed to be an unconstitutional act of the executive, as well as to the Senate's voluntary abandonment of its rights and privileges. The Constitution specifically limited the president's appointment rights during a recess to the filling of vacancies, and the commissioners filled no vacancies. Furthermore, the president alone had no more authority to appoint without nominating to the Senate than the Senate had to advise the appointment of one not nominated by him. The only exception would be in naming secret agents.

Despite the fact that some of the president's defenders referred to his mishandling of the Turkish mission as a "trifling" matter, Tazewell saw the possibility of many dangers stemming from this wanton disregard for the rights and privileges of the Senate. If the high-handed practice were allowed to become the rule, the president could, if he so desired, create a corps diplomatique with unlimited authority to pledge the nation and the public revenue to any extent he might choose. "I never have had, and I never can have, so much confidence in any President," Tazewell asserted, "as willingly to confide to his unchecked discretion, any important power, with even a hope that it will not be abused. It is the nature of man to covet power, and to abuse that which he has, in order to acquire more; and of all forms of government this elective monarchy of ours is least calculated to repress this natural proclivity of its temporary chief, especially if he desires to retain his place for another term." Nor did he absolve cabinet members of their accountability for unconstitutional acts of the executive. Four of Jackson's department heads, Tazewell reminded his colleagues, were in the Senate during the memorable Panama discussion. "All four united with me in the vote given upon that occasion." The secretary of state, then a senator from New York, "stood by my side in that debate" as the able advocate of the rights of the Senate, "eloquently denouncing the claim of power then preferred, as but a part of a long settled *system* covertly to increase the influence and patronage of the Executive." The political consequences of his stand, Tazewell realized, would be serious. He foresaw the wrath he would incur.[23]

Rising to Jackson's defense was Tazewell's old adversary, Edward Livingston of Louisiana, who scolded the Virginian for overreacting to the situation. Tazewell did not retreat: "My justification is, whatever I have said, I thought; and that which I think of the publick acts of publick men, I feel myself at perfect liberty to speak here, whenever a proper occasion arises so to do." John Tyler also replied to Livingston, observing that Virginians were in the habit of calling things by their right name. "If an act be done without law, they call it lawless; if in derogation of the rights of others, they say so, whomsoever it may offend." Tazewell was not responsible for the rift in the Jacksonian ranks, Tyler maintained. Rather, early in the session he endeavored to persuade the secretary of state of the dangers inherent in the manner in which the Turkish mission was being handled, but the secretary would not listen. Tazewell's only recourse, therefore, was to protest from the Senate floor. "The torch of discord," Tyler declared, "has been thrown among us, and the unity of the party with which we have with but one exception acted, is for the time broken up." Van Buren could have managed the matter with more finesse, possibly providing a private bill for the commissioners' compensation, rather than further insulting the Senate by "thrusting" the provision into the general appropriations bill.[24]

Tyler's analysis was not wide of the mark. Van Buren, plotting ahead as was his wont, encouraged Jackson to act as he did in regard to the Turkish mission, knowing from past experience what Tazewell's reaction would be and realizing the possibility of then denouncing the Virginian as a schismatic. Not only was Calhoun to be ejected from the association of the faithful, but this also was to be the fate of anyone influential enough to thwart Van Buren's ambitions. The night after Taze-well delivered his powerful speech, Tyler recalled, there had been an early thaw, causing the ice on the Potomac to break up. Pressed on by high waters from mountain torrents, the ice tore from its moorings a part of the bridge connecting the United States capital with the Virginia shore, whereupon a Jacksonian supporter archly remarked "the connexion be-tween Virginia and the President's mansion is now severed." "All the vials of wrath," Tyler anticipated, "are to be emptied on our heads."[25]

As a sequel to his remarks, Tyler suggested an amendment to Tazewell's resolution, approving compensation for the com-missioners but adamantly stating that nothing in the granting of payment was to be construed as sanctioning or in any way condoning the appointment of these persons by the presi-dent's action alone without the advice and consent of the Sen-ate. This passed by a vote of 25 to 18, triggering an outpour-ing of abuse from the Van Buren press. Tazewell was charged with trying to "vex and destroy the good old hero," and both he and Tyler were ridiculed for their "exaggerated venera-tion" of their native state. Thomas Ritchie, hesitating to make war openly on the Virginia senators, said their principles were correct but their manner offensive. "Virginia was never stronger for Jackson than she is at this moment. Around him she will rally, and support him with all her strength, let the struggle come when it may." What Ritchie really was doing, Tyler informed Tazewell, was rallying all the "red hot Jackson men" against the two of them.[26]

Governor John Floyd told Tazewell to ignore Ritchie's state-ments and, above all, to harbor no thought of resigning. "I am anxious on this subject, because I see very distinctly a tempest rising which will not only decide the fate of men, but the Union. I do not of late know the motives by which Mr. Ritchie is actuated. I know he has for some time considered you, Tyler, and myself, not of Van Buren's party, to whose car we for some time have thought him harnessed." The Virginia legislature, Floyd wrote assuringly, was in accord with Taze-well's views, "with hardly a dissenting voice," while Van Buren scarcely had a friend left in the General Assembly. Floyd was eager to have Tazewell publicly declare his approval of Calhoun and nullification. So was Benjamin Watkins Leigh, who informed Tazewell that Ritchie "wishes you would resign with all his heart. He has taken sides with Mr. Van Buren and would gladly take a chance to supply your place with a Senator from Virginia likely to be more manageable."[27]

The abuse in the press and the strain of Senate debates made Tazewell's life difficult, and as the Twenty-first Congress drew to a close, he found the night sessions, necessary for the conclusion of business, particularly trying. "I have seen the time when I could have stood this as well as anybody, but not so now," he told Wickham. "I am still infirm in health, altho much better than I have been." Because of his weariness he declined the honor of being president pro tempore of the Senate when, on March 1, he was elected on the third ballot. Webster asked him to reconsider, but Tazewell begged to be excused, and the Senate named Samuel Smith of Maryland.[28]

Upon adjournment of Congress, Tazewell departed Washington for Norfolk aboard the steamboat, rather than, as he earlier had planned, traveling overland to Richmond, where Floyd and several members of the General Assembly were anxious to confer with him. Tazewell made his excuses to the governor on the basis of his health, but very likely he wished to avoid being in Richmond at the same time as Calhoun, who stopped in the Virginia capital en route to his home in South Carolina. As Tazewell anticipated, Floyd royally entertained the vice-president, introducing him to important and sympathetic Virginia legislators and newspaper editors, including the influential Thomas Gilmer of the Charlottesville *Virginia Advocate*. Floyd's sole purpose was to have Calhoun endorsed as the presidential choice of the Virginia General Assembly. The presence of Tazewell and Tyler would have given substance to such an endorsement, but neither was prepared to join the "Calhoun for President" crusade.[29]

The day after the vice-president took leave of his Richmond admirers Floyd noted in his diary, "I have projected a public dinner to our senators, Tazewell and Tyler. The members of the General Assembly will do that thing in approval of their bold, honorable, and independent stand made by them in the Senate of the United States in defence of States Rights." Floyd was determined to associate Tazewell and Tyler with Calhoun in the public mind. He hoped to get them to Richmond quickly, while the aura of the vice-president still lingered, and commit them to the Calhoun cause. Both senators declined the invitation. Tyler's wife was ill, and he, with justification, used this as his excuse. "I chose therefore to rest upon that alone," he informed Tazewell, "being altogether sufficient in itself." Tazewell also, as graciously as possible, sent his regrets, explaining that such a dinner, at this critical moment, "might fan the flames of discord" in Virginia politics.[30]

Tazewell was not alone in his concern about discord. Van Buren's Virginia cohorts, alarmed by the warm reception accorded Calhoun, warned the secretary of state to stifle the attacks against Tazewell and Tyler now appearing in administration newspapers. But Van Buren's intrigues did not abate, and his next move against Calhoun was a bold one, which surprised many of his close associates and caught the opposition off guard. "I was prepared to expect movements against the friends of Calhoun in the Cabinet," Tyler observed to Tazewell, "but had not expected that matters would have taken the course they have."[31] To rid the cabinet of any semblance of Calhounism, Van Buren decided to eliminate Ingham, Branch, and Berrien, and to do so without seeming to force them out. According to his carefully laid plans, he himself would resign and persuade Eaton to do likewise; Jackson could then use their resignations as a pretext for restructuring the entire cabinet.

Before the end of the second week in April 1831, Jackson's objections to the sacrifice of his two favorites were overcome, and he accepted their resignations. The three who were the actual targets, however, did not fall in line and relinquish their positions as gracefully as Van Buren anticipated. Pressure had to be exerted, and Ingham, Branch, and Berrien did not hesitate to publicize the involuntary nature of their departure. Naturally, it was not Van Buren's intention to be left without an influential position. Included in his game of musical chairs was a request that the president recall Louis McLane from his post in England to become secretary of the treasury. His replacement at the Court of St. James's would be, of course, Martin Van Buren.[32]

For Tazewell the newly appointed secretary of state was no

improvement. Guided by Van Buren, Jackson selected Edward Livingston of Louisiana, who had served his New York connections well in the Senate. According to Van Buren's blue print, the War Department was to be filled by Hugh Lawson White, now completely disillusioned with the Jackson–Van Buren alliance. A cabinet post was intended to mollify him, and Eaton would step into White's place in the Senate. Unfortunately for Eaton, White refused to play according to Van Buren's rules, and the pliable Lewis Cass of Michigan became secretary of war, largely by default. Levi Woodbury, whom Tazewell still regarded as a friend, "that is to say, as much so as is usual in Washington," became secretary of the navy, and Roger B. Taney of Maryland accepted the Justice Department after Philip P. Barbour of Virginia declined to serve.[33]

No matter what one thought of Van Buren, Tyler admitted to Tazewell, his scheme had aspects of brilliance. In addition to removing three political opponents from the cabinet, he was now in a position to guide the president's actions while relieved of all embarrassment proceeding from them. He also was rid of the stigma of "secretary succession," a "precedent" increasingly frowned upon. Already speculators were giving excellent odds on Van Buren's becoming the next vice-president. Tazewell had prophesied this "12 months ago," Tyler recalled. Rudolph Bunner, a congressman from New York, assured Tazewell that Van Buren's "injudicious intrigue to injure Calhoun" had diminished the Little Magician's power, but Tazewell did not for a moment believe it.[34]

In Norfolk the summer brought a variety of anxieties. John's illness was the chief cause for distress. Weak, pale, and plagued by recurrent lung hemorrhages, he sought relief at the springs in the Virginia mountains. Tazewell thought a long sea voyage might be beneficial and planned to accompany his son to Madeira and the southern coast of the Mediterranean, but this had to be abandoned as too strenuous and confining for John to endure. It was probably just as well, for Tazewell dared not leave Norfolk, even to join his son at Warm Springs. On August 22 and 23 a slave revolt led by Nat Turner cut a bloody path through Southhampton County, some seventy miles west of Norfolk, killing and maiming more than sixty persons, including many women and children. Hys-

teria swept Norfolk, and Governor Floyd believed the community of ten thousand, half of whom were black, to be the most
panic-stricken of any place in the state. The Negroes were as
frightened as the whites, and with good cause, for in their
terror many whites saw in every black a potential Nat Turner,
to be shot or lynched on the slightest provocation. In the
weeks that followed, Turner's accomplices, actual and suspected, were hunted down and summarily executed, but
Turner remained at large for over two months. During these
uneasy days Tazewell rarely left his house. Caring only about
John's health and the safety of his family, he neglected his
plantations and all other business affairs.[35]

"Every evil is said to be attended with some good," Tazewell
told Wickham. "The anxieties of my wife and daughters concerning John, absorbed in great degree the distress they
would probably have experienced from the tales of the horror
scenes lately enacted in Southampton, and prevented much of
the alarm they must otherwise have felt, from the commotion
these tragedies produced even here." He knew reports of the
revolt were exaggerated, but even so, the Turner uprising
clearly illustrated to him what one day could be expected on a
much larger scale. The more he contemplated this horrible
possibility, the stronger became his conviction that "total abolition of slavery in Virginia, and the entire abduction of the
black population (whether bond or free) from this state" was
an absolute necessity. He advocated a slow but regular process, with slaves purchased from their owners " at a fixed and
fair price" and removed from the country along with the free
Negroes, according to a specific schedule designed to guard
against the effects of the vacuum which would be produced by
the sudden loss of so much labor. He hoped the procedure
could be implemented throughout the South.[36]

Nowhere in his letter to Wickham did Tazewell use the
word "colonization," yet this was precisely what he had in
mind. The basic ideas of the American Colonization Society,
which he rejected as unrealistic in 1828, now seemed worth a
try. Individual state governments and no other body or organization, however, should take the initiative in prescribing
emancipation and deportation regulations. Tazewell's plan
was lacking in detail, but he envisioned some federal assistance

in purchasing slaves and transporting the blacks wherever they were to be settled. Moreover, the political climate had to be favorable. Psychologically, no chief executive from the North could instigate the procedure, for "to give a fair chance of success to my scheme it is very desirable, if not indispensably necessary, that we should have a slaveholding president, who shall look for his elevation and support to the slaveholding states principally, and that the congressional representation of these states should regard the consummation of this purpose as the grand *desideratum,* to which all minor considerations, and especially their own lust for office must be sacrificed." The key question was, could the government of the United States be relied upon to adhere steadily to any system requiring time, regularity, and uniformity in its complete execution? Of this Tazewell was dubious, but even if the plan were only partially carried out, "it will at least leave us better off than we were." The black population would be reduced and danger alleviated.[37]

Wickham was not encouraging. He too had long reflected on the composition of Virginia's population and on the turmoil which inevitably would flare up among both blacks and whites as pressures from abolition opinion within and outside the state increased. Sadly he admitted he could find no solution. "Of one thing only I am certain, that the vessel will be driven sometimes in one direction and sometimes in another by the winds and the waves, and that no confidence can be placed in the skill of the pilots." The approaching session of the General Assembly, he anticipated, would be forced to consider numerous and diverse systems, brought forward in the hope of averting a repetition of the Southampton tragedy. Great excitement and violent animosities would arise, and arguments would continue for years. "The question of liberty and necessity you know, has occupied the mind of philosophers for ages without being brought to any certain conclusion. I think, however, I may venture to predict that whatever measures are adopted with regard to this most interesting subject will be the result of chance, necessity or whatever other name you may give, and not out of regular and systematic thought, wise or unwise."[38]

The Virginia legislature did consider emancipation and colonization during the 1831–32 session, as it examined a bewildering array of proposals and counterproposals. The attention of the entire nation was drawn to the unique spectacle of a southern state debating the slavery issue, but humanitarian expectations, probably illusory from the beginning, were dashed, and the attempt to solve Virginia's problems, and more important, to recognize the human rights of the blacks, came to naught.[39]

During the debate in the Virginia capital, Tazewell was in Washington, distracted by illness and by national affairs that also were to have a direct bearing on the continuity of the Union. He was anxious about the future of Virginia. The Nat Turner episode had rekindled the fears he had expressed in 1806 when he had opposed the importation of more slaves into the commonwealth.[40] In 1831 Tazewell was classified by many as a states' rights man, and this he was, insofar as he was opposed to the overweening coercive powers of the federal government; nevertheless, he was willing to turn to Washington for aid in solving the terrible problems associated with slavery, just as in 1806 he proposed seeking help from Congress for those states that wanted to control the African slave trade. He now advocated emancipation coupled with colonization. Although deportation had seemed to him out of the realm of possibility in 1828, currently he could see no other solution. The increase in his own slaveholdings from only a few domestic servants in 1806 to seventy-five or eighty on three plantations in 1831 had not convinced him of the desirability of defending the peculiar institution. Had the Turner insurrection happened a few years earlier, Tazewell might well have used his influence during the state constitutional convention to turn the tide against slavery. However, in 1831 he did not launch a crusade in support of his ideas. It is doubtful that they were known to the public. When Thomas R. Dew of the College of William and Mary, engaged in writing his conservative defense of slavery for the *American Quarterly Review*, wrote to Tazewell requesting a copy of his 1828 report on colonization, Tazewell sent it without indicating his own altered viewpoint on the subject. The arguments against colonization that Dew extracted from Tazewell's report became a forceful part of this classic proslavery essay.[41]

While Tazewell did not agree with those who looked upon slavery as a positive good, he seemd untroubled by the immorality of human bondage; at least, he voiced no qualms of conscience. He simply believed that slavery constituted a potential danger to the white population, and for this reason it was evil. On the other hand, he did not react to the Turner uprising, as did numerous slaveowners, by calling for stricter control of Negroes and greater severity of punishment for recalcitrant slaves.[42] Two months after expressing to Wickham his desire to see slavery totally abolished in Virginia, Tazewell wrote to John, asking him to attend a slave auction at Surry Courthouse and there purchase a male cook advertised as experienced and competent. "If you are not well enough to attend the sale yourself," he instructed his son, "I wish you would write to Mr. Cooke to buy him. I know nothing about the man myself, but should be willing to give more than he is worth for a cook that would suit you mother."[43] Along with so many others, Tazewell was caught in a paradoxical situation. He did not want slaves and thought the South would be better off without them. He believed in ridding the state of all blacks, and yet he purchased and utilized them. Given a choice, he would have wished the problems away, but emancipation was inexorably entwined with other sensitive issues, such as nullification, the tariff, and the abuse of presidential power. With the approach of the 1832 election, it was increasingly difficult to separate the points of contention, and the abolition movement in the North, with its potential to encourage slave uprisings, made the South's general position less flexible. Tazewell did not want the Union to split on any issue. He hoped for fair treatment from the northern majority, for help and understanding in regard to the slave problem, and for consideration on tariff matters and warned constantly against extreme positions on the part of either section.

## Chapter XII

# *Resignation from the Senate*

The tension in Washington as the Twenty-second Congress got underway was the worst in the memory of seasoned statesmen. Anticipation of a presidential election in the midst of growing party animosities and realignments did nothing to curb men's emotions or moderate their statements. The president was particularly hostile toward the Virginia senators. "I want strength in the Senate, of good men and true, not such men as Tazewell and Tyler," who, he charged, were under the spell of the "arch intriguer" Calhoun and therefore should be replaced by loyal advocates whose "zeal and patriotic ardor" would aid him in his burdensome duties, men such as Eaton and Van Buren.[1]

Governor Floyd, still attempting to persuade Virginia to endorse Calhoun as a presidential candidate on a State Rights ticket, described the South Carolinian as a "singularly strongminded man. The finest intellect, except Tazewell, I have ever met with. Well-educated, fine manners, forbearing and generous, he is bold, brave and truthful." Elated by the possibility of Virginia's support, Calhoun hoped to unite the entire South behind his candidacy, oust Jackson, and send Van Buren into oblivion. He declared he had "dissolved all ties, political or otherwise," with Jackson forever.[2] In reality, of course, the ties had been dissolved for him by Van Buren, and alienated from the president and the party, Calhoun was forced to seek friends among the more radical southern element. In July 1831, in his Fort Hill address, the vice-president openly announced his advocacy of nullification; his earlier opinions on the subject had been published anonymously. Now there was no turning back.

Tazewell understood and sympathized with many of Calhoun's sentiments: his fear of a dominant majority and the inevitability of violent minority resistance when tyranny became unbearable; his desire to reconcile sectional differences; his anticipation of the unification of West and South by a system of internal improvements, such as a canal joining the Ohio, Kanawha, and James rivers, financed by gifts of public lands to the states; his hope for convincing northern manufacturers that they must look to foreign markets and that by lowering the tariff they would have greater opportunities to sell their goods abroad. But Tazewell did not support nullification. To him there simply was no legal or constitutional way of refusing to obey a law. A state could protest or secede, but it could not veto an act of Congress and remain in the Union. In publicly advocating nullification, Calhoun had "brought his pigs to a fine market at last. All his long encouraged aspirations are already shown to be delusive, and no one speaks of him even as the next Vice President."[3] Nonetheless, Calhoun continued to muster a considerable following in Virginia. There the Democrats, mirroring the national party schism, were divided between the Jackson–Van Buren and Calhoun factions. Ritchie and Lieutenant Governor Peter V. Daniel led the administration forces (frequently referred to as the Junto-Jacksonians), while Governor Floyd spearheaded the "Virginia for Calhoun" movement. Tazewell was compatible with neither. He considered Jackson totally incompetent to administer the government, he distrusted Van Buren, and he could not abide Calhoun's theory of nullification.[4]

Nor was he happy with the Anti-Mason movement that held its convention, the first party to use this new mode of nominating candidates, in Baltimore in September 1831 and, after unsuccessfully offering the presidential candidacy to John Quincy Adams and Justice John McLean of the Supreme Court, prevailed upon William Wirt to head the ticket. Tazewell could see no logic in a campaign against the Masonic order, even if the object was the unseating of Jackson, and he could not understand why Wirt was so foolish as to allow his name to be used by such a "contemptible faction." "He has proved a sad marplot, I suspect," Tazewell ruefully remarked to Wickham. "It seems now to be well understood that his acceptance of the Anti-Mason nomination disappointed the views of that body not less than the opinion of his personal friends. But thus it always is." When all was over, Tazewell hoped Wirt would "not be 'found in the fatter' (as they say in Connecticut)."[5]

Also off to an early start, the National Republicans in December 1831 nominated Clay. Although the Democrats were not scheduled to name their candidate until the following May, Jackson obviously would run for reelection. To be sure, the president was not well, and should he succumb before the November election, Calhoun would benefit, but the Van Burenites could not believe Jackson would forsake them, even for a heavenly home, until the Little Magician was safely in a position to succeed him. The primary concern, therefore, was the selection of a vice-presidential candidate. In Virginia the names of Philip P. Barbour and Tazewell frequently surfaced, but the latter, his mind occupied with many other issues, was not interested in bidding for membership in Jackson's official family.[6]

Tazewell arrived for the opening of the Twenty-second Congress to find an influenza epidemic sweeping the city, and he promptly contracted the disease. Bled and blistered until he had scarcely any strength left, he said he felt like Job, but without the patriarch's patience to bear such afflictions. When writing to his family he casually mentioned a "slight indisposition," but through the imprudence of certain persons in the capital, news reached Norfolk of the seriousness of his illness. Ann, thoroughly alarmed, immediately made arrangements to find out for herself the nature of his malady. Accompanied by John, who was himself in no condition to travel, she set out early in January. For Ann to leave home at any time, especially during the winter when travel was so hazardous, amazed her husband. "The trip was a most disagreeable one as you may well suppose," Tazewell told Wickham, "and I fear it has done John much mischief."[7]

Convinced of her husband's steady improvement, Ann remained in Washington only until John was again halfway able to travel, a matter of slightly more than a week. On the day of her departure Tazewell was invited to dine with the president, who took "much pains" to point out that the dinner was intended for Mrs. Tazewell, whose absence was sincerely regretted. "The party was not a large one," Tazewell described the occasion for Ann, "and consisted of both ladies and gentlemen. I was directed to hand Mrs. Donnelson to the table, and of course was placed in the post of honour. I acquitted myself as well as I could, and left the party so soon as I might." He was accompanied to the dinner by Hugh Lawson White, who remarked this was the only presidential invitation he had accepted during the current season, and he had acceded to this one solely because he thought Mrs. Tazewell would be a guest. The president's gesture of conciliation impressed neither of the senators.[8]

Tazewell was deeply touched by Ann's concern for his welfare, realizing what an effort it had been for her to leave home and children, even for a short period. Since Henry's death she had become almost a recluse, but Tazewell optimistically believed the journey to Washington could be the beginning of a change in her attitude, and he hoped she would be willing to come again. "Take exercise whenever the weather will permit you to do so without incurring the hazard of taking cold," he advised. "See more company and mix more in society than you have done for many years past; and rely upon it, you will not only improve your health, but your happiness also." He went to great lengths to describe how much her visit had brightened Mrs. Peyton's boardinghouse, adding, "If any of the mess knew I was writing to you, I should be charged I am sure with all sorts of kind wishes & compliments to you. These you may easily imagine and fill the blanks as you please; but I have not heard one word from anyone in praise of your caps."[9]

To convince Ann of his continued improvement, Tazewell appeared in the Senate for at least a few hours every day despite his hoarseness, which grew increasingly worse as he was drawn into preelection intensification of debates on the tariff, nullification, and the Bank of the United States. If there were no president to elect, Tazewell thought the situation might remain fairly stable for "some time yet to come," but he was certain that upon these issues "we must some day split."[10]

To forestall such a split he considered assuming the role of arbiter between conflicting parties in the Senate, if only he had enough strength for the task. For the moment, he confided to Wickham, he could command the confidence of all the senators whose esteem he valued, but he questioned how long he could maintain this position. "If I felt any ambition to gratify my course would be a plain one. I could become a great man at any time by ceasing to be an honest one in my own opinion." To Ann he said essentially the same: "Times here are getting warm, very warm indeed, nor is there any probability that the heat will decrease as the session proceeds," but she was not to worry, regardless of what she heard or read about the state of things in Washington. He would try to keep peace between the rival parties so long as he could, and when this was no longer possible, he would take sides with neither but "let them fight it out as they please."[11]

When the matter of Van Buren's appointment to the Court of St. James's came before the Senate, Tazewell voted in favor of confirmation. This was not a magnanimous decision. Tazewell preferred having him in London rather than in Washington, and he also believed that a negative vote would give Van Buren the vice-presidential nomination. Calhoun evidently did not perceive the situation in the same way. With the Senate equally divided, Calhoun, as president of the body, cast the deciding ballot against Van Buren's appointment. Tazewell was convinced Calhoun had made a mistake and, in so doing, had destroyed his own political prospects while enhancing those of Van Buren. Both the vice-presidency and the presidency were now within the New Yorker's grasp.[12]

Tazewell was weary. During the frequently called secret sessions of the Senate he often was compelled to speak when he was so weak that his voice sunk and his knees trembled. Kindness of the members spared him unnecessary fatigue and exertion, but the Foreign Relations Committee, which he now chaired, carried a heavy and troublesome load. There was the northeast boundary dispute with England, Jackson's desire to acquire Texas, and a pending commercial treaty with Russia. The latter was complicated by the fact that the United States had no minister in Saint Petersburg. Randolph had vacated his post for a milder clime, and James Buchanan of Pennsylvania, appointed in June 1831 to succeed Randolph, delayed his departure until April of the following year.[13]

On the Senate floor the most irritating and important topic was the tariff. The "Tariff of Abominations" had caused a frightening furor, and even Webster favored reconsideration of the 1828 act. The new year was only nine days old when Clay proposed a substitute bill which, designed as a compromise, generally moved duties back to the levels of 1824 and abolished those on foreign goods not in competition with American products. Clay's recommendations did nothing to aid the South or mollify its feelings, for, quite significantly, the bill indicated a permanent retention of the protective policy. Virginia's governor was loud in his condemnation of the measure. If the federal government repealed or reduced duties on luxuries while retaining them on iron, cotton textiles, and woolens, warned Floyd, South Carolina would nullify the act. What would follow, he dared not imagine. Jackson was to blame; he "floats like a stick upon the flood," doing nothing to sway or push Congress in the direction of a substantial tariff reduction. If the protectionists were victorious, "the South will be compelled to secede."[14]

Tazewell was inundated by suggestions for arguments to use in his fight against the tariff advocates. Thomas Ritchie's brother-in-law, Richard E. Parker, a respected Virginia judge, voiced opinions similar to those of Governor Floyd. "If Mr. Clay's plan is adopted without modification, it will be resisted by the Southern States. I am satisfied Eastern Virginia will not submit to it, but will unite with South Carolina in the strongest measures she may adopt." Wickham took a different tack. It was remarkable, he observed, that the " 'Amis des Noirs,' abolitionists, colonization people & id genus omne have never thought of the sufferings of their poor favorites from the tariff." The few planters who were wealthy and free of debt would, of course, provide for their slaves as usual, but those economically blighted by the tariff would have no choice but to stint their Negroes severely. "I am told by our dealers here that the sale of blankets has diminished in quantity and quality, and [I] doubt not that this is the case with regard to this article of the first necessity throughout the southern states." Senators John Tyler and Samuel Smith spoke of "dividing the Union by the Potomac" if the northern protection policy prevailed.[15]

Tazewell preferred a positive rather than a negative approach. In his major speech against Clay's bill he neither threatened nullification and secession nor scolded the friends of the blacks. Instead he calmly stated facts and made a strong bid for support of the West in the battle for the reduction of duties. As he saw the problem, there were three great interests to be considered: first, the manufacturers, principally of the North and East, who benefited from a system of high duties; second, the producers of raw materials, largely of the South, who wished to reduce the tariff to the lowest possible rate or eliminate it altogether; third, the people of the West, who were but little affected by either high or low duties because the cost of transportation on an imported article, even if it came in duty free, was so expensive as to preclude the possibility of westerners purchasing it. They were restricted, therefore, to the use of domestic articles, regardless of tariff charges. But the West was interested in increasing its population, getting its lands on the market at the lowest price. The East opposed this. Tazewell reminded the Senate of Richard Rush's report recommending a continuation of high public land prices in order to prevent a drain of population from the manufacturing states. To keep wages down in the East, Tazewell quoted Rush, it was mandatory to keep land prices high in the West. To resist this "conspiracy," Tazewell offered southern support for reduced land costs if the West would fight for a tariff compatible with southern needs. The *Richmond Enquirer,* acknowledging the importance of Tazewell's remarks, gave him a rare compliment: "In his hands, possibly, may rest the greatest interest of the Union. We know not whether the Union itself may not depend upon his efforts."[16]

Consideration of the tariff measure continued throughout the spring months. The Democrats in Congress apparently were unwilling to act on any important items before the Baltimore convention, scheduled for the third week in May. "Every measure is made to depend upon the election of a vice president," Tazewell complained to John. "The friends of Mr. Van Buren are unwilling to risk anything which may tend to impair his hopes both from the tariff and anti-tariff parties, therefore they plan to postpone everything which may produce this effect." With Van Buren's nomination accomplished, "his friends will then shew his cloven foot, and we shall get a tariff scheme enacted, of which Virginia will very soon be sick enough. It will then be too late, however, to repent. I have done everything in my power to open the eyes of the people of Virginia upon this subject, but in vain. I now wash my hands of it forever."[17]

Without any formal nomination, the Democratic convention proclaimed Jackson its standard-bearer. Some anticipated a struggle over the vice-presidential choice, but followers of Van Buren maintained their control and obtained a unanimous endorsement for the New Yorker on the second ballot. Tazewell could not conceal his disgust. If Virginia had stood firm for Barbour, perhaps Van Buren's nomination could have been prevented. Now there was every reason to anticipate his election to the second highest position in the land, with the strong and frightening possibility of seeing him before long in the presidential chair. "To this extremity has the blind policy of Ritchie & co. brought us."[18]

While the Democrats met in Baltimore, the Senate, before coming to a decision on the tariff measure, began debate on a bill to recharter the Bank of the United States. The charter was not due to expire until 1836, but on several occasions since taking office President Jackson had indicated his hostility toward the nation's major financial institution. He spoke of "curbing" the bank's power and of the "perpetual apprehensions and discontent on the part of the States and the people" in regard to the present agency.[19] Nicholas Biddle, the bank's dapper and intellectual president, for whom Jackson felt no affinity, was understandably uneasy about the future. As the election approached, Jackson, following sound political advice, backed away from the bank issue in fear of endangering his standing in Pennsylvania, while Biddle, aided and abetted by Clay, was determined to seek rechartering immediately. From all indications the bill was certain to pass both houses, and there was a better chance, Biddle thought, of avoiding a Jackson veto in an election year than during the president's second term. Three members of Jackson's cabinet, along with a number of Democratic members of Congress, professed loyalty to both the chief executive and the Bank of the United States. Influential and important National Republicans, including

Daniel Webster, agreed with Clay and Biddle. Anything which would complicate matters for the incumbent in the upcoming election was desirable, and the bank issue looked delectable indeed. There were those, however, who warned against baiting the president during the campaign, especially if rechartering seriously was desired. Senator Willie P. Mangum of North Carolina was certain Jackson would accept a recharter bill, with slight modification, if the measure were deferred until the next session. Samuel Smith and Louis McLane agreed with Mangum. Others equally were convinced of Jackson's determined intention to destroy the "Monster."[20]

Tazewell was not avidly hostile to the bank, as were some of his fellow Virginians or those wearing the Old Republican label, such as Nathaniel Macon and John Randolph. The bank's fiscal policies, he realized, had value in restraining credit and overextension of commercial enterprises, but he was opposed to the bank's power, its seemingly unrestricted ability to act as almost an independent agent, free of all controls or supervision. Naturally, as the bank grew larger, its power and influence increased. The first Bank of the United States had been a modest affair. Tazewell had purchased large blocks of shares and tried unsuccessfully for a seat on the board of directors. He continued to be a stockholder in the second bank, chartered in 1816. However, as Jackson's antipathy toward the bank became increasingly vociferous, Tazewell, as a cautious businessman, believed bank stock to be of dubious value, and in the fall of 1830, while requesting John, then in New York, to invest $15,000 for him "in any stocks that promise a reasonable profit," he had ruled out the purchase of additional shares in the Bank of the United States. The following February he voted in favor of Senator Benton's request to introduce a resolution against rechartering the bank.[21] Whether he sincerely objected to its continuation or simply wished to have the matter investigated is difficult to say. Possibly his vote for Benton's resolution was a political move. Indications point to his willingness to offer quid pro quo: his opposition to the Bank of the United States, at least in its present form, for western support for a tariff acceptable to the South.[22]

Political maneuvering was the order of the day, and in all

his years in the Senate, Tazewell had never known it to be more complex or intense than in the spring and summer of 1832. The bank, the tariff, public land prices, and the national debt were all held in equilibrium, or so it seemed, and if one was dislodged, everything would come tumbling down. Benton, too, hoped to link tariff modification with a reduction in the price of public lands, but the Committee on Manufactures, charged with examining the tariff and headed by Henry Clay, submitted to the Senate a report which rejected the land price reduction proposal. Clay, instead, recommended a distribution plan whereby revenue from the sale of public lands (with prices maintained at a high level) would be distributed among the states to be used primarily to finance internal improvements. The distribution idea also served to bolster Clay's argument in favor of a high tariff, for with income from public lands distributed to the states, the tariff would be the exclusive source of national revenue. Southerners were troubled. Not only would the distribution plan make the national government dependent on the tariff, but the same situation also would result from a reduction in land prices. With less revenue accruing from the sale of land, the high-tariff advocates would possess a forceful argument in favor of perpetuating or increasing the current rates.[23]

Although Tazewell continued to side with Benton and the West on the land issue, a number of southerners did not, thus weakening the South-West alliance at a crucial time when solidarity was most needed. Seven southern senators also voted for Clay's distribution scheme, which Benton bitterly asserted was merely the old restrictive land policy cleverly made more palatable. Among the southern senators there was a noticeable lack of dynamic leadership. "In the Senate," Tazewell observed, "the decided preponderance of talent and skill is with the Clay men." The western Jacksonians were very strong in enthusiasm, but the southern element was floundering.[24] It had no cohesiveness. Direction was needed, particularly of the moderate variety that Tazewell might well have provided had he been willing to do so, but characteristically he shied away from that responsibility. According to his mode of operation, one presented a proposal, and if it was fair, men of reason would see the light and support it for the good of the whole.

This was the philosophy with which he ultimately approached the bill to recharter the bank, but reason and moderation, he quickly acknowledged, were rare commodities in the Senate of the United States.

One of the most serious objections to the existence of the bank, in Tazewell's estimation, was the power it possessed over the regulation of the country's currency, a power which, according to the Constitution, was a prerogative of Congress. However, if Congress was willing to delegate to the bank the right to control the currrency, Tazewell thought it advisable to limit the duration of the charter to ten years, rather than allow it to run for fifteen or twenty. During the life of the charter, Congress should not meddle in the bank's business; therefore, shortening the tenure of the charter seemed the sensible thing to do, thus allowing the government to correct with greater dispatch abuses that might develop under inept or unscrupulous management. He declared his willingness to back a proposal limiting the charter even to one year if this would rectify some of the existing evils, real or imagined. Webster's reply was instantaneous, and his was not a voice of moderation. With biting sarcasm he accused Tazewell of using the issue of limiting the duration of the charter as a delaying tactic. "No," Webster thundered, "the Senator from Virginia would prefer to limit the charter not to one year, but to one day!"[25]

Failing to convince the Senate of the necessity of curbing the bank's almost unrestricted independence, Tazewell voted to postpone indefinitely the question of recharter. After all, the bank legally could operate for four more years, and in the meantime other ideas and attitudes might arise. This proposal was defeated 24 to 20, and on June 11 the bank recharter bill, minus Tazewell's suggested modifications, passed the Senate, 28 to 20, with Tazewell voting with the minority. "God knows when we shall adjourn," he wearily wrote to Wickham. "All here is confusion. . . . The President will surely veto the Bank Bill, should it pass the House of Representatives—For what reasons time will disclose, but they will be unquestionably 'judicious,' in his estimation, if not in yours or mine."[26]

The Senate again turned its attention to the tariff. Tazewell, declaring Clay's bill unfair to the South, offered one of his own which Tyler termed "a most liberal proposition," but the tariff men in the Senate "turn up their noses at it." Yet, in the midst of the hassle, Tazewell was elected president pro tempore. Reluctantly, and in a voice so weakened by prolonged debating that his words were inaudible in the gallery, he accepted the honor, believing it ungracious to decline a second time.[27]

At this juncture, aid for tariff modification came from an unexpected quarter. John Quincy Adams, now an energetic member of the House, advocated appeasing the nullifiers by a more serious lowering of the tariff while still maintaining the principle of protection. The House accepted Adams's comparatively moderate proposal as an adjustment between the demands of the nullifiers and Clay's stronger protective measure. Clay vowed to "defy the South, the President, and the devil," if necessary, to preserve the American System. "The Puritan" and "the black-leg" had come to a parting of the ways. The Senate was not happy with the House bill, but after prolonged debate and despite loud protests from Clay and Webster, it acceded to the compromise. "As things stand now," William Wickham advised Tazewell, "I cannot but think a conciliatory course will be the wisest & safest—to repeal as many of the odious duties as you can & renew your attacks at the next session—rather than to refuse anything because you cannot get everything." He believed he spoke for "a great portion of the people, who detest the oppression of the tariff and are yet anxious to preserve the peace of the country." Tazewell thought the Adams tariff inadequate to allay the nullification movement brewing in South Carolina. Stronger action was needed. Adams's bill satisfied neither protectionists nor low-tariff advocates.[28]

In Washington political chaos intensified when, two days before the Senate's approval of the Adams tariff and only one day after Tazewell's election as president pro tempore, Congress received the president's message vetoing the act to recharter the Bank of the United States. Not merely the veto but the words in which the message was couched caused tempers to explode. As an electioneering document it was a masterpiece, appealing to patriotism, pitting poor against rich, and declaring an end to the participation of foreign stockholders in the financial affairs of the United States. Repeatedly and deliberately, emotionally charged words were used: "monopoly," "exclusive privilege," "privileged order," "the rich and powerful." For the Bank of the United States there were no kind phrases, no acknowledgment of services rendered, no appreciation of attempts made to keep the nation on a steady economic course. The president had decided to kill the bank. No matter that Congress had approved the recharter or that the Supreme Court had upheld the constitutionality of the institution, declaring it "necessary and proper" to carry into effect the powers of the general government. The president, Jackson asserted, was as justified in pronouncing an act of Congress constitutional or unconstitutional as was the Supreme Court. "Each public officer who takes an oath to support the Constitution swears that he will support it as he understands it, and not as it is understood by others. . . . The opinion of the judges has no more authority over Congress than the opinion of Congress has over the judges, and on that point the President is independent of both." Such was Jackson's astonishing declaration, and its implications shocked Tazewell to the depth of his being.[29]

The veto message touched off an outpouring of violent opinions greater than any since Webster and Hayne had engaged in verbal combat, and Tazewell, in the chair, presided over the wild scene. Webster cried "despotism" and likened Jackson to "James the Second of England, a month before he was compelled to fly the kingdom," or to Louis XIV of France, who had the audacity to declare, "I AM THE STATE." The president, Webster proclaimed, "is as much bound by the law as any private citizen, and can no more contest its validity than any private citizen. He may refuse to obey the law, and so may a private citizen, but both do it at their own peril, and neither of them can settle the question of its validity. The President may *say* a law is unconstitutional, but he is not the judge." That right was reserved for the nation's highest judicial tribunal. Nicholas Biddle characterized the veto message as a "manifesto of anarchy, such as Marat or Robespierre might have issued to the mob of the Faubourg St. Antoine; and my hope is, that it will contribute to relieve the country from the domination of these miserable people [the Jacksonians]." This, too, was Clay's burning desire. The senators from Missouri

and Kentucky exchanged abusive remarks, with Benton defending the president and Clay recalling Jackson's propensity
to take the law into his own hands by resorting to various
forms of physical violence. Both hurled charges of "atrocious
calumny" as Tazewell attempted to gavel them to order.[30]

Whether more than one-third of the Senate would sustain
the veto, Tazewell was uncertain, but when the question of
repassing the bank bill against the wishes of the president was
put to the test, there were 22 yeas and 19 nays, far short of the
necessary two-thirds. Tazewell voted to uphold the veto, or
more accurately, he again cast his ballot against recharter
under the conditions set forth in the bill.[31] The charges of
executive usurpation brought by Webster and other National
Republicans echoed those Tazewell had voiced on several occasions against both John Quincy Adams and Andrew Jackson, and he believed they were completely justified in this
instance also. Consequently, his vote on the veto did not indicate approval of the president but merely reflected his predicament in having to choose between the exorbitant power of
the bank or that of the chief executive. The decision was not
an easy one. However, a president could be removed from
office at the end of the four-year term; the bank, if rechartered under the present bill, would live for fifteen. Having failed to override the veto, Congress adjourned. The session had been the most exciting and exasperating Tazewell
had experienced.

His greatest source of anxiety was dissension within Virginia. There the political structure was more complex than
ever, with Jacksonian Democrats splitting into factions, some
clinging with varying degrees of intensity to Old Republican
ideals, others drifting into the Clay camp, while another group
listened with interest to Calhoun's panacea of nullification. No
matter how he voted on an issue, Tazewell was certain to
displease a vocal portion of his constituency, and always sensitive to abuse, he became increasingly so as time passed. Perhaps on one issue alone did he feel competent to speak for an
almost united commonweatlh, Virginia's opposition to the
removal of the remains of General Washington from Mount
Vernon to Washington, D.C., for interment in a specially constructed tomb in the Capitol. "Think you," Tazewell asked the

Senate, "that Virginia will consent to the violation of the tomb of her dearest child?" The request had been refused on prior occasions, and so it should be now. Senator Tyler concurred entirely with Tazewell's sentiments, and in the end, Washington continued to rest at Mount Vernon.[32]

As the congressional session drew to a close, Tazewell was visibly on edge. Alarming news reached Washington of a cholera epidemic slowly making its way down the east coast from Canada. Initially, Tazewell resolved to remain calm. He cautioned himself and others against fostering hysteria, and when Clay arose in the Senate to offer a resolution requesting the president to set aside a day of public humiliation, prayer, and fasting, invoking Almighty God to spare the United States of America from the ravages of the disease, Tazewell withheld his assent. In the first place, he asserted, Congress had no right to meddle in religious affairs, by either joint resolution or law. Then, to inject a note of calm, he contended that the disease would not be extensive in the United States except among the unfortunates who brought it with them from some distant country or among those who lived in squalid filth and poverty. Clay's resolution, he felt, could induce panic unnecessarily.[33]

Tazewell was more concerned than his poise indicated. After cholera was reported in Newcastle-on-the-Delaware, brought there by passengers aboard a ship from Ireland bound to Philadelphia, he daily expected to hear of its sweeping through New York, Philadelphia, and Baltimore. From Baltimore the disease could spread to Norfolk in a few days. Therefore, when the last gavel sounded, he immediately set out for home. Upon arrival, he first thought his fears had been groundless; however, within a few weeks the insidious pestilence crept into his own neighborhood, which was neither squalid nor poor but one of the healthiest and cleanest situations in the borough. A naval officer living nearby lost five of his six domestics in as many days. In all the homes in the area the disease hit hard, but almost exclusively among the blacks. "Doubtless there must be some local cause, but what is it?" asked the *Norfolk Herald*. The victims were fed and clothed better than in any other part of the city, and before being struck down by the epidemic they had been in good health; yet their cases were marked by the very worst characteristics of the disease.[34]

For a time the Tazewell household escaped the affliction. "I ascribed the exemption of mine from any disease," Tazewell explained to Wickham, "to their more comfortable habitations, to their more prudent conduct, to the open space about my dwellings, and in short to any and every cause which held out the hope that this exemption would continue." But he was clutching at straws, and the hope was delusive. Within two weeks of the appearance of cholera in the immediate vicinity, the Tazewell laundress suddenly was attacked and died in less than five hours. Four days later the gardener was stricken while walking in the street on a Sunday morning and was dead in less than twenty-four hours. Then John became ill. The physicians diagnosed his condition as the "premonitory symptoms" of cholera, but Tazewell refused to believe his son had contracted a disease which, according to his own declaration, would occur only among foreigners, the filthy, the poor, or blacks. "The cases of my servants were too strongly marked to admit of any doubt; but as to my son's, I then thought, and sitll believe that it was a simple attack of bilious fever, not of a high type either, which would yield to the ordinary treatment. The event proved the correctness of my opinion, for his fever left him in three or four days, without a resort being had to bark."[35]

John's illness was a terrible fright for the entire family. And there were other complications. As the epidemic "raged with horrible malignity" throughout the black population, the Tazewell slaves became too terror-stricken to perform the most ordinary duties. Country people refused to enter the town to supply the markets, and the entire borough was immobilized with fear. The ladies of Tazewell's household were in a constant state of agitation, causing him, for the sake of "humanity, prudence, comfort, and tranquillity," to move his family elsewhere. As a young man he always scoffed at the practice of fleeing from yellow fever epidemics, but now as soon as John was able to travel a short distance, Tazewell gathered his wife, children, and surviving servants and crossed Hampton Roads. Old Point Comfort was to be a temporary location until John gained strength and a safer place could be found. Fortunately, Tazewell was able to engage a suite of excellent rooms, and the family was established comfortably within a short time.

The change of air proved to be of great benefit to John, and the quietness and respite from worry restored the rest of the household to its "accustomed tranquillity." With the family seemingly out of danger, at least for the moment, Tazewell left for the Eastern Shore where his slaves were terrified because several shoremen, recently returned from Baltimore and Washington, had died of cholera. Unable to remove the sixty or more Eastern Shore slaves to a safer haven, Tazewell spent a week attempting to soothe their fears. A few days after he returned to Old Point Comfort, the disease made its appearance there too. As it spread beyond Fortress Monroe to the town of Hampton, the mortality rate was proportionately much greater than in Norfolk. Clearly another change of abode was mandatory. To prepare for this, Tazewell made a hurried trip to Norfolk to care for business affairs and gather a few additional belongings. There, to his delight, he found the epidemic had subsided. New cases were rare anywhere in town, and the sickness was entirely absent from the vicinity of the Tazewell house. Having satisfied himself that the danger actually had passed, he moved his entourage back to Norfolk.

The experience had shaken him. Between July 24, when the first Norfolk fatality occurred, and September 11, when the last was recorded, well over four hundred people in the borough succumbed to cholera. "Of all the scourges which have ever afflicted the human race, in the shape of disease," Tazewell wrote to Wickham, "nothing has equaled the cholera, I believe." Quite likely, he thought, if diagnosed and treated without delay, many fatalities could be averted, "but if neglected, it assumes the character of true Asiatick cholera, and it is then (I believe) beyond the reach of any mortal means of cure." In his opinion the malady was not contagious. "My wife, all of my grown children, and myself, have attended the servants we have lost, throughout the whole disease constantly; and their own fellow servants have never left them. If it had been contagious we could not have escaped it."[36]

According to the *Norfolk Herald*, well over three-fourths of the victims of the epidemic were black. Tazewell set the percentage much higher. Among the whites who died, he contended, there was not one known to him either by name or reputation. "You may infer from this fact something of the true character of the distemper." The *Herald* also mentioned that most of the white deaths occurred among "transients, or people living in obscurity."[37] Obviously, there was something disgraceful about a white person of means contracting cholera.

While Tazewell's entire attention was focused on the epidemic, South Carolina took action against the 1832 tariff bill, fulfilling his prediction of the unacceptability of the Adams compromise. For over a year South Carolina's nullifiers and secessionists had organized, and in September 1832 their struggle with local "Unionists" reached a climax. Not only the tariff but also ominous threats of abolition, accompanied by terrifying thoughts of slave insurrection, obsessed the populace. Literature published by William Lloyd Garrison and others caused escalating rumors of slave plots. President Jackson directed Secretary of the Navy Levi Woodbury to ready a squadron for possible action in the Charleston area. In the October state elections South Carolinians swept nullifiers into office, and Governor James Hamilton, Jr., issued a call for a special session of the new legislature to consider appropriate action against the tariff. Antiabolition agitators played an important part in stirring the emotions of the people. What the tyrannical majority of the North could do in regard to the economy, they cried, it likewise could do to slavery.[38]

Coincidently, on the day the special session of the South Carolina legislature convened, Tazewell resigned from the Senate of the United States, and Jackson saw the two events as parts of a sinister plot. The "reckless course of the leaders in nullification" and the "sudden resignation of Mr. Tazewell all combine to strengthen a belief that some plan of policy has dictated the measure." Against such a "combination of the wicked" one must forever be on guard.[39]

Although, in his letter to Governor Floyd, Tazewell alluded only to private affairs that would demand the major portion of his attention during the whole of the approaching winter,[40] this was not the real motivation for his resignation. Many factors contributed to his decision. The cholera epidemic was one. Never again in the face of a similar disaster did he wish to risk being an appreciable distance from his family. Homesickness, plus disenchantment with the governmental process, or the way in which it was implemented, had caused him to poise on the verge of resignation throughout much of his senatorial career, and his disillusionment became acutely severe during the years of the Jackson presidency. Perhaps, too, there was a close connection between his resignation and the South Carolina nullification movement. Tazewell felt caught up in events for which he had no liking but could not control. He was labeled a states' rights man, but he deplored nullification; he wanted to do his best to represent Virginia, but the state was torn by political upheaval, and during the last session of Congress, he felt out of step with many of the commonwealth's representatives, particularly the Speaker of the House, Andrew Stevenson, a stalwart Jacksonian. A number of Virginia congressmen, Tazewell believed, voted contrary to the "vital interests of the Commonwealth," but he failed to convince them of this. "I greatly prefer'd to avoid the approaching conflict, rather than to engage in an angry contest, where victory offer'd nothing which seemed to me worth the struggle to obtain it," he explained to Wickham. "Moreover, Virginia herself had in fact already decided against me, in bestowing her overwhelming vote in favor of Mr. Van Buren" in the Baltimore convention. "Between that gentleman and myself there never has been, and never can be, any community of political feelings, interests, or principles. Altho' there has never been the slightest cloud passing between us to interrupt our social or personal intercourse, yet the fact of our political disagreements was perfectly known, therefore we could not each represent truly the same constituents."[41]

Tazewell's position was no longer tenable. He could not withstand the Calhoun nullification pressures on the one hand and those of the Van Buren–Jackson forces on the other. Was it not better, he asked, to retire rather than to continue to misrepresent his state? He did not relish the position of "an isolated being in the midst of intriguers of every sort." He abhorred from his "inmost soul" experiments of all kinds upon the body politic, even when made by calm, disinterested, and skillful statesmen, but when such experiments were indulged in by "a wretched set of quacks, or stupid and selfish knaves, who feel no remorse in easily cutting away upon the sensitive subject with the clumsy and brutal force of a butcher's cleaver, in order to carve out some tidbit from the quivering muscle to gorge their voracious appetite," he was filled with disgust. Strange events were occurring. New political organizations were in the offing. To remain in the Senate, "hovering for a little while on the brink of my political grave already gaping to receive me, the poor epitome of what Virginia once was," was unthinkable. He felt hated and abused in his own state because he would not bow down and worship the calf (the Jackson presidency) which his own hand had assisted to create, and he was ridiculed nationally as a political alchemist, seeking to find the philosopher's stone or the "elixir vitae," political integrity![42]

Governor Floyd regretted Tazewell's decision, which deprived Virginia of a virtuous, talented man of learning and ability, no longer able to tolerate "an ignorant and vicious president who had abandoned all his principles" or the president's "low, unbred counsellors, men without minds or morals, yet sustained by a majority." Tazewell's action disturbed his friends, and they reacted in different ways. Hugh Lawson White felt the loss of Tazewell's companionship and counsel most keenly. The Tennessee senator was traveling from his home to Washington when he heard the news and was overcome by sadness, as he said, more from selfishness than from patriotism. "I feel the country has lost much by your withdrawal from the Senate—I have lost everything which made public employ tolerable." In the past, whenever he was uncertain how to act, Tazewell had been there, "a friend in whose intelligence and integrity I could safely confide." Now White felt bereft, "left entirely alone, to grope my way, with the limited resources of my own mind." Wickham thought it too early for Tazewell to retire from public life and "vegetate" at home. "Tis a pity your Eastern Shore estate is so remote. . . . If you have any thing like as much fondness for agriculture as myself, you could employ much of your time in this way with pleasure and advantage."[43]

Tazewell did intend to devote a large amount of time to his plantations, but first there was young Littleton's education to decide upon. As Harvard had proven unsatisfactory for the older boys, Tazewell selected Princeton for his third son and in November accompanied him to New Jersey. After that, he assured Wickham, there were many pleasant occupations to anticipate. During the cool weather his dog and his gun would keep him from dyspepsia, and when summer arrived he would turn angler and "read old Isaac Walton." Idle hours would be devoted to the study of La Place's *Mécanique Céleste,* which he had just ordered, or, he gibed, if he really wanted to challenge his intellect, he might read the poems of John Quincy Adams "and sundry other tracts, which will certainly exact all my acumen to find out either their ends or their means." Regardless of how he chose to spend his days, he hoped he had shaken hands with the public for the last time. He wished the parting might have been more agreeable on both sides, but "perhaps it is better as it is."[44]

Chapter XIII

# Jackson's
# *"Tyranny Unmasked"*

Jackson swept the nation in the election of 1832 and carried Virginia by more than 22,000 votes. Close on the heels of the election a state convention in South Carolina passed an ordinance of nullification, declaring the tariffs of 1828 and 1832 null and void and, as of February 1, 1833, not enforceable within the confines of the state. Moreover, should the federal government presume to collect the revenue or in any manner coerce the state, South Carolina's only recourse would be secession.[1]

Surprisingly, Jackson's initial reaction was mild. About midway through his annual message of December 4, 1832, he informed Congress of his "painful duty" to report this threat to the integrity of the Union, but the patriotism and prudence of the people involved, he trusted, would lead to a peaceful resolution of the difficulty. Although he left no doubt of his intention to enforce the law, he asked for a gradual reduction of the tariff, ultimately limiting protection "to those articles of domestic manufacture which are indispensable to our safety in time of war." The tone of the message was deceptively conciliatory and gentle.[2] A week later the storm broke, and a startled, then incensed, South read the president's proclamation against nullification, secession, and state sovereignty. Virginians, who a short time earlier had cast their votes for Jackson, were incredulous. Many southerners agreed with his views on nullification, Tazewell among them, but the president's total disrespect for cherished states' rights and his advocacy of absolute power vested in a national government controlled by a majority, with no regard for minority rights, was more than they could bear. Even Thomas Ritchie was forced to do some fancy footwork to maintain a modicum of credibility with Virginia Democrats as he endeavored to steer a "straight course between nationalism and Calhoun's variety of particularism," while continuing to support the president. Jackson's signature was on the proclamation, the general ideas were his, the document was issued in his name, but the words, supplied by Secretary of State Edward Livingston, were more nationalistic and abusive of states' rights than any Jackson had ever uttered. "Mark under what pretenses you have been led to the brink of insurrection and treason," was the ominous warning to the nullifiers. Calhoun's name was not mentioned, but the accusing finger decidedly was pointed in his direction.[3]

While South Carolina prepared to defend itself and the president dispatched troops to the Charleston area, Governor Floyd sent the South Carolina nullification ordinance to the Virginia House of Delegates. On Virginia's official response to the "unhappy state of affairs" hung the fate of the nation, of this the president was keenly aware, as he anxiously awaited news from Richmond. For the first time in the nation's history, Calhoun declared, American guns were pointed inward, and the entire country watched nervously for the next development.[4]

In the Virginia legislature Jacksonians were in the majority, as they were throughout the state, and on December 10, as yet unaware of the president's proclamation, the members elected William Cabell Rives to succeed Tazewell in the Senate. Rives characterized himself as "anti-tariff, anti-Bank, anti-nullification, and a thorough and decided friend of Jackson's administration." For him the timing of his election was propitious. After the president's proclamation circulated among the legislators, admiration for the Jackson administration markedly diminished. A political upheaval was in the making.[5]

As debate on the South Carolina ordinance developed in the Virginia legislature there were calls for Tazewell's presence. "It is the desire of very many in the house that your father should be here as a Delegate," John Murdaugh wrote from Richmond to John Tazewell. "His services are considered to be indispensably necessary to lead the State Rights party, which appears to be completely distracted between the principles of the State and devotion to General Jackson." A day later Murdaugh was more insistent, and his second letter to John reflected increasing excitement in the legislature. "The time has now arrived when Congress must be taught by resistance to restrain its action within the constitutional limits, and Andrew Jackson must be taught that his will is not yet the supreme law of the land. My opinion is that a war is inevitable, and the sooner the people can be brought to a knowledge of this fact, the better it will be for the cause of State Rights." But the majority of legislators, realizing the significance of their actions, did not wish to go this far. "Virginia is fully aware of the awful responsibility that devolves upon her at the present crisis," reported the *National Intelligencer.*[6]

Tazewell had no desire to throw himself into the maelstrom. His sentiments were not those of the states' righters who favored nullification. His health was not good. For several years during the winter months he had been afflicted with an inflammatory disease which generally resulted in pleurisy and affected the glands of his throat, depriving him of the use of his voice for long periods of time, often until the return of warm weather.[7] Rather than participate in endless, and perhaps futile, debate in Richmond, he preferred to express his views in writing. In late December the first of a series of thirteen articles entitled "A Review of the Proclamation of President Jackson" appeared in the *Norfolk Herald* under the signature of "A Virginian."[8]

Like Calhoun, Tazewell had a scholar's mind, and he enjoyed tracing historical or legal precedents or mulling over abstract political theories. The articles, however, were composed while he was ill and confined to his room "in a fit of excitement produced by reading the President's Proclamation," and in his own opinion, there were few original thoughts in the entire series. "All the rest is matter which everybody knew before, *except the President.*"[9] Although Tazewell's main thrust was against Jackson's misconception of the nature of the government over which he presided, he again rejected the theory of nullification. In toto, Tazewell's writings constituted a plea for forbearance, directed to both the president and South Carolina, but without specifically mentioning the current controversy. Rather, he reiterated the compact theory of government, that the states, instructed by their citizens, created the federal government, and that the Constitution was a covenant among the states. If the covenant was breached, a state could secede. Secession was a proper action; nullification was not. A state which desired to secede should be allowed to go in peace, but if only a single state made this move, it would soon learn the value of the Union and speedily return. Although coercion could be used to force the seceding state back into the fold, a war waged to revive a broken covenant would never attain the desired result. "It may bring conquest, may make loyal subjects or hollow-hearted pretenders allies, but it cannot make a real Union. The Union of free states can neither be made nor preserved by force." The spirit would be gone. Because of this, all who valued the Union shoud practice moderation. Tazewell did not speak lightly of dismemberment. The states, the federal government, and the people must look to the fearful consequences of their actions. The right of secession, he doggedly held, was the constitutional prerogative of each state. It could be claimed by one today and by another tomorrow. The only way to prevent this legitimate, but terrible, recourse was for all to abstain from exercising doubtful powers or pressing lawful powers until they became doubtful. For Jackson, who flaunted the sacred Constitution, Tazewell reserved his harshest words: "I utterly disclaim the authority of this self-sufficient personage, the President, to denounce me and all others from his throne, as stupid fools or cowardly knaves, because we do not concur in his new political dogmas, but dare to think for ourselves."[10]

While Tazewell wrote his articles, the Virginia Democratic party was disintegrating, not because of concerted approval of South Carolina's ordinance, but as a result of Jackson's cavalier attitude toward state sovereignty and states' rights. The western section of the state rejoiced in the president's proclamation, so bitterly refuted in the Tidewater. Thomas Ritchie, attempting to straddle the issue, urged his readers to rally around Old Hickory and expressed hope that Virginia would act as conciliator between South Carolina and the nation's capital.[11]

In Washington the turmoil was unbelievable, as were some of the coalitions being formed. The most obvious way to avert catastrophe was to lower the tariff, but Jackson preferred the threat of military action and on January 16 sent to Congress a message expressing his determination to quell by arms, if necessary, South Carolina's wanton refusal to honor and obey the laws of the land. The Force Bill, as it was called, inflicted a wound which was to fester for decades. Van Buren, understandably aghast at the thought of a broken party and an irreconcilable South, strongly advised tariff reduction. But the president insisted that "the crisis must now be met with firmness."[12]

Two days before Jackson's message, the Virginia General Assembly called for a reduced tariff and requested South Carolina to suspend the nullification ordinance until the close of the congressional session. To open a line of communication and urge moderation, Virginia sent Benjamin Watkins Leigh to the South Carolina capital. The legislature also defeated, 107 to 24, a resolution approving the president's proclamation against nullification and expressing faith in his integrity, firmness, and patriotism. After word of the Force Bill arrived, Jackson's adherents were even fewer. John Randolph, desperately ill, appeared at Charlotte and Buckingham courthouses to denounce the man on whom he formerly had showered praise. If Jackson's headstrong obstinacy and fondness for fighting brought an open rupture, "this Union is gone."[13]

Taking advantage of southern resentment against both Jackson and Webster, who also advocated force to quell the nullifiers, Clay saw a chance to seize the leadership of a coalition based on a South-West alliance and introduced a tariff bill calling for a gradual reduction of revenue between 1834 and 1842. He hoped that this long-range program would keep the sticky tariff topic out of politics for several years, until passions cooled. The Force Bill and the compromise tariff were considered simultaneously. Virginia's dichotomous condition was indicated by the pronounced positions of its two senators. Tyler, in the best speech of his senatorial career, opposed the Force Bill with all the vigor and talent he could muster, while Rives just as resolutely upheld it. Among the state's populace sympathy for South Carolina and a strong desire to be loyal to Jackson resulted in an almost schizophrenic condition. Many party leaders eventually affiliated, somewhat uneasily, with the Whigs.[14]

After weeks of tortured confrontation, the Force Bill was brought to a vote late on the night of February 20, after many senators had gone home. Calhoun and other southerners who opposed the measure requested an adjournment until the full membership could express an opinion, and when this was denied, they left the chamber. Only Tyler, determined to cast his negative vote, remained, and the Force Bill passed, 32 to 1. To Calhoun, as to Tazewell and Tyler, the will of the tyrannical majority prevailed. The compromise tariff, as Adams noted, "swept the House like a hurricane." The gradualness of the plan, its guarantee of some protection over at least a nine-year period, and its promised restoration of harmony made it at least endurable to all who preferred compromise to a calamitous sectional conflict. On March 1 the measure won Senate approval, 29 to 16. On the same day the House passed the Force Bill, and on March 2 Jackson signed both controversial transactions. The crisis had passed, or so it seemed. Tazewell was not surprised. He had anticipated a peaceful resolution of events. "The pear is not yet ripe," he assured Wickham, "but I shall not be so sanguine in my expectations, should I live to see a second edition of nullification put to press, whether the work is published in South Carolina, or anywhere else." Certainly the tariff issue was not permanently resolved. Yet, out of all the turmoil he thought much good might come, "provided a little discretion is used by the southern states." But the wounds of 1833 were not to heal.[15]

For the time being, however, Tazewell enjoyed his respite from public responsibilities. He could give unhurried attention to his plantations and spent hours reading, planning horticultural experiments, and exchanging opinions with John Wickham. Ann's depression had subsided, and upon returning from the Eastern Shore late in April, Tazewell was pleasantly surprised to find that his wife had made arrangements for a northerly excursion to accompany young Littleton back to Princeton at the close of his vacation. Going on to New York, the Tazewells purchased plants and trees for the garden, as well as household items, bonnets, and hundreds of yards of cotton cloth for the slaves' summer garments. Once imbued with the spirit of shopping, Ann found it pleasant indeed, and her husband indulged her, although "if it depended on me," he wrote John, "we would get back tomorrow if possible."[16]

John Randolph too was in the North. Terribly ill, restlessly groping for some distraction to ease his pain, he planned to sail from Philadelphia for England. Upon hearing of his friend's presence, Tazewell immediately went to Philadelphia to see if he could assist him. Randolph's appearance was shocking. He was dreadfully emaciated, "as low as a man may be to live," and looked as if he could not survive for a day. Yet, he talked confidently of going to Europe. Tazewell thought Randolph's mind was clear, but his temper extremely peevish and wayward. "I wish he had remained in Virginia where he is well known," Tazewell told Wickham. "He is a lion wherever he goes, but the queerness of his humors, and the recklessness with which he treats all who approach him, must make his time quite uncomfortable among strangers." On May 26, only hours after Tazewell's return to Norfolk, a steamboat from Baltimore brought news of Randolph's death. At first Tazewell refused to believe the report. It was so short a time since he had seen his friend alive. Perhaps, he hoped, the story was premature. "He frequently faints from mere debility and the suspension has been mistaken for the extinction of life, I conjecture." But the report was true. Randolph died on May 24. For Tazewell the loss was painful.[17]

In Norfolk the summer of 1833 was unusually healthy and the fall singularly beautiful, but Virginia was troubled as northern antislavery societies grew alarmingly clamorous and militant, spreading panic of black insurrections throughout the Tidewater. One might deplore but scorn Garrison's *Liberator* or other fanatical papers; however, it was another matter when the *North American Review* began "squinting at the state of slavery." Solemnly the *Richmond Enquirer* announced "as soon as any attempt shall be made to touch our constitutional rights, the Union will inevitably fall to pieces." Repeatedly Virginia newspapers urged northern forbearance. "We must again warn our Eastern brethren upon this solemn subject. Why should anyone be so infatuated in the North, as to touch it? *Laissez nous faire.* We beg you to let us alone. We know the evil. We alone understand whether there be a remedy." Within Virginia, antislavery sentiments continued to be heard, but these were not so disturbing as interference from the North.[18]

In Virginia politics there was vast confusion. Tyler, who at the time of his election to the Senate had to explain and agonize over his embarrassing correspondence with Clay, was reelected, at the height of congressional debates on the compromise tariff and the Force Bill, by antiadministration, pro-Clay legislators. A strange and unlikely combination of political beliefs was molding itself into a State Rights party, unmercifully ridiculed by Ritchie for allying with Clay against Jackson and for including members who favored the rechartering of the Bank of the United States. Jackson was just slightly over six months into his second term, but the Virginia State Rights party was already discussing the next presidential election, touting Benjamin Watkins Leigh as its most likely candidate. The party also named its choice for governor, to be elected by the legislature in January 1834. "I hope, my dear sir," the incumbent, John Floyd, carefully approached Tazewell, "you will not refuse to permit your friends to place your name in nomination." The position would not be difficult, Floyd assured him. Tazewell was well acquainted "with all the involutions and convolutions" of the Richmond Junto, "which has exercised such a baneful influence upon the country for some time past, but I am happy to say is now in the evening of its power, & which, with your presence, will never again do us mischief."[19]

Had it not been for another of Jackson's arbitrary actions, Tazewell might have refused the request outright, but in late September the president made the stunning announcement that public funds would no longer be deposited in the Bank of the United States, and shortly thereafter he ordered the removal of deposits from the bank and their transfer to designated state banks. This was done with flagrant disregard for the wishes of Congress, the House having voted, 109 to 46, on March 2, 1833, to leave government deposits in the bank. When Secretary of the Treasury Louis McLane advised against the action, he was shifted to the State Department. His successor, William J. Duane, refused to remove the deposits until Congress convened; thereupon, Jackson called for Duane's resignation, and when Duane did not comply, the president removed him. The third man appointed to head the Treasury Department, Roger B. Taney, was more than willing to cooperate in the removal venture, agreeing with Jackson that unless the bank was destroyed completely, it would gather enough strength during the remaining years of its chartered existence to smite the Democratic party. Faced with the destruction of his bank before its charter expired, Nicholas Biddle fought back, curtailing loans throughout the entire banking system and causing financial chaos, particularly in commercial centers. Petitions begging the president to reverse his policy poured into the executive office, but Jackson was prepared to fight to the finish. "I am ready with the screws to draw every tooth and then the stumps," he fumed to Van Buren, who, looking toward 1836, worried about another incident qualified to antagonize more Democrats. "Fear not," Jackson told his vice-president, Mr. Biddle and his Bank would be "as quiet and harmless as a *lamb* in six weeks."[20]

But in six weeks the storm scarcely had begun. In December, Clay called for Senate censure of Jackson for "open, palpable, and daring usurpation" and misuse of presidential power in removing the deposits. Jackson, in turn, indicated he was accountable only to the people who had overwhelmingly returned him to office. Obviously they approved of his actions, and they were the source of his executive power. Jackson's assertion alarmed Tazewell. This, indeed, was a new conception of the presidential office. Tazewell saw a constitutional crisis in the offing which would make the financial panic pale by comparison. "The removal of the public deposits, altho' the apparent proximate cause of the utter prostration of credit that now threatens us, is in truth but the manifestation of another cause that lies much deeper." What really disturbed Tazewell was the spirit in which the removal was accomplished. The establishment of a precedent giving to the president "absolute control over the currency, and transforming this great monied institution into a mere electioneering machine to be put in action every four years" was a frightening prospect. Victory in an election could not give a chief executive a mandate to do anything he wished, to act unilaterally, ignoring constitutional provisions for checks and balances. Instead of wasting time on long speeches, Congress, immediately upon convening, should have restored the deposits, "by a strong and indignant vote." "Their delay has aggravated the mischief."[21]

Furthermore, if the president were accountable to the people alone, majority tyranny could never be checked. This would be catastrophic, for the people, collectively, had neither the intelligence nor the wisdom to see all aspects of a complex problem. At times Tazewell, extremely agitated, referred to the masses as "the many headed beast," causing his close friend John Mercer Patton, a member of the House of Representatives from Fredericksburg, to chide, "I cannot however as yet bring myself thoroughly to the conviction that there is not a large fund of intelligence & wisdom among the body of the people—and a large stock of integrity and public spirit among the public men."[22] But Tazewell was skeptical.

To keep the "great monied institution" out of the hands of the president and prevent a perpetual fluctuation of credit, Tazewell sought an alternative. "What think you," he asked Wickham, "of re-chartering this Institution, not by Congress, but by the several states, under an arrangement to be previously agreed upon by them, containing mutual stipulations satisfactory to each, with adequate guarantees against the action of the federal government?" All the Atlantic states, except New York, he thought, could be induced to adopt the plan. "If I did not consider the case as almost desperate, I would not think of trying so strong a remedy."[23]

Clay consulted Tazewell on another major point of controversy associated with the removal of deposits, whether or not a president could remove a cabinet officer by his own action alone. Early in his senatorial career, Tazewell replied, he had examined the question carefully and concluded that whereas the Constitution gave the president the right to appoint officials only with the advice and consent of the Senate, it was "manifestly absurd to regard the President as responsible for the acts of subordinate agents, and yet to deny him the uncontrolled power of supervising them, and of removing them from office whenever they had lost his confidence." Although willing to concede to the president exclusive right to all executive powers created by the Constitution, to be exercised by him at his discretion, Tazewell tenaciously believed the president accountable to Congress, the states, and the people for every misuse of discretionary power. Under no circumstance did he have a right to abuse or usurp power; he had no right to do wrong. In the United States, where all political powers are conferred, and therefore limited, "there always exists a tribunal competent to decide upon the legitimate exercise of power."[24]

Jackson's arbitrary conduct accelerated the formation of a new party combination which had been developing for some months. It was a strange group, primarily held together by disdain for the president. National Republicans (bank, tariff, and internal improvements advocates) made up the largest component, but they were joined by nullifiers, states' righters, and various shades of Democrats, most of whom favored low tariffs and had mixed feelings about the bank. This eclectic cluster was called the Whig party, indicating, the members said, a preference for liberty over tyranny and support for "the rights and immunities of the people, as ascertained by the equity of nature, the constitution and laws of the country, against the predominance of the Crown, or Executive power."[25]

In Virginia mass meetings protesting the deposit removals were held in Petersburg, Staunton, Wheeling, Fredericksburg, Richmond, Norfolk, Lynchburg, and many other places. Several western counties, Jackson's stronghold, were as critical of the transaction as were counties east of the Blue Ridge. This time, even for them, Jackson had gone too far. The Richmond meeting adopted resolutions sponsored by Benjamin Watkins Leigh stating that as long as the bank was a safe depository, it was entitled to receive public moneys until the expiration of its charter. This was a charter right, and withdrawal constituted a breach of the public faith. Thomas Ritchie, while remaining loyal to the chief executive, also believed deposits should be restored to forestall the demise of the Democratic party.[26]

In the midst of the uproar Tazewell pondered whether or not he should accede to Floyd's persuasion and allow his name to be entered in the gubernatorial race. He was, he admitted to Wickham, in an unpleasant and embarrassing predicament. He had no desire to be governor or to commit himself to a specific political party. He did not consider himself a Whig. Floyd had tried to make him a nullifier or a member of the State Rights party. He was neither. Rather, he followed his own conscience, which now told him that if Andrew Jackson was destroying constitutional government, responsible people should try to stop him. With this in mind, what should he do? The anti-Jackson forces lacked cohesion and leadership. Should he try to pull them together? Wickham agreed it would be quite a task. The state legislature was fragmented; within that body there was great diversity of opinion and very little talent. Undoubtedly Tazewell was needed. However, Wickham was reticent about giving advice and gently reminded his friend, "when you communicated to me your resolution to retire from the Senate I did not attempt to dissuade you from it though I thought that at your time of life you might for years occupy a public station with credit to yourself." It was for Tazewell alone to decide "both of the good you might do and of the sacrifices of ease and domestic comfort you might be obliged to make."[27]

## Chapter XIV

# *"The Most Unambitious of Men"*

John Tyler, despairing over the agitated condition of the country and the "mad careers of its leaders," felt it mandatory for Virginia to place the "highest grade of intellect in the gubernatorial office," a man of public virtue and unsuspected purity, and who "unites these qualifications in so eminent a degree as L. W. Tazewell?" Tyler realized that Tazewell's past history proved him to be "one of the most unambitious of men." Yet, he begged him to "deny not to your friends the use of your name in a crisis so full of peril to the public good."[1]

After his usual plunge into a state of painful indecision, Tazewell acceded, and on January 7, 1834, the Virginia General Assembly elected him governor for a three-year term, commencing on March 31. For the first time the Jacksonians went down to complete defeat in the Old Dominion. The Richmond Junto was routed.[2] In Washington reactions were mixed. John Quincy Adams, while pleased by the president's discomfiture, could not resist sourly noting that Tazewell now had "boxed the compass of politics, from federalism to nullification." Still, Adams saw the election as "the signal for raising the standard of Virginia against Jackson." According to a reporter for the Norfolk *American Beacon*, the Senate chamber, upon hearing of Tazewell's election, "exhibited the broad lights and shadows of a Rembrandt painting," with exultation and dismay upon alternate countenances. Calhoun rejoiced in the opportunity now afforded Virginia to "stand in her old position, in the cause of liberty & the Constitution." "Movements in Virginia & particularly your election, have given them [states' rights doctrines] a great impulse." John Patton, too, was certain "that Van with all his New York tactics" was done in the state.[3]

The day after his election Tazewell spoke at a Norfolk meeting called to voice the borough's disapproval of the deposit removals. He had not intended to address the gathering, but the very large crowd was in a nasty mood, angry and emotional, and Tazewell confided to Wickham, "I saw, or thought I saw, that unless some exertion was used, the indiscretion of some of our 'antagonizing' young lawyers would produce mischief." Speaking with conviction about the jeopardy in which the president had placed the nation, he nevertheless urged his fellow townsmen to restrain their emotions. Cool heads prevailed and the frenzy was defused, but the effort made him ill for days afterward.[4]

Shortly thereafter, the Whigs in the Virginia General Assembly passed resolutions denouncing the deposit removals as "an unauthorized assumption and dangerous exercise of executive power" which inflicted "deep and lasting injury upon the people of Virginia." Senators Rives and Tyler were instructed to work toward the adoption of proper measures for restoring the public moneys to the Bank of the United States, but the resolutions clearly indicated the legislature's belief in the unconstitutionality of congressional chartering of a national bank.[5]

Again the complicated issue of the right of state legislatures to instruct senators was opened to debate. Instruction was considered by many to be an important aspect of the democratic process. Since United States senators were elected by state legislatures, they were accountable, it was maintained, to those governing bodies. Members of the House of Representatives were chosen by the people and therefore merely could be "requested," not instructed, to vote in accordance with specified legislative resolutions; but the compliance of senators to legislative direction was considered of major importance. In Virginia the only serious challenge to the practice had come in 1811 when Senators Richard Brent and William Branch Giles were instructed to vote against the recharter of the first Bank of the United States. Brent refused to bow to the wishes of the General Assembly, and Giles, while voting according to legislative dictates, spoke forcefully against the idea of mandatory instruction. Two young members of the House of Delegates, John Tyler and Benjamin Watkins Leigh, led the hue and cry against Brent and Giles for the disrespect they displayed to the body that had elected them to high office. In January 1812 Tyler's proposed resolutions of censure against the insubordinate senators were superseded by those of Leigh, who categorically stated that a senator either had to obey or resign. In a similar vein, Tazewell, in his *Review of the Proclamation of President Jackson,* listed among the prerogatives of the people the right to instruct their own representatives, "whose duty it is to observe such instructions." He did not refer specifically to directives received by senators from state legislatures, but the statement seemed to imply his approval of the practice.[6] All three, Tyler, Leigh, and Tazewell, later revised their views.

In 1834 Rives, in a letter to the speakers of both houses of the Virginia General Assembly, questioned the language of the instructions directed to him. If, he said, the instructions had required him to vote for legislation to restore the deposits, he would have acted accordingly, however inexpedient he thought such a measure to be. But if he accepted the resolution condemning Jackson's "unauthorized assumption" of executive power, he felt he would be placed in the position of having to support Clay's resolution of censure of the president. This Rives declared he could not do "without a complete compromise of personal honor," and he thereupon tendered his resignation. The legislature elected Leigh to replace him.[7]

Throughout the early weeks of 1834 the Virginia Capitol resounded with "scurrilous epithets, impotent threats, and low abuse." Tazewell had no desire to witness the partisan violence, but John Floyd thought the governor-elect should make an appearance in Richmond before the legislature adjourned. "Pray come," Floyd persisted, " 'for great events are in the gale' and our friends will like to hear your views before they go home to 'open another campaign.' " Wickham too urged Tazewell to come, and he finally agreed to do so on condition that no public dinners be held in his honor. In late February, Governor Floyd and several legislators paid a return visit to Tazewell in Norfolk.[8]

During the months before he took office Tazewell was preoccupied, above all, with finding a way to forestall national financial disaster. To Calhoun he suggested the same plan he mentioned to Wickham earlier, rechartering the bank under the auspices of the several states. Like Wickham, Calhoun thought the idea infeasible; instead, in strict confidence, he broached to Tazewell the possibility of renewing the bank's charter but with very important modifications stressing an "entire divorce between the government and the banking system, or it will certainly ruin the country." Many of the South Carolinian's ideas were similar to those Tazewell had voiced during the 1832 recharter debate. What Tazewell feared most was a general suspension of specie payment. Although Calhoun considered this unlikely, he included Tazewell's concerns in his March 21 speech to the Senate in which he tried to suggest ways to separate the bank from politics. Webster backed a bill to extend the life of the institution for six years after expiration of the charter in 1836, but both Calhoun and Tazewell were against allowing the bank to be used as a pawn in two more presidential elections. Taking shape in their minds was a vague outline of a plan which surfaced again in 1837 as the Independent Treasury system.[9]

Thomas Ritchie called on Virginians to reject all proposals which included a national bank in any form. "Will you rule the mammoth, or shall it rule you?" He urged voters to send to the legislature men who would declare the bank contrary to the sovereignty of the state and dangerous to the liberties of the people. But many Virginians appeared more skeptical about Jackson's position on state sovereignty and civil liberties, and Ritchie realized there was much convincing to do. The president's actions had not made this an easy task. "I have no doubt he acted from the best motives [in removing the deposits]," Ritchie anxiously told Rives, "but I thought he ought to have waited, at least until the Committee of Congress could have investigated & reported on the misconduct of the Bank. Things would have gone on much smoother in that way." Also, Ritchie thought the Force Bill should be rescinded, now that the "emergency" had passed. It "is only calculated to fester the feelings & excite the discord of the South," and he advised Rives to use his influence to have it abolished. Ritchie had reason to worry. The state elections in April indicated a growing antiadministration sentiment, and Clay's resolution to censure Jackson for removal of deposits, which on March 28, 1834, passed the Senate, 26 to 20, appeared to have the approval of a majority of the commonwealth's citizens. The next General Assembly was to be quite strongly Whig, a turn of events which the governor-elect found comforting.[10]

Tazewell assumed his duties on the last day of March without pomp. According to tradition the incoming governor merely went to the executive chamber and sent for the mayor or a magistrate who administered the oath. "In this plain unceremonious manner," John Floyd explained, "have all Governors been inducted into office." Tazewell heartily approved. No member of his family accompanied him to Richmond, and while the governor's mansion underwent renovation, Tazewell stayed at Mrs. Duval's boardinghouse. He felt lonely and out of sorts. "I have been here now a whole week, and have not heard directly from one of you at home, although I write by every boat." When the superintendent of public edifices sought advice on redecorating, Tazewell had no idea what to tell him. He needed his wife's recommendations and was sure he would never get settled without assistance. "Entreat your mamma and sisters to come to me speedily," he begged John. "I should rather see your mother than any body else, but if anything exists to prevent her from coming up shortly, if for a few days only, for Heaven's sake prevail upon Louisa & Sally to do so at once, the sooner the better."[11]

Ann continued to delay her departure for Richmond, preferring to shun the public eye for as long as possible, but within a few days after Tazewell's cry for help, Louisa, Sally, and young Littleton arrived, and by the end of April the governor occupied the mansion on the Capitol grounds. "We took our first dinner *at home* yesterday," he informed John on April 29, "when we found ourselves in want of many things that we had not thought of providing. . . . I shall leave all minor matters to the discretion of the home secretaries, Louisa and Sally, but the more important I must take upon myself. Our wants of this class are bacon, wine, rum, and cider." By the first steamboat John was to send a quarter cask of madeira, a couple of demijohns of rum, and as much bacon as could be conveniently spared from home.[12]

Although his domestic affairs were in better order, Tazewell felt misplaced and found life irksome. The routine duties of office gave him no trouble, but Jackson proponents created many complications, even attempting a few "low tricks" which caused the governor, in turn, to be "somewhat dictatorial." Repeatedly he entreated John to persuade his mother to "come to me as soon as her convenience will permit." He desperately needed her and the younger children. "In their society I can willingly put the world at defiance, and keep my own course." The future worried him. The state was torn by dissension, and the atmosphere in Richmond was most depressing. "You have no idea of the state of society here at this time," Peter V. Daniel, the Jacksonian lieutenant governor, told Congressman Andrew Stevenson. "I am watched throughout the day; every door I enter, every person with whom I speak, is a subject of jealous scrutiny. . . . But d—— the contemptible slaves of the Bank, I put them all at defiance." Tazewell saw "a cloud forming in the distant horizon, which I would avoid if I could." But he was determined to "weather this gale, altho' it may cost me the loss of much personal comfort to do so." By June, Ann was in Richmond. Tazewell, hoping to lessen tensions in the capital, decided to give a party, but the thought of hostessing a social event sent Ann to bed with one of her headaches. She wished to avoid all such responsibilities, but her husband persisted, set a new date for the party, and notified John to "send us by the next boat a plentiful supply of everything good which we can't get here, especially fish, fruits, and if possible a turtle."[13]

Social gatherings did little to alleviate political hostilities. As Congress intensified its pressure on Jackson, the antiadministrationists in Virginia drove the president's supporters into an increasingly defensive position. Early in the summer of 1834 the stalwart Jacksonian Andrew Stevenson resigned from the House of Representatives and accepted the post of minister to Great Britain. Although he preferred to remain in Congress, he was aware of his district's attitudes on removal and restoration of the public deposits, and "recognizing the right of the people to instruct, and the duty of the Representative to obey, or surrender up the trust, I am ready to lay down the trust whenever it may be required in a manner that I ought to listen to and respect." Not long afterward the Senate rejected Jackson's nomination of Roger B. Taney as secretary of the treasury, and Congress, fearful of the president's control over the nation's finances through his close affiliation with a relatively few pet banks, passed the Deposit Act, increasing the number of state deposit banks from twenty to ninety. Unfortunately, congressional failure to provide necessary regulations or regulatory agencies for these ninety banks led to wild extensions of credit to almost anyone who asked for it. Within a few years, when the vast federal surplus was distributed to the states, the nation was caught up in a chaotic financial cycle. Easy credit precipitated a land boom, and revenue from land sales increased the federal surplus, which went back to the states, creating easier credit. Jackson was not unaware of the dangers inherent in the Deposit Act, but believing a veto would injure Van Buren's chance for the presidency in 1836, he signed the bill. With his removal scheme the president had set in motion something he could not stop.[14]

The approaching national election cast its shadow over Jackson's entire second administration and loomed large in the thinking of almost everyone associated with government at any level. "Who can unite the whole South?" Tyler asked William F. Gordon, and then quickly proceeded to answer his own question. "I have brought myself to think that Gov. Tazewell is that very man." The Carolinas and Georgia would support him, Tyler believed, and when he mentioned Tazewell to a Pennsylvanian, a Kentuckian, and a Marylander, "they snatched at the suggestion. I should not be surprised if he is named in some public journal of each of these states, forthwith. No matter where his name may be first brought out, it will spread like lightning—that is my opinion."[15]

John Randolph's half-brother, Nathaniel Beverley Tucker, echoed Tyler, but Tazewell courteously rejected the idea, pointing out that Hugh Lawson White, one of the most frequently mentioned standard-bearers for the Whigs, was a personal friend, "and time and chance has left me so few of these that no earthly consideration shall induce me to be placed even in seeming conflict with any who remain." This remark about the loss of friends was not made lightly. Within the year Tazewell mourned the deaths of three of the closest companions of his youth: Randolph in May 1833, William Wirt in February 1834, followed by Robert B. Taylor in April. Tazewell felt bereaved and much older. He had no ambitions to fulfill; high office held no charm for him; he disliked power. Yet he was willing to serve his state. In what might be regarded as his credo, he told Tucker, "I was born in Virginia, I have lived a long life in Virginia, and I trust God, that when in his good time he shall call me hence, my earthly remains will be deposited in the land where I have ever lived, and in which it is my wish to die. While I live, I will willingly render to Virginia all she may choose to require of me, to which I may be equal. But I serve no other mistress or master, and it is gratitude and loyalty only that induce me to devote my few expiring years to her." Under no conceivable set of circumstances would he consider a nomination to the presidency. If the commonwealth believed his presence in Congress was essential for a season, he would go. "In doing it, however, I should know that I go there to die; the climate and mode of life disagree with me so much, that I could not hope to survive a long and continued abode there."[16]

Tazewell loved his state, but this did not preclude his loving the Union. States' rights and Unionism were not, in his mind, mutually exclusive but, rather, dependent on one another. The more the national government respected the states, the stronger the country would be linked together by a chain of friendship. Virginia, he firmly was convinced, should and, under the proper conditions and represented by right-thinking statesmen, could serve as the balance between North and South, the conciliator, the reasonable voice. As senator he had hoped to be instrumental in establishing a stable relationship of this nature, but he believed he had failed. Yet, he had devoted years to the service of his state and nation, years of personal anguish and loneliness. So also had many others. He was not unique, except that unlike most of his counterparts he was not ambitious. Public office was not a prize to be won, rather it was a duty to be borne. Had Ann been more supportive, life might have been easier, but she either could not or would not. After a few months in Richmond she returned to Norfolk, leaving her husband depressed and forlorn. "Every day I find new cause to deplore my folly in accepting the appointment I now fill," Tazewell told John in October 1834, "but if to its necessarily disagreeable accomplishments, these long separations from my family are to be added, I shall find them quite intolerable soon. . . . I am becoming quite petulant and dictatorial, I fear."[17]

With violence occurring in the corridors of the Capitol there was reason to be somewhat imperious. One day, sitting in his office, Tazewell "very distinctly" heard blows, as John Hampden Pleasants, editor of the *Richmond Whig*, "fell abroad" Lieutenant Governor Daniel. Pleasants "is said to have beaten him a good deal," Tazewell reported. "The Grand Jury has presented Pleasants for an assault & battery," Ritchie informed Rives. "God knows what we are coming to." Striving to prevent outbreaks of fisticuffs or worse during meetings of the Council of State, the governor presided over the body "with a perfect, if frosty, decorum, and no conflicts arose."[18]

In his message to the General Assembly in December 1834 Tazewell also indicated to the legislature how he expected it to behave. While forcefully denouncing the president for his reckless treatment of public funds, he cautioned against rash retaliation. In deliberating upon matters calculated to produce excitement, he asked the lawmakers always to remember "that the character and honor of Virginia is involved, not less in what you may do, than in the temper and manner in which this may be performed." Therefore, "act in all things as becomes this Commonwealth." But vindictiveness did surface. Ritchie was removed as public printer, a post he had held for twenty years. The editor, in turn, carried on an intemperate campaign against Leigh, but despite all efforts to the contrary, Leigh was elected to a full term in the Senate, and the Whigs removed Peter V. Daniel from the Council of State. Daniel also lost the lieutenant governorship, a position held by the senior councilor. "Blair would not believe me last August— you would scarcely listen to me in November when I predicted to you the mischievous consequences of removing the deposits," Ritchie moaned to Stevenson. "I fear we shall rue the precipitate step in sackcloth and ashes."[19]

But Ritchie was not to be thwarted, and as the presidential campaign began in earnest early in 1835, his paper bristled with insults and innuendos against the antiadministration forces. "I suppose that Ritchie & Co. are to keep the State agitated for another twelve months," Tyler sighed, and he was right. Ridicule of the strange conglomeration of beliefs represented by the Whig party was a major theme. "The Whigs," Ritchie remarked, "have materials enough to choose from; but the misfortune is that they have also too many persons to please. They have 'too many cooks'—and their 'broth may be spoilt.' "[20]

The Whigs did not call a national convention, thus avoiding, they contended, the "circus atmosphere" prevalent at those held in the past few years. Instead, legislative caucuses, state conventions, and other local meetings selected candidates. The real reason for resorting to these methods was fear of deep differences of opinion within Whig ranks that would be destructively obvious were all Whig delegates gathered under one roof. The conflicting philosophies within the party were reflected in the candidates chosen. In December 1834 a caucus of anti-Jackson congressmen from Tennessee named Hugh Lawson White. Shortly after the turn of the year, Daniel Webster was endorsed by the Massachusetts legislature, and sometime later a Pennsylvania Whig convention decided upon the candidacy of William Henry Harrison. Clay, defeated in 1832 and the focal point of controversy ever since, was ignored, and "Poor Calhoun," one of Tazewell's correspondents observed, "has nullified himself" out of position. John Tyler and Francis Granger of New York, a former Anti-Mason, were prime prospects for the vice-presidential nomination.[21]

In May 1835 Democrats traveled to Baltimore for their convention. There Van Buren's years of careful and clever planning paid off, and he slid gracefully into the top spot. The party's choice for second place on the ticket was Richard Johnson of Kentucky rather than William Cabell Rives, who was favored by a majority of southern Jacksonians, and Ritchie was deeply disappointed. "We have been beaten at Baltimore—after all that has been done," he commiserated with Rives. "But we must not divide our party. . . . You, of course will keep perfectly cool—not suffer your feelings for a single moment to move your judgment." Rives still might have a chance to return to the Senate; to this end, Ritchie in the spring of 1835 launched an all-out campaign to recapture the Virginia legislature for the Jacksonians. Conditions were favorable. With crops good and prices high, the editor was able to convince many voters that the financial panic predicted by

Tazewell and others as a consequence of the pet bank scheme was only a scare tactic designed to destroy the Democratic party. The strategy worked, and enough administration candidates were successful to enable the Jacksonians to retake control of the General Assembly.[22]

For Tazewell the times seemed absurdly out of joint. Virginia voters swung abruptly first one direction, then in another. In July the death of John Marshall added to Tazewell's apprehensions. The chief justice symbolized continuity and soundness, and even though Tazewell often disagreed with him, both men respected the law and cherished the Constitution and expected others, including presidents, to do the same. Each, in his own way, was motivated by a force above that of political ambition. Marshall's body arrived in Richmond aboard the steamboat *Kentucky.* All business ceased, and bells throughout the city tolled until the setting of the sun. Perhaps, reported the *Enquirer,* no funeral procession in Virginia had ever been more extensive and solemn. Tazewell, along with the Council of State and other officials, followed behind the clergy as the cortege wound its way to the cemetery on Shockoe Hill. It was startling to learn that Roger B. Taney, Jackson's willing instrument in removing the deposits, was likely to replace Marshall as chief justice. Without a doubt, everything was askew.[23]

There were other, more immediate, reasons for alarm. During the summer of 1835 a great surge of abusive antislavery literature poured forth from abolition presses as the reform movements obsessing Western civilization focused increasingly on the issue of human bondage. Tracts, pamphlets, and newspapers designed to open the eyes of slaveowners to their sins described in graphic detail the horrors of the peculiar institution. If abolitionists believed they could in this fashion persuade masters to renounce their evil ways, they sorely were disappointed. Most southerners were convinced that the propaganda barrage was really intended to encourage black hatred of whites; the consequences of arousing such hostile emotions were fresh in the minds of Virginians.[24]

By December, when the state legislature convened, tension was extreme, particularly in the Tidewater and Southside.

Tazewell was in a quandary. When was it justifiable, if ever, to interfere with freedom of the press? Was there a clear and present danger to the citizens of the commonwealth which obliged the governor to act to protect them? In his message to the General Assembly he tried to address these difficult and painful questions. Residents of northern and and eastern states, aided by a few foreigners, Tazewell told the legislators, had organized societies, subscribed large sums of money, and established presses to produce direct interference with slave property. Virginia, on the border of the free North, bore the brunt of propaganda "obviously designed and well-calculated to lead to insurrection, rapine, and murder." These dangerous publications were transmitted to the South by the United States postal service. Because the authors of these schemes lived outside the state, they were impervious to local laws. Furthermore, they did not stop with inciting slaves to insurrection; they contended that the Constitution of the United States endowed Congress with plenary authority to free every slave in the District of Columbia, prohibit transportation of slaves from one state to another, emancipate all slaves in the territories of the nation, and make liberation a precedent condition for admission of states into the Union.

"It is no time to temporize," Tazewell warned. "It is vain to turn away our eyes from the state of things as they now exist. We have to meet it in some form or other, and it belongs properly to you to describe as to the manner in which this shall be done." However, he offered several recommendations. The legislature should request northern states in which abolitionist organizations existed to suppress the societies and to adopt regulations to prevent or punish those who disturbed the tranquillity of the South. Southern states had no intention of interfering in the internal affairs of their northern neighbors but only appealed to them to preserve interstate peace and harmony. He advised legislators to take a stronger stand in addressing the federal government. Virginia should demand that Congress speedily ban distribution by the post offices of seditious and incendiary publications. Southern states should not have to help pay for their own destruction. To continue to act as a conveyor of harmful propaganda was a

gross perversion of the responsibilities of the Post Office Department. He exhorted the General Assembly to seek from
other slaveholding states suggestions for mutual protection.[25]

Not everyone applauded the governor's remarks. Patton
took issue with Tazewell's demand that Congress speedily pro-
scribe distribution of seditious and incendiary publications. "I
do not see how the power can be conceded without admitting
the right to define what are and what are not incendiary pamphlets. A man may write what he pleases. . . . Anything which
it is not contrary to the laws of the United States to write or
print, it seems to me, may be transported by the mails." Unless
Congress had the power to prohibit writing and printing of
antislavery papers, there was no way to prevent the publications from being carried by the postal service, and there was
not the slightest chance that laws interdicting antislavery literature could pass both houses of Congress. Patton was
shocked by Tazewell's apparent willingness to see basic tenets
of the Bill of Rights violated or destroyed; even the possibility
of servile insurrection did not warrant a sacrifice of such mag-
nitude. One reader of the *Enquirer* belabored Tazewell for
being silly enough to suppose that northern fanatics could
ever effect a general abolition of slavery, and Ritchie accused
the governor of overreacting for political purposes. But the
issue was also a concern of the president of the United States.
On December 7, 1835, the same day that Tazewell's message
was read in the House of Delegates, Jackson asked Congress
to consider the propriety of passing a law prohibiting circulation through the mails of publications intended to instigate
servile insurrection. While applauding the president's solicitude, Calhoun objected to placing such potentially dangerous
censorship power in the hands of Congress. Early in 1836 he
introduced a bill allowing each state to decide for itself what
publications were incendiary and giving local postmasters the
right to intercept those so designated. Upon request, the federal government was to aid, within constitutional limitations,
states in the enforcement of laws designed to protect internal
security. The bill did not pass.[26]

As the Virginia legislative session got underway, Tazewell
found party feeling stronger "than policy and patriotism combined," resulting "in a state of the most perfect confusion."

"What may be the result nothing short of infinite wisdom can foresee." The most bitter clashes occurred when the Jacksonian majority resolved to instruct Virginia's senators to use all possible means to push through a bill obliterating the 1834 reprimand of the president for withdrawing the deposits. Periodically since the Senate censure of Jackson, Thomas Hart Benton had moved to have the journal of 1834 brought into the chamber, where, in the presence of the entire body, black lines would be drawn around the critical passage, and the words "Expunged by order of the Senate," followed by the date of the expunction, superimposed thereon. It was this bill, verbatim, which the Virginia General Assembly directed its senators to introduce and support. The edict was to be forwarded to Leigh and Tyler by the governor of the commonwealth.[27]

The *National Intelligencer* was aghast, not only because the Virginia legislature countenanced defacing the records of the Senate but also because *"the Senators shall be made the instruments of their own disgrace."* This, cried the Washington paper, was carrying "man-worship" too far. "Is this Virginia? So long distinguished by her attachment to the true principles of liberty?" Did the state of Jefferson, Washington, and Mason have a new motto: "When Caesar says do this, it is performed?" All major newspapers printed editorials and letters for and against the right of instruction. Virginia's action, some said, exemplified the abuse of the practice, for clearly the Jacksonian legislators there, believing Leigh and Tyler would resign rather than obey instructions, hoped to force the senators out of office and to replace them with loyal proponents of the administration. Other editors declared the doctrine of instruction unconstitutional and disorganizing, arguing that the Constitution carefully specified staggered terms of office: four years for the president, two for representatives, and six for senators. The Senate was intended to be the branch of government most likely to insure stability and consistency. Instruction, if considered mandatory, could drive out of office men who could not in good conscience vote according to the current whim of a state legislature. This would make senatorial elections nothing but appointments at will. There were other facets to contemplate. The Senate, the *Intelligencer* observed, was not only one branch of the legislature but also an essential part of the treaty-making and appointing powers of the national government. Thus, "it may well be said, that the people of one state were willing to trust their own high interests to Senators chosen by the several States, because they saw security for those interests in the qualifications required, and *in the term of office prescribed.* For any State, then, to insist that she has a right to compel her Senators to resign, at her own pleasure, appears to us to be a plain infringement upon the rights of other States under the Constitution" and a dangerous departure from the true principles on which the Constitution was founded.[28]

Aside from theoretical discourses, the main question of the moment was whether Leigh and Tyler would actually resign. Calhoun was determined to prevent this from happening. "If we understand the case correctly," he advised Tazewell, "in voting for Mr. Clay's resolution [of censure], your Senators voted in fact under instructions. Should they be instructed to vote for expunging these resolutions, it would be a case of instructions against instructions." Given these circumstances, Calhoun thought it perfectly proper for Leigh and Tyler to send a communication to the governor refusing to honor the instructions until results of the spring elections were known and promising to abide by the will of the people so expressed. The primary worry was that the two senators were "disposed to pursue different directions," Tyler to obey the legislative directive and Leigh to refuse. This, Calhoun was certain, would weaken the antiadministration stand.[29]

Tazewell was faced with making an immediate and personal decision of his own. Should he or should he not accede to the legislature's directive and forward the instructions to Leigh and Tyler? He sincerely believed the censure of Jackson was a correct and proper exercise of the Senate's right and duty to check and balance executive action, and therefore, he had no choice but to refuse to be a party to its removal. Neither Virginia's constitution nor state statutes, he contended, required him to transmit instructions to senators. To do so would be a voluntary action on his part and, in the eyes of the public, would add his approbation and sanction to resolutions that he considered palpable violations of the Constitution of the United States. A censure, he held, could not be erased. It was an irrevocable fact, recorded in the journal, and there it should stand through time and eternity. The Senate, at one specific moment, thought the president guilty of wrongdoing. Unless the clock could be turned back to that precise instant, the censure could not be removed at another time by a body whose composition had been altered. Perhaps the Senate of 1836 could announce its approval of the chief executive, but it had no right to expunge an opinion of the Senate of 1834 and deface the journal. If instructions were to be sent to Virginia's senators, the task would have to be assigned to another agent.

The incensed legislature thereupon directed the presiding officers of the two houses to assume the responsibility. When news of the General Assembly's action reached Washington, Leigh announced his refusal to obey instructions. His decision had been made months earlier. "I will not be instructed out of my seat," he told Tyler during the preceding summer. He did not intend to write himself off as a "fool, knave, and slave." As he had stated in the Virginia resolutions of 1812, a senator was not bound to obey instructions that required him to violate the Constitution or commit an act of moral turpitude, and he believed the current instructions were of this character for, instead of voicing the will of the people, the legislature was attempting to shorten the senatorial terms of himself and Tyler. Submitting to the directive would establish a precedent for this "pernicious practice." "You know what I am going to do," Leigh informed Tazewell, "but as to what my colleague will do, you do not know—Neither do I, and I verily believe *he* does not, even yet. The probability is, that he will resign."[30] Tyler did relinquish his office on February 29, 1836, and was replaced by William Cabell Rives. Leigh stayed on to face the outrage of the vocal element of his constituency. Pleading ill health, he resigned on July 4, 1836; in his letter of resignation he reaffirmed his belief in the doctrine of instruction while condemning its abuse.[31]

For refusing to forward the instructions of the General Assembly, Tazewell was maligned, burned in effigy, and threatened with removal from office. On March 31, 1836, at the close of the legislative session, he resigned. "This is the first instance we recollect," announced the *Enquirer*, "of any Governor of Virginia having resigned since the Revolution." Ritchie

thought he should have been impeached, thus giving the
House of Delegates an opportunity to try the question of
whether or not a governor could decline to carry out the
wishes of the legislative branch. The state's constitution bound
the executive to take care that the laws be faithfully executed,
and a resolution of both houses "is to all intents and purposes
a law because it is the expression of the will of the supreme
power of the state." By refusing to transmit the expunging
resolutions, Ritchie contended, Tazewell indicated his con-
tempt for the legislature of the commonwealth.[32]

Tazewell did forward, according to legislative direction,
resolutions adopted in January relative to the interference of
northern abolitionists with domestic slavery in the South.
These were in line with suggestions included in his message to
the General Assembly, calling upon northern states to suppress abolition propaganda for the sake of general peace and
tranquillity. Debate on these resolutions was spirited, with politics inevitably playing a part. Ritchie thought such legislation
would embarrass Van Buren, but even the Democrats in the
General Assembly believed more was at stake than the presidency. Alarm precipitated by the circulation of abolition literature was very real. The South, and especially Virginia, was
haunted by the thought that another Nat Turner might be
triggered by an inflammatory pamphlet to rage through the
countryside. Every precaution had to be taken to prevent a
similar disaster from happening again.[33]

At times hysteria caused the lawmakers to go too far. One
example of this occurred a few days before Tazewell left office
when the General Assembly passed what has been termed the
most intolerant act adopted in Virginia. The statute went beyond the governor's recommendations. Anyone who entered
the state and advocated the abolition of slavery or maintained
by speaking or writing that owners of slaves had no right to
hold them as property was to be fined and imprisoned. If a
slave or "other colored person" circulated or caused to be
circulated printed materials that encouraged insurrection, he
was to be whipped, not exceeding thirty-nine lashes, and
transported and sold beyond the limits of the United States,
under orders of the governor. If a white person was found
guilty of doing the same, he faced imprisonment for from two

to five years in the state penitentiary. Postmasters throughout Virginia were to notify justices of the peace when inflammatory abolition materials appeared in the mails, whereupon the justice of the peace was to have the book, pamphlet, or other writing burned in his presence. Additional punishments were prescribed for subscribers to abolition publications. Vigilantism was encouraged by a stipulation giving any free white person authority to arrest purveyors of abolition doctrines.[34]

The act was harsh and suppressive, but less so than one approved a few months earlier by the Georgia legislature calling for the death penalty for publication and circulation of incendiary material. Likewise, the governor of South Carolina declared that "the laws of every community should punish this species of interference with death, without benefit of clergy." Among both the abolitionists and the proslavery advocates fanaticism was gaining ground, and as Tazewell had anticipated, reason was being thrust aside. In the past, book burning, disregard for freedom of speech, and restrictions on the press would have incensed him. Indubitably, he left the governor's office with somber thoughts of what the future held for Virginia, the South, and the nation. Fear of slave insurrection, very real in the minds of many Virginia citizens, had caused him to make distasteful recommendations to the legislature. Perhaps he was not quite at peace with his own conscience; as John Patton reminded him, "the only permanent record of a public man must be the approbation of his own conscience."[35]

## Chapter XV

# "*Where the Tree Falls, There Let It Lie*"

On a bright, beautiful March day in 1837 Martin Van Buren became president of the United States. For Tazewell the passing of Andrew Jackson from the national scene was no cause for rejoicing. Too much harm had been done. The country's psyche as well as its financial and political future had been damaged irreparably. "I think when Andrew Jackson came into power he was a very different man from what he was when he left Washington," Hugh Lawson White observed in a letter to Tazewell. "I thought him honest, with good sound judgment, and great decision of character. The last trait I think he yet possesses in a very high degree. He has all sorts of courage: physical courage to encounter any personal danger— moral courage enough to do whatever he thinks right, and immoral courage to do whatever he *pleases,* whether it be *right* or *wrong*." Van Buren, White believed, had no marked character of his own. "I view him as the *appointee of his predecessor,* willing to profess any politics most likely to elevate him to office, and willing to practice whatever will most likely gratify importunate partizans."[1]

Tazewell was tempted to agree; yet, in Van Buren's inaugural address there were encouraging statements, provided one could trust what he said. It was heartening to read the incoming president's promise to adhere strictly to "the letter and spirit of the Constitution as it was designed by those who framed it." Van Buren also reiterated his preelection declaration of opposition to "every attempt on the part of Congress to abolish slavery in the District of Columbia against the wishes of the slaveholding states" and his determination to resist the slightest interference with slavery in the states where it existed. Also, it was refreshing to have in the White House someone who appreciated protocol and decorum. Obviously, Van Buren did not intend to strain himself to relate to the common man, at least not in the fashion of Andrew Jackson. In reality, the rotund New Yorker had little chance to develop his own administration. He was far too busy plugging the Jacksonian dike. "What a legacy of trouble old Jackson has left to little Van," remarked John Patton.[2]

Only a few weeks after the change of administrations the nation's financial structure collapsed. The panic that Tazewell predicted would result from Jackson's haphazard and unsound fiscal program swept the country. Suspension of specie payments by New York banks on May 10, 1837, began a profusion of similar actions in other states. Richmond banks followed suit five days later. Initially the distress in the money market caused little concern on the Eastern Shore where Tazewell now spent most of his days. "Have you withdrawn yourself completely from any concern about the political affairs of the country?" Patton almost angrily asked. "The currency question is at present engaging the best minds. . . . Why do you not contribute something to the mass of useful and practical information which is being brought forth? No man is better qualified than yourself to take an enlarged and liberal view of our financial condition, nor to sustain the best system for the moment & for the future." But when Tazewell again rejected the ultra–states' rights stand and voiced his approval of the Independent Treasury system, or, as it was sometimes called, the Subtreasury system, Patton was distressed. To him the scheme created nothing but a great national bank. Tazewell, however, thought Van Buren was correct in attempting to separate government finances from state banks, politics, and executive control by making the Treasury Department responsible for the care of the nation's funds and, for the sake of convenience, establishing subtreasuries in several major cities.[3]

While Tazewell favored this plan, he did not intend to wage a crusade in its behalf. "I am quite out of the world," he told Wickham. His primary interest was the price Eastern Shore products could command in coastal ports, from Cape Cod to Florida. "Scarcely a day and certainly not a week elapses without some vessel passing my door, so near that it is easy to obtain the latest intelligence." Despite an occasional bad passage, he derived great benefit from his trips across the bay. To make his voyages more pleasant and have a vessel under his own control, he invested in a schooner. His acquisition made him as enthusiastic as a schoolboy. "She sails remarkably well," he boasted to Wickham, "and with a tolerable breeze, can make the passage from here [Norfolk] to my plantation [King's Creek] in about five hours, and from Old Point in less than three." Driven east of the Gulf Stream by a heavy gale while on a run to Charleston, she was kept at sea for ten days, but the cargo was not damaged or "a rope yarn strained."[4]

Tazewell sold his oats in Charleston at a fine price, fifty-three cents a bushel, but had difficulty in collecting the proceeds. Charleston paper could not be disposed of in Norfolk except at considerable loss, and the price of everything in South Carolina was so high in their inflated currency that it did not pay to purchase goods there. "Thus," he complained, "I lose in the exchange what I gain in price. Is this state of things never to have an end?" Total reliance on paper currency, he feared, would upset foreign commerce. "The politicians of the present day are determined (as it seems) to regard this subject as one of mere finance," without considering its impact on world trade.[5]

If Tazewell believed, as did Hugh Lawson White, that the country was ruined, he made no speeches, wrote no articles. Rather he increasingly devoted his time to the inspection of his plantations and the keeping of meticulous record books on day-by-day transactions, weather data, and crop information, even including names of mules and horses that departed this life. During all seasons his journeys across the bay were numerous. Every December he was on hand for hog-killing, and often he remained through January and into February. Frequently he was the only white person on the plantations, especially during the Christmas season when his overseers left to visit family or friends. In late December "quite alone" appeared with regularity as an entry in his plantation book. As the years passed Louisa, a "maiden lady" now approaching middle age, insisted on accompanying her father, ostensibly to cut out garments for the slaves or direct projects such as soap-making but actually to watch over him. On occasion young

Littleton also crossed the bay for the same reason. John was occupied with the care of his own Sandhills plantation and business affairs in Norfolk or attempting to recover his health at Virginia mountain spas. Tazewell's accounts of sheepshearing, planting, harvesting, and building give a detailed picture of life on the Eastern Shore and of his careful utilization of products for his urban household. "Returned to Norfolk bringing with me 25 chickens from Old Plantation, and 12 ducks and 12 chickens from King's Creek" was a typical item in his journal.[6]

In 1837 Tazewell owned sixty slaves on the Eastern Shore: twenty-four at Old Plantation and eighteen each at New Quarter and King's Creek. Over the years the number fluctuated between sixty and eighty. When recording information about the slaves, Tazewell referred to them individually by name or collectively as "the people": "Gave all the people blankets and gave money to the negroes at King's Creek," or "Gave Martha (who is about to have a child) $1." "Sent Patrick, Solomon, and little Sam from Old Plantation to King's Creek, and Ben, old Sam, and Amy from King's Creek to New Quarter—and little George to Old Plantation." When the weather was extreme he was "seriously apprehensive for my people."[7]

The abolition movement continued to worry Tazewell, not entirely because of the threat to his property, but because he dreaded the social and economic upheaval that inevitably would be the consequence of emancipation. He was an orderly person who preferred having things done according to plan. Revolutions never go backwards, he had warned. Therefore, they should be carefully structured, with means and ends well established in the minds of all concerned. The abolitionists evinced little interest in the fate of the Negroes after liberation. Tazewell had hoped a solution to the dilemma would arise from the Nat Turner tragedy, but the time was not ripe, or so the Virginia legislature decided. Tazewell knew there would never be a "favorable" climate for complete manumission. Yet, realist that he was, he knew the problem could not be allowed to fester indefinitely. For the moment he worked within the system, without agonizing over the immorality of human bondage. He bought slaves, occasionally, but not always, at the request of

Negroes themselves, and he advised John to make timely acqui-
sitions. "You may, if you please and can do so properly, open a
negotiation for the purchase of some dozen or twenty in fami-
lies at private sale, provided you like the negroes and the prices
asked for them" he wrote his son in October 1842. "I am in
want of some house servants as you know, a man servant for the
dining room and a ladies' chamber maid. If you meet with such,
pray buy them for me at once. I should prefer an elderly man
and his wife, without children, if such may be had; but I would
submit even to the annoyance of the latter rather than not get
the former." Price, he said, would be no object. When seventeen young Negro men, fugitives from plantations north of
Eastville, wrecked the sailing vessel in which they were fleeing
and were recaptured on Chinquoteague Island, Tazewell informed John they would be sent to Norfolk for sale. "If you
want such negroes, you will have a good opp'y of buying as
many as you may wish. They are represented as being very
likely, two of them carpenters—and altho' they can't be kept on
the Eastern Shore, I should have no objection to owning them,
if they can be got low."[8]

For southerners preoccupied with the terrible dread of slave
uprisings, actions taken against abolitionists by "gentlemen of
property and standing" in the North were heartening. Tazewell received firsthand information of such activities in the
spring of 1838 when young Littleton, while escorting his
mother and sisters on a shopping trip to Philadelphia and
New York, witnessed the violence of an antiabolitionist mob in
the City of Brotherly Love. Out of curiosity he had gone to
hear an abolition address by "a Miss Grimke of South Carolina." Arriving at Pennsylvania Hall, a recently constructed
edifice housing abolition bookstores in the basement and a
large lecture room on the first floor, he saw what he estimated
to be a crowd of from fifty to seventy thousand. Many were
engaged in breaking windows, tearing down shutters, smash-
ing doors, and in other ways attempting to raze the structure,
but it was so new and substantially built, "the brick & wood
work only having been finished a week (the house not even
having been painted) it resisted all their efforts." Finally a gas
pipe was broken and ignited. The hall burst into flames, and
in two or three hours it was "a heap of ruins."

The following day Littleton took his mother and sisters to view the destruction. "The walls are still standing," he wrote John, "at the very imminent risk of the dense mob collected below. While there the alarm that the walls were falling was given and my party immediately scampered off, mamma & sisters waddling like ducks, but proving themselves quite active on such an occasion. The excitement is still excessively great and abolition is the sole topic of conversation." Later in the day, as different parts of the hall collapsed, the crowd shouted, "Huzza for the South!" "Abolition," Littleton confidently declared, "is used up in Philadelphia."[9]

While his family vacationed or went about their regular tasks, Tazewell was busy with agricultural and horticultural pursuits, but try as he might, he could not remove himself permanently from political affairs. His friends simply would not allow him this luxury. In the years following his governorship a complete reshaping of Virginia parties had taken place. Democratic Conservatives, as they were called, refused to sanction the Independent Treasury idea, insisting instead on a continued utilization of state banks as depositories for national funds. For the sake of party harmony, Thomas Ritchie initially tried to persuade Van Buren to abandon the Independent Treasury scheme, but the president declined. Ritchie accepted the decision, but William Cabell Rives launched a campaign against the chief executive, naturally seeking support from the states' rights Whigs. During the presidential election of 1840 Rives supported the Whig candidates, William Henry Harrison and John Tyler, while Tazewell, suprisingly to some, thought his erstwhile adversary, Van Buren, worthy of a second term.[10] For one thing, Tazewell could not countenance another general in the White House, especially one with whom he invariably differed on all constitutional questions. In addition, he much preferred Van Buren's Independent Treasury to either a recharter of the Bank of the United States or a continued reliance on state banks. Van Buren, in Tazewell's estimation, had not been a bad president. He had kept executive prerogatives in check, had avoided a sectional clash by choosing not to consider the Texas bid for annexation, and had endeavored to blunt the abolition movement. Moreover, in 1840 Van Buren's followers conducted a sensible campaign, quite unlike that of the Harrison-Tyler camp, which surpassed the antics of the 1828 Jacksonian bid for votes of the masses.[11] The promoters of "Tippecanoe and Tyler too" derided Van Buren for his aristocratic tastes, while insisting the Whigs stood for log cabins, hard cider, and the common man. In Virginia alone they built seventeen log cabins adorned with coonskins, gourds, and cider barrels to house Tippecanoe clubs. There were processions in which log cabins were drawn by ten or twelve horses. The crowning touch to the campaign in the commonwealth came in October 1840, when a large Whig convention in Richmond highlighted James Barbour, William Cabell Rives, Beverley Tucker, Benjamin Watkins Leigh, and Daniel Webster—all on the same platform! Many a Virginian echoed Peter Daniel's comment to Van Buren: "We are now, my dear sir, in the midst of the greatest effervescence of the political cauldron. Who is to survive, and who is to be consumed, in its furious bubblings, God knows. Sure I am that I have never witnessed anything like the scenes now passing before me."[12]

Tazewell warned Tyler about the possibility of his being one of the consumed if he insisted on running for the vice-presidency on the Whig ticket. Harrison, Tazewell pointed out, was sixty-seven (a year older than Tazewell), and not in robust health. Should the Whigs be victorious and Harrison die before the expiration of his presidential term, the dominant nationalist faction within the Whig party would pressure Tyler to act according to its wishes, and unless he yielded his conscience, judgment, and all else into the hands of political managers, he would be violently assaulted. Fearful combinations would try to force his resignation.[13]

When Harrison, a month after assuming office, succumbed to pneumonia, Tyler turned to Tazewell for counsel, even though Tazewell had not supported him in the election. Tyler apologized for intruding upon Tazewell's retirement, but the fearful combinations had materialized, and he felt alone and vulnerable. Tazewell was the person to whom he could appeal. "The late differences of opinion between us, *not of principle*, for there I am happy to believe that we entirely concur, have not for a moment lessened either my regard for you or confidence in you." A few weeks later he entreated Tazewell, "Do, my dear sir, turn over your Sibyl leaves and read to me their recorded prophecies. If they augur badly for me, I may by being forewarned become forearmed. Your early prophecy was of infinite service to me from the moment of my assuming the helm, as without it my ship, already tempest tost, might ere this have been stranded."[14]

Throughout his administration Tyler sought Tazewell's advice, and he did not complain when the latter was brutally frank. To be shown the error of his ways in a plain and downright fashion, Tyler said, was far preferable to being surrounded, as he was aware he was, "by men who have now smiles in their eyes and honey on their tongues, the better to cajole and deceive." The president, seeking respite from the Washington scene, often secluded himself at Old Point Comfort or the Rip Raps, a manmade island in Hampton Roads. At such times he requested Tazewell's company, but the latter eluded these invitations whenever possible. After one apparently unavoidable visit Tazewell complained to John that even though "nothing occur'd but the short greetings of two very old acquaintances," he had been beset with "pimps and spies" ever since his return to Norfolk. Later, when he concluded that Tyler, in shaping his policies, had only one goal in mind, that of achieving the presidency in his own right in 1844, Tazewell voiced complete disgust. Personal ambition, he was convinced, caused Tyler to compromise the nation's good.[15]

Declaring all current seekers of political office guilty of vaulting aspirations, Tazewell pronounced the outcome of the upcoming election of no consequence. Still, he was not displeased when James K. Polk emerged the victor. As a freshman congressman boarding at Mrs. Peyton's, the young man from Tennessee had admired Tazewell's "great purity and uprightness of character" and considered him one of the greatest men he had ever known. As president he retained this view and was eager for the Virginian's approval of his performance. "Mr. Tazewell will have great weight with Mr. Polk," John Strode Barbour, a prominent Virginia Democrat, told Calhoun. But not until August 1846 did the two friends meet to discuss national affairs. Then, a vacation at Fortress Monroe, across Hampton Roads from Norfolk, gave Polk an opportunity to invite Tazewell to join him for a day, much of which was devoted to an appraisal of administrative accomplishments. Later that evening a gratified president recorded in his diary that Tazewell said "my administration had successfully disposed of and settled more important public subjects of great interest in the first eighteen months of my term than any of my predecessors had ever done in eight years." Among the achievements enumerated by Tazewell were settlement of the Oregon boundary, annexation of Texas, reduction of the tariff, and reestablishment of the Independent Treasury.[16]

Almost as an afterthought Polk added that Tazewell "approved, too, my action in relation to Mexico." A war with that country had been underway since May. Perhaps Polk was hearing what he wanted to hear, for in a letter to R. M. T. Hunter, Tazewell later expressed grave disapproval of the military venture. "The Statesman must be deficient in political sagacity," he said, "who does not foresee that all the nations holding territories adjacent to the US must feel anxiety for the safety of their dominions, when such principles if not openly avowed are acted upon systematically by the Government of the US."[17]

Tazewell had sad forebodings concerning problems already arising from the anticipated acquisition of Mexican territory. Two weeks before the Polk-Tazewell conference at Fortress Monroe, David Wilmot of Pennsylvania threw "an apple of discord," as Calhoun called it, into the House of Representatives by proposing to ban forever the institution of slavery from any territory acquired from Mexico. This proviso launched a four-year debate which aroused the ardor of abolitionists and proslavery advocates, left the nation torn and suspicious, and the South convinced of its permanent minority status as long as it remained in the Union. Countering the Wilmot Proviso, Calhoun offered resolutions declaring that the territories of the United States were the possessions of all the states, held by them as joint property, and that Congress, "as the joint agent and representative of the States of this Union," had no right to make any law or do any act whatever which would directly or indirectly discriminate against any of the states by depriving them of their full and equal rights in territory, acquired or to be acquired.[18]

The rise of third-party movements presaged a serious sectional break. In 1840 and 1844 abolitionists entered the political arena with the formation of the Liberty party, which attracted relatively few voters. Of greater significance was the Free-Soil party of 1848. Designed to isolate the South and ally the North and West, it appealed to those who wished to aid free white labor by keeping slaves and slaveholders out of the territories and to those who wanted free land and federally sponsored internal improvements. Thomas Ritchie called it "the vilest and most mischievous party which has ever arisen in the republic," and when Van Buren, probably to his own amazement, accepted the Free-Soilers' invitation to be its first standard-bearer, he "bid defiance to the South." Polk's sad verdict was, "Mr. Van Buren is the most fallen man I have ever known."[19] The same year brought suggestions of a Tazewell-Jefferson Davis ticket. "Will they do?" William Yancey of Alabama asked Calhoun. "Will you write to Tazewell for us? and write me fully your opinions? The skies are brightening. I was despondent a week ago, I am hopeful now. We are all so. We will move in force and effectively." Tazewell refused to give the proposal the slightest consideration. Since his retirement from active political life, he had been mentioned for numerous posts. In 1840 there were those who wanted him to run for the vice-presidency, joining Van Buren on the Democratic ticket. President Tyler considered Tazewell for the State Department twice, first as a successor to Daniel Webster and again following the untimely death of Abel P. Upshur. But he had absolutely no intention of reentering public affairs. "The difficulty with Mr. Tazewell," John Strode Barbour remarked to Calhoun, "is to rouse him to service, an inertion, consequent on age, with most men; and to whom there is a natural proclivity with him at all times, defies every attempt to stimulate him into active life." Tazewell considered himself too old. He had done what he could, and now the days of his existence were numbered, but as he told John, he had learned long since that "everything which has a beginning must have an end, and the question as to the time when, is one of too little consequence to deserve much attention from one so old as I am."[20]

These were sad years too. He missed John Wickham, who died in 1839. While others sought Tazewell's advice, he invariably had relied on Wickham's opinion. "My excellent friend Littleton Waller Tazewell," was how Wickham had referred to him in his last will and testament,[21] and their association had been, indeed, superior. Its termination was cause for deep sorrow, but it did not bring the heartbreak which came with the death of young Littleton in the spring of 1848, at the age of thirty-two. Three years earlier Littleton had taken a bride considered unsuitable by his father, and Tazewell disinherited him.[22] There had been bitterness, an emotion which now turned to terrible grief. Only two of the Tazewell daughters married, Ann to Edmund Bradford and Mary to Mathew Page Waller. John remained a bachelor, and although ill much of the time, he was his father's main support, a dependable associate and a patient sounding board.

Tazewell needed comfort and encouragement. As the South's problems escalated, he feared what the future might bring. "The day that the balance between the two sections of the country—the slaveholding States and the non-slaveholding States—is destroyed," Calhoun warned, "is a day that will not be far removed from political revolution, anarchy, civil war, and widespread disaster."[23] Everyone knew the balance was no longer a reality. For twenty years the scales had been tipping in the North's favor. Population growth had given that section superior power in the House of Representatives. In addition, control of the Senate was slipping away from the South and, when the California gold rush brought requests from that newly won area for admission to the Union as a free state, the danger of the South's imminent oblivion was obvious to all informed citizens.

Undoubtedly Tazewell and Daniel Webster discussed these threats to the nation's future when the New Englander came to Norfolk in the spring of 1849. On a Sunday morning after church Webster called on Tazewell, and the two had a lengthy conversation. Webster considered Tazewell the ablest man in Virginia, "certainly the most fluent and eloquent talker," and "twenty years earlier, one of the best-looking men in the country." Toward evening, of the same day, to everyone's amazement, Tazewell, who long ago had foregone all social affairs, returned Webster's courtesy by going to the hotel where the Massachusetts senator was staying. Tazewell said he especially wanted to see Mrs. Webster and remained for three hours, "talking finely and laughing heartily all the time." "He and I have been personal friends a great while," Webster explained to his sister-in-law, "though always differing on political matters. He endured me, notwithstanding my distaste for Virginia notions, and I admired him for his knowledge, his talents, his vivacity, and his infinite volubility of discourse."[24]

When Clay attempted to hold the Union together with another compromise, Webster supported the effort, while Tazewell, along with Calhoun, believed the South was being handed the short end of the stick. Attempting to provide something for everyone, Clay suggested, among other measures, the admission of California as a free state, and popular sovereignty on the question of slavery in the remainder of the territory acquired from Mexico. In March 1850 a dying Calhoun made his last two appearances on the Senate floor in opposition to the compromise. Too weak to deliver his dissent, he had Senator James Mason of Virginia read his speech. "I have, Senators," Calhoun's words rang out, "believed from the first that the agitation of the subject of slavery would, if not prevented by some timely and effective measure, end in disunion." Certainly now the Union was in danger. Could the balance between North and South be preserved? California was the test question. "If you admit her, under all the difficulties that oppose her admission, you compel us to infer that you intend to exclude us from the whole of the acquired territories, with the intention of destroying, irretrievably, the equilibrium between the two sections. We would be blind not to perceive in that case, that your real objects are power and aggrandizement, and infatuated not to act accordingly."[25]

Webster, while favoring the admittance of a free California, urged the North to consider the consequences of further disturbing the balance between the sections. He too spoke for the preservation of the Union, "not as a Massachusetts man, nor as a northern man, but as an American, and a member of the Senate of the United States." "Hear me for my cause," he pleaded. Webster also condemned the abolition societies. "I do not think them useful," he told the Senate. "I think their operations for the last twenty years have produced nothing good or valuable. . . . I cannot but see what mischiefs their interference with the South has produced." Webster's statements were more forceful than Tazewell anticipated, and he welcomed the New Englander's viewpoints. While Tazewell was unwavering in his belief that a state had the right to secede, he concurred with Webster as to the awful sequel to such a move. "I see," said Webster, "that it must produce war, and such a war as I will not describe, *in its twofold character*," meaning, of course, the rising of blacks against whites, as well as section against section. But Tazewell could not join him in support of Clay's compromise package, which, in his eyes, relegated the South to an inferior position in the Union.[26]

The southern states, Tazewell told R. M. T. Hunter, "have long accustomed themselves to regard the Senate of the US as the only body upon which any reliance could be placed for the conservation of their political rights and interests. They will now see, I suppose, that this was mere delusion; that these rights and interests have been wantonly sacrificed by members of that body in whom they had good reason to repose confidence; and like the dying Caesar, struck down at the foot of Pompey's statue by the daggers of pretended friends, they may well cry out *et tu quoque Brute*." He advised southern states to abstain from any hypothetical declaration of how they intended to react to recent developments, but whatever they decided to do, he was sure they would not be influenced by craven fears. For his part, he would abide by Virginia's judgment. "I have often invoked my God to witness the solemn pledge I willingly gave to be 'faithful and true' to her," he told Hunter, "and when I forget the sacred obligation of this vow of allegiance, may God forget me."[27] It was not restrictions on the expansion of slavery that Tazewell railed against, but the Senate's final acquiescence to the rule of the numerical majority, an assent fatal to the future of the South. In Tazewell's remonstrance there was a mixture of injured pride and genuine alarm at the specter of perpetual northern domination of the economic, political, and social life of the nation.

Internally, Virginia was faced with a somewhat similar situation. Demands for majority rule and calls for a constitutional convention were again heard from the western section of the state. Advocates demanded reapportionment of the state legislature, recognition of the preponderance of the western counties, white manhood suffrage, election of the governor and other officials, including judges, by the people, elimination of the Council of State, and the establishment of a public school system. As in 1829–30, the basis of representation was the most vexing issue. The Tidewater clung to the mixed basis, counting both blacks and whites, while the west wanted representation calculated from the white population alone. Although a compromise was reached on the apportionment of delegates to the General Assembly, the constitution of 1851 was, on the whole, a victory for the more liberal element in the commonwealth. White male suffrage, regardless of property or tax qualifications, was adopted. Likewise, there was no property stipulation for the governor, who was to be chosen by popular vote rather than by the legislature. The Council of State was abolished, and as the rejoicing victors contended, all vestiges of aristocratic colonialism were eliminated. Majority rule was the order of the day. Considering the character of political campaigns since 1828, Tazewell wondered on what whims and selfish motives the people would make their judgments. How would they use their unrestrained power? He thought it might be preferable for the state to divide, thus allowing westerners to go their way without involving many from the eastern section who were opposed to innovations; but among reformers there was a feeling that Virginia, in shedding the "relics of feudalism," finally was becoming "permeated with the spirit of the age."[28]

All this made Tazewell extremely weary, rather than bitter or alienated as were Beverley Tucker or Edmund Ruffin, the agricultural reformer, who was inclined to attribute "base motives" to any southerner who advocated continuance of the Union. For Tazewell secession was the very last resort. As a shrewd businessman, he fully realized the economic chaos that would accompany separation. Moreover, he was devoted to the Union, at least to a Union which respected the rights of the South as well as those of the North. Years before, he had expressed fears that his children would reap the whirlwind sown by others. Now he felt discouraged, out of step with the times. Except for rare occasions, he no longer traveled across the bay to the Eastern Shore. John purchased King's Creek from his parents, and the other plantations were placed in his care. Tazewell occupied himself with playing chess by mail, reading, especially the ancient classics, providing information for biographers of John Randoplh and Stephen Decatur, and, at the request of Richard Crallé, examining the proof sheets of Calhoun's *Disquisition on Government* and *Discourse on the Constitution.* But the restraints of old age and ill health dispirited him. Ann refused to take her husband's complaints seriously. "Your Papa groans more than ever and eats heartily and sleeps well—it is a habit with him now and I don't think he will ever relinquish it," she wrote to Sally, away from Norfolk, visiting the Bradfords.[29] There were accolades. The College of William and Mary conferred on him the honorary degree of Doctor of Laws as an acknowledgment on the part of the faculty of the prominent and useful position he had occupied in the councils of the state and nation, of his high character, and great abilities. The Virginia Historical Society made him an honorary member.[30]

In the last years of his life Tazewell rarely ventured outdoors but on pleasant summer days sat on the porch or in the hall near the front door to catch the breeze from the Elizabeth River. It was there Edmund Ruffin found him one sultry July afternoon in 1858. Ruffin, who had not seen Tazewell in thirty years, was anxious to hear his views on current political affairs, but Tazewell refused to be drawn into a discussion of explosive issues with the ardent secessionist. Instead, he talked about the impending removal of the remains of James Monroe from New York, where they had reposed since 1831, to Richmond for reburial in Hollywood Cemetery. "They are about to make a great parade with removing the body of my old friend Monroe," he told his visitor. "Yes," Ruffin replied, "and very foolishly." Tazewell was silent for a moment, then said, "It had better be let alone. Where the tree falls, there let it lie."[31]

Later Ruffin disparagingly commented that Tazewell "has had no ambition." "With all his ability & power, & the readiness of the people & the government to recognize & to use his services, he has been of scarcely any use to the public." Perhaps this was true, according to Ruffin's measure of "utility." He could not understand a man who avoided the limelight, who worked often behind the scenes to preserve the checks and balances necessary to keep government on an even keel, whose major concern was to restrain power within limits wherever or whenever he saw it getting out of bounds. Nor could Ruffin imagine someone believing in the legitimacy of secession, yet dreading its coming. Tazewell did not have within him a hatred of all things northern. The two men were dissimilar also in their solutions to the South's economic problems. Ruffin's progressive agricultural ideas were commendable, and Tazewell practiced them, but Ruffin saw little for the region beyond agrarianism, while Tazewell advocated the development of a multiplicity of economic ventures to remedy the sad financial plight of the slaveholding states. Perhaps one of Tazewell's most serious miscalculations was in refusing to sanction federally supported internal improvements. On this, as well as on several other matters, he was inclined to cling too closely to a doctrinaire interpretation of the Constitution. A rational, moderate man, at a time when such traits were becoming unfashionable, he feared the force of a numerical majority, prone to emotionalism in decision making. Unchecked democracy, he often reiterated, could trample underfoot minority rights, local government, individual liberties, and the South's fair claim to the nation's resources. Alexis de Tocqueville had sensed this also. The majority in the United States, he wrote in his classic interpretation of democracy in America, "exercise a prodigious actual authority, and a power of opinion which is nearly as great; no obstacles exist which can impede or even retard its progress, so as to make it heed the complaints of those whom it crushes upon its path. This state of things is harmful in itself and dangerous for the future."[32]

Tazewell's concern for the nation's welfare was sincere, and he spent many years, at great personal sacrifice, serving his government to the best of his ability. "Altho' I have no care to conceal anything that I have ever thought or said or done in my whole life," he confided to R. M. T. Hunter, "yet I have ever felt a morbid horror at becoming a subject of notoriety." He was a sensitive, private man, deeply devoted to family and friends. The deaths of those close to him caused him intense grief, which he rarely could bring himself to express to anyone, thus making his pain all the more devastating. His "ice rests on a volcano," John Randolph once observed. In the fall of 1858 Tazewell suffered his greatest loss. Ann died on September 15. Louisa and Sally, still "secretaries for domestic affairs," carefully attended to their father's needs, but he failed rapidly. Early in May 1860 he contracted pneumonia and deliriously called for his son Henry and for Ann. On Sunday morning, May 6, he died.[33]

After the funeral service, held at the Tazewell residence on Granby Street, a procession was formed and the casket escorted to the Elizabeth River where it was placed aboard the steamer *Northampton* for Tazewell's last trip to the Eastern Shore. Because of a difficult bay crossing, darkness fell before the boat reached King's Creek, site of the family burial ground. The service was read by candlelight, the familiar words from the Book of Common Prayer carrying out over the dark bayside waters.[34]

For years Tazewell had an impending dread of civil war. He died on the eve of the tragic conflict that brought both great gains and irreparable losses, freedom for people who never should have been enslaved, humiliation and heartbreak for others in the South. The end of an era had come. Much evil was blotted out, many good things were no more. And like the characters in Anton Chekhov's play, Tazewell, before he died, distinctly heard "the strokes of the ax against a tree far away in the orchard."

*Notes*

*Select Bibliography*

*Index*

# Notes

## Chapter I

1. Littleton Waller Tazewell (hereafter LWT), "Sketches of His Own Family," MS, dated Norfolk, Va., 1823, pp. 1–7, Virginia State Library, Richmond.
2. Ibid., Introduction and pp. 36–101.
3. Hugh Blair Grigsby, *Discourse on the Life and Character of the Hon. Littleton Waller Tazewell* (Norfolk, Va., 1860), 11.
4. LWT, "Sketches," 106–7.
5. Hugh A. Garland, *The Life of John Randolph of Roanoke*, 2 vols. (New York, 1856), 1:20–21.
6. Grigsby, *Tazewell*, 82.
7. LWT, "Sketches," 109–10.
8. Ibid., 111–12.
9. Ibid., 121–23.
10. Lyon G. Tyler, *The Cradle of the Republic: Jamestown and James River* (Richmond, 1906), 234–35; Thomas Jefferson to Peter Carr, Aug. 10, 1787, *The Works of Thomas Jefferson*, ed. Paul L. Ford, 12 vols. (New York, 1904), 5:322; Dumas Malone, *Jefferson and His Time* (Boston, 1948–81), 2:82.
11. Hugh Blair Grigsby, *The History of the Virginia Federal Convention of 1788*, 2 vols. (Richmond, 1890), 1:306–7; Jefferson to Dr. Richard Price, Aug. 7, 1785, Jefferson, *Works*, 4:447–48; Julian P. Boyd, *The Murder of George Wythe* (Philadelphia, 1949), 1–9; Richard Beale Davis, *Intellectual Life in Jefferson's Virginia, 1790–1830* (Chapel Hill, N.C., 1964), 126; Theodore Cox, s.v. "George Wythe," *Dictionary of American Biography.*
12. LWT, "Sketches," 127–28; William Mumford to John Coalter, June 12, July 22, 1791, "Glimpses of Old College Life," *William and Mary Quarterly*, 1st ser., 8 (1899): 154–55; Charles Crowe, "Bishop James Madison and the Republic of Virtue," *Journal of Southern History* 30 (1964): 60–62.
13. Lyon G. Tyler, "School Days of John Randolph," *William and Mary Quarterly*, 1st ser., 24 (1915): 4–5; William Cabell Bruce, *John Randolph of Roanoke, 1773–1833*, 2 vols. (New York, 1922), 1:124–25.
14. LWT, "Sketches," 133–36.
15. Ibid., 137–40; Grigsby, *Tazewell*, 15.
16. LWT, "Sketches," 145.
17. LWT, "Sketches," 148–49.
18. Ibid., 149–51; "Glimpses of Old College Life," 155.
19. LWT, "Sketches," 151; Mary N. Stanard, *Richmond: Its People and Its Story* (Philadelphia, 1923), 92–95.

20.  LWT, "Sketches," 152–61; Robert Greenhow to Henry Tazewell, March 15, 1797, Tazewell Papers.

21.  Noble E. Cunningham, Jr., *The Jeffersonian Republicans: The Formation of Party Organization, 1789–1801* (Chapel Hill, N.C., 1957), 77–85.

22.  LWT, "Sketches," 82; *Biographical Directory of the American Congress, 1774–1927* (Washington, D.C., 1928), 54; Henry Tazewell to Bishop James Madison, March 6, 1796, quoted in Cunningham, *Jeffersonian Republicans: Formation,* 89–90.

23.  LWT to Henry Tazewell, Jan. 5, 1797, Tazewell Papers.

24.  Ibid., Jan. 21, 1797.

25.  Henry Tazewell to LWT, June 12, 1797, LWT to Henry Tazewell, Feb. 16, 1798, and documents of appointment, June 12, 22, 1797, ibid.

26.  Henry Tazewell to LWT, Nov. 28, 1797, LWT to Henry Tazewell, Dec. 22, 1797, Jan. 1, 1798, ibid.

27.  Grigsby, *Tazewell,* 22; LWT to Henry Tazewell, April 10, 1798, Tazewell Papers.

28.  Adrienne Koch, *Jefferson and Madison, the Great Collaboration* (New York, 1964), 179; *The Virginia Report of 1799–1800 Touching the Alien and Sedition Laws* (Richmond, 1850), 156–57; Robert B. Tunstall, s.v. "Henry Tazewell," *DAB.*

29.  Nathan Schachner, *Thomas Jefferson, a Biography* (New York, 1951), 603–4; Tazewell, "Sketches," 82–83; Henry Tazewell to LWT, Jan. 22, 1799, John Beckley to LWT, Feb. 14, 1799, bills charged to the Estate of the Honorable Henry Tazewell, deceased, Jan. 25, 1799, and bills in account with John Beckley, Jan. 30, 1799, Tazewell Papers; Jane Carson, *James Innes and His Brothers of the F.H.C.* (Charlottesville, Va., 1965), 159–60; Edmund Berkeley and Dorothy Smith Berkeley, *John Beckley, Zealous Partisan in a Nation Divided* (Philadelphia, 1973), 189.

30.  LWT, "Sketches," 84.

31.  Henry Tazewell's will, Tazewell Papers; Grigsby, *Tazewell,* 78.

32.  Theodore S. Cox, s.v. "John Wickham," *DAB.*

33.  LWT to Elizabeth McClurg, Aug. 1799, John Wickham Papers (microfilm), University of Virginia Library, Charlottesville (hereafter UVa Lib.).

34.  Ibid., Nov. 12, 14, 1799.

35.  LWT to Thomas Jefferson, March 29, 1800, Jefferson to LWT, April 10, 1800, Coolidge Papers, Massachusetts Historical Society, Boston (hereafter MHS); *Virginia Argus,* Aug. 8, 1800; Lisle A. Rose, *Prologue to Democracy: The Federalists in the South, 1789–1800* (Lexington, Ky., 1968), 234–35; Norman K. Risjord, "The Virginia Federalists," *Journal of Southern History* 33 (1967): 504.

36.  Stanard, *Richmond,* 113.

37.  *Virginia Argus,* Aug. 1, 5, 8, 1800; Albert J. Beveridge, *The Life of John Marshall,* 4 vols. (New York, 1919), 2:515; Rose, *Prologue to Democracy,* 264; James Bayard to Alexander Hamilton, Aug. 11, 1800, *Papers of James A. Bayard,* ed. Elizabeth Donnan (Washington, D.C., 1915), 113.

38.  *Annals of Congress,* 6th Cong., 2d sess., 789; Malone, *Jefferson and His Time,* 3:474–75.

39. *National Intelligencer,* Nov. 3, 24, 1800; Henry Adams, *Life of Albert Gallatin* (New York, 1879), 252–53.

40. Bruce, *Randolph,* 1:115–75.

41. Ibid.; *Biographical Directory of Congress, 1774–1927,* 64, 67; *National Intelligencer,* Dec. 5, 1800.

42. Malone, *Jefferson and His Time,* 3:499; Cunningham, *Jeffersonian Republicans: Formation,* 241–43; *National Intelligencer,* Jan. 14, 16, 1801.

43. LWT to James Monre, Feb. 12, 1801, Monroe Papers, Library of Congress (hereafter LC).

44. Ibid., Feb. 13, 1801.

45. *National Intelligencer,* Feb. 16, 18, 20, 23, 1801; Malone, *Jefferson and His Time,* 3:504; *Annals of Congress,* 6th Cong., 2d sess., 1029.

46. *Annals of Congress,* 6th Cong., 2d sess., 915.

47. *National Intelligencer,* March 11, 1801.

## Chapter II

1. LWT, "Sketches of His Own Family," typed copy with addenda by his daughter, Ann Bradford, and his grandson, 71–72, 165, Sargeant Room, Kirn Memorial Library, Norfolk, Va.; Oscar M. Voorhees, ed., *Phi Beta Kappa General Catalog, 1776–1922* (Sommerville, N.J., n.d.), 749; Thomas J. Wertenbaker, *Norfolk, Historic Southern Port* (Durham, N.C., 1962), 91–92; Grigsby, *Tazewell,* 22.

2. Wertenbaker, *Norfolk,* 84–86; Grigsby, *Tazewell,* 24, 92; Hustings Court Records, Norfolk Borough, Order Books, 1804–27, and Corporation Court Records, Office of the Clerk of Court, City Hall, Norfolk, Va.

3. Grigsby, *Tazewell,* 41, 115–16, 118; Davis, *Intellectual Life,* 355, 382.

4. Richard Beale Davis, *Francis Walker Gilmer: Life and Learning in Jefferson's Virginia* (Richmond, 1939), 88; [Mrs. Anne Riston], *A Poetical Picture of America* (London, 1809), 101; Talbot Hamlin, *Benjamin Henry Latrobe* (New York, 1955), 95–98; Rabbi Malcolm H. Stern, "Moses Myers and the Early Jewish Community of Norfolk," typescript, 8 pp., Myers House, Norfolk; Wertenbaker, *Norfolk,* 92–93, 124.

5. *Norfolk Herald,* March 6, 1802; William S. Forrest, *Historical and Descriptive Sketches of Norfolk and Vicinity* (Philadelphia, 1853), 272.

6. Wertenbaker, *Norfolk,* 88–89; John Cowper to Gov. James Monroe, March 11, 1802, *Calendar of Virginia State Papers,* 11 vols. (1875–92; rept. New York, 1968), 9:287 (hereafter *CVSP*).

7. Wyndham B. Blanton, *Medicine in Virginia in the Nineteenth Century* (Richmond, 1933), 224–26.

8. LWT, "Sketches" MS, 92, Tazewell Papers; *Norfolk Herald,* July 17, 1802.

9. Grigsby, *Tazewell,* 71–73; John P. Kennedy, *Memoirs of the Life of William Wirt,* 2 vols. (New York, 1869), 1: 57–62, 92, 98; William Wirt to LWT, Aug. 31, Nov. 16, 1803, Tazewell Papers.

10.  William Wirt to Dabney Carr, June 8, 1804, to Mrs. Wirt, May 10, 1805, Kennedy, *Wirt,* 1: 113–17, 133; Grigsby, *Tazewell,* 40; Wirt to LWT, July 23, Aug. 20, 1804, Tazewell Papers.

11.  Malone, *Jefferson and His Time,* 4:367–92; Beckles Willson, *Friendly Relations: A Narrative of Britain's Ministers and Ambassadors to America, 1791–1930* (Boston, 1934), 38–39.

12.  Lucy Ludwell Paradise to LWT, Feb. 24, 1805, Tazewell Papers; Archibald Bolling Shepperson, *John Paradise and Lucy Ludwell of London and Williamsburg* (Richmond, 1942), 433, 441–43, 446.

13.  *Norfolk Gazette and Publick Ledger,* Nov. 8, 1805, April 6, 1816; Alexander Slidell Mackenzie, *The Life of Stephen Decatur* (Boston, 1846), 134–35, 294–366.

14.  Wilson Cary Nicholas to LWT, June 29, 1804, Tazewell Papers.

15.  John Waller to LWT, April 5, 1804, ibid.; Records, Elmwood Cemetery, Norfolk.

16.  LWT to John Randolph, Nov. 13, 1803, Tazewell Papers.

17.  Ibid., Dec. 29, 1803.

18.  John Randolph to LWT, Jan. 8, 1804, ibid.

19.  Ibid., Feb. 26, 1804; LWT to Randolph, March 4, 1804, ibid.; *Virginia Argus,* March 3, 1804.

20.  John Randolph to LWT, April 21, 1804, Tazewell Papers; Harry Ammon, *James Monroe: The Quest for National Unity* (New York, 1971), 158–60.

21.  John Randolph to LWT, April 21, 1804, Tazewell Papers.

22.  *Virginia Argus,* April 28, 1804; John Randolph to LWT, June 8, 1804, James Semple to LWT, Feb. 23, 1804, Thomas Jefferson to LWT, Jan. 26, 1804, copy, Tazewell Papers. Norman K. Risjord, *The Old Republicans: Southern Conservatism in the Age of Jefferson* (New York, 1965), 21–22, explains the liberal-conservative division in the Republican party: "The vestiges of mercantilism and the commercial flavor of Jeffersonian Liberalism tended to breed suspicions in the less flexible, agrarian wing of the Republican party."

23.  J. Stratton to LWT, March 10, 1804, Tazewell Papers; LWT to St. George Tucker, May 8, 1804, Tucker-Coleman Papers, Swem Library, College of William and Mary; *Norfolk Gazette and Publick Ledger,* Nov. 16, 1804.

24.  LWT to John Randolph, May 8, 1804, Wilson Cary Nicholas to LWT, Aug. 21, 1804, Tazewell Papers; William Thomson to Nicholas, Sept. 1, 15, 1804, William Pennock to Nicholas, Aug. 10, 1805, Wilson Cary Nicholas Papers, UVa Lib.

25.  Wilson Cary Nicholas to LWT, July 31, 1804, Tazewell Papers; *Norfolk Gazette and Publick Ledger,* Aug. 23, 1804.

26.  *Norfolk Gazette and Publick Ledger,* Dec. 17, 1804; Wilson Cary Nicholas to LWT, Dec. 17, 1804, Tazewell Papers.

27.  *Norfolk Gazette and Publick Ledger,* Dec. 21, 1804; *Virginia Argus,* Dec. 29, 1804; LWT to St. George Tucker, Dec. 24, 1804, Tucker-Coleman Papers.

28.  Thomas Jefferson to LWT, Jan. 5, 1805, Jefferson Papers, UVa Lib.

29.  *Virginia Argus,* Jan. 21, 1806.

30.  *Richmond Enquirer*, Jan. 15, 1805; *Virginia Argus*, Feb. 7, 1806.

31.  *CSVP*, 9:293–94, 296–310, 320; Winthrop D. Jordan, *White over Black: American Attitudes toward the Negro, 1550–1812* (Chapel Hill, N.C., 1968), 382–84, 396–97; John D. Russell, *The Free Negro in Virginia, 1619–1865* (Baltimore, 1913), 65; *Virginia Argus*, Feb. 29, 1804.

32.  LWT to John Randolph, March 4, 1804, John Nivison to LWT, Jan. 5, 15, 1805, Tazewell Papers.

33.  James Hugo Johnson, *Race Relations in Virginia and Miscegenation in the South, 1776–1860* (Amherst, Mass., 1970), 120.

34.  Russell, *Free Negro in Virginia*, 61, 67; St. George Tucker, *A Dissertation on Slavery with a Proposal for the Gradual Abolition of It in the State of Virginia* (Philadelphia, 1796), 70. A 1782 Virginia statute made it possible for individual owners to free slaves without permission from the state legislature.

35.  *Richmond Enquirer*, Jan. 15, 1805; *Virginia Argus*, Jan. 17, 21, 1806; *Journal of the House of Delegates of Virginia, 1805–1806* (Richmond, 1806), 68, 77.

36.  *Richmond Enquirer*, Jan. 18, Feb. 4, 1806; *Journal of the House of Delegates of Virginia, 1805–1806*, 77; *Virginia Argus*, Jan. 28, 1806.

37.  LWT to Henry Tazewell, Jan. 5, 1797, Tazewell Papers.

## Chapter III

1.  LWT to James Monroe, Jan. 3, 1807, Monroe Papers, LC.

2.  Charles H. Ambler, *Thomas Ritchie: A Study in Virginia Politics* (Richmond, 1913), 38; Malone, *Jefferson and His Time*, 4:406; Thomas Perkins Abernethy, *The Burr Conspiracy* (New York, 1954), 36–56, 188–90; Thomas Jefferson to William Branch Giles, April 20, 1807, Jefferson, *Works*, 10:383–88; Walter F. McCaleb, *The Aaron Burr Conspiracy* (New York, 1903), 285–311.

3.  LWT to James Monroe, Jan. 3, 1807, Monroe Papers, LC. The "Randolph revolt" is described in Noble E. Cunningham, Jr., *The Jeffersonian Republicans in Power: Party Operations, 1801–1809* (Chapel Hill, N.C., 1963), 78–88.

4.  Counsel for the prosecution included George Hay, William Wirt, and Alexander MacRae; Burr's attorneys were Edmund Randolph, John Wickham, Benjamin Botts, John Baker, and Luther Martin. David Robertson, *Reports of the Trials of Colonel Aaron Burr*, 2 vols. (1808; rept. New York, 1969), 1:31, 97; Paul S. Clarkson and R. Samuel Jett, *Luther Martin of Maryland* (Baltimore, 1970), 245–47.

5.  *Norfolk Gazette and Publick Ledger*, June 8, 1807; Washington Irving to Mrs. Hoffman, June 4, 1807, *The Life and Letters of Washington Irving*, ed. Pierre M. Irving, 2 vols. (New York, 1862), 1:191–92; Robertson, *Trials of Burr*, 1:44–46, 113–89; John Nivison to LWT, May 27, 1807, Tazewell Papers.

6.  LWT to ——, Feb. 4, 1811, Tazewell Papers; Abernethy, *Burr Conspiracy*, 179–82.

7.  LWT to ——, Feb. 4, 1811, Tazewell Papers.

8. Samuel H. Wandell and Meade Minnigerode, *Aaron Burr*, 2 vols. (New York, 1925), 2:196; Bruce, *Randolph*, 1:304–5; John Randolph to Joseph Nicholson, June 25, 1807, quoted in Henry Adams, *John Randolph* (Boston, 1892), 221–22.

9. *Annals of Congress*, 10th Cong., 1st sess., 627–33.

10. Beveridge, *Marshall*, 3:466; Clarkson and Jett, *Luther Martin*, 272; Abernethy, *Burr Conspiracy*, 259; John Randolph to LWT, Dec. 24, 1807, LWT to ——, Feb. 4, 1811, Tazewell Papers.

11. Malone, *Jefferson and His Time*, 5:276, states: "While Jefferson cannot escape the charge of gullibility in his relations with Wilkinson, the simplest explanation of his course is that one seemingly necessary step followed another until he had reached a position from which it would have been extremely difficult to withdraw." In other words, Jefferson, in order to thwart one culprit, apparently found himself allied with another.

12. Log of the *Chesapeake*, LC; *Proceedings of the General Court Martial Convened for the Trial of Commodore James Barron, Captain Charles Gordon, Mr. William Hook, and Captain John Hall of the United States Ship* Chesapeake *in the Month of January, 1808* (Philadelphia, 1822), 209; James Fenimore Cooper, *The History of the Navy of the United States of America*, 2 vols. (Philadelphia, 1839), 2:95–97.

13. Leonard D. White, *The Jeffersonians: A Study in Administrative History* (New York, 1951), 265–68; Malone, *Jefferson and His Time*, 4:102–3, 248–49, 442; Mackenzie, *Decatur*, 145; *American State Papers: Foreign Relations*, 3:12.

14. *Norfolk Gazette and Publick Ledger*, June 24, 1807; Log of the *Chesapeake*, LC; *American State Papers: Foreign Relations*, 3:6–7.

15. *Norfolk Gazette and Publick Ledger*, June 29, 1807; Edwin M. Gaines, "The *Cheasapeake* Affair: Virginians Mobilize to Defend National Honor," *Virginia Magazine of History and Biography* 64 (1956):131–35; William Wirt to Dabney Carr, July 2, 1807, Kennedy, *Wirt*, 1:196; *CVSP*, 9:522–26.

16. Grigsby, *Tazewell*, 54. Grigsby states that Tazewell dictated the letter signed by Richard E. Lee, July 4, 1807. The letter in its entirety is found in *CVSP*, 9:526–27.

17. LWT to Richard E. Lee, July 6, 1807, to William H. Cabell, July 6, 1807, *CVSP*, 9:528–33.

18. Malone, *Jefferson and His Time*, 5:432–36; Thomas Mathews to William H. Cabell, July 28, Aug. 3, 1807, to LWT, July 26, Aug. 1, 1807, to Sir Thomas Hardy, July 26, 1807, Hardy to Mathews, Aug. 4, 1807, LWT to William Dudley, July 28, 1807, to Mathews, July 28, Aug. 3, 1807, *CVSP*, 9:553–57, 567–73; Hardy to LWT, Aug. 2, 1807, Tazewell Papers.

19. William Henry Allen letter, dated June 24, 1807, "Letters of William Henry Allen, 1800–1813," pt. 2, *Huntington Library Quarterly* 1 (1938): 215; Robert Smith to LWT, Sept. 12, 1807, Miscellaneous Letters Sent by Secretary of the Navy, RG 45, M-209, roll 3, National Archives, Washington, D.C. (hereafter NA).

20. John Nivison to LWT, Sept. 21, 1807, Tazewell Papers; LWT to Robert Smith, Oct. 6, 1807, Miscellaneous Letters Received by Secretary of the Navy, RG 80, M-124, roll 17, NA.

21.   LWT to Robert Smith, Oct. 6, 1807, RG 80, M-124, roll 17, NA; Smith to LWT, Oct. 12, 1807, RG 45, M-209, roll 3, NA; "Report of Court of Enquiry, held on board the *Chesapeake*, Oct. 5, 1807–Nov. 4, 1807, to Secretary of the Navy," *American State Papers: Foreign Affairs*, 3:21–23.

22.   Robert Smith to LWT, Nov. 18, Dec. 4, 1807, RG 45, M-209, roll 3, NA; LWT to Smith, Nov. 27, 1807, RG 80, M-124, roll 18, NA; Stephen Decatur to Smith, Dec. 17, 1807, Letters Received by Secretary of the Navy from Captains, RG 80, M-125, roll 9, NA; Smith to Decatur, Dec. 26, 1807, Letters from Secretary of the Navy to Officers, RG 45, M-149, roll 7, NA.

23.   *Proceedings of the General Court Martial*, 24–33, 167–69; *Norfolk Gazette and Publick Ledger*, Feb. 4, 1808.

24.   Sentence of the General Court Martial in the Case of Commodore James Barron, Records of General Courts Martial and Courts of Inquiry, 1799–1867, RG 125, M-273, roll 4, NA; *Proceedings of the General Court Martial*, 333–50.

25.   *Proceedings of the General Court Martial*, 98–99, 111, 351–56, 413–36; Leonard F. Guttridge and Jay D. Smith, *The Commodores* (New York, 1969), 165–70; Records of General Courts Martial and Courts of Inquiry, RG 125, M-273, roll 4, NA.

26.   Cooper, *History of the Navy*, 2:110.

27.   Charles Oscar Paullin, *Commodore John Rodgers, Captain, Commodore, and Senior Officer of the American Navy, 1773–1838* (Annapolis, 1967), 194.

28.   *Notes to the Trial of Commodore Barron*, 8 pp, pamphlet in Eleutherian Mills Historical Library, Greenville, Del.

## Chapter IV

1.   *Norfolk Gazette and Publick Ledger*, Dec. 14, 1807; James Monroe to LWT, Oct. 30, 1808, *The Writings of James Monroe*, ed. S. M. Hamilton, 7 vols. (New York, 1898–1903), 5:71; Merrill D. Peterson, *Thomas Jefferson and the New Nation* (New York, 1970), 863; Ammon, *Monroe*, 263; John Nivison to LWT, May 27, 1807, Tazewell Papers.

2.   Malone, *Jefferson and His Time*, 5:150–58; Harry Ammon, "Monroe and the Election of 1808 in Virginia," *William and Mary Quarterly*, 3d ser., 20 (1963): 39–42; Noble E. Cunningham, Jr., "Who Were the Quids?" *Mississippi Valley Historical Review* 50 (1963): 252–63.

3.   LWT to Monroe, May 30, 1807, Monroe Papers, LC; Risjord, *Old Republicans*, chaps. 1 and 2.

4.   Cunningham, *Jeffersonian Republicans in Power*, 86, 230; Ammon, "Monroe and the Election of 1808," 33–34; Harry Ammon, "The Richmond Junto, 1800–1824," *Virginia Magazine of History and Biography* 61 (1953): 395–418; Joseph H. Harrison, Jr., "Oligarchs and Democrats—The Richmond Junto," ibid., 78 (1970): 184–98; LWT to Monroe, Oct. 8, 1808, Monroe Papers, LC. See also LWT to Monroe, Jan. 3, 1807, ibid.

5.   Malone, *Jefferson and His Time*, 5:483–84; Wertenbaker, *Norfolk*, 104–9; *Norfolk Gazette and Publick Ledger*, Sept. 8, Nov. 16, Dec. 14, 1808.

6.   Garland, *Randolph*, 1: 233; *Norfolk Herald*, April 6, 1827.

7.  LWT to Monroe, Oct. 8, 1808, Monroe Papers, LC.

8.  Ammon, "Monroe and the Election of 1808," 46; *Norfolk Gazette and Publick Ledger,* Jan. 30, 1808; LWT to Monroe, Oct. 8, 1808, Monroe Papers, LC.

9.  LWT to Monroe, Oct. 8, 1808, Monroe Papers, LC.

10.  Monroe to LWT, Oct. 30, 1808, Monroe, *Writings,* 5:66–81.

11.  *Norfolk Gazette and Publick Ledger,* Nov. 7, 14, 1808.

12.  LWT to Monroe, Jan. 26, 1809, James Monroe Papers, Rare Books and Manuscripts Division, New York Public Library, Astor, Lenox and Tilden Foundations.

13.  Malone, *Jefferson and His Time,* 5:646–49, 655–56; Irving Brant, *James Madison,* 6 vols. (Indianapolis, 1941–61), 5:35; Ammon, *Monroe,* 280; William Wirt to Monroe, Dec. 20, 1808, Monroe Papers, LC; Monroe to Wirt, Dec. 20, 1808, Monroe, *Writings,* 5:84–85.

14.  LWT to Monroe, Feb. 13, 1811, Monroe Papers, LC.

15.  Ibid., Dec. 30, 1810.

16.  This was before Giles's break with Madison, which cost Giles considerable support in Virginia. Dice R. Anderson, *William Branch Giles: A Study in the Politics of Virginia and the Nation from 1790 to 1830* (Menasha, Wis., 1914), 165–67.

17.  Monroe to LWT, Feb. 6, 1811, Monroe, *Writings,* 5:167–68.

18.  LWT to Monroe, Feb. 13, 1811, Monroe Papers, LC.

19.  Ibid.;Benjamin Rush to John Adams, April 26, 1810, *Letters of Benjamin Rush,* ed. L. H. Butterfield, 2 vols. (Princeton, N. J., 1951), 2:1042.

20.  John S. Pancake, "The 'Invisibles' ": A Chapter in the Opposition to President Madison," *Journal of Southern History* 21 (1955): 17-37.

21.  LWT To Monroe, Feb. 13, 1811, Monroe Papers, LC.

22.  Monroe to LWT, Feb. 25, 1811, Chapman Johnson to Monroe, Jan. 12, 1811, Monroe to Johnson, Jan. 14, 1811, Monroe, *Writings,* 5:172-77, 164-65.

23.  Monroe to Richard Brent (U. S. senator from Virginia), March 18, 1811, ibid., 5:178-80; Brant, *Madison,* 5:273-87.

24.  LWT to Monroe, March 17, 1811, Monroe Papers, LC.

25.  Monroe to Madison, March 23, 1811, Monroe, *Writings,* 5:181-83.

26.  LWT to Monroe, March 24, 1811, Monroe Papers, LC; Bruce, *Randolph,* 1:348.

27.  Deed Book 29:115-16, Deed Book 30:15-17, Court house Records of Princess Anne County, Circuit Court, city of Virginia Beach, Va.; *The Lower Norfolk County Virginia Antiquary,* ed. Edward W. James, 5 vols. (Charlottesville, Va., 1895), 1:77, 5:104.

28.  Record of Inscriptions on the Tombstones in St. Paul's Church Yard, no. 215, *St. Paul's Church, 1832, Originally the Borough Church, 1739, Elizabeth River Parish, Norfolk, Virginia* (Norfolk, 1934), 103.

29.  LWT to Thomas Jefferson, July 3, Aug. 28, 1810, Jefferson Papers, Coolidge Collection, MHS.

30.  Legal papers of Henry and Littleton Waller Tazewell, UVa Lib.; LWT to Jefferson, Sept. 11, 1811, Jefferson Papers, Coolidge Collection, MHS; LWT to Jefferson, Oct. 13, 1811 (copy), Tazewell Papers.

31. *American State Papers: Public Lands*, 2:5-8, 12-102.

32. William B. Hatcher, *Edward Livingston, Jeffersonian Republican and Jacksonian Democrat* (Baton Rouge, La., 1940), chap. 8; Peterson, *Jefferson and the New Nation*, 944-47; Jefferson to James Madison, May 25, 1810, Jefferson, *Works*, 11: 139-41.

33. Wirt to LWT, Oct. 24, 1810, Tazewell Papers.

34. George Hay to LWT, March 6, 1811, Jefferson to LWT, March 23, 1811 (copy), ibid.; Kennedy, *Wirt*, 1:265; LWT to Jefferson, Sept. 27, 1810, quoted in Edward Dumbauld, *Thomas Jefferson and the Law* (Norman, Okla., 1978), 188.

35. LWT to Jefferson, May 15, 1812, quoted in Dumbauld, *Jefferson and the Law*, 43. Tazewell believed Jefferson's "interests ought not to be put in hazard, even for the benefit of settling either abstract political questions, or of trying a right of property in others who seemed to take no interest in the controversy." Jefferson had hoped that the federal government or the Territory of Orleans would assist him financially in opposing the Livingston claim. Neither would do so.

36 Jefferson to Madison, May 25, 1810, Jefferson, *Works*,11:139-41; Peterson, *Jefferson and the New Nation*, 945-46.

37. George Hay to LWT, May 25, 1811, Tazewell Papers.

38. *Virginia Argus*, Dec. 5, 1811; LWT to Jefferson, Dec. 4, 1811, Jefferson Papers, Coolidge Collection, MHS.

39. Jefferson to LWT, May 12, 1812 (copy), Tazewell Papers; *Reports of Cases Decided by the Honourable John Marshall in the Circuit Court of the United States for the District of Virginia and North Carolina*, ed. John W. Brockenbrough, 2 vols. (Philadelphia, 1837), 1:206-12; Beveridge, *Marshall*, 4:112-16.

40. Jefferson to Wirt, April 12, 1812, Jefferson, *Works*, 11:226-31.

## Chapter V

1. LWT to James Monroe, May 10, 1811, Monroe Papers, LC; *Norfolk Gazette and Publick Ledger*, Feb. 25, 1811; *Norfolk Herald*, June 3, 1811.

2. *Norfolk Herald*, Aug. 30, 1811; Monroe, "written in the fall of 1811, and addressed to some person of high influence in England," *Writings*, 5:191–92.

3. *Annals of Congress*,12th Cong., 1st sess., 441–55; Brant, *Madison*, 5:356.

4. LWT to Monroe, Jan. 17, 1812, Monroe Papers, LC; Brant, *Madison*, 5:358.

5. LWT to Monroe, Jan. 17, 1812, Monroe Papers, LC.

6. Edwin Gray to LWT, Mar. 20, 1812, Tazewell Papers; LWT to Monroe, Jan. 17, May 10, 1812, Monroe Papers, LC; Brant, *Madison*, 6:280–83.

7. *Norfolk Gazette and Publick Ledger*, April 8, 1812; *Annals of Congress*, 12th Cong., 1st sess., 1451–63.

8. Monroe to John Taylor, June 13, 1812, Monroe, *Writings*, 5:205–12; Wirt to Monroe, June 21, 1812, Monroe Papers, LC.

9. Quoted in Risjord, *Old Republicans,* 145.

10. Stephen Decatur to Luke Wheeler and LWT, June 20, 1812 (copy), Tazewell Papers.

11. *Norfolk Herald,* June 19, 1812; *Norfolk Gazette and Publick Ledger,* July 29, 1812; *Virginia Argus,* June 29, 1812; F. Lee Benns, *The American Struggle for the British West India Carrying-Trade, 1815–1830* (Bloomington, Ind., 1923), 27; Wertenbaker, *Norfolk, 110.*

12. Addendum by Ann Tazewell Bradford to LWT, "Sketches," typed copy, 166, Kirn Memorial Library, Norfolk; Norman K. Risjord, "Election of 1812," *History of American Presidential Election,* ed. Arthur M. Schlesinger, Jr., 4 vols. (New York, 1971), 1:255–69.

13. *Virginia Argus,* Feb. 11, 1813; Robert B. Taylor to Gov. James Barbour, March 4, 1813, Monroe Papers, LC.

14. *Norfolk Gazette and Publick Ledger,* Dec. 11, 1812, Jan. 8, Feb. 10, 1813; Nivison to LWT, March 6, 9, 18, 1813, bill from LWT to the United States government for the use of slaves, animals, and equipment, Jan. 23, 1814, and LWT, "Sketches," MS, 3, Tazewell Papers; Frank A. Cassell, "Slaves of the Chesapeake Bay Area and the War of 1812," *Journal of Negro History* 58 (1972), 144–55.

15. Wertenbaker, *Norfolk,* 113–14; *Norfolk Gazette and Publick Ledger,* Jan. 4, 1815.

16. Richard Cocke to LWT, Jan. 12, 1814, Henry Tazewell to LWT, Nov. 9, 1814, Nivison to LWT, June 4, 1815, Tazewell Papers.

17. Wirt to LWT, Aug. 11, 1814, ibid.

18. Wilson Cary Nicholas to LWT, Oct. 10, 1814, ibid.

19. Ibid., April 18, Aug. 26, 1815; Victor D. Golladay, "The Nicholas Family of Virginia, 1722–1820" (Ph.D. diss., University of Virginia, 1973), 420–22.

20. Wertenbaker, *Norfolk,* 145–46; John Nivison to LWT, June 4, 1815, Tazewell Papers.

21. LWT to John Randolph, March 14, 1815, Tazewell Papers.

22. Ibid.

23. Ibid., Dec. 30, 1814, March 14, 1815.

24. John Nivison to LWT, June 4, 1815, ibid.; Paullin, *Commodore John Rodgers,* 304–5.

25. Mackenzie, *Decatur,* 244–92, 295–96, 386–89; Secretary of the Navy Benjamin Crowninshield to LWT, June 29, 1816, RG 45, M-209, roll 4, NA; *Norfolk Gazette and Publick Ledger,* April 6, 1816.

26. *Richmond Enquirer,* Jan. 28, 1817.

27. *Norfolk Gazette and Publick Ledger,* April 23, 1816.

28. *Journal of the House of Delegates of Virginia, 1815–1816* (Richmond, 1816), 17–18; *American Beacon,* Nov. 6, 1816.

29. *Richmond Enquirer,* Feb. 15, 1816; *Niles' Weekly Register,* Feb. 24, 1816; John Nivison to LWT, Nov. 28, 1816, Tazewell Papers.

30. William E. Dodd, *The Life of Nathaniel Macon* (Raleigh, 1903), 294; Bruce, *Randolph,* 1:430; George Dangerfield, *The Awakening of American Nationalism, 1815–1828* (New York, 1965), 97–99.

31.  *American Beacon,* Dec. 24, 1816; *Richmond Enquirer,* Dec. 24, 1816.

32.  Merrill D. Peterson, ed., *Democracy, Liberty, and Property: The State Constitutional Conventions of the 1820's* (Indianapolis, 1966), 273–74; *American Beacon,* Sept. 4, 1816; *Niles' Weekly Register,* Sept. 7, 1816; Fletcher M. Green, *Constitutional Development in the South Atlantic States, 1776–1860* (Chapel Hill, N.C., 1930), 173–76, 183–92; Risjord, "The Virginia Federalists," 514–16.

33.  *Richmond Enquirer,* Jan. 14, 1817.

34.  Tazewell's speech, in its entirety, is found in the *Richmond Enquirer,* Jan. 28, 1817.

35.  *Richmond Enquirer,* Oct. 2, 1816, Jan. 23, 30, Feb. 1, 13, 1817; *Niles' Weekly Register,* March 8, 1817; Charles Ambler, *Sectionalism in Virginia from 1776 to 1861* (Chicago, 1910), 96. The anomaly of the Federalist and Jeffersonian positions is discussed at length in Risjord, "The Virginia Federalists," 486–517.

36.  William Wickham to LWT, May 2, 1817, Tazewell Papers.

37.  Ibid.; *American Beacon,* May 29, 1816; *Norfolk Gazette and Publick Ledger,* June 8, 11, 1816.

38.  William Tazewell to LWT, July 23, 1817, and balance sheet of the steamboat *Powhatan,* Sept. 4, 1817, Tazewell Papers; *American Beacon,* Oct 9, 1817; Samuel Ward Stanton, "Baltimore and Norfolk Boats from the Early Days to the Present," *Steam Navigation on the Carolina Sounds and the Chesapeake in 1892* (Salem, Mass., 1947), 23; William Wirt to Mrs. Wirt, Nov. 3, 1817, Kennedy, *Wirt,* 2:29–31.

39.  *Norfolk Herald,* April 10, Aug. 10, 1818; *American Beacon,* April 18, 20, Aug. 8, 1818.

40.  Forrest, *Norfolk,* 115–17; Wertenbaker, *Norfolk,* 157–58.

41.  *American Beacon,* July 31, 1818; *Norfolk Herald,* Aug. 3, 1818; LWT to Robert Walker, July 18, 19, 1820, Tazewell Papers.

# *Chapter* VI

1.  Lynn W. Turner, "Elections of 1816 and 1820," *History of American Presidential Elections,* ed. Schlesinger, 1:304.

2.  William Wirt to James Monroe, Nov. 8, 1817, Monroe Papers, LC; Wirt to LWT, Dec. 18, 1817, Tazewell Papers.

3.  Stephen Decatur to LWT, March 9, 1818 (copy), Wirt to LWT, Oct. 15, 1818, Tazewell Papers.

4.  *The Old Bachelor* was first published as a series of essays in the *Richmond Enquirer.* The essay on Tazewell (whom Wirt called "Sidney," but who clearly was identifiable as Tazewell) appeared in the issue of Aug. 13, 1811.

5.  Francis Walker Gilmer, *Sketches, Essays, and Translations* (1816; rev. ed., Baltimore, 1828), 35. Written in 1815, Gilmer's work was published in 1816 under the title *Sketches of American Orators.* A revised edition was published posthumously in 1828. Davis, *Gilmer,* 289, 291.

6.  John Nivison to LWT, July 24, 1819, William Nivison to Sarah Nivison, Sept. 2, 23, 1819, William Nivison to Louisa Nivison, Aug. 2, 26, Sept. 26, 1819, Tazewell Papers.

7. Francis Corbin to LWT, April 12, 1820, ibid.

8. William Nivison to Louisa Nivison, Oct. 2, 1819, ibid.; "Correspondence between Commodore James Barron and Commodore Stephen Decatur," app. no. X, Mackenzie, *Decatur*, 398–441; *St. Paul's Church,* 102.

9. Quoted in *Early History of the University of Virginia as Contained in the Letters of Thomas Jefferson and Joseph C. Cabell,* ed. Nathaniel Francis Cabell (Richmond, 1856), 212.

10. William F. Gordon to James Barbour, Feb. 18, 1820, John Tyler Papers, LC; Glover Moore, *The Missouri Controversy, 1819–1821* (Lexington, Ky., 1966), 237, 243.

11. LWT to John Randolph, Jan. 25, 1821, Tazewell Papers.

12. John Bassett Moore, *History and Digest of the International Arbitrations to Which the United States Has Been a Party,* 6 vols. (Washington, D.C., 1898), 5:4497–4500; statement of Dec. 1822, quoted in Grigsby, *Tazewell,* 120.

13. Notation by LWT on Farmers' Bank account and statement, Aug. 8, 1827, Tazewell Papers.

14. Moore, *International Arbitrations,* 5:4502; Nancy N. Scott, *A Memoir of Hugh Lawson White* (Philadelphia, 1856), 34–35; Robert Ernst, *Rufus King* (Chapel Hill, N.C., 1968), 346, 353n; Thomas Perkins Abernethy, s.v. "Hugh Lawson White," *DAB;* Robert E. Moody, s.v. "William King," *DAB.* Later, as fourth auditor of the treasury during the John Quincy Adams administration, Watkins was found to have been "peculating upon the public money, to the amount of nine or ten thousand dollars at least." Adams was "more shocked at hearing this than I could be at the loss of ten elections." *Memoirs of John Quincy Adams,* ed. Charles Francis Adams, 12 vols. (1874–77; rept. New York, 1970), 8:141.

15. William Wickham to LWT, Sept. 20, 1821, Tazewell Papers; *American Beacon,* Aug. 17, 25, Sept. 4, 5, 6, Oct. 25, 1821; *St. Paul's Church,* 102.

16. Tobias Watkins to LWT, Nov. 5, Dec. 15, 1821, Tazewell Papers.

17. "Commissioners' Final Report," Moore, *International Arbitrations,* 5:4507–18.

18. Adams, *Memoirs,* 5:361–63.

19. *The Diary of John Quincy Adams, 1794–1845,* ed. Allan Nevins (New York, 1951), 291–92; Ben. Perley Poore, *Reminiscences of Sixty Years in the National Metropolis,* 2 vols. (Philadelphia, 1886), 1:70–71.

20. Wirt to Francis Gilmer, May 9, 1822, Kennedy, *Wirt,* 2:121–22; 7 Wheaton, 283–84.

21. Grigsby, *Tazewell,* 45; Claude M. Fuess, *Daniel Webster,* 2 vols. (Boston, 1930), 1:255; LWT to John Randolph, Jan. 25, 1821, Tazewell Papers.

22. Grigsby, *Tazewell,* 43–45.

23. 7 Wheaton, 355.

24. Garland, *Randolph,* 2:170; Grigsby, *Tazewell,* 44, 118.

25. William N. Chambers, *Old Bullion Benton, Senator from the New West* (Boston, 1956), 108–9; LWT to John Randolph, Feb. 10, 1822, William Wickham to LWT, April 18, 1822, Tazewell Papers; LWT to John Wickham, April 26, 1824, Wickham Papers.

26. LWT to John Tazewell, May 24, 1823, Tazewell Papers; Ralph T. Whitelaw, *Virginia's Eastern Shore: A History of Northampton and Accomack Counties*, 2 vols. (Richmond, 1951), 1:144, 147.

27. William Floyd (overseer) to LWT, June 5, 1822, LWT to John Tazewell, April 28, 1824, Tazewell Papers.

28. Ann Tazewell to Henry and John Tazewell, Sept. 30, 1822, ibid.

29. Ibid.; Ann Tazewell to John Tazewell, Nov. 24, Dec. 8, 1822, LWT to John Tazewell, Nov. 5, 1822, ibid.

30. LWT to John Tazewell, Oct. 2, 1822, ibid.

31. Ibid., Oct. 3, Nov. 5, 1822.

32. Ann Tazewell to John Tazewell, May 14, 1823, Dec. 8, 15, 1822, ibid.

33. Ann Tazewell to Henry and John Tazewell, Sept. 30, 1822, LWT to John Tazewell, May 24, 1823, ibid.

34. George Ticknor to LWT, May 14, 1823, ibid. The board of visitors of the University of Virginia also attempted to employ Ticknor. Cabell, *Early History, University of Virginia*, 460.

35. LWT to John Tazewell, May 24, July 3, 1823, Wirt to LWT, Aug. 25, 1823, Tazewell Papers.

36. George Ticknor to LWT, Oct. 17, 1823, Henry Tazewell to LWT, Oct. 14, 1823, LWT to John Tazewell, Dec. 25. 1823, March 7, April 25, 1824, ibid.

37. LWT to John Tazewell, March 14, April 11, May 6, 1824, ibid.

38. Ibid., Dec. 22, 1823, April 28, 1824.

39. Ibid., April 11, 25, 1824.

40. Ibid., March 14, April 24, 1824.

41. Ibid., Jan. 2, 1823, May 6, 1824; Ann Tazewell to John Tazewell, Dec. 8, 1822, ibid.

42. LWT to John Tazewell, April 28, 1824, ibid.

43. Ibid., April 25, 1824.

44. Adams, *Memoirs*, 5:361; Moore, *International Arbitrations*, 5:4518; *National Intelligencer*, June 9, 1824; Edwin M. Borchard, *The Diplomatic Protection of Citizens Abroad or the Law of International Claims* (New York, 1919), 379–80.

45. *American Beacon*, Oct. 25, 1824; *Richmond Enquirer*, Oct. 29, 1824; Forrest, *Norfolk*, 164–68.

46. Henry H. Simms, *Life of John Taylor* (Richmond, 1932), 210.

## Chapter VII

1. In the *Richmond Enquirer*, June 8, 1824, Tazewell, writing under the name of "Chatham," expressed his disgust with the nation's leaders. Tazewell's authorship was revealed by Wirt. See Adams, *Memoirs*, 6:378.

2. Robert V. Remini, *Martin Van Buren and the Making of the Democratic Party* (New York, 1959), 38–41; Ammon, "Richmond Junto," 408–9; Wil-

liam E. Dodd, "Chief Justice Marshall and Virginia," *American Historical Review* 12 (1907): 776–87; Simms, *John Taylor*, 170–71; Peterson, *Jefferson and the New Nation*, 990–91.

3.  Marshall to Story, June 15, July 13, 1821, quoted in Dodd, "Marshall and Virginia," 784; Ammon, "Richmond Junto," 410–11.

4.  *Richmond Enquirer*, June 8, 1824.

5.  Chase C. Mooney, *William H. Crawford, 1772–1834* (Lexington, Ky., 1974), 255, 258–59.

6.  LWT to John Wickham, April 26, 1824, Wickham Papers; James F. Hopkins, "Election of 1824," *History of American Presidential Elections*, ed. Schlesinger, 1:361; Wirt to William Pope, Nov. 12, 1824, Kennedy, *Wirt*, 2:161.

7.  Mooney, *Crawford*, 240–48; Charles M. Wiltse, *John C. Calhoun*, 3 vols. (Indianapolis, 1944–51), 1:277. The national popular vote: Jackson, 152,901; Adams, 114,023; Crawford, 46,979; Clay, 47,217. The electoral vote: Jackson, 99; Adams, 84; Crawford, 41; Clay, 37. Schlesinger, *History of American Presidential Elections*, 1:409.

8.  Richard E. Parker to LWT, Dec. 1, 1824, Tazewell Papers.

9.  "Letter to the Members of the Virginia Legislature," *Richmond Enquirer*, Dec. 7, 1824. See also ibid., Dec. 9, 1824.

10.  "Extracts from the Letters of Mr. Tazewell Respecting Public Office," Grigsby, *Tazewell*, app. IV, 120–21; LWT to Henry Baldwin, Feb. 4, 1825, Tazewell Papers.

11.  The debate on Tazewell's nomination is covered in the *Richmond Enquirer*, Dec. 9, 1824.

12.  Ibid.

13.  Waller Taylor to LWT, Dec. 17, 1824, Tazewell Papers.

14.  Mary Cable, *The Avenue of the Presidents* (Boston, 1969), 86; Charles K. Sellers, *James K. Polk*, 2 vols. (Princeton, N.J., 1957–66), 1:116–17, 2:486. Jackson resigned from the Senate on Oct. 14, 1825, and White took his place on Dec. 12, 1825. Polk was elected to the 19th Congress. *Biographical Directory of Congress, 1774–1927*, 142.

15.  Verplanck, Woodbury, and Ellis did not arrive in Washington until the 19th Congress, while Bell was elected to the 20th Congress. *Biographical Directory of Congress, 1774–1927*, 142, 149; George Ticknor to Mrs. Ticknor, April 22, 1828, *Life, Letters, and Journals of George Ticknor*, ed. George S. Hillard, 2 vols. (Boston, 1876), 1:381; Chambers, *Benton*, 137.

16.  LWT to John Tazewell, Feb. 27, 1825, to Henry Baldwin, Feb. 4, 1825, Tazewell Papers. Baldwin, from Pennsylvania, served in Congress from 1817 to 1822 and was appointed to the United States Supreme Court in 1830.

17.  Henry Tazewell to Andrew Jackson, July 20, 1798, *Correspondence of Andrew Jackson*, ed. John S. Bassett, 7 vols. (Washington, D.C., 1926–33), 1:50–54; John S. Bassett, *The Life of Andrew Jackson*, 2 vols. (New York, 1916), 1:28–32, 54.

18.  *Register of Debates*, 18th Cong., 2d sess., 303–18; *National Intelligencer*, Jan. 24, 1825.

19.  *National Intelligencer*, Feb. 4, 1825; John Wickham to LWT, Feb. 20, 1825, Tazewell Papers.

20. Wertenbaker, *Norfolk*, 158–61.

21. Ralph D. Gray, *The National Waterway: A History of the Chesapeake and Delaware Canal, 1769–1965* (Urbana, Ill., 1967), 55, 63–64; John Cowper to LWT, Feb. 12, 1825, George Newton to LWT, Feb. 12, 1825, Tazewell Papers.

22. *Register of Debates*, 18th Cong., 2d sess., 672–78, 19th Cong., 1st sess., 710–20.

23. Peterson, *Jefferson and the New Nation*, 855–58; Wiltse, *Calhoun*, 1:133–34; Risjord, *Old Republicans*, 246.

24. Ambler, *Ritchie*, 95; John Wickham to LWT, Feb. 20, 1825, Tazewell Papers.

25. Quoted in Risjord, *Old Republicans*, 242.

26. *National Intelligencer*, Feb. 9, 1825.

27. Ibid., Feb. 10, 11, 1825; Margaret Bayard Smith, *The First Forty Years of Washington Society*, ed. Gaillard Hunt (New York, 1965), 185–87; Glyndon G. Van Deusen, *The Life of Henry Clay* (Boston, 1937), 190–91.

28. Samuel F. Bemis, *John Quincy Adams*, 2 vols. (1949–56; rept. New York, 1965), 2:47–48, 57–58; Wiltse, *Calhoun*, 1:311–12; Adams, *Memoirs*, 6:506–8; Andrew Jackson to William B. Lewis, Feb. 14, 1825, to Squire Grant, Feb. 18, 1825, Jackson, *Correspondence*, 3:276.

29. "Monroe on the Adams-Clay Bargain," ed. Barnes F. Lathrop, *American Historical Review* 42 (1937): 273–76; Adams, *Memoirs*, 6:505, 520; Kennedy, *Wirt*, 2:166–67.

30. *A Compilation of the Messages and Papers of the Presidents*, ed. James D. Richardson, 10 vols. (Washington, D.C., 1903), 2:294–99; Adams, *Memoirs*, 6:525; *National Intelligencer*, March 9, 1825.

31. LWT to John Tazewell, Feb. 27, 1825, Tazewell Papers.

32. Ibid.; Francis Gilmer to John Tazewell, April 5, 1825, John Tazewell to LWT, April 6, 1825, ibid.

33. LWT to Jefferson, March 1, 1825, Jefferson Papers, Coolidge Collection, MHS; Jefferson to LWT, Nov. 25, 1825 (copy), Tazewell Papers; Peterson, *Jefferson and the New Nation*, 988.

34. Ann Tazewell to John Tazewell, May 1, 1825, Jacob G. Parker to LWT, April 9, 1825, Tazewell Papers.

35. Benjamin Watkins Leigh to LWT, Aug. 22, 1825, ibid.

36. Peterson, *Jefferson and the New Nation*, 992–93.

37. Ann Tazewell to John Tazewell, June 10, 1825, LWT to John Tazewell, June 10, 1825, John Wickham to LWT, Dec. 28, 1825, Tazewell Papers.

## Chapter VIII

1. *Messages and Papers*, 2:299–317; Bemis, *J. Q. Adams*, 2:65–70; Adams, *Memoirs*, 7:58–64; George Loyall to LWT, Dec. 10, 1825, Tazewell Papers.

2. Bemis, *J. Q. Adams*, 2:69–70; Grigsby, *Tazewell*, 59.

3. John Wickham to LWT, Dec. 28, 1825, Tazewell Papers.

4. *Messages and Papers*, 2:302, 318–20; Thomas Hart Benton, *Thirty Years' View*, 2 vols. (Boston, 1854), 1:65; Wiltse, *Calhoun*, 1:322–23.

5. Benton, *Thirty Years' View*, 1:65–69; Dodd, *Macon*, 351. Dodd blames Clay for "Adams' blunder"; Clay "took up the invitation with his usual gusto and urged Adams to accept it and promised to send representatives without so much as consulting Congress."

6. Benton, *Thirty Years' View*, 1:65–69; Adams, *Memoirs*, 7:103–5; Wiltse, *Calhoun*, 1:325; Bemis, *J. Q. Adams*, 2:76–77; Remini, *Van Buren*, 105–6.

7. LWT to John Randolph, Feb. 10, 1826, Randolph to LWT, Feb. 12, 1826, Tazewell Papers.

8. LWT to Randolph, Feb. 12, 1826, ibid.

9. Randolph to LWT, Feb. 12, 14, 15, 1826, ibid.

10. LWT to Randolph, Feb. 16, 17, 1826, ibid.

11. Ibid., Feb. 16.

12. Ibid., Feb. 20, 26, 27, March 8, 13, 1826.

13. Ibid., Feb. 23, 27, 28, 1826; Hugh Lawson White to LWT, Feb. 17, 20, 23, 24, 1826, Randolph to LWT, Feb. 21, 24, 28, 1826, ibid.; Remini, *Van Buren*, 109; *Register of Debates*, 19th Cong., 1st sess., 115–31, 154–74.

14. LWT to Randolph, March 6, 1826, Tazewell Papers; *Register of Debates*, 19th Cong., 1st sess., 389–406; Benton, *Thirty Years' View*, 1:70–77; Van Deusen, *Clay*, 219–20.

15. *Register of Debates*, 19th Cong., 1st sess., 597–619; LWT to John Wickham, May 9, 1826, Wickham Papers. Tazewell was speaking in favor of a resolution introduced by John Branch of North Carolina "that the President of the United States does not, constitutionally, possess either the right or the power to appoint ambassadors or other public ministers, but with the advice and consent of the Senate, except when vacancies may happen in the recess."

16. Henry St. George Tucker to LWT, June 23, 1826, Tazewell Papers; Risjord, *Old Republicans*, 261–66.

17. Wiltse, *Calhoun*, 1:328; LWT to Randolph, March 4, 1826, John Wickham to LWT, June 3, 1826, Tazewell Papers.

18. John Tazewell to LWT, April 29, 1826, H. P. C. Wilson to LWT, Aug. 8, 1826, S. Wilkins to LWT, Sept. 23, 1826, William S. Smith to LWT, Sept. 28, 1826, John Wickham to LWT, Oct. 14, 1826, William Wickham to LWT, Oct, 31, 1826, Tazewell Papers; *Norfolk Herald*, Sept. 22, 1826.

19. John Wickham to LWT, July 8, 1826, Tazewell Papers; Risjord, *Old Republicans*, 256–59; Arthur P. Hayne to Andrew Jackson, July 20, 1826, James K. Polk to Jackson, Dec. 4, 1826, Jackson, *Correspondence*, 3:306–7, 321–22.

20. Benjamin Watkins Leigh to LWT, Jan. 24, 1827, John Wickham to LWT, Dec. 17, 1826, Tazewell Papers.

21. Robert V. Remini, *The Election of Andrew Jackson* (Philadelphia, 1963), 52–53.

22. LWT to John Wickham, Dec. 23, 1826, Wickham Papers.

23. Adams, *Memoirs*, 7:193; Wiltse, *Calhoun*, 1:343–44; George Loyall to LWT, Jan. 1, 1827, Tazewell Papers; Henry Clay to Francis Brooke, Dec.

23, 1826, *The Private Correspondence of Henry Clay,* ed. Calvin Colton (New York, 1855), 153.

24. W. H. Fitzhugh to LWT, Dec. 18, 1826 (copy), Tazewell Papers; *The Autobiography of Martin Van Buren,* ed. John C. Fitzpatrick (Washington, D.C., 1920), 514. Van Buren always remembered the visit "as a green spot in the pilgrimage of life," as, indeed, for him it was.

25. LWT to John Wickham, Dec. 23, 1826, Wickham Papers.

26. Oliver Chitwood, *John Tyler, Champion of the Old South* (New York, 1939), 76; Leigh to LWT, Jan. 24, 1827, Tazewell Papers; *Richmond Enquirer,* Jan. 16, 1827.

27. Leigh to LWT, Jan 24, 1827, Tazewell Papers.

28. Van Buren to Thomas Ritchie, Jan. 13, 1827, quoted in Remini, *Van Buren,* 132–33.

29. Tazewell's letter to Ritchie, quoted in Ambler, *Ritchie,* 108–9; Wiltse, *Calhoun,* 1:349–50.

30. Ritchie to LWT, Feb. 28, 1827, Tazewell Papers; *Richmond Enquirer,* April 27, 1827.

31. John C. Calhoun to James Edward Calhoun, Dec. 24, 1826, *Correspondence of John C. Calhoun,* ed. J. Franklin Jameson (Washington, D.C., 1900), 237; *Norfolk Herald,* April 4, 11, 1827; *Register of Debates,* 19th Cong., 1st sess., 586.

32. Benns, *BWI Carrying Trade,* 104; Bradford Perkins, *Castlereagh and Adams: England and the United States, 1815–1823* (Berkeley, Calif, 1964), 237.

33. *Register of Debates,* 19th Cong., 1st sess., 589, 708–9; Frank A. Cassell, *Merchant Congressman in the Young Republic: Samuel Smith of Maryland, 1752–1839* (Madison, Wis., 1971), 238–39; Benns, *BWI Carrying Trade,* 119.

34. John Cooper to LWT, Dec. 8, 1826, Tazewell Papers; *Richmond Enquirer,* Dec. 12, 1826; Adams, *Memoirs,* 7:213–14; *Register of Debates,* 19th Cong., 2d sess., 399, 403–62, 486, 495–96, 501, 504–6, 1465; Benns, *BWI Carrying Trade,* 136–41; *Norfolk Herald,* Feb. 5, 1827.

35. *Messages and Papers,* 2:375–76; Adams, *Memoirs,* 7:249; *Richmond Enquirer,* March 20, 1827; *Norfolk Herald,* March 31, 1827; Wertenbaker, *Norfolk,* 151.

36. *Norfolk Herald,* March 28, May 30, April 6, 1827; Benns, *BWI Carrying Trade,* 162.

37. Adams, *Memoirs,* 7:224; *National Intelligencer,* Feb. 14, 21, 1827; Van Buren, *Autobiography,* 169; Remini, *Van Buren,* 134–36; *Register of Debates,* 19th Cong., 2d sess., 496.

38. Van Buren, *Autobiography,* 209–10.

39. John Wickham to LWT, March 17, 1827, Tazewell Papers.

40. Remini, *Van Buren,* 137–38.

## Chapter IX

1. Mahlon Dickerson to LWT, March 21, 1827, Tazewell Papers; John C. Calhoun to LWT, April 1, 1827, Calhoun Papers, L.C.

2. Calhoun to LWT, July 1, 1827, Calhoun Papers.

3. Remini, *Van Buren*, 148–53.

4. Calhoun to LWT, Aug. 25, 1827, Calhoun Papers.

5. Ibid., Nov. 9, 1827; John Wickham to LWT, Dec. 9, 30, 1827, Tazewell Papers; Risjord, *Old Republicans*, 267. Risjord notes that Tazewell, writing to Ritchie earlier in 1827, clearly saw the Van Buren alliance as merely a "temporary coalition" which could succumb to northern entrepreneurial interests.

6. Remini, *Election of Jackson*, 101–2; John Wickham to LWT, Dec. 30, 1827, Tazewell Papers; Richard Hofstadter, *Anti-intellectualism in American Life* (New York, 1963), 158–59; Hugh Blair Grigsby, *Letters of a South Carolinian* (Norfolk, 1827), 5–10.

7. Remini, *Election of Jackson*, 118; John Wickham to LWT, Dec. 30, 1827, Tazewell Papers.

8. Remini, *Election of Jackson*, 171–72; Adams, *Memoirs*, 7:366–67.

9. *Norfolk Herald*, Jan. 9, Feb. 4, 8, 11, 1828; LWT to John Tazewell, Jan. 5, 1828, Tazewell Papers.

10. LWT to Ann S. Tazewell, Feb. 27, 1828, Tazewell Papers.

11. Remini, *Van Buren*, 170–72; John Wickham to LWT, March 23, 1828, Tazewell Papers.

12. John Wickham to LWT, Dec. 30, 1827, Tazewell Papers.

13. Tazewell read the report to the Senate on April 28, 1828. It was printed in the *Norfolk Herald*, May 21, 23, 1828.

14. Littleton Waller Tazewell, "Sketches," typed copy, 165, Kirn Memorial Library, Norfolk.

15. John Wickham to LWT, March 23, 1828, Tazewell Papers.

16. Richard Parker to LWT, May 4, 1828, W. B. Giles to LWT and John Tyler, May 21, 1828, ibid.; John C. Calhoun to James Edward Calhoun, May 4, 1828, Calhoun to James Monroe, July 10, 1828, Calhoun, *Correspondence*, 264–67.

17. Remini, *Election of Jackson*, 178–79; *The Letters and Times of the Tylers*, ed. Lyon G. Tyler, 3 vols. (1884–96; rept. New York, 1970), 3:69n; *The Works of John C. Calhoun*, ed. Richard K. Crallé, 6 vols. (New York, 1854–57), 6:1–57.

18. William S. Smith (overseer) to LWT, Oct. 16, 1827, Tazewell Papers; *American Beacon*, July 7, 17, 28, 1828.

19. LWT, "Sketches," typed copy, 190, Kirn Memorial Library, Norfolk. The information concerning Henry was provided by Tazewell's grandson Littleton Waller Tazewell, who, although the son of Ann and Edmund Bradford, took the Tazewell name. Whitelaw, *Virginia's Eastern Shore*, 1:203, has a brief statement on the suicide.

20. Schlesinger, *History of American Presidential Elections*, 1:492; Charles H. Ambler, *The Life and Diary of John Floyd* (Richmond, 1918), 78–79; *Richmond Enquirer*, Nov. 7, 14, 1828.

21. Remini, *Election of Jackson*, 183–95, 203.

22. John Wickham to LWT, Dec. 10, 1828, Theodore Miller to LWT, Dec. 17, 1828, Hugh Blair Grigsby to LWT, Dec. 5, 1828, Tazewell Papers.

23. John Wickham to LWT, Dec. 21, 1828, ibid.; James K. Polk to Andrew Jackson, Dec. 5, 1828, *Correspondence of James K. Polk*, ed. Herbert Weaver and Paul H. Bergeron (Nashville, 1969—), 1:213–14.

24. Scott, *Memoir of White*, 35, 416–19; LWT to Ann Tazewell, Dec. 25, 1828, Tazewell Papers.

25. John C. Calhoun to Patrick Noble, Jan. 10, 1829, Calhoun, *Correspondence*, 269–70; Claude G. Bowers, *The Party Battles of the Jackson Period* (Boston, 1928), 41; *Richmond Enquirer*, Dec. 6, 1828; *Norfolk Herald*, Jan. 7, 1829; Hugh Blair Grigsby to John Tazewell, Jan. 3, 1829, Tazewell Papers.

26. LWT to John Tazewell, Jan. 9, 1829, Tazewell Papers.

27. John Tazewell to LWT, Jan. 18, 1829, LWT to John Tazewell, Jan. 9, 1829, ibid.

28. LWT to John Wickham, Feb. 11, 1829, Wickham Papers. Tazewell's correspondence with his wife, Wickham, and Jackson belies Van Buren's contention, stated in his *Autobiography*, that Jackson regretted his too hasty action in offering Tazewell the diplomatic post without first consulting Van Buren and hoped Tazewell would not accept. Regardless of the fact that Van Buren made many pleasant references to Tazewell, he obviously had no affection for the Virginian. Van Buren, *Autobiography*, 256–59.

29. Ann Tazewell to LWT, Feb. 21, 1829, Tazewell Papers.

30. *Norfolk Herald*, March 4, 1829; James A. Hamilton, *Reminiscences of James A. Hamilton; or, Men and Events, at Home and Abroad, during Three Quarters of a Century* (New York, 1869), 90–91; John A. Munroe, *Louis McLane: Federalist and Jacksonian* (New Brunswick, N.J., 1973), 253; Ambler, *Ritchie*, 127–28.

31. *National Intelligencer*, March 3, 4, 5, 1829; LWT to Ann Tazewell, Dec. 25, 1828, Tazewell Papers.

32. *National Intelligencer*, March 5, 1829; Adams; *Memoirs*, 8:105; *Messages and Papers*, 2:436–38.

33. *National Intelligencer*, March 7, 10, 11, 1829; Wiltse, *Calhoun*, 2:19–23; William Wirt to William Pope, March 22, 1829, Kennedy, *Wirt*, 2:228–29; Smith, *First Forty Years*, 287.

34. Andrew Jackson to LWT, March 12, 1829 (copy), Tazewell Papers; LWT to John Wickham, April 9, 1829, Wickham Papers.

35. LWT to Andrew Jackson, March 30, 1829, Jackson, *Correspondence*, 4:15–17.

36. Jackson to LWT, April 6, 1829 (copy), Tazewell Papers; John M. Berrien to Jackson, April 9, 1829, Jackson, *Correspondence*, 4:22; Munroe, *McLane*, 253–55; John C. Calhoun to LWT, April 14, 1829, Calhoun Papers. For background on Berrien, see Thomas P. Govan, "John M. Berrien and the Administration of Andrew Jackson," *Journal of Southern History* 5 (1939): 447–67.

37. John Wickham to LWT, April 24, 1829, Tazewell Papers; LWT to John Wickham, June 3, 1829, Wickham Papers.

38. LWT to John Wickham, April 9, June 3, 1829, Wickham Papers.

# Chapter X

1. LWT to John Wickham, April 9, 1829, Wickham Papers.

2. Ibid., June 3, 1829; Deed Book 36:269, Courthouse Records of Princess Anne County, Circuit Court, city of Virginia Beach.

3. *Norfolk Herald,* April 30, 1828; Green, *Constitutional Development,* 210; Peterson, *Democracy, Liberty, and Property,* 274.

4. *Richmond Enquirer,* Dec. 16, 1828; Ambler, *Ritchie,* 117–18; Theodore Miller to LWT, Dec. 22, 1828, Tazewell Papers.

5. *Richmond Enquirer,* Feb. 10, 12, 1829; Green, *Constitutional Development,* 211–17.

6. John Wickham to LWT, Dec. 21, 1828, Jan. 18, 1829, Tazewell Papers; LWT to Wickham, Jan. 7, 1829, Wickham Papers.

7. Hugh Blair Grigsby to John Tazewell, Jan. 10, 17, 1829, Tazewell Papers.

8. *Norfolk Herald,* May 27, 1829; LWT to John Wickham, June 3, 1829, Wickham Papers; Wickham to LWT, June 23, 1829, Tazewell Papers.

9. John Wickham to LWT, July 25, 1829, LWT to John Tazewell, Aug. 13, 1829, Benjamin Watkins Leigh to LWT, Sept. 30, 1829, LWT to Mr. Allien, April 2, 1830, Tazewell Papers.

10. *Norfolk Herald,* Oct. 5, 1829; Grigsby to John Tazewell, Oct. 6, 1829, Tazewell Papers.

11. *Proceedings and Debates of the Virginia State Convention of 1829–30,* 2 vols. (1830; rept. New York, 1971), 1:1–5, 2:588; Grigsby to John Tazewell, Oct. 6, 1829, Tazewell Papers; Ammon, *Monroe, 563–66.*

12. *Richmond Enquirer,* Oct. 31, 1829; Grigsby to John Tazewell, Oct. 6, 1829, Tazewell Papers.

13. *Proceedings and Debates,* 1:15–22; *Norfolk Herald,* Oct. 14, 1829.

14. LWT to John Tazewell, Oct. 20, 1829, Tazewell Papers.

15. *Proceedings and Debates,* 1:326–35.

16. Ibid., 222–24, 234–35.

17. Ibid., 331–32.

18. Grigsby to John Tazewell, Dec. 8, 1829, Tazewell Papers; *Proceedings and Debates,* 2:580–82.

19. Beveridge, *Marshall,* 4:485–88; *Proceedings and Debates,* 2:582; Green, *Constitutional Development,* 220.

20. *Proceedings and Debates,* 2:615–19, 871–72.

21. Ibid., 619.

22. Ibid., 764–65; Grigsby, *Tazewell,* 67.

23. *Proceedings and Debates,* 2:901.

24. Ibid., 777, 882, 885–86, 895; *Richmond Enquirer,* Jan. 16, 1830.

25. *Proceedings and Debates,* 2:897–99; Green, *Constitutional Development,* 221–22.

26. *Proceedings and Debates,* 2:900; Leonard Baker, *John Marshall: A Life in Law* (New York, 1974), 711; Peterson, *Democracy, Liberty, and Property,* 284.

27. Beveridge, *Marshall*, 4:492–93. This was done with the support of the west. See Robert P. Sutton, "Sectionalism and Social Structure: A Case Study of Jeffersonian Democracy," *Virginia Magazine of History and Biography* 80 (1972): 83–84.

28. *Proceedings and Debates*, 2:903; Ambler, *Sectionalism in Virginia*, 172–74; Peterson, *Democracy, Liberty, and Property*, 284–85.

29. Risjord, *Old Republicans*, 3–4.

30. From Randolph's speech on the county courts, *Proceedings and Debates*, 2:533.

## Chapter XI

1. LWT to Mr. Allien, April 2, 1830, Tazewell Papers; *National Intelligencer*, Feb. 25, 27, 1830.

2. LWT to Mr. Allien, April 2, 1830, Tazewell Papers. For a reproduction of the Healy painting, see Wiltse, *Calhoun*, 2: opp. p. 30.

3. LWT to John Tazewell, March 24, 1830, Tazewell Papers.

4. LWT to Mr. Allien, April 2, 1830, ibid.; Adams, *Memoirs*, 7:179; John Tyler to Conway Whittle, May 22, 1853, *Letters of the Tylers*, 1:410; Remini, *Election of Jackson*, 78–80; Ambler, *Ritchie*, 129.

5. John Wickham to LWT, April 6, 1830, Tazewell Papers.

6. LWT to John Wickham, April 25, 1830, Wickham Papers; *National Intelligencer*, April 20, 1830; Richard R. Stenberg, "The Jefferson Birthday Dinner, 1830," *Journal of Southern History* 4 (1938): 337; Wiltse, *Calhoun*, 2:67–71.

7. LWT to John Wickham, April 25, 1830, Wickham Papers.

8. Sellers, *Polk*, 1:149; Adams, *Memoirs*, 8:222; Ambler, *Ritchie*, 136.

9. LWT to John Tazewell, April 30, May 7, 1830, Tazewell Papers; *National Intelligencer*, April 29, May 13, 17, 1830; *Norfolk Herald*, May 5, 14, 1830.

10. Hugh Lawson White to LWT, May 22, 28, 1830, Tazewell Papers.

11. Van Buren, *Autobiography*, 320; Bassett, *Jackson*, 2:490–91.

12. John Tyler to LWT, May 28, 1830, *Letters of the Tylers*, 1:412; Thomas Ritchie to Archibald Ritchie, June 8, 1830, "Unpublished Letters of Thomas Ritchie," ed. Charles H. Ambler, *John P. Branch Historical Papers of Randolph-Macon College* 3 (1911): 208; Van Buren, *Autobiography*, 320–23; Wiltse, *Calhoun*, 2:75.

13. Van Buren to Jackson, July 25, 1830, Jackson, *Correspondence*, 4:166; Van Buren, *Autobiography*, 326; John Wickham to LWT, June 3, 1830, Tazewell Papers.

14. Wiltse, *Calhoun*, 2:74–75; John Tyler to Rober W. Christian, May 13, 1830, John Tyler to LWT, May 22, 1830, *Letters of the Tylers*, 1:408–9; Jackson to Calhoun, May 13, 30, 1830, Jackson, *Correspondence*, 4:136, 140–41.

15. Jackson to John Overton, Dec. 31, 1829, Jackson, *Correspondence*, 4:108–9; Gerald M. Capers, *John C. Calhoun, Opportunist: A Reappraisal* (Chicago, 1969), 127–28; Mooney, *Crawford*, 318–19; Ambler, *Ritchie*, 108–9.

16.  LWT to Randolph, May 26, 1830, Tazewell Papers; LWT to John Wickham, Oct. 12, 1830, Wickham Papers.

17.  Wertenbaker, *Norfolk*, 152–53; Benns, *BWI Carrying Trade*, 177–78, 184; *Norfolk Herald*, Nov. 16, 1835; LWT to John Wickham, Oct. 12, 1830, Wickham Papers.

18.  LWT to John Tazewell, Jan. 8, 1831, Tazewell Papers; Henry Clay to J. S. Johnston, Nov. 14, 1830, Clay, *Private Correspondence*, 288.

19.  *Messages and Papers*, 2:500–529; *Washington Globe*, Dec. 7, 1830.

20.  LWT to John Tazewell, Feb. 13, 18, 1831, Benjamin Watkins Leigh to LWT, Feb. 22, 1831, Tazewell Papers; John C. Calhoun to James H. Hammond, Feb. 16, 1831, Calhoun, *Correspondence*, 289–90; Henry Clay to Francis Brooke, April 24, 1831 [misdated 1830], *Life, Correspondence, and Speeches of Clay*, 4:262–64; Wiltse, *Calhoun*, 2:96.

21.  Wiltse, *Calhoun*, 2:98–99; Adams, *Memoirs*, 8:327.

22.  Chitwood, *Tyler*, 103; Wiltse, *Calhoun*, 2:98; *Messages and Papers*, 2:504; *National Intelligencer*, Dec. 29, 1830; *Register of Debates*, 21st Cong., 2d sess., 215–41. The speech also was printed for distribution: *Speech of Mr. Tazewell in the Senate of the United States on the Motion to Amend the General Appropriations Bill* (Norfolk, Va., 1831).

23.  *Register of Debates*, 21st Cong., 2d sess., 241–60.

24.  Ibid., 274–75, 260–70.

25.  Ibid., 261.

26.  Ibid., 310; *Niles' Weekly Register*, May 14, July 30, 1831; *Richmond Enquirer*, March 8, 1831; Tyler to LWT, May 8, 1831, Tyler Papers.

27.  John Floyd to LWT, Feb. 22, 1831, Benjamin Watkins Leigh to LWT, Feb. 22, 1831, Tazewell Papers.

28.  LWT to John Wickham, March 4, 1831, Wickham Papers; *Niles' Weekly Register*, March 5, 1831; *Richmond Enquirer*, March 5, 1831.

29.  LWT to John Wickham, March 4, 1831, Wickham Papers; Ambler, *Life and Diary of Floyd*, 125–26; Henry H. Simms, *The Rise of the Whigs in Virginia, 1824–1840* (Richmond, 1929), 45; Wiltse, *Calhoun*, 2:100–101.

30.  Ambler, *Life and Diary of Floyd*, 128, entry of March 13, 1831; Tyler to LWT, May 8, 1831, Tyler Papers; *Richmond Enquirer*, April 8, 1831.

31.  Wiltse, *Calhoun*, 2:101; Tyler to LWT, May 8, 1831, Tyler Papers.

32.  Jackson, *Correspondence*, 4:257–79; Bassett, *Jackson*, 2:520–32; Govan, "Berrien and the Administration of Jackson," 455–60.

33.  Bassett, *Jackson*, 2:533–38; LWT to John Wickham, Dec. 28, 1831, Wickham Papers.

34.  Tyler to LWT, May 8, 1831, Tyler Papers; Rudolph Bunner to LWT, March 23, 1831, Tazewell Papers.

35.  LWT to John Wickham, Sept. 23, Oct. 29, 1831, Wickham Papers; Stephen B. Oates, *The Fires of Jubilee: Nat Turner's Fierce Rebellion* (New York, 1975), 126; Ambler, *Life and Diary of Floyd*, 165, entry of Oct. 17, 1831. According to the *Richmond Enquirer*, Aug. 27, 1831, the current population of Norfolk was: whites, 5,131; slaves, 3,757; "free persons of color," 928.

36.  LWT to John Wickham, Sept. 23, Oct. 29, 1831, Wickham Papers.

37.  LWT to Wickham, Oct. 29, 1831, ibid.

38. John Wickham to LWT, Nov. 26, 1831, Tazewell Papers.
39. John Clarke Robert, *The Road from Monticello: A Study of the Virginia Slavery Debate of 1832* (Durham, N.C., 1941), 17–21; Ambler, *Life and Diary of Floyd*, 174–75, entries of Jan 21, 24, 25, 1832.
40. LWT to John Wickham, Jan 6, 1832, Wickham Papers; LWT to Ann Tazewell, Jan. 14, 1832, Tazewell Papers; *Richmond Enquirer*, Jan. 18, 1806.
41. Thomas R. Dew to LWT, May 9, 1832, Tazewell Papers. Dew's essay, "Abolition of Slavery," was published in the *American Quarterly Review*, 12 (Sept. 1832): 189–265. An enlarged version, *Review of the Debates in the Virginia Legislature of 1831 and 1832* (Richmond, 1832), includes Tazewell's 1828 views on colonization with full credit to the senator, pp. 81–86.
42. Patricia P. Hickin, "Antislavery in Virginia, 1831–1861" (Ph.D. diss., University of Virginia, 1968), 107, observes that many southerners, "perhaps irrationally," viewed the insurrection "not as a sign of the impracticality of slavery but of the impracticality of freedom. Slaves, because they could be more easily controlled than free men, could more easily be kept from violence than could free Negroes." This was true of Calhoun, who, unlike Tazewell, reacted harshly to news of the Turner rebellion and immediately ordered thirty lashes for one of his runaway slaves. See Wiltse, *Calhoun*, 2:117–19.
43. LWT to John Tazewell, Dec. 26, 1832, Tazewell Papers.

## Chapter XII

1. Andrew Jackson to John Coffee, April 24, 1831, Jackson, *Correspondence*, 4:268–69.
2. Ambler, *Life and Diary of Floyd*, 142, diary entry of April 26, 1831; Memorandum by James H. Hammond, March 18, 1831, "Documents on Nullification in South Carolina," *American Historical Review* 4 (1901): 741–45.
3. LWT to John Wickham, Dec. 28, 1831, Wickham Papers. Tazewell agreed with Madison, who in the 1830s repeatedly denied that either he or Jefferson, in the Virginia and Kentucky Resolutions, intended to set forth the idea that a single state could veto a law and remain in the Union. For Madison's views, see Brant, *Madison*, 6:487.
4. Ambler, *Life and Diary of Floyd*, 136, entry for April 11, 1831; John P. Frank, *Justice Daniel Dissenting: A Biography of Peter V. Daniel, 1784–1860* (Cambridge, Mass., 1965), chap. 4. See also Richard P. McCormick, *The Second American Party System: Party Formation in the Jacksonian Era* (Chapel Hill, N.C., 1966), 184–92.
5. LWT to John Wickham, Oct. 29, Dec. 14, 1831, Wickham Papers.
6. John Floyd to John C. Calhoun, Jan. 2, 1832, Floyd Papers, L.C.
7. LWT to John Wickham, Dec. 14, 28, 1831, Jan. 6, 1832, Wickham Papers.
8. LWT to Ann Tazewell, Jan. 14, 1832, Tazewell Papers.
9. Ibid., Jan. 29, 1832.
10. LWT to John Wickham, Dec. 14, 1831, Wickham Papers.

292                                                            NOTES

11.  Ibid., Jan. 6, 1832; LWT to Ann Tazewell, Jan. 29, 1832, Tazewell Papers.

12.  LWT to Ann Tazewell, Jan. 29, 1832, Richard E. Parker to LWT, Feb. 6, 1832, ibid.

13.  LWT to John Wickham, Jan. 6, 1832, Wickham Papers; Hatcher, *Livingston*, 395–418.

14.  *Register of Debates*, 22d Cong., 1st sess., 55; F. W. Taussig, *The Tariff History of the United States* (New York, 1964), 105; Ambler, *Life and Diary of Floyd*, 172–73, 175–76, entries of Dec. 29, 1831, and Jan. 27, 1832.

15.  Richard E. Parker to LWT, Feb. 6, 1832, John Wickham to LWT, March 18, 1832, Tazewell Papers; Adams, *Memoirs*, 8:455.

16.  *Register of Debates*, 22d Cong., 1st sess., 635–38, 676–78; *Richmond Enquirer*, May 1, 1832.

17.  LWT to John Tazewell, May 8, 1832, Tazewell Papers.

18.  Ibid., May 23, 1832.

19.  *Messages and Papers*, 2:528–29.

20.  Robert V. Remini, *Andrew Jackson and the Bank War: A Study in the Growth of Presidential Power* (New York, 1967), 74–77; Bray Hammond, *Banks and Politics in America, from the Revolution to the Civil War* (Princeton, N.J., 1957), 384–86.

21.  LWT to John Tazewell, Sept. 5, 1830, Tazewell Papers; *Register of Debates*, 21st Cong., 2d sess., 78. The resolution lost, 23 to 20.

22.  *Register of Debates*, 22d Cong., 1st sess., 1161–67.

23.  Chambers, *Benton*, 190.

24.  *Register of Debates*, 22d Cong., 1st sess., 1174; Chambers, *Benton*, 191; LWT to John Wickham, Dec. 28, 1831, Wickham Papers.

25.  *Register of Debates*, 22d Cong., 1st sess., 1014–15, 1019–20.

26.  Ibid., 1071, 1073; LWT to John Wickham, June 18, 1832, Wickham Papers.

27.  *Register of Debates*, 22d Cong., 1st sess., 1174, 1205; LWT to John Wickham, June 18, 1832, Wickham Papers; John Tyler to John B. Seawell, June 15, 1832, *Letters of the Tylers*, 1:436–37.

28.  Bemis, *J. Q. Adams*, 2:244–47; William Wickham to LWT, June 18, 1832, Tazewell Papers; *Register of Debates*, 22d Cong., 1st sess., 1023–24; Francis F. Wayland, *Andrew Stevenson, Democrat and Diplomat, 1785–1857* (Philadelphia, 1949), 90. Tazewell also was concerned about the effect of the bill on Norfolk's ocean trade, and, quite likely, Adams's authorship did nothing to endear the measure to him.

29.  *Messages and Papers*, 2:576–91; *Register of Debates*, 22d Cong., 1st sess., 1220.

30.  *The Works of Daniel Webster*, ed. Edward Everett, 6 vols. (Boston, 1853), 3:432–35; Nicholas Biddle to Henry Clay, Aug. 1, 1832, *Life, Correspondence, and Speeches of Clay*, 4:341; Poore, *Reminiscences*, 1:144.

31.  LWT to John Tazewell, July 11, 1832, Tazewell Papers; *Register of Debates*, 22d Cong., 1st sess., 1295.

32.  *Register of Debates*, 22d Cong., 1st sess., 297, 371–73.

33.  Ibid., 1130–32.

34.  LWT to John Tazewell, June 22, 1832, Tazewell Papers; LWT to John Wickham, Sept. 17, 1832, Wickham Papers; *Norfolk Herald*, Aug. 6, 1832.

35.  LWT to John Wickham, Sept. 17, 1832, Wickham Papers.

36.  Ibid. Yet Tazewell thought it prudent to consider the purchase of a plantation inland to which he could remove his family in case of future need.

37.  *Norfolk Herald*, Sept. 17, 1832; LWT to John Wickham, Sept. 17, 1832, Wickham Papers.

38.  William H. Freehling, *Prelude to Civil War: The Nullification Controversy in South Carolina, 1816–1836* (New York, 1968), 252–60; Jackson to Woodbury, Sept. 11, 1832, Jackson, *Correspondence*, 4:474–75. Not all nullifiers were secessionists. In fact, a number of southerners supported nullification in an attempt to preserve the Union, while others used it as a first step toward secession.

39.  Jackson to Van Buren, Nov. 18, 1832, Jackson, *Correspondence*, 4:489. The date of Tazewell's resignation often is cited incorrectly as July 16, 1832. This was the last day he served in the Senate; however, he did not resign until Oct. 22, 1832.

40.  LWT to John Floyd, Oct. 22, 1832, *CSVP*, 10:579–80.

41.  LWT to Wickham, Dec. 17, 1832, Wickham Papers.

42.  Ibid.

43.  Ambler, *Life and Diary of Floyd*, 199–200, entry of Oct. 27, 1832; Hugh Lawson White to LWT, Dec. 19, 1832, John Wickham to LWT, Dec. 8, 1832, Tazewell Papers.

44.  LWT to John Wickham, Nov. 17, 1832, Wickham Papers.

## Chapter XIII

1.  Freehling, *Prelude to Civil War*, 263–64.

2.  *Messages and Papers*, 2:598–99. The moderate tone of the annual message is explained by the fact that Jackson did not see the nullification ordinance until after the message had gone to press. Sydney Nathans, *Daniel Webster and Jacksonian Democracy* (Baltimore, 1973), 52.

3.  Ambler, *Ritchie*, 153–54; Hatcher, *Livingston*, 383–87. For the full text of the president's proclamation, see *Messages and Papers*, 2:640–56.

4.  Margaret Coit, *John C. Calhoun, American Portrait* (Boston, 1950), 239.

5.  John W. Murdaugh to John Tazewell, Dec. 13, 1832, Tazewell Papers; Raymond Dingledine, "The Political Career of William Cabell Rives" (Ph.D. diss., University of Virginia, 1947), 179–86; Simms, *Rise of Whigs*, 64–65.

6.  John W. Murdaugh to John Tazewell, Dec. 13, 14, 15, 1832, Tazewell Papers; *National Intelligencer*, Dec. 18, 1832.

7.  LWT to John Wickham, March 3, 1833, Wickham Papers.

8.  Tazewell's articles appeared in the *Norfolk Herald* in late December 1832 and throughout January 1833 and also, years later, in a 112-page

book, *A Review of the Proclamation of President Jackson of the 10th of December, 1832* (Norfolk, 1888).

9. LWT to John Wickham, March 3, 1833, Wickham Papers.

10. LWT, *Review of the Proclamation*, 4–5, 7, 10–11, 111–12.

11. Simms, *Rise of Whigs*, 74; *Richmond Enquirer*, Dec. 25, 1832.

12. *Messages and Papers*, 2:610–32; Van Buren to Jackson, Dec. 27, 1832, Jackson to Van Buren, Jan. 13, 1833, Jackson to Joel Poinsett, Jan. 16, 1833, Jackson, *Correspondence*, 4:506–8, 5:2–6.

13. Simms, *Rise of Whigs*, 67; Freehling, *Prelude to Civil War*, 290; Bruce, *Randolph*, 2:22–25.

14. *Register of Debates*, 22d Cong., 2d sess., 462–73, 477–78, 519; *National Intelligencer*, Feb. 13, 1833; Van Deusen, *Clay*, 267–69; Claude H. Hall, *Abel Parker Upshur, Conservative Virginian, 1790–1844* (Madison, Wis., 1964), 88–89, 232; Simms, *Rise of Whigs*, 86.

15. *Register of Debates*, 22d Cong., 2d sess., 688; Chitwood, *Tyler*, 114–17; Adams, *Memoirs*, 8:527; Van Deusen, *Clay*, 268; LWT to John Wickham, March 3, 1833, Wickham Papers.

16. Ann Tazewell to children, May 12, 1833, LWT to John Tazewell, May 13, 1833, John Wickham to LWT, May 14, 1833, Tazewell Papers; LWT to John Wickham, Aug. 11, 1833, Wickham Papers.

17. John Wickham to LWT, May 14, 1833, Tazewell Papers; LWT to John Wickham, May 26, 1833, Wickham Papers; Bruce, *Randolph*, 2:30–48; *Richmond Enquirer*, May 28, 1833.

18. LWT to John Tazewell, Sept. 22, 1833, Tazewell Papers; *Richmond Enquirer*, July 19, 26, Aug. 2, 1833.

19. Simms, *Rise of Whigs*, 76; *Richmond Enquirer*, July 2, 1833; John Floyd to LWT, Nov. 8, 1833, Tazewell Papers.

20. Munroe, *McLane*, 386–88; Remini, *Jackson and Bank War*, 122–24; Thomas P. Govan, *Nicholas Biddle, Nationalist and Public Banker, 1786–1844* (Chicago, 1959), 244–53; Jackson to Van Buren, Oct. 5, 1833, Jackson, *Correspondence*, 5:216–17.

21. Van Deusen, *Clay*, 278–80; Remini, *Jackson and Bank War*, 138, 143–48; LWT to John Wickham, Jan. 14, 1834, Wickham Papers.

22. John M. Patton to LWT, Oct. 20, 1833, Tazewell Papers.

23. LWT to John Wickham, Jan. 14, 1834, Wickham Papers.

24. LWT to Clay, Feb. 19, 1834, *Life, Correspondence, and Speeches of Clay*, 4:378–81.

25. Arthur C. Cole, *The Whig Party in the South* (Washington, D.C., 1914), 30–31; *Richmond Whig*, April 8, 1834.

26. Cole, *Whig Party*, 28–29; Simms, *Rise of Whigs*, 79; Wayland, *Stevenson*, 100; *Richmond Enquirer*, Dec. 31, 1833.

27. John Wickham to LWT, Dec. 10, 1833, Tazewell Papers.

## Chapter XIV

1. John Tyler to Thomas W. Gilmer, Jan. 7, 1834, Tyler to LWT, Dec. 3, 1833, *Letters of the Tylers*, 1:480–81, 479–80.

2. William Maxwell to LWT, Jan. 7, 1834, Tazewell Papers. See also *Richmond Enquirer*, Jan. 9, 1834, and Frank, *Daniel*, 125.

3. Adams, *Memoirs*, 9:73; *American Beacon*, Jan. 17, 1834; John C. Calhoun to LWT, Jan. 16, Feb. 9, 1834, Calhoun Papers; John M. Patton to LWT, Jan. 16, 1834, Tazewell Papers.

4. LWT to John Wickham, Jan. 14, 1834, Wickham Papers.

5. *Journal of the House of Delegates of Virginia, 1833–1834* (Richmond, 1834), 234; Wayland, *Stevenson*, 98–99.

6. Clement Eaton, *The Freedom-of-Thought Struggle in the Old South* (New York, 1964), 353–55; Anderson, *Giles*, 160–67; LWT, *Review of the Proclamation*, 75.

7. William Cabell Rives, "Letter to the Speakers of Both Houses of the Virginia General Assembly, Feb. 21, 1834," *Richmond Enquirer*, Feb. 25, 27, 1834.

8. LWT to John Wickham, Jan. 14, 1834, Wickham Papers; Wickham to LWT, Jan. 23, 1834, John Floyd to LWT, Jan. 26, 1834, Tazewell Papers; LWT to Henry Clay, Feb. 19, 1834, *Life, Correspondence, and Speeches of Clay*, 4:378; *American Beacon*, Feb. 22, 24, 1834.

9. Calhoun to LWT, Feb. 9, March 27, 1834, Calhoun Papers; Wiltse, *Calhoun*, 2:226–29.

10. *Richmond Enquirer*, April 4, 1834; Ritchie to Rives, Jan. 6, 1834, "Unpublished Letters of Ritchie," 215–16; Van Deusen, *Clay*, 284; LWT to John Tazewell, April 29, 1834, Tazewell Papers.

11. John Floyd to LWT, Jan. 26, 1834, LWT to John Tazewell, April 5, 1834, Tazewell Papers.

12. LWT to John Tazewell, April 29, 1834, ibid.

13. Ibid., May 4, June 17, 1834; Frank, *Daniel*, 125–26.

14. *Richmond Enquirer*, May 27, July 1, 1834; Wayland, *Stevenson*, 101; Remini, *Jackson and Bank War*, 141–42, 169–71.

15. John Tyler to William F. Gordon, Nov. 6, 1834, *Letters of the Tylers*, 3:65–66.

16. LWT to Nathaniel Beverly Tucker, Dec. 7, 1834, Tucker-Coleman Papers.

17. LWT to John Tazewell, Oct. 3, 1834, Tazewell Papers.

18. Ibid., Aug. 19, 1834; Ritchie to Rives, Aug. 23, 1834, "Unpublished Letters of Ritchie," 217–18; Frank, *Daniel*, 127.

19. *Richmond Enquirer*, Dec. 2, 9, 1834, Jan. 31, Feb. 2, 1835; Ambler, *Ritchie*, 160.

20. John Tyler to Mrs. Tyler, Feb. 1, 1835, *Letters of the Tylers*, 1:509–10; *Richmond Enquirer*, Jan. 22, 1835.

21. Joel H. Silbey, "Election of 1836," *History of American Presidential Elections*, ed. Schlesinger, 1:584–86; John M. Patton to LWT, Dec. 18, 1834, Tazewell Papers.

22. Ritchie to Rives, May 19, June 5, 1835, "Unpublished Letters of Ritchie," 219–22; Ambler, *Ritchie*, 169.

23. *Richmond Enquirer*, July 10, 1835; Carl B. Swisher, *Roger B. Taney* (Hamden, Conn., 1961), 316–17; Beveridge, *Marshall*, 4:588–89.

24. Hickin, "Antislavery in Virginia," 173–74.

25. *Richmond Enquirer*, Dec. 8, 1835.

26. John M. Patton to LWT, Jan. 16, 1836, Tazewell Papers; *Richmond Enquirer*, Dec. 7, 12, 19, 1835; *Messages and Papers*, 3:175–76; Wiltse, *Calhoun*, 2:274–77.

27. LWT to John Tazewell, Jan. 19, 1836, Tazewell Papers; *National Intelligencer*, Jan. 6, 12, 1836; Van Deusen, *Clay*, 285–86.

28. *National Intelligencer*, Jan. 6, 12, 1836.

29. Calhoun to LWT, Jan. 24, 1836, Calhoun Papers.

30. *Richmond Enquirer*, Feb. 25, 1836; *National Intelligencer*, Feb. 26, 1836; *American Beacon*, Feb. 23, 27, 1836; Leigh to Tyler, July 5, 1835, *Letters of the Tylers*, 1:523; Leigh to LWT, Feb. 18, 1836, Tazewell Papers.

31. John Tyler to Robert Tyler, Feb. 15, 1836, *Letters of the Tylers*, 1:534–35; *American Beacon*, March 7, 1836; Eaton, *Freedom-of-Thought Struggle*, 364–66; *Biographical Directory of Congress, 1774–1927*, 175.

32. John M. Patton to LWT, May 4, 1836, Tazewell Papers; *Richmond Enquirer*, April 1, 5, 1836.

33. *Acts of the General Assembly of the Commonwealth of Virginia, 1835–36* (Richmond, 1836), 395–96; Oates, *Fires of Jubilee*, 143–45.

34. Eaton, *Freedom-of-Thought Struggle*, 127; *Acts of the General Assembly*, 44–45.

35. Russel B. Nye, *Fettered Freedom: Civil Liberties and the Slavery Controversy, 1830–1860* (East Lansing, Mich., 1963), 41–85; David Biron Davis, *The Slave Power Conspiracy and the Paranoid Style* (Baton Rouge, La., 1969), 38; John M. Patton to LWT, May 4, 1836, Tazewell Papers.

## Chapter XV

1. Hugh Lawson White to LWT, May 17, 1838, Tazewell Papers.

2. *Messages and Papers*, 3:318–19; James C. Curtis, *The Fox at Bay: Martin Van Buren and the Presidency, 1837–1841* (Lexington, Ky., 1970), 62–63; John M. Patton to LWT, Nov. 21, 1837, Tazewell Papers.

3. John M. Patton to LWT, Nov. 21, 1837, Feb. 18, 1838, Tazewell Papers.

4. LWT to John Wickham, Dec. 14, 1837, Feb. 11, 1838, Wickham Papers.

5. Ibid., Feb. 11, 1838.

6. White to LWT, Feb. 18, 1838, LWT to John Tazewell, Dec. 26, 30, 1836, Aug. 16, 1838, and Plantation Book, entries for Dec. 25, 26, 1836, Aug. 18, 1837, Tazewell Papers.

7. Plantation Book, entries for Jan. 1, 3, 1837, ibid.

8. LWT to John Tazewell, Oct. 3, 1843, Dec. 29, 1848, Oct. 5, 1849, ibid.

9. Littleton Tazewell, Jr., to John Tazewell, May 18, 1838, Ann Tazewell to John Tazewell, May 31, 1838, ibid.

10.  Thomas Ritchie to Martin Van Buren, July 2, 1838, Ritchie to William Cabell Rives, Sept. 21, 1837, June 5, 1838, "Unpublished Letters of Ritchie," 229–30, 225–28; LWT to Dr. J. P. Young, published in *Winchester Virginian*, Sept. 9, 1840, cited in Simms, *Rise of Whigs*, 155; James Roger Sharp, *The Jacksonians versus the Banks: Politics in the States after the Panic of 1837* (New York, 1970), 215–73.

11.  C. J. Ingersoll to LWT, Oct. 3, 1840, Tazewell Papers; Curtis, *Fox at Bay*, 158–60, 168.

12.  *American Beacon*, Oct. 12, 1840; Peter V. Daniel to Van Buren, Sept. 28, 1840, quoted in Simms, *Rise of Whigs*, 157.

13.  "Extract from a Letter Addressed by President Tyler to the Norfolk Democratic Association, dated Sept. 2, 1844," *Letters of the Tylers*, 2:95–96.

14.  Tyler to LWT, Oct. 11, Nov. 2, 1841, ibid., 127–31.

15.  Tyler to LWT, Aug. 26, 1842, ibid., 183–84; LWT to John Tazewell, Oct. 24, 1842, Aug. 15, 1843, Tazewell Papers.

16.  William Wickham to LWT, Aug. 30, 1844, Tazewell Papers; John S. Barbour to Calhoun, Dec. 18, 1844, *Correspondence Addressed to John C. Calhoun, 1837–1849*, ed. Chauncey S. Boucher and Robert Brooks (Washington, D.C., 1930), 271; *The Diary of James K. Polk during His Presidency, 1845 to 1849*, ed. Milo M. Quaife, 4 vols. (Chicago, 1910), 2:94–96, entry of Aug. 22, 1846.

17.  Polk, *Diary*, 96; LWT to Robert M. T. Hunter, Aug. 18, 1850, *Correspondence of Robert M. T. Hunter, 1826–1876*, ed. Charles H. Ambler (Washington, D.C., 1918), 115–18.

18.  LWT to Robert M. T. Hunter, Aug. 18, 1850, Hunter, *Correspondence*, 115–18; Calhoun to Lewis S. Coryell, Nov. 7, 1846, Calhoun, *Correspondence*, 710; Calhoun, *Works*, 4:342, 348; Holman Hamilton, *Prologue to Conflict: The Crisis and Compromise of 1850* (New York, 1966).

19.  Wiltse, *Calhoun*, 3:368–69; Polk, *Diary*, 4:67; Holmes Alexander, *The American Talleyrand: The Career and Contemporaries of Martin Van Buren, Eighth President* (New York, 1935), 404–5.

20.  William Yancey to Calhoun, June 21, 1848, Calhoun to Armistead Burt, Nov. 2, 1840, Calhoun, *Correspondence*, 1177, 465–66; Isaac Van Zandt to Anson Jones, April 19, 1843, *Diplomatic Correspondence of the Republic of Texas*, ed. George P. Garrison, pt. 2 (Washington, D.C., 1911), 164; Hall, *Upshur*, 117; Wiltse, *Calhoun*, 3:162; Barbour to Calhoun, Dec. 18, 1844, *Correspondence Addressed to Calhoun*, 271; LWT to John Tazewell, Sept. 25, 1842, Tazewell Papers.

21.  John Wickham's will, Jan. 9, 1839, Wickham Papers. "I desire my excellent friend Littleton Waller Tazewell to accept as a small token of my affection and respect Wilson's Ornithology with Bonaparte's continuation thereof, or if he prefers it, the choice of a male and female of my original stock of cattle or the like choice out of my pure Devonshire Breed. The remoteness of his residence prevents my asking of him the favor—to be one of my Executors." Tazewell chose Wilson's *Ornithology*.

22.  *American Beacon*, Nov. 16, 1844; LWT to Ann Tazewell, Dec. 10, 1844, Tazewell Papers; *Southern Argus*, March 4, 1848.

23.  Calhoun, *Works*, 4:343.

24.   Daniel Webster to Mrs. Paige, April 23, 1849, *The Private Correspondence of Daniel Webster*, ed. Fletcher Webster, 2 vols. (Boston, 1857), 2:320.

25.   Hamilton, *Prologue to Conflict*, 54–59; Calhoun, *Works*, 4:542–78.

26.   Webster, *Works*, 5:325–66; James Hamilton to LWT, May 15, 1850, Tazewell Papers.

27.   LWT to Robert M. T. Hunter, Aug. 18, 1850, Hunter, *Correspondence*, 115–18.

28.   Green, *Constitutional Development*, 287–96; Barton H. Wise, *The Life of Henry A. Wise* (New York, 1899), 151.

29.   Hugh Garland to LWT, Jan. 3, 15, 1844, Alexander S. Mackenzie to LWT, Nov. 28, 1846, Richard Crallé to LWT, Dec. 21, 1850, John Cocke to LWT, May 27, 1856, Ann Tazewell to Sally Tazewell, Sept. 27, 1856, Tazewell Papers.

30.   Notification of election as honorary member of the Virginia Historical Society, Dec. 20, 1847, Benjamin S. Ewell, President of the College of William and Mary, to LWT, July 24, 1854, ibid.

31.   *The Diary of Edmund Ruffin*, ed. William K. Scarborough (Baton Rouge, La., 1972), 1:207–8.

32.   Ibid., 208–9; Alexis de Tocqueville, *Democracy in America*, 2 vols. (New York, 1954), 1:266.

33.   LWT to Robert M. T. Hunter, Aug. 18, 1850, Hunter, *Correspondence*, 118; Grigsby, *Tazewell*, 91–99; *Southern Argus*, May 8, 1860.

34.   *Southern Argus*, May 8, 1860. Shortly after the Civil War, Tazewell's remains, along those of other members of his family interred at King's Creek, were removed to Elmwood Cemetery in Norfolk. John Tazewell outlived his father by nine years. Louisa died in 1873, Mary and Ella in the mid 1880s, Sarah in 1892, and Ann in 1898. In 1862, when the Union forces occupied Norfolk, Sandhills plantation was seized and given over to the superintendent of Negro affairs. The Eastern Shore plantations were sold in 1883 to William L. Scott, a northern railroad and coal magnate who had invested heavily in Union bonds during the Civil War.

# Select Bibliography

Although a number of additional sources are cited in notes, listed below are only those of greatest importance to this study.

## Primary Sources

### Manuscript Sources

John C. Calhoun Papers, Library of Congress.
John Floyd Papers, Library of Congress.
Thomas Jefferson Papers, University of Virginia Library.
Thomas Jefferson Papers, Coolidge Collection, Massachusetts Historical Society, Boston.
James Monroe Papers, Library of Congress.
James Monroe Papers, Rare Books and Manuscripts Division, New York Public Library, Astor, Lenox and Tilden Foundations.
Wilson Cary Nicholas Papers, University of Virginia Library.
Tazewell Papers, Virginia State Library, Richmond.
Tucker-Coleman Papers, Swem Library, College of William and Mary.
John Tyler Papers, Library of Congress.
Martin Van Buren Papers, Library of Congress.
John Wickham Papers (microfilm), University of Virginia Library.
William Wirt Papers (microfilm), Maryland Historical Society, Baltimore.

### Memoirs and Correspondence

*Memoirs of John Quincy Adams*. Ed. Charles Francis Adams. 12 vols. 1874–77; rept. New York, 1970.
*Correspondence of John C. Calhoun*. Ed. J. F. Jameson. Washington, D.C., 1900.
*The Works of John C. Calhoun*. Ed. Richard K. Crallé. 6 vols. New York, 1854–57.
*The Life, Correspondence, and Speeches of Henry Clay*. Ed. Calvin Colton. 6 vols. New York, 1864.
*The Private Correspondence of Henry Clay*. Ed. Calvin Colton. New York, 1855.
Ambler, Charles H. *The Life and Diary of John Floyd*. Richmond, 1918.
*Correspondence of Andrew Jackson*. Ed. John S. Bassett. 7 vols. Washington, 1926–33.

*The Writings of Thomas Jefferson.* Ed. Andrew A. Lipscomb and Albert E. Bergh. 20 vols. Washington, D.C., 1903.

*The Works of Thomas Jefferson.* Ed. Paul L. Ford. 12 vols. New York, 1904.

*The Writings of James Monroe.* Ed. Stanislaus M. Hamilton. 7 vols. New York, 1898–1903.

"Unpublished Letters of Thomas Ritchie." Ed. Charles H. Ambler. *The John P. Branch Historical Papers of Randolph-Macon College* 3 (June 1911).

*The Letters and Times of the Tylers.* Ed. Lyon G. Tyler. 3 vols. 1884–96; rept. New York, 1970.

*The Private Correspondence of Daniel Webster.* Ed. Fletcher Webster. 2 vols. Boston, 1857.

Kennedy, John P. *Memoirs of the Life of William Wirt.* 2 vols. New York, 1869.

## Contemporary Writings

Gilmer, Francis Walker. *Sketches, Essays, and Translations.* Baltimore, 1828.

Grigsby, Hugh Blair. *Discourse on the Life and Character of the Hon. Littleton Waller Tazewell.* Norfolk, 1860.

——. *Letters of a South Carolinian.* Norfolk, 1827.

Tazewell, Littleton Waller. *A Review of the Negotiations between the United States and Great Britain, Respecting the Commerce of the Two Countries.* London, 1829.

——. *A Review of the Proclamation of President Jackson of the 10th of December, 1832.* Norfolk, 1888.

——. *Speech of Mr. Tazewell in the Senate of the United States on the Motion to Amend the General Appropriations Bill.* Norfolk, 1831.

Wirt, William, *The Old Bachelor.* Richmond, 1814.

## Documents

*Acts of the General Assembly of the Commonwealth of Virginia, 1835–1836.* Richmond, 1836.

*Annals of Congress.* 6th Cong., 2d sess.; 9th Cong., 1st sess.; 10th Cong., 1st sess.; 12th Cong., 1st sess.

*Calendar of Virginia State Papers.* Vols. 9 and 10. Ed. H. W. Flournoy. Richmond, 1890–92; rept. New York, 1968.

*A Compilation of the Messages and Papers of the Presidents.* Ed. James D. Richardson. 10 vols. Washington, D.C., 1903.

*Journal of the House of Delegates of Virginia, 1805–1806, 1815–1816, 1833–1834.*

*Proceedings and Debates of the Virginia State Convention of 1829–30.* 2 vols. 1830; rept. New York, 1971.

*The Register of Debates in the Congress of the United States.* 18th Cong., 2d sess.–22d Cong., 1st sess.

Robertson, David. *Reports of the Trials of Colonel Aaron Burr.* 2 vols. 1808; rept. New York, 1969.

*Santissima Trinidad Case.* 7 Wheaton, 283–355.

*The United States and Officers, etc., of the Schooner Grampus v. the Brig Palmyra.* 12 Wheaton, 1–17.

## Newspapers

*American Beacon,* (Norfolk, Va.)
*National Intelligencer* (Washington, D.C.)
*Niles' Weekly Register* (Baltimore)
*Norfolk Herald*
*Norfolk Gazette and Publick Ledger*
*Richmond Enquirer*
*Richmond Whig*
*Southern Argus* (Norfolk, Va.)
*Virginia Argus* (Richmond)
*Washington Globe*

## Secondary Sources

### Books

Abernethy, Thomas Perkins. *The Burr Conspiracy.* New York, 1954.
Ambler, Charles H. *Thomas Ritchie: A Study in Virginia Politics.* Richmond, 1913.
Ammon, Harry. *James Monroe: The Quest for National Unity.* New York, 1971.
Anderson, Dice R. *William Branch Giles: A Study in the Politics of Virginia and the Nation from 1790 to 1830.* Menasha, Wis., 1914.
Bassett, John S. *The Life of Andrew Jackson.* 2 vols. New York, 1916.
Bemis, Samuel F. *John Quincy Adams.* 2 vols. 1949–56; rept. New York, 1965.
Benns, F. Lee. *The American Struggle for the British West India Carrying-Trade, 1815–1830.* Bloomington, Ind., 1923.
Beveridge, Albert J. *The Life of John Marshall.* 4 vols. New York, 1919.
Bruce, William Cabell. *John Randolph of Roanoke, 1773–1833.* 2 vols. New York, 1922.
Chitwood, Oliver. *John Tyler, Champion of the Old South.* New York, 1939.
Coit, Margaret L. *John C. Calhoun: American Portrait.* Boston, 1950.
Cole, Arthur C. *The Whig Party in the South.* Washington, D.C., 1914.
Cunningham, Noble E., Jr. *The Jeffersonian Republicans: The Formation of Party Organization, 1789–1801.* Chapel Hill, N.C., 1957.
——. *The Jeffersonian Republicans in Power: Party Operations, 1801–1809.* Chapel Hill, N.C., 1963.
Curtis, James C. *Andrew Jackson and the Search for Vindication.* Boston, 1976.
Davis, Richard Beale. *Intellectual Life in Jefferson's Virginia, 1790–1830.* Chapel Hill, N.C., 1964.
*Democracy, Liberty, and Property: The State Constitutional Conventions of the 1820's.* Ed. Merrill D. Peterson. Indianapolis, 1966.
Frank, John P. *Justice Daniel Dissenting: A Biography of Peter V. Daniel, 1784–1860.* Cambridge, Mass., 1964.
Freehling, William W. *Prelude to Civil War: The Nullification Controversy in South Carolina, 1816–1836.* New York, 1968.

Garland, Hugh A. *The Life of John Randolph of Roanoke*. 2 vols. New York, 1856.

Hall, Claude H. *Abel Parker Upshur, Conservative Virginian, 1790–1844*. Madison, Wis., 1964.

Hatcher, William B. *Edward Livingston, Jeffersonian Republican and Jacksonian Democrat*. Baton Rouge, La., 1940.

Kirk, Russell. *John Randolph of Roanoke: A Study in American Politics*. Chicago, 1964.

McCormick, Richard P. *The Second American Party System: Party Formation in the Jacksonian Era*. Chapel Hill, N.C., 1966.

Mackenzie, Alexander Slidell. *The Life of Stephen Decatur*. Boston, 1846.

Malone, Dumas. *Jefferson and His Time*. 6 vols. Boston, 1948–81.

Peterson, Merrill D. *Thomas Jefferson and the New Nation*. New York, 1970.

Remini, Robert V. *Andrew Jackson*. New York, 1969.

——. *Andrew Jackson and the Bank War: A Study in the Growth of Presidential Power*. New York, 1967.

——. *The Election of Andrew Jackson*. Philadelphia, 1963.

——. *Martin Van Buren and the Making of the Democratic Party*. New York, 1959.

Risjord, Norman K. *The Old Republicans: Southern Conservatism in the Age of Jefferson*. New York, 1965.

Robert, John Clarke. *The Road from Monticello: A Study of the Virginia Slavery Debate of 1832*. Durham, N.C., 1941.

Sellers, Charles K. *James K. Polk*. 2 vols. Princeton, N.J., 1957–66.

Simms, Henry H. *Life of John Taylor*. Richmond, 1932.

——. *The Rise of the Whigs in Virginia, 1824–1840*. Richmond, 1929.

Van Deusen, Glyndon G. *The Life of Henry Clay*. Boston, 1937.

Wertenbaker, Thomas J. *Norfolk, Historic Southern Port*. Durham, N.C., 1962.

Wiltse, Charles M. *John C. Calhoun*. 3 vols. Indianapolis, 1944–51.

## *Articles*

Ammon, Harry. "Monroe and the Election of 1808 in Virginia." *William and Mary Quarterly*, 3d ser., 20 (1963): 33–56.

——. "The Richmond Junto, 1800–1824." *Virginia Magazine of History and Biography* 61 (1953): 395–418.

Crowe, Charles. "Bishop James Madison and the Republic of Virtue." *Journal of Southern History* 30 (1964): 58–70.

Cunningham, Noble E., Jr. "Who Were the Quids?" *Mississippi Valley Historical Review* 50 (1963): 252–63.

Dodd, William E. "Chief Justice Marshall and Virginia." *American Historical Review* 12 (1907): 776–87.

Gaines, Edwin M. "The *Chesapeake* Affair: Virginians Mobilize to Defend National Honor." *Virginia Magazine of History and Biography* 64 (1956): 131–42.

Harrison, Joseph Hobson, Jr. "Martin Van Buren and His Southern Supporters." *Journal of Southern History* 22 (1956): 438–58.

——. "Oligarchs and Democrats—The Richmond Junto." *Virginia Magazine of History and Biography* 78 (1970): 184–98.

Risjord, Norman K. "The Virginia Federalists." *Journal of Southern History* 33 (1967): 486–517.

Stenberg, Richard R. "The Jefferson Birthday Dinner, 1830." *Journal of Southern History* 4 (1938): 334–45.

Sutton, Robert P. "Sectionalism and Social Structure: A Case Study of Jeffersonian Democracy." *Virginia Magazine of History and Biography* 80 (1972): 70–84.

# Index